INTERNAT

China's Policy in Africa 1958-71

INTERNATIONAL STUDIES

PUBLISHED FOR THE CENTRE FOR
INTERNATIONAL STUDIES, LONDON SCHOOL OF
ECONOMICS AND POLITICAL SCIENCE

Editorial Board
Dr Coral Bell
Professor G. L. Goodwin
Professor J. B. Joll
Professor P. J. de la F. Wiles
Professor L. B. Schapiro
Mr D. C. Watt
Mr P. Windsor

The Centre for International Studies at the London School of Economics was established in 1967 with the aid of a grant from the Ford Foundation. Its aim is to promote research and advanced training on a multi-disciplinary basis in the general field of International Studies, particular emphasis being given initially to contemporary China, the Soviet Union and Eastern Europe and the relationship between these areas and the outside world. To this end the Centre offers research fellowships and studentships and, in collaboration with other bodies (such as the Social Science Research Council), sponsors research projects and seminars.

The Centre is undertaking a series of publications in International Studies, of which this volume is the second.

Whilst the Editorial Board accepts responsibility for recommending the inclusion of a volume in the series, the author is alone responsible for the views and opinions expressed.

ALSO IN THIS SERIES
BLIT: The Origins of Polish Socialism
STEINER: The Slovak Dilemma
VAN CREVELD: Hitler's Strategy 1940–1941: The Balkan Clue

China's Policy in Africa
1958-71

ALABA OGUNSANWO

CAMBRIDGE UNIVERSITY PRESS

CAMBRIDGE UNIVERSITY PRESS
Cambridge, New York, Melbourne, Madrid, Cape Town, Singapore,
São Paulo, Delhi, Dubai, Tokyo

Cambridge University Press
The Edinburgh Building, Cambridge CB2 8RU, UK

Published in the United States of America by Cambridge University Press, New York

www.cambridge.org
Information on this title: www.cambridge.org/9780521134408

© Cambridge University Press 1974

This publication is in copyright. Subject to statutory exception
and to the provisions of relevant collective licensing agreements,
no reproduction of any part may take place without the written
permission of Cambridge University Press.

First published 1974
This digitally printed version 2010

A catalogue record for this publication is available from the British Library

Library of Congress Catalogue Card Number: 72-89810

ISBN 978-0-521-20126-1 Hardback
ISBN 978-0-521-13440-8 Paperback

Cambridge University Press has no responsibility for the persistence or
accuracy of URLs for external or third-party internet websites referred to in
this publication, and does not guarantee that any content on such websites is,
or will remain, accurate or appropriate.

To my loving parents, brothers and sisters and Helen

CONTENTS

	Preface	ix
	Acknowledgements	xi
	Abbreviations	xiii
1	The Background to Chinese Policy	1
2	Breaking New Ground 1958–9	15
3	Adjustment and Reappraisal 1960–2	61
4	1963–5 Commitments, Consolidation, Reflection	112
5	Darkening Clouds: The Cultural Revolution	180
6	After the Cultural Revolution	241
	Conclusion	258
	Appendix I	269
	Appendix II	278
	Select Bibliography	287
	Index	292

PREFACE

I decided to write this book in 1968 after attending a stimulating course on War and Crisis in International Relations at the London School of Economics and Political Science. Initially, I considered the possibility of writing on the applicability of Mao's theory of people's war to the various liberation movements in Africa. However after giving some thought to how useful so narrow a study would be and to the availability of concrete material, I decided instead to work on the present book.

As it stands, this book examines China's policy in Africa between 1958 and 1971 tracing how that continent developed in importance in China's overall foreign policy. From the peripheral status it occupied in the middle fifties, China's policy in Africa rapidly achieved a self-propelling and compulsive momentum. This momentum, resulting from the logic of Chinese policy, led to the undertaking to construct and finance the Tanzania–Zambia railroad – the largest single Chinese and indeed Communist aid project in Africa.

Chinese policy in Africa does not of course operate in a vacuum. Its objectives, aspirations and the implementation or achievement of these necessarily interact not only with the parallel and often rival efforts of the United States and the Soviet Union, but also with the policy choices and aspirations of the African states. This book examines the various ways in which Chinese policy was implemented together with the limitations and successes.

The line of approach is analytical and situational, in a general historical framework. At a glance, one sees the process of metamorphosis in Chinese policy: from opposition to Khrushchev's massive economic assistance to bourgeois nationalist governments, to, in the last three years, Chinese annual aid to non-Communist countries exceeding that of the giant Soviet Union; from encouraging violent uprising in order to bring about revolutionary change to the tacit acceptance of the status quo in most African states; and

x *Preface*

finally the change in policy which led to receiving President Nixon as a guest in China in February 1972.

I have called Chapter 1 'The Background to Chinese Policy'. It examines the antecedents and setting of China's Africa policy, and the importance of the general international situation in this policy. Chapter 2, 'Breaking New Ground', examines Chinese performance in 1958 and 1959, the effect of China's interpretation of the international situation on their African policy, and the ways in which they implemented this policy. Chapter 3, 'Adjustment and Reappraisal', which covers the period 1960-2 examines Chinese reaction to the changes in Africa which followed the creation of independent African states in 1960 and discusses the effect on China's policy of the current open Sino-Soviet disagreement on crisis management. Chapter 4, 'Commitments, Consolidation, Reflection', covers the period 1963-5. This has been, to date, the most active period in China's African policy, and witnessed triangular competition between China, the Soviet Union and the United States in several sectors of the international arena. It saw the expansion of Chinese commitments to several African states. Chapter 5, 'Darkening Clouds: the Cultural Revolution', looks at Chinese policy in the period 1966-8, the setbacks which began late in 1965 and the effects of the Cultural Revolution on the different facets of China's African policy. The final chapter, 'After the Cultural Revolution', deals with the period 1969-71; the evolution of Chinese policy after the turbulence of the later sixties, the new approach which led in October 1971 to the admission of Peking's representatives to the United Nations and President Nixon's visit to China in February 1972.

In this book I have tried to analyse the various aspects of Chinese policy in Africa, governmental and non-governmental; the interaction with African events, attitudes and policies and the consequent success or failure of Chinese policy. In foreign policy these terms are relative but I hope this book will contribute to the process of distinguishing the woods from the trees. If it does that then it will have succeeded. An earlier version of this work – 'China's Policy in Africa 1958–1968' – was presented to the University of London as a doctoral thesis in March 1971.

Institute of Administration,   Alaba Ogunsanwo
University of Ife, Nigeria.

ACKNOWLEDGEMENTS

In writing this book I am indebted to many. First, I wish to express my sincere gratitude to Mr James Mayall of the London School of Economics and Political Science who provided invaluable guidance, suggestions and criticisms. My profound gratitude also goes to Dr Coral Bell formerly of the same School who initially suggested the possibility of my writing on China. All along, her enthusiastic encouragement and support provided the necessary fillip in times of difficulty and her multidimensional help has been priceless.

I also wish to express my gratitude to the Centre for International Studies at the London School of Economics for providing me with the necessary financial assistance. I also wish to thank its members particularly Professor G. L. Goodwin for the advice and help rendered. My highly eventful fieldwork in East Africa in 1969–70 was financed by the Centre and for this I am grateful.

I am particularly grateful to the Tanzanian government officials, ministers, and members of parliament who rendered considerable help to me while I was in that country. I cannot mention their names here but I am sure they will understand. My gratitude also goes to Chinese personnel in Tanzania and London and to Nigerian diplomats in East Africa.

I much appreciated the services provided by the staff of the Library and Press Archives of the Royal Institute of International Affairs, the Library of the School of Oriental and African Studies the Library of the Institute of Administration, University of Ife, and I would particularly like to thank Miss K. Duff and Mrs C. Linehan who edited the typescript.

I also express my appreciation of the kind efforts made by S. K. Panter-Brick of the London School of Economics who in the first instance encouraged me to study at the London School of Economics. At an early stage, I looked through the files of Mr Colin Legum of the *Observer* and for this I am grateful. My gratitude also goes to all those whose names, for various reasons, I have not been able to mention. I have also utilised the valuable insights I gained from discussions with my colleagues at the Institute of Administration, University of Ife.

I greatly appreciate all the help rendered to me; any shortcomings in this book are however mine alone.

ABBREVIATIONS

A.A.P.S.O.	Afro-Asian People's Solidarity Organisation
A.A.T.U.F.	All African Trade Union Federation
A.C.F.T.U.	All China Federation of Trade Unions
B.B.C. S.W.B.	British Broadcasting Corporation *Summary of World Broadcasts*
C.A.R.	Central African Republic
C.B.	Current Background
C.C.P.	Chinese Communist Party
C.N.T.G.	Confédération Nationale des Travailleurs Guinéens
C.P.M.	Communist Party of Morocco
C.P.P.	Convention People's Party
C.P.S.U.	Communist Party of the Soviet Union
FRELIMO	Front for the Liberation of Mozambique
G.R.A.E.	Government of the Republic of Angola in Exile
I.A.D.L.	International Association of Democratic Lawyers
I.C.F.T.U.	International Confederation of Free Trade Unions
I.O.J.	International Organisation of Journalists
I.U.S.	International Union of Students
K.A.N.U.	Kenya African National Union
M.E.N.A.	Middle East News Agency
M.P.L.A.	Movimento Popular de Libertaçaõ de Angola
N.A.T.O.	North Atlantic Treaty Organisation
N.C.N.A.	New China News Agency – also known as Hsinhua News Agency
N.E.P.U.	Northern Elements Progressive Union
N.L.F.	National Liberation Front
N.P.C.	National People's Congress
O.A.U.	Organisation of African Unity
P.A.I.G.C.	African Independence Party of Guiné and the Cape Verde Islands
P.D.G.	Parti Democratique de Guinée
P.G.R.A.	Provisional Government of the Republic of Algeria
P.R.C.	People's Republic of China
S.A.N.U.	Sudan African National Union
S.C.M.P.	Survey of China Mainland Press
T.A.N.U.	Tanganyika African National Union
T.F.L.	Tanganyika Federation of Labour
T.U.C.G.	Trade Union Congress of Ghana

Abbreviations

T.U.C.N.	Trade Union Congress of Nigeria
U.A.R.	United Arab Republic
U.G.T.A.N.	Union Générale des Travailleurs d'Afrique Noire
U.M.T.	Union Marocaine du Travail
U.N.	United Nations
U.P.A.	Popular Union of Angola
U.P.C.	Union des Populations du Cameroun
W.F.D.Y.	World Federation of Democratic Youth
W.F.T.U.	World Federation of Trade Unions
W.P.C.	World Peace Council

1 THE BACKGROUND TO CHINESE POLICY

On the whole Chinese policy in Africa has resulted from the diplomatic initiative of the People's Republic of China, rather than of the African States themselves. This immediately suggests questions requiring examination. Why is China interested in Africa? Has there been a coherent policy towards Africa in the period under consideration or is it simply a policy of fomenting revolutions everywhere and especially in places where revolution is detrimental to the interests of imperialism? Is there a genuine desire for the independence and welfare of the African people or is there a grand strategy aimed at bringing the whole continent under the aegis of China? Again, is the Chinese record in Africa merely a chain of failures resulting from their lack of understanding, their lack of communication with, and misperception of, the situation in Africa and the way the leaders of the new states choose to conceive their national interests?

In this book, I shall argue that Chinese policy in the period under consideration is both a reaction to the international environment as interpreted by the Chinese and an attempt to change those aspects of the environment which were inimical to China's interests. I shall also show that its different phases display the sort of flexibility which normally results from a state's experiences in the international political system. What is therefore striking is not so much the extent of Chinese diplomatic failure in Africa as the extent of her success in a situation manifestly hostile to Chinese interests.

Although the history of the Chinese empire goes back 3,000 years, China's current participation in the modern international system only started with the accession to power of the Chinese Communist Party (C.C.P.) in October 1949 and her diplomatic activity abroad has been conducted since in the teeth of American and Western opposition – her task, however, has not been eased by the Sino-Soviet conflict. That Chinese diplomacy has been a reaction to the international environment as seen by the Chinese does not of course mean that whatever diplomatic blunders have been made must be laid at the door of factors beyond the control of the Chinese leaders.

China's policy in Africa is not carried out in a vacuum. The newly independent African states also have their aspirations, the desire for economic development and welfare and the stability of their policies. Methods have varied with the attitudes and approaches of the leaders in the various countries and the objective and subjective factors with which those leaders have had to deal. Their response to Chinese initiatives has therefore depended on how far they considered their national interests would be served by dealing with China; what concessions the Chinese were demanding and how compatible these were with their own aspirations; how they perceived the 'real' interests of China in offering them economic and technical aid; their own philosophy of development and evaluation of the adequacy or inadequacy of the Chinese model of development for their countries.

A subsidiary will be that on the economic and diplomatic levels, China has been more successful in those countries where the natural wealth has not been such as to attract large-scale investment from what China calls the 'imperialist vultures', and where the leadership has adopted a philosophy of development more compatible with the Chinese ideal of self-reliance.

Chinese diplomatic activity is, of course, carried out on two levels: 'intergovernmental' and 'people's diplomacy'. The presence in many African states of groups sympathetic to China has provided her with a useful avenue for influence and activity. The continuing wars of national liberation in the remaining colonial territories provide a testing ground for the Chinese advocacy of acquiring power and independence through revolutionary struggles.

Since Chinese activity in the main began with front organisations before most African states achieved independence, the impact of activity on this level on the attempt to cultivate normal diplomatic relations with the governments of the new states will be examined.

How much 'real' economic aid has China given to the various African states and what has been its effect on the foreign policy stance? Has China more permanent interests in Africa than other big powers or does her interest merely lie in the revolutionary movements and is it therefore likely to wane with the liberation of those territories still under colonial rule? To what extent has China's behaviour been determined by the desire to play the role of a big power and what impact does the conflict with America and the Soviet Union have on her African policies? What was the impact of 'Great Proletarian Cultural Revolution' which involved the recall to Peking of all Chinese diplomats, except the ambassador to the U.A.R., for re-education and remoulding? It will be shown that contrary to popular belief, Chinese commitment to Africa has not been adversely affected by the Cultural Revolution. Although the number of African delegations visiting China and Chinese delegations visiting Africa has declined considerably, a greater technical and economic commitment has been made, concentrating on six States: Mali, Guinea, Tanzania, Zambia, Mauritania and Congo Brazzaville. Further, many of the projects already initiated were completed between 1966 and 1968.

To place Chinese policy in Africa between 1958 and 1971 in its correct perspective it is necessary to examine the context in which the policy was formulated. An important factor is, for example, China's awareness of the interlocking of her African policy with her international strategic interests and thus the relative incomprehensibility of the former without the latter. Since the proclamation of the People's Republic in October 1949, China's international policy has gone through a sort of metamorphosis – a metamorphosis reflected in the ebb and flow of revolutionary strategic initiative and of selective tactical caution. Her African policy in this period can be viewed more clearly by first analysing the pre-1958 period.

In a major pronouncement on foreign policy, *On the People's Democratic Dictatorship* written in June 1949, Mao Tse-tung, Chairman of the Central Committee of the Chinese Communist Party laid down the following guiding principle for the regime that was soon to take over the central administration of the country:

Internationally we belong to the anti-imperialist front, headed by the Soviet Union.... The Chinese people must either incline towards the side of imperialism or that of socialism. There can be no exception to the rule. It is impossible to sit on the fence. There is no third road. [He went on to say that] It would be the task of the new regime to: unite in a common struggle with those nations of the world which treat us as equals and unite with the peoples of all countries...[1]

[1] Mao, *Selected Works*, IV, 415.

4   China's Policy in Africa 1958–71

Given the continuing intensification of the cold war between the Soviet bloc and the Western countries, and the implacable hostility the Chinese Communists developed during this period towards the United States as a result of U.S. help to the Kuomintang in the Civil War,[1] the new regime's policy could hardly have been different. Neutrality was rejected on the grounds of both prudence and morality. The newly emerging states, notably India, which claimed to be neutral in the East–West struggle, were accused of being appendages of imperialism, without real independence. This conformed to the current policy of the international Communist movement and of Moscow.

The changes Chinese foreign policy has passed through since the 1949 proclamation reflect that interaction of internal and external factors which normally shapes foreign policy. For China, the process was complicated by the existence of two dichotomous factors, which, as in the Soviet Union, have led to speculation on policy motivation – the existence of the revolutionary interests of the regime and the conventional concepts of national interests.

Inevitably, there is a wide gap between declaratory and operational policies – the result on the one hand of idealistic revolutionary aims, and on the other of tactical caution. The latter is dictated by the limited resources of the country and the proportion of those resources the leaders are prepared to commit to achieving grandiose aims in their external affairs.

Initially, however, the new regime was more concerned with obtaining the maximum international recognition, claiming the Chinese seat on the U.N. Security Council, and securing from the Soviet Union the economic and technical aid necessary for the rapid development of an industrial infrastructure at home. Political consolidation, liquidation of the remnants of the Kuomintang forces, as well as various rectification campaigns, still had to be carried out. The regime's attention was therefore centred on Asia, and a positive African policy was non-existent – it was virtually so for the Soviet Union too. Apart from the question of geographical distance, the new regime was not yet strong enough to adopt any meaningful policy towards Africa, despite its ambition to universalise its revolutionary experience. Its tasks were further complicated

[1] Total U.S. aid to the National Government was more than £3,000 m. See *The China White Paper*, U.S. Department of State, Aug. 1949. Reissued by Stanford University Press, 1967, p. 969.

by being called upon to take a decision of vital international importance only months after taking office.

In June 1950, the North Korean armed forces advanced across the thirty-eighth parallel, the temporary demarcation line between North and South Korea. They did not seem to have anticipated the resolute response of the United States and some members of the United Nations, who intervened militarily to support the South Korean war effort under a Security Council resolution, passed in the absence of the Soviet Union. While the available evidence suggests that the Chinese Government was not consulted before the attack was carried out, it did enthusiastically support the North Koreans and at first the outbreak of the war did not seem to be dangerous to China. Initially, the North Koreans advanced rapidly as the South Korean forces began to collapse. However, the committal of a U.N. force under United States command, and the Inchon landing by General MacArthur's forces turned the tide of the war and the North Koreans began their strategic retreat.[1] At this stage, the General Assembly of the United Nations called for the forcible unification of Korea, even though the Soviet Union had returned to the Security Council specifically to prevent such a resolution going through. The United Nations' initial aim of safeguarding South Korea was thus changed into unification by force.[2]

The Chinese Government let it be known that it would not retaliate if South Korean forces alone crossed the demarcation line in pursuit of North Korean forces, but that it could not remain indifferent if United States troops did so. Considerable effort was made to communicate this resolute intention to the United States and the other participating countries, and the U.S. Joint Chiefs of Staff urged restraint on General MacArthur.[3]

In mid-October China issued a final warning through the Indian Ambassador to Peking, and when this was not heeded Chinese troops entered the conflict, at first cautiously to see whether the U.N. forces would halt their advance. With General MacArthur's 'home by Christmas' order to his forces to advance towards the Yalu River, the Chinese 'Volunteers' counterattacked inflicting a

[1] On the Korean War see David Rees, *Korea: The Limited War*, Macmillan, London, 1964.
[2] Leland Goodrich, *Korea*, Council on Foreign Relations, New York, 1956, pp. 128–33.
[3] *Ibid.* pp. 140f. See also W. A. Zelman, *Chinese Intervention in the Korean War: A Bilateral Failure of Deterrence*, University of California Press, Los Angeles, 1967.

6 China's Policy in Africa 1958–71

heavy tactical defeat on the U.N. forces and compelling them to withdraw.[1] Despite this setback, which put the U.N. camp into disarray on the political front, the U.N. forces soon recovered and in 1951 began to push the Communists back. Stalemate was eventually reached in the war, with Armistice talks dragging on from 1951 to 1953.

By not participating in the war, India in particular, and non-aligned countries in general, limited and helped to terminate it. They also proved their usefulness to Peking. The existence of neutralism in a supposedly two-camp world gave China favourable opportunities in her policies towards the Asian countries and later towards Africa.

The strategy of the united front – of uniting with as many people as possible, even if temporarily, in order to isolate and destroy the enemy – was one which the Chinese Communists used to great advantage in the course of their own revolutionary civil war. They also have had recourse to it with some success in their foreign policy. Mao Tse-tung declared in his 'Analysis of the Classes in Chinese Society':[2] Who are our enemies and who are our friends? This question is one of primary importance in the revolution. The method of analysing the contradictions within society and making use of this analysis to select the main targets for attack was one the Chinese leadership intended to apply in their foreign policy. When hostilities ended in Korea in 1953, they turned their attention to another theatre of war in Asia, this time to Indochina, where the Nationalist forces had been waging a liberation war against the French authorities since the end of the Second World War. The end of the war in Korea permitted an influx of weapons from China to the Vietmin forces led by Ho Chi Minh and the French army was defeated in the battle for Dien Bien Phu in 1954. This defeat demonstrated the fact that a colonial people could win a struggle of national liberation against the French and it had an impact on the Algerian war of independence which erupted in November 1954[3] and on the decision to grant independence to Morocco and Tunisia.

[1] Allen Whiting, *China Crosses the Yalu: The Decision to Enter the Korean War*, Macmillan, New York, 1960.
[2] Mao, *Selected Works*, I, p. 13.
[3] See John Dunn *Modern Revolutions: an introduction to the analysis of a political phenomenon*, Cambridge University Press, 1972, pp. 146 and 147.

The new (1952) American Administration, which had blamed the previous government for 'losing' China, soon embarked on a policy of isolating the Communists throughout the world. An economic and commercial embargo had already been placed on activities with China; and to persuade other countries to follow suit was an objective of American foreign policy. By July 1950 the Government extended full protection to the defeated Chinese Government in Taiwan (a step which the new Chinese Government regarded as interference in the Civil War), and it now proceeded to organise military alliances in Asia with the states surrounding China.

With this new threat it was clear to the Chinese Government that the rigid two-bloc division of the world had to be temporarily abandoned. Their new policy was now not so much to isolate the United States and destroy her, as to prevent the isolation of China herself by showing her neighbours that they had nothing to fear and that she was prepared to be on friendly terms with them. Then it was hoped they would not sign military pacts with the United States which might make it possible for American military bases to be set up around China. In this attempt, the Chinese Government sought to utilise the neutralist policy of many States in the area. While the U.S. Secretary of State, John Foster Dulles, condemned neutrality on moralistic grounds thus alienating Nehru and other leaders, China achieved a diplomatic masterstroke in 1954 by including the so-called 'five principles of co-existence' (Panch Sheel), in instruments relating to India's trade with the Tibet region of China.[1] The two countries pledged themselves to maintain:

Mutual respect for each other's territorial integrity and sovereignty;
Mutual non-aggression;
Mutual non-interference in each other's internal affairs;
Equality and mutual benefit;
Peaceful co-existence.

This document was widely publicised, and to many it seemed to herald a new peaceful China whose attitudes would make the contemporary American efforts to form an anti-Communist united front in Asia superfluous and irrelevant. This new diplomatic initiative was soon to bear fruit with the convening of an Asian-

[1] On India's connection with Tibet see N. Maxwell, *India's China War*, Jonathan Cape Ltd, London, 1970, pp. 39-135.

8   *China's Policy in Africa 1958–71*

African Conference of Heads of States and Governments in Bandung, Indonesia (18–27 April 1955). The decision to call the conference was announced in a communiqué issued after the meeting of the Colombo Powers (Burma, Ceylon, India, Pakistan and Indonesia). At first, even the announcement aroused anxiety in the wider Communist camp lest it should turn out to be an anti-Communist crusade, though China and North Vietnam were invited.[1] Opinions in the Western countries on the possible achievements of the proposed conference varied, but the majority probably agreed with the Western diplomat who predicted that it would 'be a Babylonic cacophony ending up in a rising crescendo of confusion and indecision',[2] because of the apparent incompatibility of interests among the participants.

However, contrary to expectations that China would be in the dock at Bandung, Chou En-lai gained prestige with a triumph of personal diplomacy. Disarming all hostility with a display of moderation and benevolence, he held aloof from all wrangling and steadfastly identified China with the common cause. He then played his 'master card' by offering to negotiate with the United States on the Taiwan issue. This offer to negotiate, with China's arch-enemy, was made at precisely the right moment to achieve the maximum effect on the participants in the conference.[3]

Bandung also marked a watershed in Chinese diplomacy, especially with regard to the evolution of a policy in Africa. Henceforth, Afro-Asian solidarity and the 'spirit of Bandung' became a prominent theme in Chinese pronouncements. Six African states were represented at the conference – Egypt, the Sudan, Ethiopia, Liberia, Libya and the Gold Coast (now Ghana). It was of more immediate importance that Gamal Abdul Nasser led the Egyptian delegation to the conference. Chou En-lai seized the opportunity to establish a working relationship with him and to impress some of the other African delegates. The contacts made at Bandung were a successful beginning and a measure of Chou's success was the publication in the Cairo press of pictures of Chou En-lai, Nehru and Nasser as 'the three champions of Afro-Asian independence'.[4]

[1] F. Schatten *Communism in Africa*, 1966, p. 269.
[2] *Survey of International Affairs*, 1955, p. 61.
[3] Charles Neuhauser, *Third World Politics: China and the Afro-Asian People's Solidarity Organisation 1957–1967*, 1968, p. 6.
[4] G. F. Hudson, 'Balance Sheet on Bandung', *Commentary*, June 1955, p. 565.

The Bandung Conference was followed by Chinese efforts to increase diplomatic, economic and cultural contacts. In 1956, Chinese cultural missions visited Egypt, the Sudan, Morocco, Tunisia and Ethiopia. China also made commercial inroads into Africa with large cotton purchases from Egypt, followed by her first commercial contracts with other African countries – beginning with the Sudan and Morocco. On the diplomatic front, she succeeded in obtaining diplomatic recognition from Egypt in May 1956, and the first Chinese embassy in Africa was established in Cairo, with the wider function of contacting as many African groups as possible and making a concrete analysis of the general African situation. Ambassador Ch'en Chia-k'ang was sent to Cairo, where he remained till December 1965.

From Cairo, China's diplomats observed the situation on the continent. On most points, they seem to have conformed to the Soviet analysis, although probably disagreeing about parliamentary roads to Socialism in the ex-colonies. China was now beginning to examine specific African countries, though events in Africa were still of peripheral, not direct, interest, and only a small proportion of her foreign trade was with African states.[1]

With the outbreak of the Suez crisis in October 1956 China offered an outright gift of $4.7 million[2] to Egypt, coupled with a promise to send volunteers if asked to do so by the Egyptian Government.[3] Even though the latter offer could hardly have been taken seriously by the French, British and Israeli Governments, this did not seem to detract from the cheap popularity China wanted to gain in North Africa. From this time Chinese broadcasts in Arabic increased, and the China Islamic Association sent more Chinese pilgrims to Mecca, calling fortuitously at Cairo.[4] In 1957 China stepped up her cultural exchanges with Africa, and her stand at the Casablanca Trade Fair in Morocco gave a good impression of her achievements.

However, in 1956 and 1957 considerably more attention was devoted to events in the Communist camp and to developments affecting the balance of forces between the so-called imperialist

[1] In 1956 China's trade with non-Communist countries was not yet very important to her development and trade with Africa was still less so.
[2] See Table 1 in Appendix I.
[3] Z. Brzezinski, *Africa and the Communist World*. Article by R. Lowenthal, p. 157.
[4] See Table 1 in Appendix I.

camp and the camp of peace; these events together with the 'hundred flowers' campaign in China, have considerable effect on Chinese policy in Africa.

Events in the Communist camp affected China's policy towards Africa and the rest of the world because of the 'common' ideological outlook which Communist countries are said to share. It is a prismatic outlook which sees the world as passing through an incessant process of dialectical conflict and change, inevitably propelling it towards the desired Communist millennium. This Marxist-Leninist analysis does not, however, provide unimpeachable and rigid rules of do's and don't's, as it is often necessary in the face of overwhelming odds to take a tactical step backwards in order to take two strategic steps forward at the opportune moment. Marxism-Leninism then, as a guide to action and not as dogma, necessarily requires continuous penetrating analysis of the situation as well as appropriate action at the right moment. The dilemma of Marxism-Leninism arises when a Communist party assumes absolute power in a state. The demands of proletarian internationalism sometimes conflict unavoidably with the traditional concept of national interest or *raison d'etat*, and at that point the government has to make a choice between priorities – ideological mission or 'realpolitik'. No doubt an ideological rationalisation is always provided whenever it is necessary to retreat on the ideological front. Complications arise, however, when there is no longer one Communist state but many, and when the element of nationalism refuses to disappear before the idealistic demands of proletarian internationalism.

For a long time after the October Revolution of 1917 in Russia, there was no other Communist state, and Moscow acted as the supreme guardian of Marxism-Leninism as well as the real dictator of the strategy and tactics to be adopted by other Communist parties. The Chinese Communist Party had more than its 'fair' share of misfortune and calamities resulting from wrong directives emanating from Moscow, directives which did not take into consideration the actual situation in China and sometimes simply resulting from conflict in the Russian leadership.[1]

---

[1] The clearest example of this was Stalin's insistence in 1927 that the C.C.P. must continue its united front policy with the KMT even after the party had been decimated by the massacre of thousands of its members; and his frequent calls for revolutionary

The C.C.P. was not in in 1949, as a result of Stalin's assistance and generosity, but in spite of him and the 'advice' he had given to the Chinese Communists at the end of the Second World War[1] – advice dictated by what he considered to be Soviet imperial interests in the Far East. It could have been seen from the beginning that the interests of a strong and united China would conflict both ideologically and materially with those of the Soviet Union. A careful perusal of Mao's statements in Yenan in the late 1930s might also have suggested that this conflict would extend to Africa,[2] in view of the evident Soviet interest in continuing as the chief if not the only guide of Communist activities throughout the world.

Though initially the Chinese leaders claimed their revolutionary experience was relevant to the movements which will be considered later in colonial and semi-colonial areas the Chinese were in general prepared to defer to Soviet dominance of the Communist movement, if only as a tactical concession. On Stalin's death, however, in March 1953 'ended the era when a decision by one man could change abruptly the whole course of foreign policy of the Soviet Union and world Communism. His successors neither collectively nor singly would ever again have that power.'[3] From the struggle for leadership within the Soviet Party Khruschev eventually emerged as the leader of the Party and Government. In the process, Chinese support had been deemed very useful and the new Russian leaders saw the need to be more generous to China in terms of economic aid.[4]

action when this would smack of high adventurism to the local Communists, who were aware of the actual situation.
[1] As Stalin revealed to a Yugoslav delegation in Moscow, his 'advice' to the CCP was to disband their army and co-operate with the KMT Government rather than fight another civil war – advice in direct contradiction to Mao's saying: 'Without a people's army, the people have nothing.' See Milovan Djilas, *Conversations with Stalin*, Harcourt Brace, 1962, p. 182.
[2] Interview at Pao An in 1936 with Edgar Snow, *Red Star Over China*, London, 1937, p. 421. 'The victory of the Chinese national liberation movement will be part of the victory of world Communism, because to defeat imperialism in China means the destruction of one of its most powerful bases. If China wins its independence, the world revolution will progress very rapidly.'
[3] Adam B. Ulam, *Expansion and Co-Existence: The History of Soviet Foreign Policy, 1917–1967*, Secker & Warburg, London, 1968, p. 538.
[4] Following the Khruschev-Bulganin visit to Peking in 1955, the Soviet share in the Joint Stock Companies was abandoned, Port Arthur was returned to China and more credits were offered, but the Russians refused to discuss the return of Outer Mon-

With Stalin's death, the only giant left in the Communist world was Mao Tse-tung, and the Chinese expected him to play the role Stalin had played, giving ideological guidance to the rest of the Communist world. Khrushchev's denunciation of Stalin in his address to the 20th Congress of the C.P.S.U. in 1956 came as a great shock to the Chinese leaders, the more so as they were not consulted before the speech was made. Moreover, a corollary of the speech was the new policy of so-called peaceful co-existence with the capitalist world, the non-inevitability of world war and the possibility of the parliamentary road to power in other non-Communist states. Khrushchev's pronouncement on peaceful co-existence might seem to conform with the contemporareous Chinese adoption of the five principles and the 'spirit of Bandung'. In reality, however, his move was an attempt to prevent Asia falling by default into the Chinese orbit. It was a counter-challenge. The immediate impact within the Soviet world of Khruschev's de-Stalinisation policy was felt in Eastern Europe. As a result of Stalin's firm grip being loosened Gomulka rose to power in Poland and the uprising against the Communist Party and government in Hungary took place in October 1956 – a popular uprising which was ruthlessly suppressed by Soviet troops. Although the polycentrism of ideas in the Communist world unleashed by de-Stalinisation could not be easily reversed, it was left to Mao Tse-tung, the philosopher, to provide the ideological under-pinning for the continuance of conflict in a supposedly Socialist society.

Following Chou En-lai's tour of East European countries early in 1957 – which in effect constituted intervention by China in the disenchantment between Moscow and the East European countries, Mao Tse-tung delivered his momentous speech *On the Correct Handling of Contradictions Among the People*[1] at the Eleventh Session of the Supreme State Conference on 27 February. Here he explained why contradictions will continue to exist even in the

---

golia. For the role played by Chinese intervention in the Soviet power struggle see Uri Ra'anan, *The U.S.S.R. Arms the Third World*, M.I.T. Press, Cambridge, Mass., 1969.

[1] Mao Tse-tung, *Four Essays on Philosophy*, Peking, 1966, p. 79. He based his thinking on an earlier essay 'On Contradiction' written in August 1937, where he discussed fully such concepts as the universality and particularity of Contradiction, the principal Contradiction and the principal aspect of a Contradiction, and the place of antagonism in Contradiction.

Communist society, and how contradictions among the people[1] can, if not properly handled, easily acquire an antagonistic nature in spite of their basically non-antagonistic character. While the theory provided the much needed ideological underpinning for the Communists, it also implied that doctrinal authority could emanate from Peking as it had done in the past from Moscow. This implication was to become particularly clear later on with the Sino-Soviet rivalry for influence, not only within the Socialist states and the Communist parties in Western Europe but, more importantly for this study, in the developing countries of Asia, Africa and Latin America.

With the abortive 'hundred flowers campaign'[2] in the late spring and early summer of 1957, Chinese internal, and, of necessity, external, policies shifted to the Left. This shift was particularly important coming at the moment when the international situation was about to undergo a 'dramatic change' because of the Soviet Union's technological achievements. By September 1956, Mao Tse-tung had already pointed in the direction of militancy when in his address to the opening session of the Eighth Congress of the C.C.P.: he said: 'We must give active support to the National Independence and Liberation Movements in Asia, Africa and Latin America, as well as to the Peace Movement and righteous struggle in all countries throughout the world.'

To do this, however, the international situation had to be taken into consideration. Already at the beginning of 1957 the Chinese had declared that the Socialist camp headed by the Soviet Union was 'as strong as the imperialist bloc, if not stronger'.[3] What occurred in the autumn of that year was seen as marking a decisive shift in the balance of forces between Socialism and imperialism – a shift which called for the adoption of appropriate strategy and

[1] The definition of 'the people' varies with circumstances and situations, but is always such as to encompass at least 80 per cent of the population. This flexibility in definition gives a leeway to the Chinese in deciding whether or not to support so-called 'patriotic' regimes in developing countries, and makes Chinese policy border on opportunism rather than dogmatism.
[2] This was a call by Mao for free and open criticisms of the regime so that the 'few' grievances among the people not yet met by the Communist Party might be brought to the surface. The vehemence of the criticisms in the press against both the Communist system and the high-handedness of the party functionaries shook the regime. A halt was called to the campaign with the *post facto* explanation that it was an attempt to trap the anti-party elements in the country.
[3] *Hsieh Hsi*, No. 1, 2 Jan. 1956.

tactics in the struggle against imperialism on all fronts including Africa, Asia and Latin America. As this marked a significant phase in China's policy stance, this study begins with the meeting of the Communist and Workers' Parties in Moscow in November 1957 and considers its implications for Chinese policy in Africa in the years ahead. It also looks at the convening in Cairo in December 1957 of the Afro-Asian Peoples' Solidarity Conference – a conference which decided to establish a permanent secretariat in Cairo.

2 BREAKING NEW GROUND 1958-9

The International Situation and its Implications for Chinese Policy in Africa

The significant shift to the left in Chinese domestic politics in the autumn of 1957 was accompanied by a similar shift in foreign policy. Signified internally by the anti-right campaign in late summer and externally by the advocacy of more militant confrontation with the United States in those areas of the world where the Communists had 'genuine' grievances, it coincided with a significant technological break-through in Soviet armaments. The successful launching of an earth satellite and an intercontinental ballistic missile in October and November 1957 was regarded by the Chinese as a mark of decisive international change in the balance of forces between 'Socialism' and 'imperialism'. Mao Tse-tung led a C.C.P. delegation to the celebration of the 40th anniversary of the October Revolution in Moscow. Addressing the Moscow meeting of Communist and Workers' Parties on 18 November 1957, Mao made his now famous speech on the East Wind.

It is my opinion that the international situation has now reached a new turning point. There are two winds in the world today, the East Wind and the West Wind. There is a Chinese saying 'Either the East Wind prevails over the West Wind or the West Wind prevails over the East Wind.' I believe it is characteristic of the situation today that the East Wind is prevailing over the West Wind. That is to say, the forces of socialism have become overwhelmingly superior to the forces of imperialism.[1]

For Africa, the implications of this analysis of the international situation in terms of tactics and strategy in the struggle against imperialism were made more explicit in various editorials and commentaries in the *People's Daily* and *Red Flag*. The important point was not whether the Socialist camp really had achieved over-

[1] Mao Tse-tung: Speech at the Moscow Meeting of Communist and Workers' Parties, 18 Nov. 1957. *Quotations from Chairman Mao Tse-tung*, 1st Edition, 1966, p. 80, Foreign Languages Press, Peking, 1966.

whelming superiority vis-à-vis imperialism, but that the Chinese believed this had happened. In his Address to the Fifth Session of the First National People's Congress, in February 1958, Prime Minister Chou En-lai laid great emphasis on the decisive change in the international balance of forces and connected the strength of the socialist bloc with the revolutionary opportunities in Africa by saying that 'The existence of this Socialist Camp and its powerful support to national independence movements has inspired all those peoples striving to win or preserve their freedom and independence, and provides increasingly favourable conditions for them to wage successfully their heroic struggle against imperialism and colonialism.'[1]

The Chinese viewpoint thus expressed was based on the dialectical conception of society which sees human and material relationships in terms of contradictions. According to Leninist postulates the three contradictions of capitalism are (a) between labour and capital; (b) between imperialists competing for world markets and raw materials; and (c) between colonial peoples and imperialists. These three kinds of contradictions lead to three kinds of conflict and wars: (i) between the proletariat and the capitalists; (ii) imperialist wars; and (iii) wars of liberation. From it follows the Leninist view that imperialism can be weakened by engaging the imperialist forces on one of three fronts. Thus, objectively, the struggle of the colonial peoples for freedom from imperialist exploitation contributes to the eventual and inevitable success of the proletarian revolution and should therefore be promoted. Stalin gave a doctrinal formulation to this view when he wrote that

> If Europe and America may be called the front or the arena of the major battles between Socialism and imperialism, the unequal nations and the colonies with their raw materials, fuel, food and vast store of manpower must be regarded as the rear, the reserve of imperialism. To win a war it is necessary not only to triumph at the front, but also to revolutionise the enemy's rear, his reserves. Hence the victory of the world proletarian revolution may be regarded as assured only if the proletariat is able to combine its own revolutionary struggle with the liberation movement of the labouring masses of the unequal nations and the colonies against the rule of the imperialists.[2]

Significantly, he did not claim that support for the anti-imperialist struggle in the colonial areas was altruistic; this was to come later,

[1] *Current Background*, No. 492, pp. 6–7.
[2] J. V. Stalin, *Works*, Vol. v, p. 57.

when the Chinese claimed love for and solidarity with the African peoples in their struggle for absolute independence. Since imperialism can be attacked on any of three fronts, victory is more likely if the front chosen is the weakest link in the imperialist chain. It is from this point that a correct analysis of the international situation is important. The so-called overwhelming superiority of the Socialist forces over imperialism did not mean that the Soviet Union and the Socialist countries should launch an attack on the imperialist camp and precipitate a war. Rather that the Soviet advance in armaments should be used to provide a nuclear umbrella for members of the camp who had 'legitimate grievances' against imperialism. China did feel she had a case herself against the United States with regard to Taiwan and the off-shore islands. At the same time, just wars of national liberation, if waged in Asia, Africa and Latin America, would inevitably dissipate the efforts of imperialism, enable the 'people's forces' to engage it at each point and thus defeat it. More important still they would prevent an undesirable detente between U.S. and U.S.S.R. as this would also be incompatible with active support for the liberation movements.

In practice, therefore, Chinese interests would be furthered by the agitation of the African peoples for independence, particularly where such agitation had reached the 'advanced' stage of armed struggle. As in the years 1958-9 the Chinese began to analyse more intensively the situation in Africa and the possibilities for furthering their interests, they came to understand that a rigid approach could not succeed and that there would have to be compromises. By examining the similarity between the early stages of the Chinese revolution and the revolutionary situation in Africa,[1] they realised the need to take one step backwards in order to take two forward.

Tactics and Strategy

With the establishment of their embassy in Cairo in 1956, the Chinese were able to contact the various exiled political leaders who had offices there. They now divided their activities in Africa accord-

---

[1] The concept of 'one step backwards and two steps forward' was essentially a Leninist principle. The idea is to reach a compromise on an issue of principle with the belief that an opportune moment in the future will enable one to achieve the original objective. It is adopted where rigidity on an issue is likely to block the achievement of an objective permanently. This of course can easily degenerate into mere opportunism.

ing to the status of each area. Essentially there were three broad categories:
  1. Politically independent African states, classified into 'progressive' and 'pro-imperialist'.
  2. 'Advanced' colonial areas such as Algeria, Cameroun and to a lesser extent Kenya.
  3. Colonial territories which were at present relatively quiet although growing in political awareness and in some cases actively clamouring for independence.

I shall consider the instruments of policy in the next section, but wish to emphasise here that Chinese objectives in Africa were both short range and long range. The short range objective in states of the first category was to break through the barrier of suspicion created by 'imperialist' propaganda, establish diplomatic relations, extend trade and eventually aid, while trying to persuade the government to adopt an anti-western brand of neutralism. The long range objective would be to help train indigenous revolutionary cadres whose function would be to transform the African nationalist political temperament into a Communist one. The contradiction between these two objectives was shown in worsening relations with the United Arab Republic in late 1958 and during much of 1959.[1] All-out Chinese support would be given to countries in the second category, 'advanced' colonial areas, to enable them to carry the struggle against imperialism to complete victory. As for the third category, the Chinese claimed to be under an obligation to help them advance towards the stage of armed struggle, and to persuade those countries which had won political independence to regard support for the 'struggling masses' as their obligation too. To speed the process towards a revolutionary situation in Africa, various analogies were made with the Chinese revolution – analogies which became more persistent in 1958 and 1959.

Addressing the opening session of the World Federation of Trade Unions (W.F.T.U.) Conference in Peking on 16 November 1949, Liu Shao-chi[2] had declared that

> The course followed by the Chinese people in defeating imperialism and its lackeys and in founding the People's Republic of China is the course that should be followed by the peoples of the various colonial and semi-colonial countries

[1] See below pp. 21–7.
[2] China's Head of State (1959–68). In 1949 he was second in command to Mao Tse-tung.

in their fight for national independence and people's democracy.... If the people of a colonial or semi-colonial country have no arms to defend themselves they have nothing at all. The existence and development of proletarian organisations and the existence and development of a national united front are closely linked to the existence and development of such an armed struggle. For many colonial and semi-colonial peoples, this is the only way in their struggle for independence and liberation.[1]

Although emphasis on the need to emulate the Chinese revolution was muted after 1950, it was revived with full vigour in the late fifties when the Chinese felt that it was again time to arouse the revolutionary consciousness of the colonial and semi-colonial peoples. Commenting on the meeting of delegates from Asian and African countries in December–January 1957–8, the *People's Daily* said

Although these countries or areas have different social systems, ideologies, languages and customs, the people share a similar experience and a common desire. The overwhelming majority have suffered or are suffering from imperialist oppression, enslavement and slaughter.... Their common demand is to fight for and safeguard independence and freedom, consolidate world peace and promote friendly co-existence among the peoples of all countries.[2]

Though stress was still being laid on the 'Afro-Asian nature' of the struggle against imperialism, the Chinese were also well aware that: 'the tide of the national independence movement has spread from Asia to Africa'.[3]

At this stage the Soviet Union did not object to China's emphasis on the special relevance of their own experience for the underdeveloped countries, or what they called the exploited areas of the world, since this clearly furthered general Communist goals. Indeed Western observers[4] were quick to assume that a formal division of revolutionary labour had been agreed by Moscow and Peking.

Since China considered the United States to be the main enemy at this time, it was not enough for the African struggle to be against imperialism in general. In one way or the other, the United States had to be brought into the scene and condemned by the African people not merely as the leader of imperialism but as the bulwark

---
[1] Quoted in *China Quarterly*, No. 7, July–Sept. 1961, and in Z. Brzesinski (Ed.) *Africa and the Communist World*, article by R. Lowenthal, p. 143.
[2] Hsinhua (New China News Agency) p. 17, 27 Dec. 1957.
[3] N.C.N.A. 2 Jan. 1958, p. 2. Editorial of 1 Jan. 1958 of *People's Daily*.
[4] For instance, the Cairo Correspondent of the *Japan Times* reporting as late as 13 June 1959.

of the activities of French, Portuguese and British colonialism and thus the chief enemy of the African people. Africans were therefore warned of the double tactics the United States was adopting, pretending to be in sympathy with the African peoples while at the same time helping the colonial powers to maintain oppression.

The United States was an arch supporter of colonialism. It had all along supported France's colonialist policy toward the Algerian people and subsidised the French government's heavy war expenditure. Through N.A.T.O. the U.S. had continuously supplied France with arms which were used to slaughter the Algerian people. The Algerian people have taken up arms against the French colonialists because they can no longer endure colonial slavery.[1]

Although these vehement attacks were later to be seen in the light of the Sino-Soviet conflict on the desirability of detente with America, at this time the Soviet Union and China both seemed to have mutual interests in ensuring that the United States was presented to Africa in the most unfavourable light. Arousing the revolutionary consciousness of the African people by turning their hatred of colonialism into positive action was to characterise Chinese policy in Africa in pursuit of both short and long range objectives.

Before dealing with China's practical policy in this period and the responses made to concrete events on the continent, it is, I think, important to stress again the inter-relationship of her African policy with her government's overall objectives and aspirations. The foreign policy of any country is, after all, designed to promote as far as possible the interests of that country as perceived at each particular moment by the country's leaders. Changes in some aspects of foreign policy may not necessarily reflect changes in the concrete situation but rather a change in the perception of the policy-makers or a calculation that such change would have desirable results. China's African policy in this period, and more particularly in the sixties, was a function of her triangular relationship with the United States and the Soviet Union. Since this relationship has not been unchanging, China has had to modify her policy accordingly. Of course this is not to say that the African states have been used merely as pawns on the international chessboard: the Chinese were jolted by certain steps taken by these governments and have consequently steered their policy on a different course. Such events occurred in the years 1958 to 1959 and will be dealt with in the next section.

[1] S.C.M.P. No. 1474, 16 Feb. 1957.

Policy Implementation

China's attempts to attain her objectives in Africa, involved: efforts to obtain diplomatic recognition and extend trade and cultural exchanges with Africa; concrete support for revolutionary groups on the continent; invitations to African delegations to visit China and reciprocal visits to Africa by various Chinese delegations; the use of 'front' organisations in lieu of Communist parties in most African states and in lieu of diplomatic recognition. The choice of instrument depended on the status of each area – independent African states, 'advanced' colonial areas or other colonial territories.

By January 1958, there were nine independent African states – Ethiopia, Egypt, Morocco, Libya, the Sudan, Ghana, Liberia, Tunisia and South Africa. Of these countries Morocco and Tunisia (which were not then independent) and South Africa had not attended the Bandung Conference of Asian and African States in April 1955. In his closing remarks at that conference, Chou En-lai had stated that 'once again the Chinese people extend their full sympathy and support to the struggle of the peoples of Algeria, Morocco and Tunisia for self-determination and independence . . . and to the just struggles waged by all the peoples of Asia and Africa to shake off colonial oppression and win national independence and the people's freedom'.[1] After the conference the Chinese consistently stated that the cornerstone of their foreign policy was peaceful co-existence and Afro-Asian solidarity in the spirit of Bandung. By January 1958, however, Egypt alone had granted diplomatic recognition to the Chinese People's Republic though this did not in practice inhibit Chinese contacts with the other independent African states.

Events in 1958 and most of 1959 tended to direct Chinese attention to North Africa and the Middle East. This meant that the vagaries of Arab politics and nationalism affected Chinese policy in North Africa and led to a deterioration in relations with Egypt. Relations with Egypt were of particular importance for a number of reasons. On the one hand recognition by Egypt in 1956 made it possible for China to establish her first mission in Africa and so make contact with other African groups – contacts which were to prove important in future. After the Suez crisis of October 1956 she granted $4.7 million of aid to Egypt and offered to send volunteers

[1] *China and the Asian-African Conference*, Peking F.L.P., p. 30, 1955.

to fight side by side with the Egyptian forces. On many colonial issues, too, the Chinese found themselves on the same side as the militant Egyptians. On the other hand, President Nasser was, and continued to be, an Arab nationalist whose philosophy of Arab socialism was pointedly incompatible with Communism. By itself this incompatibility did not account for the deterioration of Sino-Egyptian relations since Nasser was also militantly anti-imperialist.

Policy towards Egypt was, however, part of the debate between the Soviet Union and China on the desirability of extending large-scale economic aid to those newly independent Afro-Asian states which were headed by bourgeois nationalists. Following the Khrushchev and Bulganin Asian tour in 1955, the Soviet Union decided to extend aid to Indonesia, India and Egypt and to establish a working relationship with the governments of these countries. This new policy of peaceful co-existence (which incidentally the Chinese were also championing) negated the old two-camp policy and made it possible for Khrushchev to include the nationalist states in what he called 'the zone of peace', thus separating them from the imperialist zone. But the establishment of a working relationship immediately begged the question of the role of the Communist parties in these newly independent states. Were they to be asked to join forces with the bourgeois governments, to promote anti-imperialism independently of them, or to work for the violent overthrow of the new leadership by beginning the second phase of the people's revolution?

The ideological issue apart, it seems to me that it was the economic implications of such a policy that were important in the debate. Obviously the Soviet Union could not support violent overthrow by indigenous Communists of governments which she was simultaneously providing with substantial economic aid. On the other hand it was also difficult for her to have good relations with a government which was currently waging an all-out campaign against its own Communists. The Chinese emphasised the need to give complete support to Communists who were prepared to carry out the second phase of the revolution. This stand, though ideological, was in fact motivated by reasons of national interest and by sound economic reasons, although the latter did tend to negate the very principles of proletarian internationalism. The economic reasons behind the Chinese arguments can be reconstructed thus:

The Soviet Union was not endowed with unlimited resources. Those she had must first be used to promote the 'vigorous' economic development of the Soviet Union and the members of the Socialist camp who needed such aid for their development – China, Albania and the other Communist countries in genuine need. The development of strong Communist nations would increase the overall strength of the Socialist camp which would then be in a better position to help the exploited masses of the developing countries. Any unilateral extension of Soviet resources to bolster the bourgeois nationalist regimes (e.g. the £250m for the Aswan High Dam)[1] would subtract from the ability of the Soviet Union to help other members of the camp. Moreover thus shifting the force of competition to the economic front would inevitably mean domination of Socialist camp policy by the Soviet Union, a situation not justified by the 'quality' of Soviet leadership, since China was not strong enough economically to participate at all. Furthermore it might give the United States an edge, since the latter was better equipped to wage this kind of competition in the developing areas than the economically less developed Soviet Union.

The African leaders of course viewed the situation differently since they believed that they had to rule in the interests of their people and not in the interests of Communism – militant anti-imperialism notwithstanding. In April 1958 Nasser gave an interview to a Columbia Broadcast Service correspondent in which he stated the views of Arab Nationalists on national and foreign policy. In the recent elections he had told the people 'frankly' to oppose 'those whom we considered to be unfit to represent the people. We did, in fact, object to some reactionaries and communists [placing the two at par]. Then we left the door open to the nationalist elements.'[2] If political parties were allowed to function the reactionaries and feudalists would propose an alliance with the West and the Communists with the East. That would leave a nationalist party strongly advocating non alignment. Such a policy, he contended, would lead the parties to 'wage a violent battle which will destroy the unity of our country.... I do not want to destroy the unity

---

[1] The Russians provided an industrial loan of $175m in January 1958. On soviet aid to Egypt, Indonesia and India, see I. Marshall Goldman, *Soviet Foreign Aid*, Praeger Publications, London, 1967.
[2] Cairo 'Voice of the Arabs', B.B.C. *S.W.B.* Part IV, 7 Apr. 1958.

of our homeland in the interests of this or that foreign country.'[1]

The stand taken by Nasser was to be echoed later by other African leaders, including Sekou Touré, Nkrumah, Modibo Keita, Nyerere, in fact by all those who have adopted the one party state. China learned a lesson from the Egyptian position as can be seen in their later attitude to these leaders, but by that time Sino-Egyptian relations had already deteriorated.

In mid 1958 Nasser clamped down on the Egyptian Communists and imprisoned their leaders. The issue was complicated by the existence of Communist parties in Syria (which joined Egypt in 1958 to form the United Arab Republic) and Iraq. On 23 December Nasser launched an attack on Syrian Communists in a speech at Port Said,[2] and Egyptian comments described them as opportunists. Relations between Nasser and the Iraqi revolutionary Government under General Quassim (with whom China had excellent relations) deteriorated and so did Sino-Egyptian relations.

An article by Yu Chao-li in the C.C.P. theoretical journal *Red Flag* (*Hung Chi*) of 1 April 1959 declared that

President Nasser, who once won the people's respect, has recently made vicious attacks on Iraq, the communist parties and the Soviet Union.... At present, Iraq and the U.A.R. are two independent and Sovereign countries.... If one ... insists on annexing the other, this will only harm the very interests of Arab unity. Those doing so, no matter how much they talk about Arab national interests, are in fact making it easy for the imperialists to carry out their scheme of getting Arabs to fight Arabs.... 'Neither East nor West' is only a deliberate attempt to confuse friends with enemies. It is tantamount to saying 'neither enemies nor friends'. But those who want no friends will naturally not be feared by any enemy. Indeed this will become a step toward going over to the enemy.[3]

The article thus in effect opposed Nasser's policy of Arab unification if the results would be anti-Communist and detrimental to the anti-imperialist cause. Although Khrushchev had attacked the U.A.R. in his speech to the 21st Congress of the C.P.S.U. in January he had nevertheless insisted that relations between the two states should not be affected by Nasser's internal policies. China adopted a more uncompromising attitude. The U.A.R. should be reminded that to

realise Arab unity, the first thing, of course, is to help the people of Algeria,

[1] Cairo 'Voice of the Arabs', B.B.C. *S.W.B.*, Part IV, 7 Apr. 1958.
[2] B.B.C. *S.W.B.*, Part IV, 28 Dec. 1968.
[3] B.B.C. *S.W.B.* Part V, 7 Apr. 1959. Article 'Imperialism as Enemy of Arab Liberation'.

Jordan, Oman and the other countries now under direct imperialist aggression to attain their independence.... How is it that just when the anti-imperialist struggles of the oppressed peoples in Asia, Africa and Latin America – especially in the very continent of Africa where Cairo is located – are surging ahead overwhelmingly and incessantly expanding, the U.A.R. authorities that *were* in the forefront of the anti-imperialist struggle remain silent in face of imperialist aggression and yet launch so fierce an attack on Iraq in Western Asia which resolutely opposes imperialism?

Since the tour of the Middle East by the U.S. envoy in December 1958, official and semi-official organs of the U.A.R. had stopped attacking imperialism seriously.

We do not find it strange that from the moment when the U.A.R. authorities stopped their struggle against imperialism... they began conducting frantic anti-communist activities. Our people know from their own history that whoever deviates from a people's standpoint, from the standpoint of anti-imperialism, invariably opposes communism because the communist party is the staunchest defender of the people's interests and the most resolute fighter against imperialism.[1]

This direct attack on the anti-Communist policy of the U.A.R. was partly aimed at making Khrushchev delay the large scale economic aid promised to Nasser, thus using the economic weapon as a direct instrument of foreign policy. Relations became even more difficult in April 1959 when the U.A.R. gave what amounted to verbal approval of the rebellion in Tibet, that troubled area of China. In a sixty page pamphlet the U.A.R. Information Department described events in Tibet as amounting to revolution and disapproved of its suppression. Paradoxically, the New China News Agency described the U.A.R.s attitude as interference in the internal affairs of China.

Borrowing fabrications churned out by the imperialist propaganda machine, the pamphlet called the rebellion in Tibet 'an Eastern version of the Hungarian revolution'. It described the quelling of the rebellion as another step in international Communism's 'creeping domination and determination to enforce Communist rule by force of arms and bloodshed'.[2]

The connection between China's criticism of Nasser's anti-communist activities and U.A.R. criticism of Chinese handling of the Tibetan rebellion was not made. The U.A.R.s attitude was even more galling as it came at a time when Chinese relations with India

[1] B.B.C. *S.W.B.*, Part v, No. 856, 26 Mar. 1959. *People's Daily* (long) editorial on U.A.R. attack on Iraq under the heading 'What are the real national interests of the Arab people?'.
[2] S.C.M.P. No. 2002, 29 Apr. 1959, p. 42.

were getting worse. The logical move, of the U.A.R. towards India, was not a welcome spectacle to China.

Strained relations continued. In October U.A.R. Government officials boycotted the National Day celebrations at the Chinese Embassy in Cairo, because Peking also invited the Syrian Communist Khalid Bakdash. On 30 September Cairo radio criticised China for having allowed Khalid Bakdash to speak at the ceremonies connected with the National Day – he had taken advantage of that opportunity to attack 'Arab Nationalism' and to advocate the break-up of the U.A.R. into its component parts. The U.A.R. Chargé d'Affaires in Peking walked out of the ceremonies. The U.A.R. protested strongly to China and asked for clarification of Bakdash's speech,[1] since this was also broadcast over Radio Peking. China was criticised for her 'discourteous aggressive and undiplomatic attitude', for her ingratitude towards the U.A.R. which had been the first African country to recognise Peking, and for having abandoned the Bandung principles by interfering in the U.A.R.s internal affairs. In an interview with the Associated Press on 7 October,[2] Nasser said that the U.A.R. regarded the Chinese Government's action over Bakdash as an insult and interference which could not be condoned from any quarter, but he stressed that there was no evidence of Chinese subversive activities against the U.A.R. and he did not think that the episode would lead to a break in diplomatic relations. While he was pained by the Chinese action he did not regret recognising China in 1956.

The quarrel had repercussions elsewhere in the Arab world. Tunis Radio for example asserted that U.A.R. attacks on China were unjustified in that Cairo itself continued to shelter and help Arab citizens from Jordan, Iraq and Tunisia who were opposed to their governments. It was hypocritical of Cairo to talk about the Bandung spirit.[3]

Commenting on the Bakdash issue the Chinese Government explained that it had never thought he would say what he did and that it was the Chinese Communist Party, not the Government, which had invited him to the National Day celebrations.[4] On the

[1] B.B.C. S.W.B. Second Series, Part IV, No. 144, 1 Oct. 1959.
[2] B.B.C. S.W.B. Second Series, No. 153, Part IV, 12 Oct. 1959.
[3] B.B.C. S.W.B. Second Series, No. 152, Part IV, 10 Oct. 1959.
[4] B.B.C. S.W.B. Second Series, No. 165, Part IV, 26 Oct. 1959.

25 October the U.A.R. press reported that the crisis was now considered over and that the U.A.R. Chargé d'Affaires in Peking was returning to the post from which he had earlier been recalled. Although the official Chinese explanation was hardly credible, the U.A.R. displayed its willingness to bury the hatchet, to overlook the fact that Bakdash's statement was broadcast three times in Arabic over Radio Peking, and to save Chou En-lai the embarrassment of having to disclaim his government's responsibility for the Communist Party's activities. The Chinese explanation however is instructive in that it shows clearly a contradiction between the policy of revolutionary action on the one hand and tactical pragmatism on the other. Though this kind of explanation was never used again, it did illustrate the significant fact that what may be desirable from the Communist Party's viewpoint in its debate with the Soviet Communist Party may in fact be detrimental to the somewhat remarkable pragmatism which the government of Premier Chou En-lai has been prepared from time to time to adopt. This down-to-earth approach is more apparent in the economic and trade relations China has cultivated with the African states.

In its political relations with the African states, China adopted an attitude aimed at obtaining diplomatic recognition. It did this by associating Chinese and African interests where a similarity of purpose made this possible by making use of visits by political and cultural delegations[1] and, where desirable, by attempting first to establish trade relations. These attempts were directed at making the new states as anti-Western and therefore anti-imperialist as possible by showing that China had consistently supported, and would continue to support, the emancipation of the African peoples from both political and economic domination. It was claimed, however, that Chinese support was rewarded by the efforts of the African people to 'wipe out all remnants of the colonialist economy and build their own independent economy',[2] as well as by the support they gave to China in her struggles against United States imperialism in the Far East. When Ghana became independent in 1957, the Chinese reminded her that the struggle was just beginning

[1] See pp. 31–6.
[2] *People's Daily*, 24 May 1958 on 'Anti-Colonialism Day'. Quoted by Radio Peking and related by N.C.N.A. 25 May.

and that there should be no relaxation of vigilance. In a message to Nkrumah on the first anniversary of independence in 1958, Chou En-lai said that the 'Chinese people are very glad to see that new successes have continuously been gained by the people of Ghana during the past year in consolidating national independence and safeguarding state sovereignty'.[1] Although Ghana had not yet officially recognised Peking her vote in the United Nations General Assembly in the winter of 1957 supported discussion of the China question. Moreover Nkrumah's militant anti-colonialism was in accord with the Chinese campaign against imperialism. He took the initiative in summoning a conference of Independent African States, held in Accra in April 1958, as a mark of Ghana's interest in promoting action on an African basis. The resolutions passed in the conference on the national independence movements and in particular on the Algerian question showed the desire for a free Africa. The conference (attended by Ghana, Liberia, Ethiopia, the Sudan, the U.A.R., Libya, Morocco and Tunisia, with a three-member delegation from the Algerian F.L.N. and a Cameroun delegation led by Félix Moumie), achieved unanimity on the fundamental aims and principles designed to safeguard 'the hard won independence, sovereignty and territorial integrity of the participating States', 'deplored the division of the greater part of the world into two antagonistic blocs'.[2] The conference also expressed its adherence to the Bandung principles and urged participating states to avoid any commitment which might be detrimental to their interests and freedom. If their expressed interests tended to coincide with those of China, this did not in any way reflect Chinese 'influence'. Like any other major power, China wanted political gains and if this could be achieved by an opportunistic association of Chinese and African interests, then this would be done.

Although Tunisia did not formally recognise Peking until 1964 China's efforts to win friends in Tunisia and Morocco increased in 1958 and 1959, the more so because of the importance of these two countries geographically and emotionally in the Algerian conflict.[3] When, in February 1958, French aircraft fighting in Algeria attacked

[1] N.C.N.A., 6 Mar. 1958, p. 9.
[2] Resolutions of the Accra Meeting of Independent African States, Foreign Policy Section. N.C.N.A., 22 Apr. 1958, p. 27.
[3] See below, p. 29.

a Tunisian village which was providing sanctuary for Algerian nationalists, the Chinese Government condemned the action and the Chinese Chargé d'Affaires in Cairo called on the Tunisian Ambassador to express the 'Chinese people's resolute support to the Tunisian people in their just struggle against the colonialists'.[1] The Chinese tried to maintain a correct attitude towards the Tunisian Government while making efforts to obtain recognition through visits by delegations and trade relations.[2]

Chinese efforts vis-à-vis Morocco and the Sudan were rewarded in 1958 when Morocco, on 31 October, and then the Sudan, on 29 November, officially recognised the Chinese Government. In both cases this followed 'considerable' improvement in trade relations.[3] It is also worth noting China's behaviour towards these two countries, both of which restricted their own Communist parties. Although all political parties in the Sudan were banned by General Aboud's military regime, the persecution of Arab Communists which had started in the U.A.R. gradually spread to the Sudan with the arrest of local Communists who were said to be distributing propaganda. It is remarkable that China did not condemn the action of the Sudanese government except in so far as her general attacks on the U.A.R.s persecution of Communists might be said to extend to them. This attitude contradicted the current Chinese attitude which favoured Communist parties in the developing countries embarking on revolution.

The Moroccan situation was also interesting because the Communist Party there was speaking out more openly and tended to analyse the situation in terms of nationalism. In March 1959 the *People's Daily* published an article by Ali Yata, first secretary of the Central Committee of the Communist Party of Morocco on the immediate tasks and problems facing the country. Drawing attention to the fact that, although nominally independent, Morocco still had foreign military bases, was subject to imperialist subversion, he pointed out that 'The most immediate task for the whole of the Moroccan people of all strata is to safeguard and consolidate the

[1] N.C.N.A., 17 Feb. 1958, p. 24.   [2] See below, pp. 31–6.
[3] Morocco's imports from China had risen from $11m in 1957 to $15m in 1958 and exports to China from nil in 1957 to $3.1m in 1958. In the case of the Sudan, imports from China had risen from $0.7m in 1957 to $1.4m in 1958, and exports to China from $1.7m in 1957 to $2.1m in 1958. See Alexander Eckstein *Communist China's Economic Growth and Foreign Trade*, 1966.

national independence of Morocco.'[1] The C.P.M. should therefore adopt a 'united front' strategy with all other patriotic parties and elements in the country in their struggle against imperialism. The fact that the article was published in Peking indicated support for the C.P.M.; this was in line with the argument which stated that Morocco was in effect a semi-colonial country. Activities against the Western military bases were anti-imperialist and therefore part of the proletarian-socialist world revolution. However, when the Moroccan Government banned the Communist Party later in the year, Chinese representatives in Morocco ceased to have any contact with C.P.M. members. This was because Chinese presence in Morocco was necessary in rendering military aid to the Algerian nationalists from the Chinese consulate in Ouida. Thus, support for revolutionary activity in Algeria received priority.

While relations with the U.A.R. were deteriorating late in 1958, events in the French territories seemed to hold promise of effective Chinese activity in sub-Saharan Africa. In a referendum at the end of September 1958 most of the French territories voted to remain in the new French Community which President de Gaulle had devised to stave off the inexorable move towards independence on the part of the African leaders. Although 'most' of the territories voted 'oui' Ahmed Sekou Touré persuaded an overwhelming majority of his people to vote 'non' and to obtain their independence from France. Consequently the National Assembly proclaimed the Republic of Guinea on 2 October 1958. This was followed by the withdrawal of French civil service personnel, economic aid, office equipment, including telephones, electric light bulbs etc., all of which made the French Government look most ungenerous. The embarrassed Western governments could not come to Guinea's aid lest they should thus offend de Gaulle. The Communist countries, of course, had no such misgivings and in fact they welcomed this opportunity to show their 'genuine' friendship.

In a message to Sekou Touré, Chou En-lai gave his support to the new state and declared: 'The fact that the people of Guinea have attained independence is another important evidence that the national independence movement in Africa is rising to a new upsurge. May your Excellency and the people of Guinea achieve new successes in your cause of safeguarding national independence.'[2] Although the

[1] B.B.C. S.W.B. No. 849, Part v, 3 Mar. 1959.   [2] N.C.N.A., 9 Oct. 1958.

Chinese offered no immediate economic aid there was no doubt that they recognised Guinea's importance. On his first visit there in June 1959 the Chinese Ambassador to Morocco brought with him 5,000 tons of rice as a gift from the Chinese people to the people of Guinea – at a time when China herself was in need of grain. Guinea's official recognition of China on 4 October 1959 heralded a period of intense Chinese diplomatic activity in sub-Saharan Africa. Under the joint cultural co-operation agreement signed in October 1959 the Guinean Minister of Education visited Peking in December.[1] On his return he declared that he was

quite convinced of the efficacy of Chinese methods. I was greatly impressed by the similarity of the economic problems that China has succeeded in solving and those that are now facing the peoples of Africa. In China, I saw what can be done if you mobilise the vital forces of a nation. With all due regard to the difference in magnitude we now propose to do the same thing.[2]

Remarkably enough the visit occurred when the shortcomings of the Great Leap Forward in China were becoming more apparent. Nevertheless this comment reflects the attitude which China was to adopt in the sixties presenting her economic reconstruction and experiences as a model to be followed by the new African states.

An examination of relations between China and the African governments deals with only a small part of Chinese activity in Africa from 1958–9. Greater efforts were made to influence important African personalities – politicians, intellectuals and even businessmen – to make sure that, among other things, they would be favourably disposed towards China, both before and especially after independence. The use of political and cultural delegations was, of course, not only directed to areas which were still under colonial rule. It also extended to independent countries whether or not such countries recognised Peking. If a country recognised Peking the nature of the delegations invited to visit China was rather different from where the government concerned was staunchly anti-China and therefore 'reactionary'.

There were two sorts of delegations – Chinese delegations to Africa dealing with cultural, political and economic affairs, and African delegations visiting China, in most cases at the invitation of

[1] Johnston and Chiu *Agreements of the People's Republic of China 1949–67*, 1968, p. 98.
[2] Quoted by Jacquet-Francillon in *Le Figaro*, 25 Dec. 1959, 'En Afrique-la Chine arrive'.

and with the financial support of Chinese political and 'cultural' organisations.[1] Those of the latter sort, together with activities in various African organisations, were defined as 'people's diplomacy'.

Addressing the session of the National People's Congress on the establishment of cultural relations with other countries, Chang Hsi-jo, President of the Chinese People's Institute of Foreign Affairs,[2] said that, since the Bandung Conference, cultural exchanges with Afro-Asia and Latin America had increased.

> In the past year alone (1958) countries with newly established cultural exchanges with us included Morocco, Ghana, Senegal, Nigeria, Somaliland, Uganda, Angola.... In the past few years, especially last year (1958), cultural delegations of our country went to many Asian, African and Latin American countries one after another with scarcely any break in between.[3]

In 1958 twenty such delegations visited African countries and in the following year ten.[4] The total number does not of course reflect the importance and nature of each delegation or the length of time spent in Africa. For instance, an 'acrobatic ensemble' made a tour of the Middle East and Africa lasting more than six months from late 1957 to March 1958. It spent five weeks in Morocco[5] putting on performances in various cities. Sports teams, youth delegations, 'song and dance ensembles' (theatre groups) and trade unionists visited Tunisia, the Sudan, Ghana, the U.A.R. and Guinea during these years. While most of these may be regarded as the sort of activities which other states also engage in, China's use of such delegations was rather more political than is usual. The Chinese meant to show that the African peoples felt warmly towards them whether or not their governments recognised Peking officially.

---

[1] China footed the bill: Interviews with Hon. H. N. Kida and Oscar Kambona. Kambona was at one time Tanganyika's Minister for Youth and Culture and later Foreign Minister. Kida visited China as a trade unionist before Tanganyika achieved independence in 1961.
[2] B.B.C. S.W.B. Second Series, Part III, Weekly Supplement No. 3, 6 May 1959.
[3] Ibid.
[4] These figures have been compiled from press and radio announcements (1958–68) as related in N.C.N.A. dispatches. Survey of China Mainland Press and B.B.C. S.W.B., correlating this where possible with official reports from the African countries concerned. Where, for instance, there are ten people in a delegation it is still regarded as one delegation. In some cases, in the interests of 'good' relations and the personal safety of the individuals, no announcement of a visit to China was made. In such cases the delegations are not known and the number is not included in this compilation.
[5] N.C.N.A., 4 Mar. 1958 announcing the departure of the delegation from Morocco for Ghana on 23 Feb. 1958.

A favourable impression of China was created and the contacts made helped to urge the governments concerned to grant recognition. The visits were also intended to help counter the effects of imperialist propaganda which had been going on for a long time. This was particularly so in the case of Chinese Muslim delegations going on pilgrimages to Mecca. After a pilgrimage the Chinese pilgrims would spend up to two and sometimes three months visiting their Muslim brethren in Tunisia, the U.A.R., the Sudan, Morocco and Guinea; later the visits were extended to Senegal, Mali, Mauretania, Niger and Northern Nigeria.[1] The aim was to stress that Muslims in China enjoyed the same freedom of worship as their brethren in the Middle East and Africa. For the same reason African Muslim delegations were invited to visit China during Muslim festivals and to participate in religious ceremonies in Chinese mosques. The long detour from Saudi Arabia to Guinea and Senegal would hardly have been justified had there been no political motivation. The President of China's Islamic Association, Burham Shahidi, was included in many of the visits and the fact that he is also a Communist Party member was not allowed to prejudice his usefulness.

Moreover political delegations visited Africa to take part in various conferences dealing with trade unionism,[2] youth solidarity and economic affairs. Trade delegations,[3] though manifestly economic, also aimed at improving political relations.

Africa delegations to China fall into two categories – official or semi-official and non-governmental. Delegations of the first type went to China either under cultural exchange agreements providing for mutual visits by teachers, technicians, scientists, government officials and ministers or under individual and group invitations extended by China to parliamentarians, leaders of cultural societies and other notable personalities. Delegations of the second type were made up of members of political parties, exiled groups living in places like Cairo, Conakry and Accra, trade unionists, opposition party members, leaders of the various China friendship societies which, by 1965, existed in most African countries, and finally and most important representatives of struggling Africans in the forefront of the battle against imperialism.[4]

For the government delegations the usual pattern was a round of

[1] The visits to these other countries came after 1959
[2] See below pp. 44 & 45.   [3] See below p. 36–40.   [4] See below p. 51.

discussions with their Chinese counterparts in the equivalent ministries, followed by visits to factories and industries or other projects falling within their professional competence. There were opportunities to meet Chairman Mao and invariably to meet the Foreign Minister. The Egyptian military delegation which visited China in April and May 1958 was personally received by Mao Tse-tung, who told them that 'the Chinese people feel very happy to have the friendship of the U.A.R. . . . We stand on the same front in the struggle against colonialism.'[1]

In December 1958 for example a U.A.R. teachers' delegation led by the Assistant Under Secretary of the Ministry of Education visited China for three weeks under the cultural agreement.[2]

However, it was the non-governmental visits that were regarded as more significant since most of the African countries thus involved were not yet independent. A total of forty-four delegations visited China in 1958 (and fifty in 1959)[3] from groups ranging from the 'Black Africa Youth Delegation', received by Chairman Mao in July 1958,[4] to the more important visit by the Provisional Government of the Republic of Algeria. Many of the delegations were invited to participate in the May Day rallies or in the National Day celebrations on 1 October. There is thus a definite pattern, the majority of delegations arriving in April and September. During these visits, delegations would be asked for their impressions about China and these would be broadcast over Radio Peking in its programme for Africa and used as propaganda. For instance eight African writers from Senegal, Angola, Nigeria, Somalia, Uganda and Ghana visiting China in November 1958 sent a letter to the *People's Daily* 'expressing satisfaction with China's astonishing progress especially in the fields of economic construction and industrial development'.[5]

African visitors were often greatly impressed by the ability of the Chinese to organise and mobilise hundreds of thousands of people to achieve a desired and defined objective quickly. The large scale of the people's communes and the rigid discipline shown by the Chinese masses impressed many African visitors who dreamed of a quick way to 'catch up' with the West in the economic and industrial

[1] S.C.M.P. No. 1766, p. 30, May 1958.
[2] S.C.M.P. No. 1921, p. 50, 24 Dec. 1958.
[3] My compilation.
[4] N.C.N.A., 13 July 1958, p. 25.
[5] S.C.M.P. No. 1889, 5 Nov. 1958.

sense. The visitors were convinced that Chinese proclamations of support for and solidarity with the Africans in their desire for independence from the colonial yoke were genuine. Attending mass rallies to celebrate such occasions as 'Algeria Day' and 'Congo Week', African visitors were impressed by the thousands of people who turned out for such demonstrations in China; like the Ugandan Nationalist leader Kiwanuka most of them were anxious to express their gratitude to 'the Chinese people for their support of the Ugandan people's fight for freedom and hope that both peoples will be united in future'.[1]

Such visitors were naturally expected to support diplomatic recognition and the opening of trade relations after independence.

In 1958 and 1959 delegations from twenty-seven African countries (states and dependent territories) visited China: Algeria, Angola, Cameroun, Congo (L), Central African Republic,[2] Chad, Ghana, Guinea, Mali, Mauretania, Kenya, Malagasy,[3] Libya, Morocco, Nigeria, South Africa, Senegal, Mauritius, Somali,[4] the Sudan, Sierra Leone, Togo, Tanganyika, Tunisia, Uganda and the U.A.R. The invitations issued to members of various overseas friendship and cultural organisations are centrally controlled in China under the joint supervision of the International Liaison and Organisation Departments of the Central Committee of the C.C.P. and the State Council's Commission for Cultural Relations with foreign countries. There were however various other organisations which had contacts with Africa. According to the *China Handbook* published by Peking in 1957 the Chinese People's Association for Cultural Relations with Foreign Countries

was founded in May 1954 with the aim of fostering friendly relations between the Chinese people and the peoples of other lands by increasing cultural contacts between them. It sponsors the exchange of cultural delegations, and visits of writers, artists and scientists, the holding of exhibitions and commemoration meetings of outstanding cultural figures of different ages and different countries, and the staging of theatrical performances. Through these and other channels, Chinese cultural achievements are introduced to the peoples of other countries whilst those of other peoples are introduced into China.

The other important organisation is the Chinese People's Institute for Foreign Affairs which was established in December 1949 as a

[1] N.C.N.A., 22 July 1959.   [2] Names adopted after independence.
[3] *Ibid*.   [4] *Ibid*.

people's organisation devoted to the study of international affairs. It extended invitations to foreign political leaders to visit the country, and through personal contacts helps to promote international understanding and friendship.[1]

Apart from these two, other organisations also played host to African delegations visiting China in 1958–9. They included the All China Federation of Trade Unions (A.C.F.T.U.), All China Youth Federation (A.C.Y.F.), the Women's Federation of the P.R.C., the Chinese Peace Committee, the Chinese Committee for Afro-Asian Solidarity, the China Federation of Literary and Art Circles, the Union of Chinese Writers, the All China Journalists Association, the China Council for the Promotion of International Trade, the China Islamic Association, the All China Students Federation, the Political Science and Law Association of China.[2] On 13 April 1960 the N.C.N.A. reported that all these organisations and a few others had joined together to form the Chinese African People's Friendship Association.[3]

On the official side a Research Commission for African Subjects is responsible for studying and financing the control of operations in African countries. With the Commission for Social Relations with the Peoples of Africa it operates under the State Office of the Government of the C.P.R. I will consider the functions and activities of these government departments later.

China is shown at her most pragmatic in her attitude towards external trade. Although for a long time after 1949 most of this was with the socialist countries, particularly with Soviet Union, the pattern began to change as she successfully broke through the series of barriers placed in her way by the United States embargo. Even then her most important non-communist trading activities were for a long time confined to Asia and Europe: Hong Kong, Malaysia, Singapore, Japan, and Indonesia, and of course the United Kingdom (which has consistently tried to divorce the question of trade from the nature of the political regime). The embargo imposed by the United States and urged upon other countries enhanced the importance to China of the British colony of Hong Kong.[4] Countries which would otherwise have preferred

[1] China Handbook (Peking), Apr. 1957.   [2] See below pp. 41–6.
[3] Hsinhua News Agency, 13 Apr. 1960.
[4] For a fuller discussion of the U.S. trade embargo see A. Eckstein *Communist China's*

Breaking New Ground 1958–9 37

not to oppose the United States found a way out by buying and selling via Hong Kong while in fact the actual trading partner was China. Thus Hong Kong stood and still stands as a source of foreign exchange for China.[1]

China's trade with African countries was no less affected by the United States' attitude, but in fact a greater difficulty was geography and the nature of the Chinese and African economies. Most African countries exported agricultural products and raw materials for industry; what they welcomed most were consumer and capital goods. These China could not provide in the quantity and quality necessary to match Africa's traditional European suppliers. Nevertheless trade between China and Northern Africa began to move forward as China made positive attempts to display her products to prospective African buyers. This development was aided by her large cotton purchases from Egypt in 1956 which were followed by commercial contracts with other African countries, notably Morocco and the Sudan. After the establishment of the Cairo Embassy in 1956, the Commercial Officer, Chan Hiang-Kang, succeeded in establishing trade relations with Tunisia, Libya, Nigeria, Ghana, Ethiopia and Tanganyika in 1957. Following a trade mission to North Africa early in 1957 its head, Chi Wei-li, claimed that prospects were good and that considerable interest was shown in 'China's tea, silk and other commodities. Chinese green tea has been very popular in those countries for a long time.'[2] China's trade with Afro-Asian countries during 1956 was said to have increased by 39.4% and its total volume to be 64% of China's trade with non-socialist countries; she had 'official trade agreements with twenty-one nations while over sixty-eight countries and regions had trade relations with her'.[3]

Thus by the end of 1957, China was already trading with a

Economic Growth and Foreign Trade, 1966. During the Korean War, the United States and other N.A.T.O. states placed an embargo on all trade with China. This embargo was more stringent in application than the one imposed on other Communist states with respect to strategic materials. After the war many countries were very reluctant to continue with the embargo and some states gradually opted out of the policy. By 1957, formal embargo on all trade with China was abandoned by the United States and restriction limited to products described as 'strategic'.

[1] See Derek Davies 'China Earns from Hongkong', *Far Eastern Economic Review*, Vol. 40, No. 12, 20 June 1963.
[2] S.C.M.P. No. 1468, 12 Feb. 1957, p. 33.
[3] N.C.N.A. Feb. 1957, quoted in S.C.M.P. No. 1480, p. 31.

number of African countries. In January 1958[1] a Sudanese trade mission to China signed an agreement on the reciprocal exchange of goods and products on condition that the products were of good quality and reasonable price. Under another agreement signed in September, the Sudanese government undertook to export cotton in return for textiles, sugar and chemicals.[2] In 1958 Chinese exports to the Sudan were £½ million[3] – 0.9% of Sudanese imports[4] – while China imported some £0.7 million worth of goods – 1.8% of Sudanese exports.[5] In the following year exports to the Sudan rose to £0.9 million (1.6%) and imports from the Sudan to more than £1m (1.6%).[6] Trade with the Sudan was to continue to increase in the years which followed.

In an international exhibition at Casablanca, Morocco, in April 1958, China's main items on display included tea, light industrial goods and handicrafts. Tea was in fact to become her main export to Morocco, her largest trading partner in Africa after the U.A.R. Moroccan exports to China have included phosphates, sardines and lorries assembled in Morocco.[7] In 1959 China sold £1.9m of goods to Morocco and bought £1.5m worth.[8]

As in Asia where Malaysia and Singapore have considerable trade with China, though not recognising her, so in Africa, Nigeria, which did not recognise China till 1971, has been the third largest importer of Chinese goods. The volume of trade had been increasing before 1958. In that year Nigeria bought £1.4m worth of goods from China and increased this to £1.86m in 1959, although selling nothing to her.[9] This pattern of trade was to be followed elsewhere, especially in the French-speaking countries. It made it possible for China to build up with these African countries external reserves which were then used for industrial purchases in Western Europe. It also does reflect the non-availability of goods which some of these African countries could sell to China. This, however, means that these countries could cut off trade with China without being adversely affected, as has in fact happened in some cases.

---

[1] N.C.N.A., 10 Jan. 1958.   [2] S.C.M.P. No. 1849, 9 Sept. 1958, p. 38.
[3] *Sudan Annual Foreign Trade Statistics*, Department of Statistics, Khartoum, 1959 (inclusive of 1958).
[4] *Ibid.*   [5] *Ibid.*   [6] *Ibid.*
[7] S.C.M.P. No. 2102, 29 Sept. 1959.   [8] See Table 5, Appendix 1.
[9] *External Trade of Nigeria 1958–60*, Lagos, Federal Dept. of Statistics.

The U.A.R. has been by far China's largest trading partner in Africa since the cotton purchases of 1956. While the trade agreements have always referred to the desirability of balancing imports and exports, China has, in fact, in most cases bought just less than she has sold,[1] though the total value is in favour of the U.A.R. China's trade with the U.A.R. has not been marred by the practices which affected Egypt's trade with the Soviet Union in this period. In August 1959 Radio Cairo announced a new 'policy of taking steps to prevent re-export of Egyptian Cotton and illegitimate competition on the world market'.[2] This would also end barter and channel transactions through the Central Bank. This statement was directed against the Soviet practice of re-selling the cotton at greater profit in Europe. (This should be contrasted with the Chinese practice as seen in the sugar deal with the Sudan, see below p. 151.) In 1959, 7.7% of U.A.R's exports went to China while her imports from China was 3.8% of the total imports to the value of £11.7m. and £8.2m. respectively.[3] It is noticeable that the political disagreement over Nasser's treatment of Egyptian Communists and the attacks on Communism as such did not affect trade relations in 1958-9. This is another aspect of China's reluctance to let trade be effected by political relations.

In 1958-9 the Chinese were primarily interested in increasing the volume of their trade with African countries. As yet there was no hint of the sizeable economic aid programme which they embarked upon in the sixties. China's ability to mount an economic offensive was limited and the political decision to make sacrifices at home in order to give economic aid to Africa had not been made. Besides, most of the African countries were still dependent territories and while it was easier to begin trade relations in such circumstances, economic aid programmes assume acceptance by the government of the country concerned. Moreover, at a time when the Chinese were attacking Khrushchev for 'squandering' the economic resources of the Soviet Union on bourgeois nationalists who were locking up their Communists, such an economic offensive was not politically feasible. Further, in 1958-9 the Great Leap Forward and the establishment of people's communes designed to

---
[1] See Table 6, Appendix I.   [2] B.B.C. *S.W.B.* No. 119, Part IV, 2 Sept. 1959.
[3] U.A.R. (Egypt) *Annual Statement of Foreign Trade*, 1959, Dept. of Statistics and Census 1961.

industrialise and communise China at breakneck speed began. The disorganisation of the economy which resulted, together with natural disasters lasting for three years, meant that China's ability to give foreign aid was reduced even further.[1] As yet, the competitive nature which aid was to assume in the sixties had not emerged, and Communist aid offered to Guinea when Sekou Touré took his country out of the French Community came from the Soviet Union and the East European countries.

Nevertheless, although the scale was modest, the Chinese did employ aid as an instrument of foreign policy.[2] Their efforts were often spectacular and quite explicitly directed towards political rather than economic ends. Thus, during the Suez crisis in 1956 the Chinese made an immediate $4.7m grant to Egypt, apart from offering to send volunteers. If anything yielded political gains for China, it was this grant and the earlier cotton deal.

Given the treatment Guinea received from France after she declared her independence in 1958, China's gift of 10,000 tons of rice was commendable. On his visit to Guinea in April 1959,[3] the Chinese Ambassador to Morocco brought with him 5,000 tons of the promised rice and in the following year a much more substantial and remarkable aid commitment was made to Guinea; with that China entered the economic race in Africa.[4]

The conference maintains that all peoples are entitled to the sacred rights of freedom, self-determination, sovereignty and independence. These resolutions without doubt voiced the common will of the hundreds of millions of people in Asia and Africa. There is still a long struggle ahead in the national independence movements in Asia and Africa and there will inevitably be more twists and turns in their future development, but the Asian and African peoples have already stood up and will never again be crushed.[5]

In these words Premier Chou En-lai summed up the results of the Afro-Asian People's Solidarity Conference held in Cairo in December–January, 1957–8.

[1] For the effects of the Great Leap Forward on Chinese economy see A. Eckstein, *op. cit.*, pp. 29–86. Before 1958 China had extended economic assistance to North Korea, North Vietnam, Mongolia, Albania and Hungary. The total value was about $507.5m (Eckstein, *op. cit.* p. 306).
[2] Financial credits to the Algerian Nationalists and various donations to the Red Cross in Tunisia and Morocco will not be treated under economic aid but under revolutionary activity. (See below, pp. 52–4.)
[3] N.C.N.A. report from Conakry, Apr. 1959. [4] See p. 87.
[5] N.C.N.A. Feb. 1958, reporting Chou En-lai's speech to the National People's Congress on the conference.

In the field of propaganda and agitation, Marxist-Leninists have always found 'people's' organisations indispensable. These can perform adequately the necessary activities without incurring the odium normally attached to Communist parties in many countries. No doubt many such organisations created to further Communist causes support noble and commendable issues which would normally distract attention from their origin, finance and structure. Such causes as 'peace', 'disarmament', democratic freedoms and 'women's rights' appeal to well-meaning individuals and groups who would normally ignore campaigns from Communist parties. It has been a logical step, therefore, for Communists to set up or sponsor the creation of organisations which behind a facade of altruism can act as transmission belts for Communist ideas and aims. These organisations are of major importance where communist parties are non-existent, newly-founded or prohibited and where open canvassing is dangerous.

The Chinese and the Russians have resorted to this device in their activities in Africa. Naturally the establishment of such organisations and their choice of issues must take into consideration the actual situation there. In the late fifties the educated and knowledgeable sections of the African community favoured independence from colonialism. (Any organisation would have to take note of this.) It was in this context that the decision to convene a conference of Afro-Asian peoples in Cairo was taken. Its aim was to co-ordinate the efforts of Asian and African peoples fighting for national independence.

The Afro-Asian People's Solidarity Conference opened on 27 December 1957 with delegations from several Asian countries and from Algeria, British Somaliland, Chad, Egypt, Ethiopia, French Somaliland, Ghana, Cameroon, Kenya, Libya, Madagascar, Morocco, Nigeria, Senegal, the Sudan, Tunisia, Uganda, Zanzibar and Italian Somaliland attending. In his greeting to the conference, Chairman Mao said that 'it would contribute tremendously to the enhancement of the Bandung spirit, the promotion of the solidarity of the Asian and African peoples, the striving for and safeguarding of the national independence in Asia and Africa and the great cause of defending peace in Asia, Africa and the rest of the world'.[1] He did not state, of course, that since the conference would lead to the

[1] N.C.N.A., 27 Dec. 1957, p. 15.

creation of an organisation it would also promote the foreign policy aims of the Soviet Union and China – both of whom were among the sponsor nations. Nor did he mention that the Communists would use subtle means to gain control of that organisation. In his own address to the conference the chief Soviet delegate Rashidov declared that it would 'hardly be possible to exaggerate the importance of this conference in which more than forty Afro-Asian countries are taking part. ... This Afro-Asian Solidarity Conference, its spirit, and its ideas are supported by all honest men throughout the world, because it is anti-imperialist, anti-colonial and anti-militarist and thus at the same time just, progressive and humane.'[1] He went on to state that the Soviet people wholeheartedly supported the aim of the Afro-Asian peoples to belong to the zone of peace and independence. In his own address the chief Chinese delegate, Kuo Mo-jo, associated China with the movement for independence surging forward in the various countries and proclaimed that there would be a 'bright state of lasting peace' when imperialism, colonialism, colonies or semi-colonies no longer existed throughout the world. The Afro-Asian peoples must therefore unite in solidarity to achieve their common aim: the liquidation of colonialism.

It is notable that in addition to the official delegations from the Communist countries, Egypt, Morocco and Tunisia also sent official delegations, while semi-official delegations came from Ghana and the Sudan. Other countries were represented by political parties and groups. Though the conference was organised by the U.A.R. Government, it was already clear from the preparatory meetings that it would be ideologically linked to the Communist camp; the attendance of many official and semi-official delegations was thus significant. It was of course argued that the mere fact of Communist support for genuine African and Asian grievances was no reason for the aggrieved peoples to drop their demands and such answers to Western criticisms of the conference's failure to discuss Hungary carried weight with enlightened African opinion. However, perhaps because so many official and semi-official delegations attended the tone of the resolutions was rather less militant. There was a call for negotiations in the Cameroons, Kenya and Uganda and an appeal for the cessation of all nuclear tests from January

[1] Minutes of the First Afro-Asian People's Solidarity Conference, Cairo, Jan. 1958, quoted by F. Schatten, *op. cit.* p. 273.

1958 as well as the inevitable condemnation of racial discrimination and imperialist warmongering. The conference paid tribute to China and India by declaring that the five principles proclaimed by Nehru and Chou En-lai and the ten principles of Bandung 'are the best means of reducing world tension and putting an end to the cold war'.

Of paramount importance for the future activities of China in Africa was the decision of the conference to approve the establishment of two permanent organs – a Solidarity Council and a Permanent Secretariat – to act when the solidarity organisations were not in session and to ensure that the conference's decisions and recommendations were carried out. The first Secretary General of the Permanent Secretariat was an Egyptian, Yousef el Sebay, with representatives from Cameroon, Ghana, Sudan, India, Japan, Indonesia, Iraq, Syria, Soviet Union and China.[1] The Communists succeeded in gradually gaining control of the Secretariat; it was to play a vital role in their activities in the future. Funds were to be channelled through it to national liberation movements in Africa and to African students for study in the Soviet bloc countries. Peking Radio announced in April 1958 that the Asian Solidarity Committee of China, the A.C.F.T.U. and the Chinese Islamic Association had decided to give the Algerian National Liberation Front the sum of half a million Chinese yuan – via the Secretariat in Cairo – as a token of solidarity.[2] The Secretariat was also used to extend invitations to groups of African visitors to China, something which would normally have been done by a functioning Communist party. It is noticeable that during the Egyptian clamp-down on Arab Communists in 1958–9 the organisation did not receive the same treatment, as an Egyptian was the Secretary General, and its activities were not thought to be inimical to the interests of the U.A.R.

From time to time the Secretariat issued statements on current events, particularly on events in Africa and Asia, though during 1958 and 1959 its activities did become increasingly limited to Africa. The importance attached to the organisation was shown by the Chinese pledge of $28,000[3] to the annual budget of the Council

[1] Charles Neuhauser *Third World Politics: China and the Afro-Asian People's Solidarity Organisation 1957–1967*, Harvard, 1968.
[2] Peking Radio, N.C.N.A. report 8 Apr. 1958.
[3] Reported in *Rose al Yusuf* (Cairo), No. 17, 1958.

and the Soviet Union's of $25,000. It soon became clear that finance from the Soviet Union and China was keeping it going. These countries also took the initiative in convening conferences. (The Afro-Asian Youth Conference held in Cairo in February 1959 received contributions of £2,500 from each of them.)[1] It was not just the convening of these conferences that was important but the opportunity of contacting delegates from African countries and inviting them to visit the Communist countries and even study there.

Though the A.A.P.S.O. has been prominent in Communist activities in Africa, other international organisations acting as 'fronts' for Communism have also been active in arranging conferences and seminars and sponsoring group visits. The World Peace Council (W.P.C.), the World Federation of Democratic Youth (W.F.D.Y.), Women's International Democratic Federation (W.I.D.F.), International Union of Students (I.U.S.) and the International Organisation of Journalists (I.O.J.) were all involved in 1958–9 in arranging conferences. The W.F.D.Y. assisted by the I.U.S. organised a World Youth Festival in July–August 1959, with delegates attending from all over the world including twenty-eight African countries. The Chinese Youth Delegation[2] had a 'get-together' with delegates from many African countries including Madagascar, Togo, Ivory Coast, Uganda, Ghana, Mali, Kenya, Guinea, Senegal and the Belgian Congo and they were told that the Chinese youth and people shared the just aspirations of the African youth and peoples for independence. In the sixties these international organisations were to play an increasingly important role as more African territories became independent.

Of all sections of African opinion, the Workers' Movement has received by far the greatest attention from the international front organisations. That the African working class was small was a partial disadvantage but the Communists were encouraged by the fact that the workers were not just limiting their demands to higher wages but extending them to the attainment of political independence. In activities concerning the penetration of the various trade unions in Africa, the World Federation of Trade Unions (W.F.T.U.) has been most important. Set up at the initiative of the British

[1] M.E.N.A., 29 Jan. 1959.
[2] S.C.M.P. No. 2068, 4 Aug. 1959. N.C.N.A. Correspondent reporting from Vienna on 28 July.

Trade Union Congress in October 1945, the organisation lost its Western affiliates in January 1949, following the intensification of the cold war and the Communists successful takeover of the organisation. The Western trade unions set up the International Confederation of Free Trade Unions (I.C.F.T.U.) in November 1949 and have been competing since then with the W.F.T.U. for the affiliation of national trade union movements all over the world.[1] Competition to gain affiliated members in Africa was complicated by the efforts of trade union leaders and politicians to steer clear of the cold war and to guide the African Workers' Movement towards pan-Africanism. Before the break in 1949 both American and Soviet trade unions had been regarded as the militants in matters of colonial labour. The Americans continued in this role in their attitude to the Kenyan, Moroccan and Tunisian trade unions – but changed in the late fifties to anti-Communism and anti-nonalignment. The I.C.F.T.U. paid less attention to helping the trade unions in Africa achieve their political goal and more to preventing the W.F.T.U. from gaining a strong foothold. As a result of this competition the Ghana T.U.C. disaffiliated from the I.C.F.T.U. and a meeting to inaugurate an All-African Trade Union Federation (A.A.T.U.F.) was summoned in Accra in November 1959.[2]

Before that time, however, the Russians and the Chinese had increased the level of their activities among trade union leaders in Africa. The All China Federation of Trade Unions acted as hosts to trade union delegations for the U.A.R., Mali, Morocco, French Equatorial Africa, Madagascar, Mauritius, Algeria, Nigeria, Guinea and a so-called trade union delegation from Black Africa in 1958 and 1959. The A.C.F.T.U. also sent delegations to the U.A.R. and Guinea to participate in and act as observers at international conferences. The conference of International Trade Unions in solidarity with the People of Algeria, which was held in the U.A.R. in September 1958, set up a committee for solidarity with the workers and people of Algeria. In 1959 the committee issued a supposedly world-wide appeal for help for Algerian refugees. In response, the A.C.F.T.U. and the Chinese National Women's Federation sent 'medicines and children's clothing worth fifty thousand yuan'.[3]

[1] For a fuller treatment see I. Davies, *African Trade Unions*, 1966.
[2] See G. E. Lichtblau, *The Politics of African Trade Unionism*, 1967.
[3] S.C.M.P. No. 2153, 10 Dec. 1959, p. 44. N.C.N.A. report from Peking of 5 Dec. on the message of thanks from the General Union of Algerian Workers.

In his efforts to extricate African trade unionism from the W.F.T.U.–I.C.F.T.U. rivalry, Sekou Touré sponsored the launching in January 1959[1] of the All-Black African Federation of Trade Unions (U.G.T.A.N.) in Conakry. The Federation was said to have a quarter of a million members and was not to be affiliated to either of the two world organisations. However the Chinese representative of the I.C.F.T.U. Secretariat[2] attended the conference as an observer and successfully invited a delegation from the new organisation to visit China for the May Day celebrations of 1959. However this did not retard the efforts of the U.G.T.A.N. to remain free of formal affiliation to the W.F.T.U. or the I.C.F.T.U. Though the W.F.T.U. established a Labour College at Budapest in 1959[3] for training African trade union leaders in response to the one established in Kampala in 1958 by the I.C.F.T.U., the U.G.T.A.N. went on to establish a third one in Conakry in 1960 under African management.[4]

With the disaffiliation (which I have already mentioned) of the Ghana T.U.C. from the I.C.F.T.U. in 1959 and the inauguration of the A.A.T.U.F. in November, the struggle for the trade unions was intensified. As the A.A.T.U.F. was being called to implement the resolution of the first conference of the All-African People's Organisation held in Accra in December 1958, most of the I.C.F.T.U. affiliates who were supposed to be attending a regional conference at the same time in Lagos sent observers to the Accra meeting. The Chinese hailed the inauguration of the A.A.T.U.F. in Accra as a manifestation of the 'advance of African workers' and condemned the regional meeting in Lagos of the I.C.F.T.U.[5] At the Accra meeting a steering committee comprising the Ghana T.U.C., the C.N.T. de Guinée, the Egyptian Confederation of Labour, Moroccan U.M.T. and the Imoudou wing of the T.U.C. of Nigeria, was set up to prepare for a full scale meeting and the formal creation of the A.A.T.U.F., which was not to occur until May 1961. That the Chinese and other Communist trade unions supported the creation of the A.A.T.U.F. was enough to give the I.C.F.T.U. cause for concern. The latter stood to lose by the new and non-affiliating All-African Federation. This support also

[1] B.B.C. *S.W.B.* Part III, 16 Jan. 1959. N.C.N.A. report of 14 Jan. 1959.
[2] *Ibid.*   [3] I. Davies, *African Trade Unions*, 1966, p. 210.
[4] *Ibid.*   [5] N.C.N.A., 23 November 1959 on the Peking Press.

indicated that apart from the possibility that the new organisation would be infiltrated it could not but take an anti-imperialist stand, since most African issues involved the Western states. The struggles that followed belong to a later period; so also does the Sino-Soviet struggle that was to develop within each national trade union organisation in the sixties. The foundation had, however, been laid through the granting of scholarships of all sorts to various trade unionists and subventions to their national funds. I will discuss this in the next chapter.

War is the highest form of struggle for resolving contradictions, when they have developed to a certain stage, between classes, nations, states or political groups...[1]

History shows that wars are divided into two kinds, just and unjust. All wars that are progressive are just, and all wars that impede progress are unjust. We Communists oppose all unjust wars that impede progress, but we do not oppose just wars, we actively participate in them.[2]

Very few Chinese statements have been as blunt on the issue of war than these quotations from Chairman Mao's writings dating as far back as 1938. That they were made a long time ago does not make them irrelevant, as they are still being quoted today in Chinese writings on revolutionary struggles in Asia, Africa and Latin America. That they are still quoted, however, does not itself mean that the Chinese have consistently and indiscriminately supported all just revolutionary struggles. In fact, they have had on occasion to modify their support for some groups in the interest of good relations with the regimes concerned.[3]

In 1958, the fiercest struggle going on in the colonial areas was that of the Algerian Nationalists against the French colonial authorities. The fighting, which started on 1 November 1954, was referred to by Chou En-lai in his speech to the Bandung conference in April 1955.[4] By late 1957, however, Chinese foreign policy had moved to the left, a shift which called for all-out support for the revolutionary struggles of the peoples in colonial areas – struggles which would objectively weaken imperialism both politically and militarily by multiplying the various fronts on which it was engaged. This multiplication would be intensified by increasing material

[1] Mao Tse-tung, 'Problems of Strategy in China's Revolutionary War', *Selected Works* Vol. I, p. 180, 1967.
[2] Mao 'On Protracted War', *Selected Works* Vol. II, p. 150, 1967.
[3] See Ch. 4.   [4] See above, p. 21.

aid in various forms to national liberation movements already fighting in Algeria and the French Cameroun.

After the establishment of the A.A.P.S.O. Secretariat in Cairo in January 1958, 30 March was declared 'Algeria Day'. The Algerian National Liberation Front (F.L.N.) sent a delegate, Ibrahim Ghafa,[1] to the celebrations in Peking, which included a mass rally and exhibition of maps and photographs, and statements from Chinese leaders. Those addressing the rally included Burham Shahidi, Chairman of the China Islamic Association, and Kuo Mo-jo of the Chinese-Asian Solidarity Committee.[2] From this time the Chinese increased their contacts with the Cairo personnel of the N.L.F. and also with the Cameroun U.P.C. and Uganda offices in Cairo. The Chinese mission in Cairo thus served not only Chinese-U.A.R. relations but also other parts of the continent which could be dealt with from there.

Meanwhile the Chinese had to convince the Russians that the struggles in Africa needed more than verbal support and half-hearted material help. A *People's Daily* editorial, 'Light of Freedom Rises in Africa', asserted that: 'The awakened African people are concerned not only with African affairs but also with the destiny of the whole world. Events in Africa show once again that the anti-imperialist national independence movement is a force of peace.'[3] In other words the struggle in Africa was worth supporting, and maximum pressure should be brought to bear upon the imperialists in that part of the world. That support for revolution in Africa would complicate Sino-Soviet relations was soon to be shown by the events which engulfed the Middle East in July 1958, the visit of Khrushchev to Peking, the Taiwan Straits crisis of late August and September, and the proclamation of the provisional government of the Republic of Algeria on 19 September.

The Iraqi revolution in July 1958 which disrupted the new Bagdad pact sponsored by the United States was followed within days by American and British troops landing in the Lebanon and Jordan. Cairo Radio reported Soviet military manoeuvres on the Iranian and Turkish borders as well as Soviet and Chinese warnings to the United States, France and Britain. The movement of Soviet ships in the Mediterranean previously reported, and apparently

[1] S.C.M.P. Nos. 1744 and 1745, pp. 44–50 and p. 43, 31 Mar. 1958.
[2] *Ibid.*   [3] N.C.N.A., 25 Apr. 1958.

meant to deter U.S. military action, meant that a more positive Soviet response than mere talk and sabre-rattling was expected. In an attempt to defuse the situation Khrushchev called for a summit meeting, to include India but not China, to handle the crisis. China made it plain that in her view Khrushchev had taken an entirely inadequate approach – pulling back from a showdown when he in fact had the 'superiority'. The least he could have done was to land troops in Iraq in a show of solidarity and as proof of readiness and determination to protect a people's revolution.

> The balance of strength was extremely unfavourable to the American and British imperialists. Imperialism had lost its superior position not only in the political but also in the military fields. Its rule in the world could be broken at any time and at any place. Its long war front could not be defended and had numerous loopholes.... Only by waging a resolute struggle against them could they be made to learn their lessons and accept peace. History has time and again shown that aggressors must be dealt resolute blows;... Imperialist aggression could be defeated and war conspiracy halted when the peoples throughout the world took to action.[1]

This tone was still maintained in Chinese comment when Khrushchev visited Peking from 31 July to 3 August. His talks with Mao Tse-tung were said to have taken place in an 'atmosphere of perfect sincerity and cordiality',[2] with full agreement on both sides. The communiqué said *inter alia* that the

> events in the Near and Middle East and other parts of the world prove that the national liberation movement is an irresistible trend, that the age of colonialism is gone for ever, and that any attempt to maintain or restore colonial rule in contravention of the trend of history is detrimental to the cause of peace and is doomed to failure.[3]

However, Khrushchev refused to give way or to admit to mishandling the situation in the Middle East. The crisis was regarded by China as very important since it was the first confrontation with imperialism since November 1957, when the international situation was said by China to have reached a turning point in favour of Socialism. In an article on the 'Decay of Imperialism' in the C.C.P. theoretical journal *Red Flag*,[4] the Chinese continued to stress the paper-tiger thesis on imperialism and the need to give a resolute

[1] *People's Daily*, 20 July 1958. N.C.N.A., 21 July 1958.
[2] N.C.N.A., Mao-Khrushchev Communiqué, 3 Aug. 1958.
[3] *Ibid.*
[4] *Red Flag*, 16 Aug. 1958 Also *People's Daily* of 8 August calling for resolute struggle.

rebuff to it, using the alleged Soviet missile superiority to impose 'peace' on the imperialists and to serve as an umbrella under which the various national liberation movements in the world could proceed without too much hindrance from imperialism. The only concession Khrushchev made was to refuse to go to New York for the meeting of heads of governments which he had at first called for to deal with the Middle East situation.

However at the end of August a crisis of greater significance for China developed in the Taiwan Straits. This followed a Chinese attempt to take over the offshore islands of Quemoy and Matsu. In response the United States fleet in the straits was reinforced and the U.S. Government declared on 4 September that the islands would be defended.[1] Chou En-lai then suggested – on 7 September – that Sino-American talks in Warsaw be resumed. Although *Pravda* had earlier supported the Chinese case,[2] Khrushchev did no more than state on 8 September in a letter to Eisenhower that an attack on China would be regarded as an attack on the Soviet Union;[3] there was nothing in his letter to indicate he supported Chinese use of force to liberate Taiwan. Thus once again as far as China was concerned Soviet missile 'superiority' did not act as an umbrella for a member of the Socialist camp attempting to redress a just grievance.

Chinese policy towards wars in Algeria and Cameroun should be seen in the light of these developments. The provisional government of the Republic of Algeria (P.G.R.A.) was proclaimed in Cairo on 19 September.[4] On 23 September China joined other Arab countries in recognising it, in a message sent by Chen Ti, the Foreign Minister.[5] Chairman Mao also sent a congratulatory message to Ferhat Abbas, the P.G.R.A. Premier, wishing the Algerian people more outstanding and greater victories in their struggle for national independence and the defeat of colonialism.[6] A *People's Daily* editorial of 23 September spoke of the proclamation of the P.G.R.A. as an event which

> will exert a tremendous influence on the national independence movement of the African people. The armed struggle of the Algerian people has always

[1] Dulles' statement in *Survey of International Affairs 1956–58*, London, 1962, p. 567.
[2] *Ibid.* p. 568. [3] *Ibid.* p. 569.
[4] N.C.N.A., 21 Sept. 1958, p. 14.
[5] N.C.N.A., 23 Sept. 1958, p. 4. [6] *Ibid.*

been a source of great inspiration for the other African people under the yoke of colonialism.... By founding their own republic through heroic struggle, the Algerian people have set a glorious example for the other African people, who demand independence, in how to deal with the bloody repressions of the colonialists and fulfil their desire for independence.[1]

The Soviet Union did not recognise the P.G.R.A. and a broadside in the *People's Daily* against the colonial powers also reflected on the Soviet position.

Compared with the excitement and rejoicing over the proclamation of the Algerian Republic in the Asian and African countries and of the progressive forces in every corner of the world the 'non-recognition' of the colonial powers is trifling and impotent. By promptly recognising the P.G.R.A. the Chinese Government and people demonstrate once again their sympathy and support for the Algerian people and all other people fighting for their national independence.[2]

Chinese efforts to obtain diplomatic recognition from Morocco were helped by recognition of the P.G.R.A. and by the aid which she was sending to the nationalists on the fighting fronts. Once recognition had been granted a Chinese consulate was established at Ouida near the Algerian border.

A P.G.R.A. Ministerial delegation led by Ben Yussef Ben Khedda left Cairo on 28 November on a mission to China. On its arrival in Peking, on 3 December, Algerian Radio, broadcasting from Cairo, recalled 'that China was the first Asian country which recognised the Algerian Government, and that it always supported Algeria's case at international conference, [the] Algerian people could never forget the Chinese people's friendly stand and effective support for their struggle for freedom and independence'. To back up this statement the Chinese Foreign Minister declared at a banquet held by the U.A.R. envoy to China for the visiting Algerian delegation that 'Algeria, the U.A.R., all countries and areas of Asia, Africa and Latin America which are striving to win or safeguard national independence as well as the Socialist countries, headed by the Soviet Union, are all sources of the East Wind.'[3] The Chinese did not fail to note that Ferhat Abbas, while stating that the Algerians would continue to fight until their national sovereignty was recognised, had also stressed Algeria's desire to solve the Algerian question through peaceful negotiations; it was, he insisted, France's

[1] N.C.N.A., 23 Sept. 1958. [2] *Ibid.*
[3] Hsinhua News Agency, 21 Dec. 1958.

obstinate refusal to negotiate which caused the continuation of the war.[1] The Chinese therefore urged on the P.G.R.A. delegation the absolute necessity of continuing the struggle until final victory. This attitude on the part of the Chinese was to lead in 1959 to the first open clash with Moscow over the policy to be pursued in Africa. The occasion was de Gaulle's offer to negotiate on self-government, which was accepted by Khruschev but rejected by the Chinese. The latter agreed that it was the familiar attempt of imperialists on the verge of defeat resorting to every means to extricate themselves and deceive the people.

Meanwhile an Algerian military delegation headed by Omar Oussedik, Secretary of State and an experienced guerilla fighter who operated in the neighbourhood of Algiers, arrived in Peking on 29 March at the invitation of Marshal Peng Teh-huai, then the Defence Minister.[2] The delegation, which included soldiers, was in China until May touring military academies and installations. Welcoming the delegation the *People's Daily* said that the 'persistent armed struggle of the Algerian people against the French colonialists has laid the foundation for the final victory of freedom and independence of their own motherland. It has an inestimable influence on the national liberation movements in Asia and Africa, particularly in the African continent.'[3] China had sought to link the revolutionary struggles of the African peoples to her increasingly open opposition to Khrushchev's attempt to improve relations with the United States administration and de Gaulle's regime in France.

Apart from quoting from the Moscow declaration of Communist and Workers' Parties of November 1957 to the effect that the United States was the chief enemy of the world's people, the Chinese referred to the fact that 'many of the best sons and daughters of Algeria are being killed by the French aggressive forces with weapons supplied by the United States. While the U.S. imperialists pose with a sympathising face before the Algerian people, their real purpose is to replace the French colonialists.'[4] In his own report to the first session of the second National People's Congress on 18 April, Chou En-lai stressed that Asia, Africa and Latin America,

[1] Algerian Radio, 26 Sept. 1958.
[2] S.C.M.P. No. 1984, 2 Apr. 1959, p. 52.
[3] Hsinhua, 5 Apr. 1959.
[4] General Huang Chang at a banquet for the Military Delegation. Hsinhua, 1 Apr. 1959.

which used to be the imperialist rear, had now come to the forefront in the fight against aggression and colonialism. The imperialists would naturally not step down from the stage of history of their own accord and the struggle to achieve independence must therefore continue vigorously. While the struggles would meet with twists and turns the various underhand schemes and machinations of the colonialists must be defeated. He pledged China's full support by saying 'We are ready to give support and assistance to the full extent of our capabilities to all national independence movements in Asia, Africa and Latin America.'[1]

This pledge was followed by grants to the P.G.R.A. after the visit of another delegation in September. It was reported that China had granted a $10 million credit for the purchase of military equipment and the financing of administration and propaganda, and had at the same time agreed to supply large quantities of U.S. weapons seized during the Korean war.[2] This report was confirmed in 1960 by Iraq's General Qasim, when he was praising Chinese aid to the P.G.R.A. He gave the figure of 'more than 12 million dollars by way of aid and backing for this blessed struggle which is sapping the strength of colonialism'.[3] He also indicated that the Chinese had given other aid to the Algerians of which he had no personal knowledge.

From the Chinese point of view, however, the revolutionary situation was not limited to Algeria. An anti-colonialist struggle was already being conducted in the French Cameroun, by the Union des Populations du Cameroun (U.P.C.) led by the exiled Dr Félix Moumie. Lack of adequate funds, arms and tactical experience and the strong desire to sustain violent action had driven Dr Moumie and his party into the Soviet camp, which financed and maintained the movement until independence in 1960. In 1958, and for much of 1959, China and Moscow agreed on policy towards the war in Cameroun. Nevertheless, the Chinese did fear that the Soviet Union might, as in other areas, 'abandon' their obligations towards the U.P.C. in an attempt to reach a general relaxation of tension with the West (a development which seemed likely) if the colonial

[1] *Current Background*, 559.
[2] B.B.C. *S.W.B.* Second Series, Part IV, Weekly Supplement No. 30, 12 Nov. 1959, Tel Aviv Radio.
[3] B.B.C. *S.W.B.* Second Series No. 843 Part IV, 8 Nov. 1960.

power granted 'independence' to Cameroun. Chinese apprehension was justified in the sixties, when China had to take over from the Soviet Union financing and arming the U.P.C. In September 1958[1] a U.P.C. delegate arrived in Peking ostensibly to attend the National Day celebrations but in fact to pave the way for the visit to China of other delegations from the party. Thus in the following year delegations of Cameroun students, writers[2] and women visited China, culminating in a visit by Dr Moumie himself in October 1959. Dr Moumie's visit was important as it took place at a time when the French had decided to grant independence to Cameroun. This, the Chinese argued, was just a political ruse aimed at disarming the Cameroun people. Dr Moumie had moved his headquarters from Cairo to Accra at the end of 1957 at the invitation of Dr Nkrumah, and he saw no prospect of the French authorities even agreeing to his and his supporters' participation in government. He was therefore definitely amenable to the Chinese argument, which 'coincided' with his views. After his move to Accra, Dr Moumie was one of those who persuaded Nkrumah to establish close relations with the Chinese, especially as regards national liberation movements and all anti-colonial forces operating in Africa.[3] There was thus close contact between China and the Cameroun politicians of the U.P.C.

On 5 December 1958 the 'All-African People's Conference' opened in Accra[4] – the result of Dr Nkrumah's fervent desire to harness the widespread nationalist sentiments in Africa towards the achievement of a Pan-African goal, and to co-ordinate the efforts of the various political groups throughout the continent. A Chinese 'fraternal delegate', Yang Shuo, attended the conference as an observer and took the opportunity of contacting some of the delegations.[5] Among the delegates was Patrice Lumumba, founder of the Mouvement National Congolais (M.N.C.). He developed a close working relationship with Nkrumah, a relationship that was to be so much in evidence in the Congolese crisis following

[1] See Table 2, Appendix I, on Delegations visiting China.
[2] See Ch. 3.
[3] Schatten *Communism in Africa*, p. 157. On the results of these activities see below, pp. 142–9.
[4] Hsinhua, 6 Dec. 1958, reporting a message sent by the Chinese Committee for Afro-Asian Solidarity expressing support for the conference.
[5] Hsinhua, 13 Dec. 1958.

independence in 1960. In the first week of January 1959, only three weeks after the All-African People's Conference, the first in a series of violent struggles broke out in the Congo The Chinese commented that

> the struggle of the people of Congo shows that today there is no longer an 'oasis' of stability in the world for the colonialists. . . . The flame of anti-colonial rule is burning in the oasis of stability. This flame though not so big at the moment will eventually develop into a scorching prairie fire. Patrice Lumumba, delegate of the National Movement Party to the All African People's Conference, said last year: 'After eighty years of colonial rule, we are determined to break with the old regime. We want to bring a new countenance to our country, that of a people free from all yokes.' Last year witnessed the upsurge of the national liberation movement. Now the new year has dawned on us with the news of the people of Congo rising against the colonial rule and the Cuban people's victory in overthrowing dictator Batista's regime. This heralds the growth both in depth and breadth of the National Liberation Movement in Asia, Africa and Latin America in the coming year.[1]

Thus the Chinese did not see the Congolese revolt as a mere isolated event in a more or less stable and quiet political situation. Events in other parts of Africa were inter-related, all pointing to general anti-imperialist feelings and popular aspirations which could and should be used by the progressive forces in the Socialist camp to weaken the overall strength of imperialism. In the clearest exposition of this view to date, the *People's Daily* stated on 24 January:

> Revolts have taken place in the French Togo and Portuguese Angola. In the Central African Federation, the Nyasaland Africans have demonstrated and the Southern Rhodesian people held an anti-colonial rally protesting against the British colonial authorities suppression and demanding for the breaking up of the C.A.F. . . . In East Africa, the Buganda National Assembly has adopted a resolution demanding the abolition of the status of a British protectorate. In Mauritania, Chad and the Cameroons, armed struggles are being waged by the people against colonialism.
> The Congolese people are not isolated in their struggle for national independence, their struggle and that of the African people have the profound sympathy and support of the Socialist camp headed by the Soviet Union the Asian countries and all progressive mankind.[2]

In these circumstances the African people who wanted to exercise their just right to bring about a revolutionary situation, deserved

---
[1] S.C.M.P. No. 1934, 15 Jan. 1959; *People's Daily* comment on the Congo, 'Oasis of Stability Aflame', 10 Jan.
[2] S.C.M.P. No. 1944, 29 Jan. 1959: 'Victory Belongs to Congolese, African People'.

the organizational and political help of the Socialist countries. Although the situation showed that the African people were coming to 'maturity step-by-step politically and organisationally by their own practical experience',[1] China would make her revolutionary know-how available to the African people who desired it.

Meanwhile China had to make her policy more attractive to the African nationalists. One of her methods was to discard the facade of Marxist interpretation when it came to issues involving the European settler populations in Southern Africa. She employed instead the language of African nationalism, which did not involve any Marxist analysis of the situation. The Soviet Union was to attack China for this in the sixties when the racial issue was turned against it in the various 'front' organisations. Writing on South Africans fighting for freedom *Kuang-ming Jih-pao* said on 30 June 1959 that

> The policy of racial discrimination and oppression is aimed at further enslaving all people other than the whites, turning them into the cheapest labour force for the mines, factories and farms owned by the white men. It aimed at turning them into slaves deprived of all rights so as to maintain the reactionary and predatory rule of the facists and monopolists.[2]

Apart from using this tactic the Chinese felt that they had to prepare to take over leadership of the national liberation movements in Africa: it was becoming increasingly clear that Khrushchev's relentless effort for a detente with the West would lead to unwillingness to fulfil his internationalist obligations to the people's movements. China thus resuscitated the theme of the special applicability of their revolutionary experience to the colonial and semi-colonial areas. Writing on 'The Victory of the Marxism-Leninism in China', Liu Shao-chi claimed that the Chinese revolution 'has a great attraction for peoples in *all* the backward countries that have suffered, or are suffering from imperialist oppression. They feel that they should also be able to do what the Chinese have done.'[3]

The experiences of the Russian Revolution were of immense importance to the socialist struggles of the proletariat in advanced countries and consequently the Soviet Union should take the lead

[1] N.C.N.A., 15 Apr. 1959.
[2] S.C.M.P. No. 2048, 6 July 1959, p. 44.
[3] *World Marxist Review*, No. 8, Oct. 1959.

in promoting revolution in that section. China's leadership however should be recognised when it came to the colonial and semi-colonial areas: the Soviet Union should limit itself there to providing the required material and political support without interfering with the organisation.

The celebrations of the 10th anniversary of Communist rule were marked by bitterness over Khrushchev's visit to the United States, his repudiation of the nuclear agreement in June, his connection with Marshal Peng Teh-huai who had recently been dismissed as Defence Minister, and his advice to Peking not to test the fierceness of imperialism on the Taiwan issue – one in which he was told that he had no right to interfere.[1] During the celebrations Minister Chen Yi claimed that the Chinese successes in revolution and construction were a tremendous encouragement to all the oppressed nations and peoples of the world fighting for their liberation. 'In the Chinese people they see their own tomorrow and the Chinese people see in all oppressed nations their own yesterday.'[2] They would therefore continue the resolute support they were giving to the various national liberation movements in Africa. This was a prelude to the declaration made very cogently in 1960 that together with Asia and Latin America Africa had become the world storm centre of revolution. That the Chinese 'see in all oppressed nations their own yesterday' was Chen Yi's way of saying that the national wars of liberation being waged in Africa should take on the character of a protracted military, political, psychological and ideological engagement which would ensure victory to the 'people' in the long run. This would mean the infiltration of the nationalist movements by Communist cadres which would in due course take over and ensure the transformation of the national democratic struggles into socialist struggles. It would also mean that a 'hasty independence' would not be accepted. The strategy of uninterrupted revolution was the Chinese way to power and was thus recommended as the

---

[1] Lin Piao's Order of the Day, 1 Oct. 1959. 'Our armed forces are a powerful force in defence of peace. . . . The integrity of the Sovereignty of the P.R.C. over its sacred territorial land, air and water must be respected; the aspirations of the Chinese people in one way or another to liberate their own territory of Taiwan and the coastal islands and to achieve the complete unification of the great motherkind, must be realised and *no foreign countries are allowed to interfere in this.*' B.B.C. *S.W.B.* Second Series No. 145, 2 Oct. 1959, Part III.

[2] Hsinhua, 3 Oct. 1959; also in *Ten Glorious Years*, Peking, 1959.

'classic' model for revolutionaries in the colonial and semi-colonial areas. Whether this was feasible in the African context is another matter; the important thing was that the Chinese believed it to be feasible and consequently argued against any negotiations which might result in a peaceful settlement before 'the people' were assured of 'absolute victory'.

This attitude largely explained their hostility to de Gaulle's proposal in September 1959 regarding negotiations with the P.G.R.A., as well as their disgust at Khrushchev's acceptance of that offer in his speech to the Supreme Soviet at the end of October.[1] It also explained their generous offer of a $10m credit to the P.G.R.A. in October 1959[2] – an expression of their determination to foot the bill if the Soviet Union and other fraternal parties reneged, as appeared likely. In their altercations both the Soviet Union and China seemed to have given little consideration to the genuine aspirations of the Africans. That they were in no way dealing with completely monolithic opinion groups in these countries introduced another complication and was to lead in the sixties to conflicts with some of the African regimes they attempted to influence. A policy according to which 'the firm grasping of the hegemony in the democratic revolution by the proletariat through the Communist Party is the key to ensuring the thorough victory of the democratic revolution and the successful switchover from the democratic revolution to the Socialist revolution'[3] may be ideologically correct according to the Chinese experience in revolution, but it is hardly one that would be looked upon with favour by the new African elite. I will consider the changing situation and the Chinese response to such changes in the following chapters.

Since 1949 therefore the Chinese Communist Party had been forced to reconcile its attitudes towards the outside world with the demands of national interest. At times it was found necessary to compromise when advancing her ideas would be detrimental to China's perceived short-term interests. In 1958 and 1959, the Chinese were still in the process of breaking new ground in Africa –

[1] Radio Moscow Broadcast, 31 Oct. 1959. Khrushchev also mentioned the 'historic' links between France and Algeria.
[2] See above p. 53.
[3] Liu Shao-chi, *World Marxist Review* No. 8, Oct. 1959.

a process which was very much influenced by the sharp leftist shift in internal policy and its influence on foreign policy.

Chinese analysis of the international situation, its incompatibility with reality notwithstanding, affected their policy in Africa in terms of the tactics and strategy adopted. However, in pursuing their objectives, the Chinese did make use on the one hand of the traditional methods of statecraft, involving the promotion of diplomatic, cultural and trade relations, and on the other of the proven Communist devices of propaganda, and infiltration of dissident movements and the organisational apparatus. While the first diplomatic foothold was secured in Cairo in 1956, the organisational breakthrough occurred with the setting up of the Afro-Asian People's Solidarity Organisation in January 1958 following a conference attended by official, semi-official and nationalist groups.

Chinese trade and economic efforts were peripheral to the overall objectives during this period and the economic aid programme was affected by the capabilities of the government and the current argument with Khrushchev over the need to devote bloc economic resources to the development of the economies of the Communist states. This led to a period of strain in relations with Nasser's Egypt, ostensibly over the issue of imprisoned Communist Party members in the U.A.R. But the Chinese response to similar situations in Morocco and the Sudan suggested an awareness of the need for flexibility in treatment, a lesson that was to be of use in the sixties when the Chinese had to adopt policies for which Khrushchev had been blamed.

As regards the revolutionary struggles on the continent and the movements for independence in various territories, the Chinese believed themselves to be in a strong position because of their ability to pass on their revolutionary experiences to Africans and to direct nationalist sentiment in a way favourable to Chinese interests. That these interests were not in the short term economic helped to reinforce the purportedly altruistic nature of the support given to these movements in the spirit of Afro-Asian solidarity. As the year 1959 drew to an end, the Chinese stood on the verge of a new challenge in Africa – that of 17 African states being made politically independent in 1960 and the attitude to be adopted towards such a development. Sino-Soviet relations were aggravated by, among other things, conflicting attitudes towards the Algerian war of liberation. Sino-Soviet conflict was also to produce an open challenge to ideological purity, and therefore, leadership of the Soviet Communist Party – a challenge that was to greatly affect Chinese policy in Africa in the future.

ized states, states which are absolutely dependent upon them
3 ADJUSTMENT AND REAPPRAISAL 1960-2

1. The New Dimensions of the International Situation – the Changing African Scene

In the 1960s a new perspective opened on the international situation. In the next few years this was to produce a drastically altered voting pattern in international conferences and in the United Nations General Assembly. As the clamour for independence gathered momentum in Africa and as violent struggles continued in Algeria and the Cameroun, the British and French colonial authorities realised it was in their interests to answer the demands of the African nationalists in one way or another. The year 1960 thus witnessed the granting of political independence to seventeen African countries, bringing the total number of independent African states to twenty-six.

The new situation was not, however, without problems and dilemmas both for the old colonial powers and for the other great powers who had hitherto considered themselves excluded from the colonial territories. China had contemplated the possibility of such a situation arising – one which presented doctrinal and practical problems, especially in the light of the running debate with Khrushchev which was soon to become public knowledge. Ideologically, Chinese referred to Lenin's thesis that:

> It is necessary steadily to explain and expose among the broadest masses of the toilers of all countries, and particularly of backward countries, the deception which the imperialist powers systematically practice by creating, in the guise of politically independent states, states which are absolutely dependent upon them economically, financially and militarily.[1]

In a dispatch from the Cairo correspondent of the N.C.N.A. entitled 'Africa looks confidently forward to the New Year' the Chinese described the preceding year as having witnessed 'a sweeping advance of the African people's struggle for national indepen-

[1] V. I. Lenin, *Preliminary Draft of the Theses of the National Colonial Questions*, 1920.

dence'.[1] Conceding that imperialism granted some countries only 'nominal independence and retains control in the political, economic, cultural and social fields'[2] they argued that 'the fact that the imperialists were compelled legally to recognise their past colonies as independent states, surrender some of the powers and withdraw themselves to the background testifies to the irrepressibility of the national independence movement and the impending doom of the colonial system'.[3] But even this optimistic forecast did not at that stage include the granting of 'independence' to the large number of French African states – as occurred later in the year. Ideologically, it was not a difficult situation to explain and the Chinese made an incisive and thorough analysis of the situation.

In practical terms the Chinese had to choose whether or not to recognise the newly 'independent' states. In other words they had to decide whether their ideological analysis should prevent the new African states being accepted and treated as equal states fully in control of their internal and external policies. Eventually, they decided to offer immediate diplomatic recognition and to express the hope that such recognition would be reciprocated. This was important in view of China's efforts to obtain representation in the United Nations and her rivalry with the Taiwan regime, which was also cultivating good relations with the new states. Inevitably China's other aspirations and aims in Africa were related to this – the arguments with Khrushchev on the desirability of extending economic aid to bourgeois governments; the continuation of the revolution till absolute victory; the question of the colonial territories which were still fighting for independence.

The Chinese also had to consider the relationship the new states would maintain with the Soviet Union and the United States, and the prospects for revolution in Africa at this time. How far the new states really were independent could be assessed from their reaction to the imperialist powers, who, 'under the strong pressure of the African national independence movement, are attempting to maintain their toppling colonial rule by deceiving the African people with offers of certain forms of sham independence'.[4] A more important test would be whether they showed their real

[1] B.B.C. *S.W.B.*, Second Series No. 222, 2 Jan. 1960.
[2] *Ibid.* [3] *Ibid.*
[4] *Red Flag*, 15 Mar. 1960. 'Victory Belongs to the Great African People.'

independence by according diplomatic recognition to Peking in the face of opposition from the former colonial countries.

But 1960 was not only the year African states entered the United Nations, it was also the year of the Congo crisis. This crisis was to be one of China's weapons in the struggle against the United States and in the conflict with Krushchev.

The changing situation in Africa, then, fitted in very well with overall Chinese policy vis-à-vis the other two great powers. It also faced the new states with the difficult problem of trying to obtain economic aid from abroad and at the same time maintaining cordial relations with the former colonial countries. The attitude of the U.S. administration to African problems was to make China's task more difficult in this period – but only in terms of the goals Peking set herself. Nevertheless, despite the impression of doctrinaire dogmatism given in the debate with Khrushchev, China's policy remained essentially pragmatic. Thus the instruments of policy which had already been developed continued to be used – the number of reciprocal delegations visiting Africa and China increased, trade increased in volume, and China found that it was necessary to enter the economic aid race in spite of the disastrous internal economic situation in the years 1959, 1960 and 1961.

The situation in Africa was a dynamic one and changes had to have an appropriately flexible response if foreign policy was to succeed. New tactics had to be adopted to combat the United States' efforts to 'keep the Cold War out of Africa' – a euphemism, in effect, for keeping out Communism. Africa became the battle ground of the Western states and the Socialist bloc; gradually towards the end of this period it turned openly into a three-dimensional struggle.

2. The Chinese Analysis of the International Situation – The Role of Africa.
As Khrushchev continued in his efforts to achieve a limited détente with the U.S. in order to relax international tension the Chinese tried even harder to prevent him from bargaining away their interests. In this respect China's analysis of the international situation and the strategy to be adopted by the 'peace' forces in their confrontation with imperialism differed from that of the Soviet Union. Seeing 'peace' as a goal to be reached only with great effort the Chinese contended that there existed an 'excellent situation for the

peace struggle' and that 'the national democratic movement in Asia, Africa and Latin America is an important force in defence' of world peace. In an article in *Red Flag*, 1 January 1960, with the title 'An Excellent Situation for the Peace Struggle', Yu Chao-li, (a pseudonym for a high-ranking official of the Chinese Communist Party), pointed out that the Western countries had always used the resources, human and financial of their colonies and semi-colonies to support them in war.

Since World War II, the national democratic movement has spread over Asia, Africa and Latin America. The movement caused and continues to cause the disintegration of the imperialist colonial system, so what was originally a rear for imperialism in war has become a front in the struggle against imperialism. . . . In defence of the interest in the peace movement, it is necessary to continue to heighten the fighting will of the world's people, rely on the mass of the world's people and win and defend peace through broad, just struggles. The enemies of peace are still feverishly active. It is necessary to explore their schemes and weaknesses so as to enable the masses to recognise their true colours and have full courage and confidence to defeat them instead of being afraid of them or begging them for peace.[1]

Yu went on to say that the Socialist camp was still superior to the West and that the aggressive nature of U.S. imperialism had not changed despite Khrushchev's claims that Eisenhower was a man of peace. The African people should not be left under the illusion that independence would be bestowed on them. Foreign Minister Chen Yi took up the same theme in February when he claimed ironically that the Sino-Soviet alliance was the 'strong bulwark of world peace'.[2] The United States had not changed its 'policy and goals of aggression against the Soviet Union and China and only tactics had been changed'.[3] Chen Yi used the occasion of the convocation of the Second All-African People's Conference, and the resolution it passed, to express 'pleasure that the national independence movements in Africa. . . . have continuously won new victories'.

Despite China's indirect warnings that Khrushchev could not negotiate on behalf of the whole Socialist bloc, the latter showed no sign of relaxing his attempts at summitry. This he believed would ease tension and pave the way towards disarmament agreements.

[1] *Red Flag*, 15 Mar. 1960. 'Victory Belongs to the Great African People.'
[2] *Red Flag*, 2 Feb. 1960. 'Sino-Soviet Alliance is the strong bulwark of world peace'.
[3] *Ibid.*

The Chinese on the other hand contended that this would lead to accommodation with imperialism – detrimental not only to the nationalist struggles in Africa but, more importantly, to China's own vital interests. The Moscow meeting of the Political Consultative Committee of the Warsaw Treaty in February was used to tell Khruschev and the world that China would not go along with any decision deemed to be detrimental to her interests wherever those interests might be. While the Chinese ideologue Kang Sheng admitted that 'certain tendencies toward relaxation in the international tension created had appeared by imperialism' he nevertheless stated at the meeting on 4 February that 'the Chinese Government has to declare to the world that any international agreements which are arrived at without the formal participation of the C.P.R. and the signature of its delegates cannot, of course, have any binding force on China'.[1]

The Chinese felt that their stand on the nature of the struggle against imperialism and the tactics to be used was shown to be justified by events in Africa, and therefore the links between the Chinese struggle against the United States and the Africans' struggle against colonialism had to be demonstrated concretely. China claimed that they were supporting every struggle of the Africans for independence and freedom and that

China and Africa have both been subjected for a long time to imperialist plunder and oppression... The peoples of China and Africa are waging a common struggle on two fronts against the same enemy – imperialism. Victories won by either are a support and encouragement to the other.[2]

Although the Africans would encounter various obstacles, even setbacks, in their struggle for independence and freedom, these would only be temporary and the people would move inexorably forward to total victory provided they persevered and were united. 'No force on earth can hold in check'[3] this trend, not even Khruschev. Having achieved their own liberation the Chinese people would follow closely the struggles of the African peoples and actively support them. They considered it their 'noble international obligation to extend support to the liberation struggles of all oppressed nations'.[4]

[1] N.C.N.A. Monitored by B.B.C. *S.W.B.*, Part III, Second Series No. 253, 8 Feb. 1960.
[2] Hsinhua News Agency, 3 Feb. 1960.
[3] 'Victory Belongs to the Great African People', *Red Flag*, 15 Mar. 1960 in S.C.M.P. No. 2221, p. 34, 22 Mar. 1960.   [4]*Ibid.*

It was thought important that the situation be made crystal clear to the African people and that they should be warned of the deceptive methods which the colonial authorities might use. As Macmillan the British Prime Minister embarked on his famous tour of Africa in February 1960, the Chinese pointed out in broadcasts to Africa that he had three main points in mind.

(i) By the end of this year there would be more Africans ruling themselves, at least nominally, than under direct white rule.
(ii) Since the Second World War, British Governments, both Conservative and Labour, had been turning increasingly towards the exploitation of Africa as the British hold over Asia weakened.
(iii) The United States was hoping to oust the other colonialist powers from Africa.

The British ruling class, however, was clever enough to see that changes were needed in Africa, though Macmillan had so far made only formal ones. The African people 'must intensify their struggle until they have thrown over completely the colonialist yoke once and for all'.[1]

The French, facing armed revolt in Algeria and the Cameroun, were equally concerned with the security of their African territories. In the Chinese view, this was not the time to offer comfort to imperialism by recklessly pursuing a chimeric peace through summitry. Despite Chinese misgivings, Khrushchev went to visit President de Gaulle in March in preparation for the Four Power Summit scheduled for May. The Soviet Union continued to lay emphasis on the possibility and desirability of 'relaxing' world tension and achieving peace through negotiations with imperialism, thus 'peddling' revisionist ideas which were likely to dampen the spirit of the oppressed peoples struggling for independence in Africa, Asia and Latin America.

In their celebrated article in commemoration of the ninetieth anniversary of the birth of Lenin, the Chinese launched an ideological challenge to the Soviet Union on many issues, including the struggles of the oppressed peoples. Referring covertly to Soviet revisionism they asked 'But what is the real situation in the world?'

Can the exploited and oppressed people in the imperialist countries 'relax'?
Can the people of all the colonies and semi-colonies still under imperialist

[1] Peking Radio broadcast to Africa 24 Feb. 1960. B.B.C. *S.W.B*. Part III, Second Series, No. 269, 26 Feb. 1960.

oppression 'relax'? Has the armed intervention led by the U.S. imperialists in Asia, Africa and Latin America become 'tranquil'? Is there 'tranquility' in our Taiwan Straits when the U.S. imperialists are still occupying our country Taiwan? Is there 'tranquility' on the African continent when the people of Algeria and many other parts of Africa are subjected to armed repression by the French, British and other imperialists? Is there 'tranquility' in Latin America when the U.S. imperialists are trying to wreck the people's revolution in Cuba by means of bombing, assassination and subversion?[1]

The obvious answer to these rhetorical questions was of course 'no'. But the Chinese also found it necessary to make it clear that they were not advocating the unleashing of a world war by the Socialist camp. This would be a contradiction since Socialist states, by definition, could never commit aggression. It was nothing more than deception to confuse the issues of peaceful co-existence and revolution as Khrushchev insisted on doing.

Peaceful co-existence between nations and people's revolutions in various countries are by nature two different things, not the same thing; two different concepts not one; two different kinds of questions not the same kind of question. Peaceful co-existence refers to relations between different nations; revolution means the overthrow of the oppressors as a class by the oppressed people within a country, while in the case of colonial and semi-colonial countries, it is first and foremost a question of the overthrow of alien oppressors, namely the imperialists...

We have always considered that the question of revolution is a nation's own affair. We have always held that the working class can only depend on itself for its emancipation, and that the emancipation of the people of any country depends on their own political consciousness, and on the ripening of revolutionary conditions in that country. Revolution can neither be exported nor imported. No one can prevent the people of a country from carrying out a revolution, nor can one manufacture a revolution in a foreign country.[2]

Since agreements reached through negotiation necessarily involve concessions on both sides, it was inevitable that the Soviet Union would have to sacrifice some of its interests. The worse possible outcome would be if as a result of Western pressure Khrushchev reneged his obligations to the Chinese and African peoples – which would be absolutely unacceptable. At the moment, struggles in the developing countries and oppressed areas were dealing 'telling' blows to imperialist interests, and were fast becoming the front line in the battle against the imperialist forces of war and oppression. To abandon these struggles under the pretext that world peace was being achieved would mean abandoning completely the struggle

[1] *Red Flag*, 22 Apr. 1960. 'Long Live Leninism'. [2] *Ibid*.

against imperialism and throwing overboard the sacred principles and teachings of the great Lenin.

Naturally such a course, if followed, would deprive the Chinese of the noble right and obligation to pass on the fruits of their revolutionary experiences to the struggling masses of Africa and would leave the field to the Soviet Union on the one hand, and the 'imperialists headed by the United States' on the other. Moreover, to fail to stand up to imperialist warmongering, and for the people to put their trust in a chimeric peace, would only increase the 'effrontery' of the imperialists and keep the people in perpetual subjugation.[1] Obviously one could point to setbacks in the peoples' struggles in an attempt to discredit them, forgetting that history develops unevenly, 'yet twists and turns, and stagnations are but partial and temporary phenomena in the long course of development of human history'.[2]

The African people should rest assured that the Chinese people who had always resolutely supported them in their struggle for national independence, would in future 'continue to stand by them unswervingly to carry the struggle against imperialism and colonialism to its end'.[3]

The Chinese thesis on the unchanging nature of imperialism and the concomitant strategy to be adopted by the 'people' was provided with live ammunition by the shooting down of the U2 spy plane over Soviet territory in May. President Eisenhower accepted responsibility for the flights over the Soviet Union rather than allow some 'warmongers' in the Pentagon to take the blame. The Chinese pointed out to Khrushchev that Marxism-Leninism

holds that aggression and war are the very nature of imperialism. It is of especially important realistic significance for the struggle to safeguard world peace today that this irrefutable, never outmoded truth should be recognised. The more thorough the exposure of the aggressive activities, arms expansion and war preparations of the imperialists, and the more resolute the struggle against them, so that imperialism falls more and more into isolation, the more guarantee there is for carrying out the tasks of relaxing international tension and safeguarding world peace. On the contrary, if one evades the struggle, that can only promote the growth of imperialist effrontery and make their aggressive activities more rabid. If we cover up the evil of the imperialists, then that can only

[1] See also below p. 98.
[2] *People's Daily* editorial on Leninism, 23 Apr. 1960.
[3] Vice Premier Ho Lung's Speech commemorating May Day. Hsinhua News Agency, 3 May 1960.

paralyse the people, so that the danger of imperialism launching a war increases and the people will suffer.[1]

Paradoxically, this was the same kind of argument as that put forward by the American analysts who advocated negotiation from a position of strength, and the attainment of military superiority over the Soviet bloc. Faced with the free world's overwhelming military strength the Communist expansionists would not then be tempted to launch an attack on one of its flanks in the belief that they could confront the West with a quick fait accompli.

At a reception at Wuhan for 'friends' from Latin America and Japan, on 14 May 1960 – two days before the opening of the abortive Summit Conference in Paris – Chairman Mao commented on the shooting down of the U2. He said the incident exposed the United States in its true colour and confirmed that 'no unrealistic illusion should be cherished with regard to imperialism'. Some people [ie Khrushchev] had described Eisenhower as 'a man who cherished peace'; he hoped that these people would be awakened by these facts. The Chinese people supported [add not] the holding of the Summit Conference, no matter whether this sort of conference made achievements or not [he hoped not] or whether the achievements were big or small. 'But the winning of world peace depends mainly on the resolute struggle carried out by peoples of all countries.'[2]

On the day the conference opened, the Chinese Communist Party's theoretical journal, *Hung Chi*, called for the formation of a 'broad United Front [to] defeat imperialism' in view of the fact that imperialist activities had caused

oppressed people everywhere to rise up in a wave of anger and conduct revolutionary struggles. The great waves of the national democratic movements in Asia, Africa and Latin America are rolling forward one after another, fiercely, sweepingly and irresistibly . . .
On the African continent several countries have either proclaimed independence or won a certain degree of independence. They are continuing their fight against imperialism [*if they are not they ought to be and must be helped to do so*] in an effort to consolidate the fruit of their struggle and achieve complete independence.

In view of the United States' activities all over the world 'oppressing the people and waging counter-revolutionary subversion' it was

[1] *People's Daily*, 9 May 1960. Editorial on U2 spy plane.
[2] B.B.C. *S.W.B.* Second Series, No. 335 Part III, 17 May 1960.

imperative that all anti-imperialist forces in the world should form a broad united front to defeat U.S. imperialism – 'the main enemy of the peoples of the world'.

The break-up of the Summit Conference was followed by enthusiastic Chinese support through mass demonstrations and rallies for the Soviet Government's stand on the issue of a public apology from the United States President. It was clear, however, that the rejoicing was more for the failure of the summit than in appreciation of Khrushchev's 'resolute' stand in Paris. In fact, the *People's Daily* of 20 May 1960 claimed that the breakdown of the conference by the action of the United States was 'nothing strange to all those who observe the international situation from the viewpoint of class analysis and are not misled [like Khrushchev] by certain superficial phenomena, and to all those who see clearly the nature of imperialism. For it is the result of the policies of aggression and war which the U.S. Government has long pursued.'

In contrast the Chinese showed themselves to be aware of the rapidly changing situation in Africa and the fact that the colonial powers could resort to and were already resorting to various methods which would minimise the loss of material interests while acceding to the demands of the nationalists. In examining the changing situation in Africa and the interests of the Western countries there, it was argued that:

the imperialists themselves have found it unprofitable to rely solely on armed forces as a means of suppressing the African national independence movement. As a matter of fact, in the past year and more, there has been no instance in which the colonialists succeeded in putting down the people's struggle with violence in a single African colony. . . . In the face of this situation the imperialists are being compelled to change their tactics and adopt more cunning methods in an attempt to bait and inveigle the right wing of the African bourgeoisie and paralyse the fighting will of the African people to win genuine independence. . . .

Africa is today still a very important market and source of new materials for imperialism. . . .

As everyone knows, important mineral resources in Africa account for major portion of those found in the capitalist world.[1]

This was the last analysis made of the situation before the Congo crisis which was to continue throughout this period and to provide opportunities for Sino-Soviet collaboration as well as for conflicts on policy and strategy. The crisis would also 'validate' the Chinese

[1] Feng Chih-tan, *Peking Review*, No. 27, 5 July 1960. 'The Awakening of Africa'.

thesis on the unwillingness of colonialism to relinquish its control over the financial, economic and military resources of newly 'independent' states.[1]

3. **Diplomatic and Friendly Relations with the New African States.**
For China, various advantages would result from diplomatic recognition by the newly independent African states. Despite the continued underlying dependence of these states on the imperialist powers, Chinese policy makers decided that to take the fact of independence for granted and to act accordingly might yield incalculable rewards. A break-through in Africa would remove the automatic power of the United States, resulting from her control of votes, to block China's entry to the United Nations. Solidarity of Afro-Asian states would effectively destroy the U.S. attempt to perpetuate the isolation of China and would thus in effect inflict a set-back on U.S. policy.

Chinese aspirations to great power status would also be enhanced by her increased acceptance by the international comity of nations. Moreover, China's claims to leadership of the developing world would be based on firmer ground if it was seen that the new states were ignoring the wishes of the United States and recognising her This aspect of Chinese policy was to become more important as the gap between Moscow and Peking widened.

To complicate the issue, efforts to secure diplomatic recognition also had to face competition from Taiwan, which already maintained diplomatic relations with South Africa, Libya, Liberia and Tunisia. Peking, of course, saw Taiwan's success as a result not of her own efforts but of pressure from the Western states. However, it is also fair to point out that non-recognition of Peking was in some cases a result of Peking's support for the revolutionary activities of opposition groups as, for instance, in the Cameroun and later, Congo Leopoldville.

In January 1960, Taiwan sent a friendship delegation to West African countries to lay the foundation for official recognition from those states which were soon to become independent. This resulted in the establishment of diplomatic relations with Cameroun in March and the raising of the status of the Taiwan delegation in

[1] On the Congo episode see below pp. 101–4.

Liberia to that of an Embassy. Peking denounced the Taiwan tour as an 'imperialist attempt to sabotage friendship between Chinese and African peoples'[1] and to promote a 'two-Chinas' policy, and attempted to explain the situation to the African people by claiming the C.P.R. was the sole legitimate government of the 650 million Chinese people. Peking had offered Cameroun immediate diplomatic recognition when it obtained independence at the beginning of January, with Chou En-lai expressing the hope that the Cameroun people would achieve more victories in future. This gesture was, however, not reciprocated by Cameroun because among other things China still gave material support to the struggles being waged by the U.P.C. Khrushchev was already withdrawing support from the U.P.C. and China would probably have done the same if Cameroun had recognised her. (This is supported by the attitude of Peking to other liberation struggles, for example in the southern Sudan where China did not lend any support to the movement, and in Iraq, where she did not support the Kurdish struggle for independence from Iraq. Both the Sudanese and Iraqi governments had recognised Peking.)

Seventeen African States gained political independence in 1960; of these only Mali and the Somali Republic recognised Peking. Ghana, which granted China recognition in July, had been independent since 1957. It is misleading, however, to regard this as a total failure, since Chinese aims in improving relations were many. When performance in the United Nations General Assembly in the autumn of 1960 is examined, the caution with which most African regimes approached the question of recognition was not as damaging as the record suggests. The situation was being closely followed by the United States. The Democratic National Chairman Henry Jackson said that voting on 8 October showed that 'the U.S.A. failed for the first time to get a majority in the U.N. Even more ominous for the future is the fact that we did not win a single vote of any of the new African nations.'[2]

For the United States it was not, of course, a hopeless situation as only Mali, Senegal and Nigeria voted against the United States' resolution (the latter two did not recognise Peking) and the other twelve African states abstained. Although apprehension was

[1] *People's Daily*, 9 Feb. 1960 in S.C.M.P. No. 2195, 12 Feb. 1960.
[2] B.B.C. *S.W.B.* Part III, Second Series, No. 460, 12 Oct. 1960.

Adjustment and Reappraisal 1960–2   73

expressed in the United States, China rightly recognised that the decreasing efficiency of the U.S. voting machinery in the U.N. did not mean that admission was imminent.[1] In fact it seemed to some decision-makers that Peking's total freedom to manoeuvre would be curtailed if she joined the United Nations. 'If our country joins the United Nations, we cannot have a majority in voting; formally the difficult situation may be moderated to some extent, but actually the struggle that arises will be more violent and we shall lose our present freedom of action. Though standing outside of the U.N. we could still participate in the Bandung Conference.'[2]

Though this was contained in a secret briefing of People's Liberation Army Commanders it simply confirmed what had already been stated earlier, that China would not feel bound by any agreement to which she was not a party.

The case of 'radical' Ghana was particularly interesting as Nkrumah refused to recognise China after Ghana's independence in March 1957. This decision was not reversed until July 1960. There were both external and internal reasons for this. First competitive radicalism with Guinea demanded that Ghana's moderation on such issues as South Africa's role in the Commonwealth and non-recognition of the Algerian Government in exile should be abandoned. Second, the presence of young Ghanaian radicals who favoured recognition together with the influence of Félix Moumie of the Cameroun U.P.C., who lived in Accra, were important factors in Nkrumah's offer on recognition to China.

The leaders of the new African states naturally considered the 'interests' of their countries before taking steps which they knew had problematic consequences. Many, like the Nigerian Prime Minister, were cautious in dealing with an unknown quantity. It was felt that some experience of international affairs was needed before entering the cloak-and-dagger game of East–West diplomacy and that former colonial power which was well-understood could be better handled than a new quantity, whose propensity for evil was not known. Other influences in favour of caution were effective

[1] *People's Daily*, 18 Oct. 1960. In fact Chinese caution proved justified in 1961, when the United States successfully introduced a resolution in the General Assembly declaring the question of China's seat an important one. This would require a two-thirds majority to seat Peking, and thus would postpone entry for as long as possible.
[2] *The Politics of the Chinese Red Army, Bulletin of Activities*, Hoover Institution for War, Revolution and Peace publication, Edited by Chester Chen, p. 480.

Western propaganda, and the close working relationships between the Civil Servants manning the top and lower echelons of the External Affairs Ministries and their British and French counterparts. For most of the French-speaking states, the issue of the Algerian war of independence and Peking's support, the Congo crisis and French attitudes on both questions played a decisive role in non-recognition at this stage. However, some of the leaders, in particular those of Gabon and the Ivory Coast, were simply conservative and did not need strong external pressure from the West.

In March 1961 Senegal recognised the Peking Government and North Vietnamese and Chinese delegations arrived in Dakar.[1] But diplomatic relations were not established as Senegal insisted on continuing relations with Taiwan. If China had accepted this decision it would have meant a drastic change in her opposition to the 'two Chinas' policy and would have affected her attitude to many issues in international relations. The question of diplomatic recognition also involved two other states in 1961 – the Congo and Tanganyika.

After the assassination of Patrice Lumumba early in 1961, President Sekou Touré of Guinea sent a message to the Chinese Government urging it to accord formal recognition to the Gizenga Government based on Stanleyville as the only legal regime in the Congo and material support.[2] China then recognised Gizenga, though a Chinese diplomatic representative did not arrive in Stanleyville until 31 July.[3] Then, on 18 September the Chinese Government announced the withdrawal of its representative from the Congo (Stanleyville) 'in view of the fact that the lawful Government of the Republic of the Congo (Stanleyville) has announced its own termination, while the Leopoldville Government in the Congo now maintains so-called diplomatic relations with the Chiang Kai Shek clique in Taiwan'.[4]

Tanganyika gained independence on 9 December 1961 and the independence celebration was attended by Huang Hua Chinese Ambassador to Ghana. He met Prime Minister Julius Nyerere and both countries decided to establish diplomatic relations at

[1] B.B.C. S.W.B. Weekly Supplement, Part IV, No. 101, 23 Mar. 1961.
[2] N.C.N.A., 21 Feb. 1961. On the Congo crisis, see below, pp. 101–4.
[3] S.C.M.P. No. 2554, 4 Aug. 1961.
[4] N.C.N.A., 18 Sept. 1961.

ambassadorial level.[1] Thus began a relationship which in time proved to be most fruitful. At that time, however, Nyerere was regarded as one of the 'moderates' among African leaders, and recognition was granted partly in an attempt to remove the steam and pressure expected from the radicals[2] and partly in a belief in the illogicality of not recognising a big country like China. Thus by the end of 1961 eight out of the twenty-nine independent African States recognised Peking.

As regards U.N. representation, China aimed to persuade as many African states as possible either to vote for her or, failing that, to refuse to vote in favour of the United States' position on the Taiwan issue. The Chinese were encouraged by the tenor of the debates at the opening sessions in October and hope was publicly expressed that the 1960 performance, when only three African states voted against the United States, would be improved.[3] In the actual voting nine African countries opposed the resolution, ten supported Peking and ten abstained.[4] This was in fact an improvement on the previous year. All the abstainers were French-speaking.

1962 saw the formal recognition of Algeria's independence by France, and Ugandan independence. The Algerian Government now formally recognised China, continuing the recognition granted by the P.G.R.A. during the fighting. Uganda also granted recognition to China on 18 October after a visit by Ho Ying the shrewd and highly intelligent Chinese Ambassador to Tanganyika.[5] In the United Nations debates of 1962 the number of African countries voting for Peking rose to fourteen with only Niger and Togo abstaining. Nevertheless, the final outcome was disappointing. While nine had voted against Peking in 1961, sixteen now voted against her thanks to mass defection by the French-speaking states who had mostly abstained in 1961.[6] In Cameroun and Congo Leopoldville, opposition could be explained as a protest against

[1] S.C.M.P. No. 2641, 18 Dec. 1961.
[2] Interview with X.
[3] Peking Review No. 42, 20 Oct. 1961. 'With the opening of the U.N. General Assembly, powerful voices have been raised demanding that China's legitimate rights in the United Nations be restored.... The devious schemes of the enemies of peace and justice are doomed to fail. The speeches at the U.N. rostrum and opinion expressed in all parts of the world foreshadow this.' Alas, success had to wait until October 1971.
[4] *Yearbook of the United Nations, 1950–64*
[5] S.C.M.P. No. 2845, 24 Oct. 1962.
[6] *Yearbook of the United Nations 1950–64.*

Peking's support for the revolutionaries in those countries: others simply followed the French lead.

(i) *Political Relations with African States: Guinea, Ghana and Mali.* Efforts to secure diplomatic recognition and representation at the United Nations constituted a relatively minor aspect of Chinese policy in Africa in this period. Though less than one-third of the African states accorded recognition, this did not mean no importance was attached to China's policy and efforts by her other rivals, notably the United States. The Chinese recognised that there were not many 'progressive' leaders and that even those who were progressive had other issues to worry about, issues which were not necessarily of interest to China. Her relationship in this period with the three West African states of Guinea, Mali and Ghana show the extent of her appeal as a revolutionary anti-colonia country in the throes of development. Apart from solidarity based on common anti-colonialism, she made efforts to increase the anti-Western stance of these states and to make them take up similar positions to hers on international issues – peace, disarmament, anti-colonialism and economic independence. She also sought to interest them in Asian issues to make sure that in a crisis Africa's voice would be added to hers and to prevent isolation and general condemnation. She was to reap significant rewards during the Sino-Indian border clashes in 1962.

No doubt the neutralist policy of most progressive African states was also anti-Western because it was anti-colonial, thus increasing the similarity of their views and Peking's. Yet it is true that China's persistent adherence to its position did eventually cause the African states to shift theirs. The Congo crisis was a prime example of this, though the Western states also did much to alienate African nationalist opinion.

In summer 1960 Chinese political activity in Africa was extended. Branches of the N.C.N.A. were set up in Conakry, Rabat and Accra.[1] The Congo crisis, the action of the Belgian troops and the dispatch of United Nations troops brought forth vociferous protests from China. While her thesis that the colonialists would not easily let go seemed to have been proved right, her condemnation of United Nations actions was not at first shared by any African state.

[1] *China Quarterly*, October/December, 1960, p. 129.

China's argument that the United States would use the U.N. operation to further her own interests, and prevent Chinese influence growing, was not at first accepted, and even the Soviet Union voted for the action in the Security Council. The disappointment of the radicals at the course of events in the Congo led to their drawing closer to the Chinese position.

In September, President Sekou Touré visited China, the first visit by an African Head of State. Addressing his hosts at Peking airport on 10 September he said that

the sentiments of fraternity that unite the people of Africa and Asia have a political and historical basis. . . . These sentiments have been reinforced by their common hatred of imperialism and colonialism and also and above all by their common will to pursue and continue the struggle until imperialism vanishes and each nation on earth can be master of its destiny with freedom and dignity.[1]

He flattered the Chinese leaders and people by telling them that his delegation came not as tourists but as fighters, and not only to measure

all the progress of your revolution, but to be able to carry away lessons that could be applied to the actual conditions of the African struggle, so as to be able, in a unity of action and in understanding, to carry out more fully our programs for justice, democratic advance and civilisation for the benefit of all society. . . . We already recognise the great contribution of your revolution and the unceasing efforts you have made at all times to push back the frontiers of misery and war, for the benefit of justice and peace.[2]

In his speaking engagements throughout the tour Sekou Touré showed himself the equal of the Chinese in platitudinous generalities. No doubt he expressed his genuine feelings but he also seemed to be aware of the high regard in China for fulsome praises.[3] Like other African leaders in the future, Sekou Touré was given a rousing welcome and the 'traditional spontaneous' Chinese hospi-

[1] S.C.M.P. No. 2338, 15 Oct. 1960.   [2] *Ibid.*
[3] Peking Review No. 37, 14 Sept. 1960, pp. 15–16. 'The contributions of the Chinese people to the clarification of revolutionary thinking, their contribution to the definition of decisive principles of a revolution at once political, social, cultural and human, are appreciated by all people of goodwill who are solely concerned with seeking and bringing about for the benefit of humanity that which is invoked by all – the happiness of mankind. . . . Every step you take, every action in which you are involved is followed closely in the thoughts of the African people who are conscious of the existence of relationships between your struggle for life and their own, who are conscious that, thanks to your political liberation and the great economic and cultural progress you have achieved, great perspectives have also been opened for them. . . .'

tality which the Chinese are accustomed to give their best friends.[1] His visit was, however, of benefit to both sides. A Treaty of Friendship was signed and also an agreement on economic and technical co-operation which was to make available to Guinea a non-interest-bearing loan of 100 million roubles ($26 million).[2] As these two agreements set the pattern for subsequent ones with Ghana, Mali, Congo (B) and Tanzania they are printed in full in Appendix II.[3] Declarations uttered in the presence of visiting Heads of State and the communiqués issued on such occasions, served two vital political purposes for the Chinese. First, the Chinese masses were shown that the views of their leaders were accepted by the leaders of other peoples in the third world and that these people looked to the Chinese for political leadership. They were reminded that every action they took in the struggle for economic and social development was being closely watched by the peoples of the world who regarded China as a model. At the same time it revived unconscious memories of the tribute-bearing foreigners who came in the past to pay homage to Chinese emperors. While the Chinese leaders could claim in their speeches that they had friends all over the world, the common man in China could think in terms of having admirers all over the world who regarded Chairman Mao as their Chairman too.

Second, such declarations demonstrated, to an international audience, the similarity between Chinese and African opinion on such vital issues as disarmament and the struggle against imperialism. The importance of this came out in the Sino-Soviet debates over these issues. Sekou Touré's saying 'That is why we hope that peace will triumph rapidly over war, that is to say that imperialism and colonialism will disappear from the whole world due to the political consciousness and struggle of the people'[4] was in complete agreement with China's attitude that while colonialism still oppressed the peoples of Africa, Asia and Latin America there could be no peace. A world without war, without imperialism and without the exploitation of man by man should be the ideal goal of mankind. Needless to say such a situation is beyond achievement.

Sekou Touré's visit and the agreements resulting from it marked

[1] Hsinhua News Agency reported that more than half a million people turned out to welcome Sekou Touré. The elated feeling on such an occasion can be imagined.
[2] On economic relations, see below pp. 87–90.
[3] See pp. 278 and 279.   [4] Sekou Touré's speech at the airport, *op. cit.*

a turning point in China's policy in Africa – the decision to enter the field of economic and technical aid had been made.[1] The improvement in the political climate and Sekou Touré's genuine desire for the liberation of the Portuguese territory adjoining his Republic made it easier to arrange for Chinese material aid to be delivered to nationalists in the Portuguese territory through Guinea.[2]

One should not, however, attribute the nationalist and 'left wing' orientation of Guinea to Chinese influence, as this would be to over-estimate Chinese capability and misunderstand Touré's views. Undoubtedly Sekou Touré's Partie Democratique de Guineé is run on Leninist lines, but he himself has always rejected 'atheism, historical materialism and class struggle as did nearly all African leaders'.[3] The Chinese were of course aware of this but to them it was the Africans' anti-colonialism, not their anti-feudalism or class consciousness which was important.[4] The more tension increased in Africa as a result of the supposed actions of the Western powers the closer the views of the African nationalists drew to China's. This was particularly so after the murder of Patrice Lumumba, and most of all among younger people. Political relations between Guinea and China benefited from the débacle over Solod, the Soviet Ambassador to Guinea, who, at the end of 1961 was involved in subversive activities against the Guinea regime and was expelled by Sekou Touré[5] for political interference. On Guinea's next anniversary of independence, the Chinese Foreign Minister Chen Yi supported her in her efforts to crush all 'subversive activities'.[6]

The political rapprochement between Ghana and China in and after 1961 was an interesting illustration of a shift of orientation on the part of an African state and at the same time of China's own activities among the young radicals of the Convention People's Party.[7] I have already referred to Nkrumah's recognition of China in July 1960, but his policy on the Congo differed dramatically from China's. He wholeheartedly supported the United Nations operations, and had himself been the first to send in troops, believing

[1] See below section 4 (i), pp. 85–7.
[2] See below, pp. 106–7.
[3] Robert C. Wesson, *Soviet Foreign Policy in Perspective*, 1969, The Dorsey Press, Homewood, Illinois, p. 264.
[4] Bulletin of Activities, *op. cit.*
[5] Wesson, *op. cit.*, p. 264.
[6] Hsinhua News Agency, 2 Oct. 1962.
[7] *Ghana's Foreign Policy 1957–1966*, 1969.

that order could be restored without drawing in the big powers. He strenuously tried to restrain some of Lumumba's extravagant aims and actions in the belief that, if properly handled, the solution of the Congo problem would reflect favourably on his pan-African aims.[1] In placing absolute trust in the head of his army, General Alexander, he was even prepared to risk the alienation of his friends in Guinea, Mali and the U.A.R. However, the impasse of the Congo issue and the thwarting of his aims by the Western powers had a traumatic effect on his thinking and position in world politics. There was a definite shift in his thinking after the murder of Lumumba. This trend was reinforced by the radical elements in the C.P.P. who were more concerned with talking about Socialism and usually gained much attention at a time of crisis. The Socialist states took advantage of this general shift to the left. For her part China made determined efforts to influence these radicals through extending invitations to visit China, ideological appeals both on radio and in international front organisations and persistent and principled opposition to the Congo operation even when most African states supported it. Nkrumah had urged Africans to 'Seek ye first the political kingdom', but he now found that all other things did not follow.[2]

It was in this mood, of movement towards the left, that Nkrumah made his extended tour of Socialist countries in the summer of 1961 visiting China in August. Like Sekou Touré before him, Nkrumah was much impressed by his reception. He also signed the symbolically significant Treaty of Friendship with China as well as numerous economic and cultural agreements. The Chinese had suggested the treaty and they knew very well that Nkrumah did not like to be outshone on the left by Sekou Touré. Its signature however, was said to have been pressed by Tawia Adamafio who insisted that 'more' of it should be signed, despite a colleague's protest that a communiqué had already been signed. 'In Russia it

[1] See also K. Nkrumah, *Challenge of the Congo*, 1967.
[2] Scott-Thompson, *op. cit.*, p. 183. 'Nkrumah had hoped to found a pan-African State by leading the Continent in a search for the political kingdom. The Congo crisis, the independence of the conservative-minded francophone states, and growing influence of radical advisers in Flagstaff House brought Nkrumah to the belief that the political kingdom alone could not resist outside forces. Neo-colonialism had become too potent in Africa ... now he became convinced that without an economic revolution political independence would be impossible, and that economic independence could only come through Socialism!' This was in agreement with China's viewpoint.

was multi-nationalism, and the industrial might that impressed him; in China it was the ideology – at least for a time.'[1] The political warmth generated on the occasion of the visit was to pay high dividends to China at the time of the Sino-Indian border clash in October to November 1962.[2]

After the break-up of the Mali Federation into Senegal and the Mali Republic in October 1960, Modibo Keita, the new President of Mali, decided to grant official recognition to China[3] and diplomatic relations were established on 27 October after talks between the two governments.[4] Mali thus joined the caucus of militantly nationalist African states – Ghana, Guinea, the U.A.R. and Morocco – and her political ideas drew nearer to China's. Official and unofficial delegations visited China more frequently, preparing for the economic aid China was to extend.[5]

(ii) *Political and Cultural Relations with African States.*
The Chinese thrust into Africa was characteristically made on all fronts – diplomatic and clandestine, conventional and unconventional; political, economic, social and cultural. The Chinese were of course under no illusions about what could be achieved through these offensives, but they tended to take a long-term view of the situation which would explain future failures as mere twists and turns in the revolutionary path. They were also aware of the dynamics of African politics and the rivalries between leaders.

'Thus Africa itself looks like the seven powers of [China's] warring States [403 B.C. to 221 B.C.] with its Nkrumah, Sekou Touré, Bourguiba and Abbas [*sic*] each with his own way of leading others. In general everyone is trying to sell his own goods. Africa is now like a huge political exhibition, where a hundred flowers are truly blooming, waiting there for anybody to pick. But everything must go through the experience of facts. History and realistic life can help the Africans to take the road of healthy developments. We must tell them about the Chinese revolutionary experience in order to reveal the true nature of both new and old colonialism. In Africa we do no harm to anyone, we introduce no illusions, for all we say is true. Africa is now both the centre of the anti-colonialist struggle and the centre for East and West to fight for the control of an

---
[1] Scott-Thompson, *op. cit.*, p. 177.   [2] See below, p. 107.
[3] N.C.N.A., 17 Oct. 1960.   [4] S.C.M.P. No. 2370.   [5] See below, pp. 87–93.

intermediary zone so that it has become the key point of world interest. The general situation is the forced withdrawal of old colonialism from Asia and the changing of the last battlefield to Africa. The entry of America's new colonialism into Africa has resulted in the crowding out of old colonialism. The present struggle will go on even for one inch of territory. We must also develop our relationship with the movement for national independence in various parts of Africa.

At present some parts of Africa are going through experiences similar to what we experienced in China sixty years ago in the Boxer rising. Some of the events were like those which occurred during the Hsin-hai of Revolution [1911], while other resembled what happened around the May 4th Movement of 1919. We had not yet begun the period of the Northern Expedition and that of the war of Resistance against Japan, and we were still far from the events of 1949 in China. Africa at present is mostly occupied with fighting imperialism and colonialism. Its fight against feudalism is not so important, and moreover, its role in the Socialist revolution is in a dormant phase. The important part of its activities lies in its national revolution and in making the United Front spread everywhere on the Continent...

After the gaining of independence by Colonies and semi-Colonies the governing parties will make some changes. Among the political leaders there are not many leaning towards the left, quite a few lean towards the right, and those truly supporting neutralism are also not many but there must be some among them who lean towards the left. Those leaning towards the right cannot basically cancel the national revolution, and this will cause them to lose the confidence of the people and be driven out of politics. We must tell them, in order to help them, about the experience of the Chinese revolution, pointing out the significance of the Taiping rising, the Boxer rising, Dr Sun Yat Sen, and the revolutionary experience of the Communists in this generation. They must depend mainly upon their own personal experience, for foreign assistance can only come second; their victory will come eventually but no immediate results should be expected. Among the independent countries in Africa, if only one or two of them complete a real national revolution, solving their own problem of resisting imperialism and reaching an internal solution of a democratic national revolution, the effect will be very great, the time ripe for action, the revolutionary wave will be able to swallow the whole African continent, and the 200 million and more Africans will advance to the forefront of the world. We should take long range views of this problem.'

Political and cultural drives were therefore aimed at creating sympathy and support for China among the African people as well as their governments. Where the governments were hostile, attention was directed at those levels of opinion which could bring pressure to bear on those governments. As in every society, there were individuals and groups who could be subsidised to promote Chinese interests openly or clandestinely. No doubt many Africans wanted Chinese support simply to help them achieve their aims and were not averse to being used for propoganda purposes as long as they were achieved. To the Western allegation that they were Communists or unconsciously Communist agents they simply replied that the mere fact of Chinese support for their noble causes should not mean that they should abandon those causes for fear of being called Communists. The Kenya nationalist leader Oginga Odinga defended himself against charges in the British press of having received funds from China and other Socialist countries by saying that he had been responsible for sending large numbers of students to the West as well as to Socialist countries including China, and would continue to do so, as long as Kenya needed more educated people.[1]

In extending invitations to African delegations, the Chinese were careful to look for dignitaries in several African countries whose voices could be heard in high government circles. Thus the Chairman of the Greater Somali League visited China in September 1960 and was well received.[2] He used his influence to secure the establishment of diplomatic relations between China and the Somali Republic in December 1960[3] after which Chinese cultural, political and commercial activity increased. The Chinese were, however, careful to avoid getting involved with Somalia's irredentist claims on Kenya and Ethiopia as this might endanger Chinese relations with Kenya.

In June 1960 the Vice President of the Chinese People's Institute

[1] B.B.C. *S.W.B.* Second Series, No. 958, Part IV, 31 May 1962.
[2] B.B.C. *S.W.B.* Part III, No. 448, 28 Sept. 1960.
[3] N.C.N.A., 14 Dec. 1960.

of Foreign Affairs, Hu Yu-Chih, was host to several political dignitaries from Congo – Leopoldville, which was soon to become independent. The delegation consisted of representatives from nationalist parties – the People's Party, Alliance des Bayanzi, the General Federation of Congo and Centre of African Regroupment – thus covering a broad section of the political spectrum in a country which had more than thirty-nine parties.[1] Thus in 1960 eleven Congolese delegations visited China where only one had done so in 1959.[2]

The number of African delegations visiting China in 1960 increased by 100% over the previous year – 105 as against 50 in 1959. They came from both dependent and independent territories and representatives also came from those peoples actually engaged in 'advanced struggle'. The phenomenal increase of 1960 was not repeated, however, in the following two years as the Chinese considered the usefulness of financing so many delegations – they generally paid the expenses of most of them. The number visiting China dropped to 51 in 1961 and to 38 in 1962. Where seven delegations came from Senegal in 1960 there was none in 1961 and only one in 1962.

On the other hand, the Chinese increased the number of their own delegations to African countries throughout the period. From a mere 10 in 1959 to 25 in 1960, 39 in 1961, and 52 in 1962. Such delegations included 'well known figures from cultural and educational, scientific, sport and art circles'[3] who visited those countries with which Peking had signed cultural agreements (Guinea, the U.A.R., Ghana, Mali, the Sudan and the Somali Republic) and also those where no such agreements existed.

The Chinese also offered scholarships to African students sponsored by trade unions and other similar bodies. In 1961 it was estimated that about 225 such students were in China's Institute of Foreign Languages in Peking where they were learning Chinese in preparation for entering Chinese universities. This number did not include those from North African countries.[4] In April 1961, Hsinhua News Agency reported that students from Somalia, Kenya,

[1] *Peking Review*, 7 June 1960, No. 23.
[2] See Table 2 in the Appendix I, p. 270.
[3] Chu Tu-nan, 'We Have Friends All Over the World', in *Peking Review*, No. 6, 10 Feb. 1961.
[4] Leon M. S. Slawecki, 'The Two Chinas in Africa', *Foreign Affairs*, January 1963.

Zanzibar, Cameroun, Chad, Ghana and Uganda had formed a 'Union of African Students in China'. Students' conditions, however, were not altogether rosy; the discipline required was considered quite intolerable by many of them and some complained of racial discrimination, just as had students sent to the Soviet Union. In August 1962 thirty Camerounian students were expelled, allegedly for reacting openly to racial discrimination.[1] The Chinese tried to minimise the impact of the situation as they did not want their image in Africa tarnished. However, Western propaganda did make use of this incident as the Chinese had vehemently and publicly opposed racial discrimination in Southern Africa and in the United States.[2] The racial issue was also to be used when rivalry with the Soviet Union in Africa intensified. It was a weapon the Soviet Union found it difficult to combat.[3]

Chinese efforts on the political front were also closely related to their efforts elsewhere, for example their promotion of trade and forced entry into the economic aid race.

4. Economic and Trade Relations

(i) *Trade Relations.*

I referred in Chapter 2, to the non-complementary nature of the Chinese and African economies. This did not, however, retard China's efforts to improve her trade relations with African countries even though 1960 and 1961 were particularly bad years for China herself, with long drought and natural calamities complicated by the disruption resulting from the Great Leap Forward of 1958–9. Chinese import needs changed drastically and it was much more difficult to deliver goods. It was necessary to import large quantities of grain from Australia and Canada and this meant diverting foreign exchange from other goods. China also had to buy more cotton from abroad (Egypt benefited from this) because of the low yield from her own crop.

[1] *Ibid.* p. 404.
[2] Some of the students referred to the lack of contact with Chinese, especially girls. Such problems invariably arise among African students abroad, especially where their number is small. In Britain on the other hand, there are 12,000 Western Nigerians and this reduces the kind of frustration one would normally meet with in China or the Soviet Union as a result of isolation.
[3] I remember a colleague of mine on first seeing a Russian in 1964 exclaimed with disappointment 'But he is white!' He was not sure what a Russian would look like but he was not expecting him to look like a British citizen!'

The Sino-U.A.R. trade protocol for 1960 called on the two sides to 'endeavour to export commodities to each other's country for an amount of fifteen million pounds sterling'.[1] In the event, China could only export £7.42m worth of goods while Egypt sold £16.75m worth, compared with her previous year's £11.76m.[2] The protocol for 1961 with the U.A.R. stated that 'the volume of mutual trade would amount to £30 million'[3] but in the event China could only export £6.75m worth while Egypt sold £5.21m worth to China.[4]

Chinese exports of green tea, rayon textiles and other products to Morocco increased from £2.53m in 1960 to £3.07m in 1961 and £3.14m in 1962.[5] At the same time China imported phosphates, superphosphates, vehicles, minerals, sardines and arts and crafts products.

In 1960 China also imported £3.32m worth of goods, mostly grain, from South Africa[6] and was to come under increasing pressure in the following years from African quarters to stop her trade relations with that country.

Chinese ability to export was also greatly hampered by the fact that even during bad years much of her produce went to the Soviet Union to pay for the loans which had been advanced in earlier years.[7]

The trade and payments agreement signed with Mali in February 1961 called for the export to Mali of machinery, farm machines and tools, scientific instruments and electrical applicances, chemicals, drugs and medical apparatus, metalware and steel products, etc.,[8] but this could better be described as aid, as Mali had at that time relatively little to export to China in return.

Chinese exports to Nigeria increased after a Nigerian Economic Mission led by the Federal Minister of Finance, Chief Festus Okotie-eboh visited Peking in June 1961. However, China's indirect offer of economic aid 'to do their small part, within their capacity, for the economic construction of Nigeria . . .'[9] was not taken up by the Nigerians who had not yet unequivocally recognised Peking.

No doubt China envied the ability of the Western countries to

[1] N.C.N.A., 24 Feb. 1960.   [2] See Table 6 in Appendix I, p. 273.
[3] N.C.N.A., 7 Feb. 1961.   [4] See Table 5, Appendix I, p. 272.
[5] See Table 6, p. 273.   [6] See Table 5.
[7] See Table 8, Appendix I, pp. 275.   [8] S.C.M.P., No. 2452, 9 Mar. 1961.
[9] Chinese Vice-Premier and Minister of Finance Li Hsien-nien at a banquet for the Mission.

extract great quantities of minerals and strategic products from Africa, and felt that she could do nothing better than replace them as an importer of these minerals. The avidity with which China quoted Western profits is a pointer: in Africa

> The amount extracted alone is startling enough. For instance, it accounts for 99% of the columbite; 98% of the diamonds; 80.1% of the cobalt; 47.7% of the antimony, 24.4% of the copper and 29.4% of the manganese ore. Africa's output of uranium exceeds the combined production of the United States and Canada and between 60% and 80% of the total output in the capitalist world is produced in the Congo alone. To a considerable extent the major imperialist countries such as the United States, Britain and France depend on Africa for the raw materials in their manufacture of weapons of mass destruction.[1]

While China has nowhere publicly expressed her desire to replace the West as the primary market for African mineral exports, such a prospect cannot be ruled out in view of the pragmatism of her economic policy-makers, who usually divorced trade from politics.

(ii) *Economic and Technical Assistance*

If there was any issue on which Chinese ideas were relatively dynamic, it was on the question of economic aid and technical assistance to countries governed by 'bourgeois nationalists'. I discussed in my last chapter the debate with Khrushchev on the advisability of extending aid to non-communist regimes. In time, however, the debate became academic as the Chinese were themselves confronted with the politics of development of the new African States and the necessity to respond to such moves if China was to remain in the field.

With the new African states came a wave of rising popular expectation. If this was not to turn in time to a counter-revolution of rising frustration, economic development, which would provide jobs, modern amenities and comfort, would have to be the main goal of the governments. Of course political independence did not bring equivalent economic independence in its train and this fact in itself placed limits on the activities of the new states. Invariably they seemed to lack sufficient manpower, capital resources and the technological know-how necessary for rapid economic development. At the same time they wanted to 'catch up with the West' by reproducing Western economies in their countries. Internally, with

[1] Feng Chih-Tan, 'The Awakening of Africa', *Peking Review* No. 27, 5 July 1960.

the drastic shortage of jobs and the constant movement of population from the countryside to the towns, and the need for politicians to satisfy their constituents, political ability became more important than technical skills in securing employment.

Confronted with these internal problems, most African governments came to regard foreign aid as the *sine qua non* of economic development. However, even assuming that the absorptive capacity of the new states for foreign aid was unlimited (which it was not), the number of foreign aid donors was itself limited, so that the new states had to compete for the limited aid available.

In this atmosphere, China stated that in granting economic aid to new countries her position compared unfavourably with that of the West. The second Afro-Asian Economic Conference, which ended in Cairo on 3 May 1960, decided to establish an Afro-Asian investment association which 'will facilitate the flow of investment by international institutions'.[1] The Chinese delegation disagreed with this move, arguing that it would simply encourage Western penetration into the Afro-Asian economies. 'The international institutions are controlled by the imperialists who seek nothing but the continued control and exploitation of the resources of the developing countries.... What is needed is increased co-operation between the Afro-Asian countries on trade and mutual aid.'[2] The Chinese, of course, stated that they were not opposed to foreign aid but could only support aid without any political conditions attached. 'The Soviet Union had given aid to many Asian and African countries. This is genuine aid. It is an aid founded on genuine equality, friendliness and mutual assistance.'[3]

The leader of the Chinese delegation, Nan Han-Chen, argued in a written statement to the Conference 'the financial and economic power of the Asian and African countries must rest in the hands of the Asian and African peoples. This road is the only road that truly leads to the development of the national economy.'[4] The favourable mention of Soviet aid was made before Khrushchev withdrew the Russian experts working in China. After that Chinese views on Soviet aid were to change.

In offering technical assistance of any kind, the Chinese were aware of the political gains accruing from such offers; especially

[1] *Peking Review* No. 19, 10 May 1960.
[2] *Ibid.*   [3] *Ibid.*   [4] *Ibid.*

where its success would largely remove the necessity to import from abroad. In this direction, Chinese technical assistance to Morocco in 1960 is worth noting. In 1958 Morocco had imported 17,000 tons of green tea, most of which came from China and thus earned foreign exchange for her. In spite of this, the Chinese responded to the Moroccan government's invitation to help in the experimental growing of green tea.[1]

Providing technical assistance to help in tea-growing was, however, qualitatively different from offering to help in the economic development of the new African states. With the Chinese economy dislocated by the Great Leap Forward and by natural disasters, China's ability to enter the aid race was severely limited. Moreover, shifting to the economic field the area of competition between the Socialist bloc and the Western countries would place the former at a disadvantage as the West had more capital and technological know-how. The acceptance of such a shift implied that within the Socialist camp itself, leadership would remain in Soviet hands in a sphere – the developing countries – where the Chinese considered they had the prerogative. In many ways the Chinese economy was similar to that of the new states: there was still considerable scope for development and great importance was attached to agriculture. But as China had not the means to give direct aid, even this similarity could not be made to yield dividends.

The Chinese argument, that only Socialist aid should be accepted, was not well received in the new states; it was even less welcome when, after the withdrawal of Soviet economic, technical and scientific aid in June 1960, China began to emphasise self-reliance and self-help.[2] As it happened, however, political considerations over-rode the dictates of the enfeebled Chinese economy. Though there was already a shortage of grain at home, Ko Hua, the Chinese Ambassador to Guinea, presented 10,000 tons of rice to Sekou Touré in May 1960 as a gift from the Chinese Government;[3] another 5,000 tons arrived in December.[4] Such a gift was a political gesture which was well received by Sekou Touré who at that time was being boycotted by the West. He said that the aid 'would help

[1] Hsinhua, 24 Mar. 1960.
[2] *People's Daily* and *Red Flag* editorial, 4 Feb. 1964. 'The Leaders of the C.P.S.U. are the Greatest Splitters of our time.'
[3] Hsinhua News Agency, 6 May 1960.   [4] Hsinhua, 28 Dec. 1960.

strengthen the common struggle of the two peoples against imperialism'.[1]

The gift to Guinea and the economic and technical assistance which the other Socialist states were already offering paved the way for the signing of the Economic and Technical Co-operation Agreement between Guinea and China in September 1960 during Sekou Touré's visit to China. The Chinese would have liked to concentrate on the ideological revolutionary level in the competition in Africa, but Guinea's positive desire for economic aid meant that China would have to respond positively if she was to remain in the triangular competition. Article 1 of the agreement stated that:

> With a view to helping the government of the Republic of Guinea to develop its economy, the government of the People's Republic of China is willing to grant the Government of the Republic of Guinea within the period from September 13th 1960 to June 30th 1963 a non-interest bearing loan without any conditions or privileges attached. The amount of the loan is 100 million Roubles.[2]

Art. 2 provided that the supply of equipment and technical assistance would be according to the 'capability of the People's Republic of China and requirement of the Republic of Guinea'. This would take care of the possibility of problems in the Chinese economy delaying implementation of the agreement. In a passage which was to become very useful in the propaganda war with the West and the Soviet Union, Art. 3 stipulated that the Chinese experts working in Guinea should have a standard of living not exceeding 'that of personnel of the same rank in the Republic of Guinea'. Although the Chinese loan of one hundred million roubles was smaller than the 140 million granted by the Soviet Union, it was free of interest and the terms of the agreement seemed to show that the Soviet Union had been moved by material self-interest, while China acted in the spirit of brotherhood. The same sort of agreement was to be made with Ghana in 1961.[3]

In February 1961 4,500 tons of rice, 10 cinema projectors, 10 electrical generators, x-ray apparatus and 100 cases of pharmaceuticals arrived in Guinea as Liu Shao-chi's gifts to Sekou Touré resulting from the latter's visit to China the previous September.[4]

---
[1] Hsinhua, 6 May 1960.
[2] Full text in Appendix II, pp. 279-80.   [3] See below, p. 91.
[4] B.B.C. *S.W.B.* Part III, Second Series No. 562, 10 Feb. 1961.

The Chinese loan to Guinea could not, of course, be compared with the United States offer to Nigeria of £80m in the same year,[1] but it is clear that the political influence China was able to generate in Africa was out of proportion to her relatively meagre economic contribution. One of the reasons for this was the style and timing of the aid and the generous terms of repayment, generally spread over a period of ten years where the aid was not gratis. Moreover Guinea's economy was relatively poor, so that an otherwise small loan assumed more significance.

During Nkrumah's visit to China in August 1961 an economic and technical co-operation agreement was signed which provided for a non-interest-bearing credit to Ghana of £7m for the five years from 1 July 1962 to 30 June 1967. The loan was to be used in instalments during the period for unspecified items of economic construction and technical assistance and was to be repaid in equal instalments during the ten years from 1 July 1971 to 30 June 1981. As in the case of Guinea, repayment could be either in export goods or in the currency of an agreed third country.[2]

The protocol to the 1961 agreement listed the following projects which were to be set up with Chinese credits – an integrated textile and knitwear factory and an enamel-ware and china-ware factory.[3] Ghanaians would also be trained in China to man these projects. The Soviet Union was greatly embarrassed by the arrangement which specified that Chinese experts in Ghana were only to be paid maintenance allowances by the Ghana Government and their standard of living was not to exceed that of their Ghanaian counterparts.[4] In January 1962, during a visit to Ghana by the Soviet Deputy Prime Minister Anastas Mikoyan, Soviet personnel salary policy was reviewed. Under the new agreement the Ghanaian Government was to pay only half the salaries of Soviet personnel in Ghana and the Soviet Union the other half.[5] For instance Soviet personnel being paid £260 a month by Ghana would now be paid £130, the rest being made up by the Soviet Union. Even if this was the only result of the agreements with China it did at least help to relieve the burden of foreign technical assistance.

[1] Of this offer only £37.7m had been utilised by Nigeria by the end of 1968 and this included the amount spent on technical assistance.
[2] *Far Eastern Economic Review*, 7 Sept. 1961, p. 449.
[3] *Ghana Today*, 7 Nov. 1962, p. 6, Accra Publication.
[4] *Ghana Treaty Series*, Vol. II 1961, pp. 28–9.   [5] *Ibid.* 1962, p. 6.

Scott-Thompson points out that by the end of 1962 little progress had been made in resolving questions raised by Ghanaian officials concerning Socialist countries' projects in Ghana; 'only the Poles and the Chinese showed real interest in accommodating the Ghanaians'.[1] The Chinese gave loans easily and were prepared to do anything the Ghanaians wished, whereas the Ghanaian civil service found the Russians tough bargainers.

The Chinese, however, were not above interfering in Ghana's internal affairs despite their claims to the contrary. This occurred whenever they felt a new development would adversely affect Sino-Ghanaian relations. Perhaps at a time when diplomacy has become competitive, interference in the internal affairs of other states was inevitable if 'good' relations are to be maintained. In late 1962 Nkrumah appointed as Managing Director of the Ghana National Trading Company, Sir Patrick Fitzgerald, who was about to leave Ghana on retiring from Unilever. It was not only the Russians who disliked this development. 'The Chinese representative was of the opinion that the newly appointed Managing Director of G.N.T.C. was likely to discourage trade between Ghana and the bi-lateral countries.'[2] The opinion was expressed but no action was taken. This kind of subtle interference will be examined when I discuss Chinese aid to Tanzania in the next chapter.

After Algeria's formal declaration of independence in the middle of 1962, the Political Bureau of the National Liberation Front issued an appeal for aid to friendly countries. The Chinese Government, which had made substantial credit available to the Provisional Government during the revolution, answered the new call with a gift of 9,000 tons of wheat, 3,000 tons of rolled steel and 21 tons of medicine 'to help the Algerian people reconstruct their country'. This set the stage for future commitments of aid to Algeria.

With Mali, the Chinese quickly followed up the signing of the Sino-Mali economic and technical co-operation agreement in September 1961. In January 1962 Chinese experts arrived in Bamako to work on irrigation projects and the planting of rice,

[1] Scott-Thompson, *op. cit.*, p. 277.
[2] Sir Patrick's letter to Secretary, Bank of Ghana, quoted by Scott-Thompson, *op. cit.*, p. 276.
[3] N.C.N.A., 5 Jan. 1960, *Peking Review* No. 34, 24 Aug. 1962, p. 7 and S.C.M.P. No. 2807, 27 Aug. 1962.

tea and sugar cane.[1] Eventually a sugar refinery would be built which would make Mali self-sufficient in sugar. The aid promised to Mali was the same as that pledged to Ghana and slightly lower than Guinea's – $19.6m compared with Guinea's $26m or 100 million roubles.

The Chinese placed emphasis on those projects which were labour-intensive rather than capital-intensive and which required a lesser period of maturity than more complicated industries. No doubt Chinese lack of abundant capital partly dictated this, but at the same time it was argued that this philosophy aimed to make use of those resources which the developing countries had in abundance – manpower, in many cases unemployed or under-employed.

5. People's Organisations and International Conferences

In the last chapter I discussed the formation of the Afro-Asian People's Solidarity Organisation, some of its activities and its use as a propaganda venue for the Soviet Union and China. In 1960–2 Sino-Soviet rivalry, which until then had been concealed, came to the surface with opposing resolutions and attempts to win Afro-Asian support in the various meetings of the Organisation. The Russians tried to have the struggle for 'peace' and disarmament accepted as the organisation's main aim, in conformity with Khrushchev's relentless effort to reach a détente with the United States. The Chinese argued that the A.A.P.S.O. was set up to co-ordinate the Afro-Asian peoples' struggle against colonialism, and that while colonialism still plagued the peoples of the two continents it was 'criminal' to try to divert their efforts to other areas.

Sino-Soviet rivalry was complicated by the fact that other African groups, such as the Cameroon U.P.C. also tried to make use of the organisation for their own purposes. This was to become more important as the Sino-Soviet differences shifted from the plane of tactics to that of policy.

In January 1960 the A.A.P.S.O. Secretariat in Cairo was faced with its first case of an African country becoming independent while a violent struggle was still going on. The U.P.C. in the Cameroons, itself a member of the Organisation, wished the Secretariat to regard the independence of Cameroun as a sham and to ignore it. However, a compromise was reached: the Secretariat

[1] S.C.M.P. No. 2655, 10 Jan. 1962.

sent messages of congratulation to the Cameroun Premier Ahmadou Ahidjo[1] and at the same time to the President of the U.P.C., Félix Moumie. However, in a move to satisfy the U.P.C., the Secretariat called, on 14 January, for the withdrawal of French troops, the release of all political prisoners, and the achievement of democracy and 'real' independence.[2] As will be shown in the section dealing with revolutionary activities, China's opinion on whether or not the struggle should go on was more important than the trivial sending of messages.

On 11 April 1960 the second Afro-Asian People's Solidarity Conference was convened in Conakry, Guinea.[3] Because of the probable shift of liberation struggles to black Africa, and the difficulty the Chinese encountered in Cairo in trying to move the Secretariat more to their side, at this meeting they attempted to have the headquarters moved to Guinea.[4] Here the atmosphere would be more cordial towards the Chinese. The first conference, held in Cairo, had been attended by delegates from 39 Afro-Asian countries and areas; at the Conakry Conference delegates from 68 African and Asian parties, associations committees and trade unions were present, the travelling expenses of many of them paid by the Soviet Union and China.[5] In his message to the conference Chou En-lai expressed the hope that it would strengthen the friendship and solidarity of the Afro-Asian peoples and take a definite line on the struggle against imperialism.[6] During the conference the Russian delegation proposed a resolution stating that the economic development of the new countries could be greatly accelerated if the cold war and arms race were ended.[7] The Chinese objected strongly to this resolution, saying they would not be a party to the spreading of illusions about the nature of imperialism.[8] Apart from the merits and demerits of the Sino-Soviet debate, the Chinese argument was based on sound logic. Events have shown that great power detentes and the relaxation of tension has usually led to a decline in competitive aid-giving to the developing countries – the Great Powers find other uses for their resources when the bogey of world Communism or imperialism has been removed. Moreover, Chinese

[1] N.C.N.A., 5 Jan. 1960.   [2] N.C.N.A., 15 Jan. 1960.   [3] S.C.M.P., 18 Apr. 1960.
[4] Interview with X.   [5] Interview with X.
[6] Hsinhua News Agency, 10 Apr. 1960.   [7] Interview with X.
[8] Z. Brzezinski, ed. *Africa and the Communist World*, p. 176.

influence in developing countries increases in direct proportion to the increase in international tension and crisis 'caused by imperialism'.

Although China's attempt to get the headquarters of the movement shifted to Guinea did not succeed, a Regional Bureau of the Organisation was set up in Conakry, together with a special 'Solidarity Fund Committee' which would, inter alia, finance movements 'resisting armed imperialist aggression'. At the Conakry meeting the Afro-Asian People's Solidarity Council was transformed into the A.A.P.S.O. with an Executive Council of fourteen African and thirteen Asian states.[1] The Fund Committee was important for the Chinese as it allowed open aid to be channelled through a 'legitimate' body. In February 1961 a meeting of the Afro-Asian Solidarity Fund Committee, of which China was a member, took place in Conakry under the Guinea Chairman.[2] It decided to create an Afro-Asian People's Solidarity Fund for

Material and financial aid to organisations and persons who participate in the struggle for the objectives and principles of the A.A.P.S. Movement. . . . Priority will be accorded to those organisations which are confronting armed aggression launched by imperialism and colonialism and are therefore in urgent need. The Committee may take all such actions as [are required] to reinforce the Solidarity of the Afro-Asian people. The Fund is destined to help in cash or kind: those political organisations, syndicates or others, national or international, of Asian and African countries which are struggling in their own countries for the liquidation of imperialism and colonial and neo-colonial systems, in all their forms and manifestations, and desire to accelerate the liberation and progressive development of the peoples of Asia and Africa; . . . and those who become victims of persecution or are obliged to leave their own countries as a result of these activities, as well as the families of the partisans of the national liberation movement who become victims in this struggle.[3]

The definition of those in need meant that practically every group which received the approval of the Committee could be legitimately helped. Colonialism and neo-colonialism implied the inclusion of dependent and independent countries like Algeria on the one hand and Cameroun on the other. The Committee launched appeals for aid to all well-meaning people all over the world and the Middle East News Agency reported on 4 August 1961 that the U.A.R. had donated $20 000 plus scholarships; Indonesia $15,000 plus scholar-

[1] Fuller discussion in F. Schatten, *Communism in Africa*.
[2] B.B.C. *S.W.B.* Part III, No. 578, 1 Mar. 1961.
[3] Peking Radio broadcast to Africa February, 26 Aug. 1961.

ships; the Soviet Union $20,000 plus material valued at 10,000 roubles plus grants; China $40,000 plus scholarships. Thus the Chinese found a useful avenue through which to channel their aid to various groups on the African continent.

The Sino-Soviet rivalry for influence was not limited to such bodies as the World Peace Council, the World Federation of Trade Unions, the World Federation of Democratic Women and other such front organisations. In February 1962 the Afro-Asian Writers' Conference held in Cairo was the scene of a bitter dispute between the Chinese and Soviet delegates on the passing of a resolution in favour of disarmament 'put forward' by a Turkish delegate.[1] The dispute was on the priority of the anti-colonial struggle over 'so-called' disarmament.[2] Mao Tun, the chief Chinese delegate and Chairman of the Union of Chinese Writers, reported that the discussion at the conference had been 'frank and warm' [a euphemism for bitter disagreement] but that it 'finally led to unanimity of understanding and enhanced solidarity'[3] – an overstatement. It was also reported that China was beginning to make use of the racial approach in trying to win support among Afro-Asian delegates.[4] Later the Russians were to accuse the Chinese of this 'crime' though they too were not free from the practice in different quarters.[5]

Africa had very few Communist parties. Those which did exist inclined to the Soviet side because of the influence on them of the French and British Communist Parties. The Communist Party of Lesotho, established in November 1961,[6] had connections with the South African Communist Party. In July 1962 Tass reported that a Communist Youth League and a Communist Party had been founded in Zanzibar. Quoting reports from the Middle East, it named the General Secretary of the Party as Abdar-Rahman Muhammad. These new parties joined the veteran Egyptian, Moroccan, Algerian, Sudanese and Tunisian Communist Parties. The Algerian Communist Party was banned in November 1962 in a move which Algiers Radio declared to be aimed at building a Socialist revolution, which would leave 'no room for reactionary

[1] B.B.C. *S.W.B.* No. 873, Part IV, 17 Feb. 1962.
[2] Colin Legum, *The Observer*, 11 Mar. 1962.
[3] B.B.C. *S.W.B.* No. 909 Part III, 31 Mar. 1962.
[4] Colin Legum, *The Observer*, 11 Mar. 1962.
[5] See below p. 165.
[6] *World Marxist Review*, Vol. 5, No. 1, Jan. 1962, p. 63.

bourgeois tendencies or for left wing organisations which sought to take advantage of difficulties'. Everybody was called upon to join the F.L.N. This was also the attitude of other one-party African states towards the setting up of Communist parties.

On the Chinese side, there was an attempt in 1960 to co-ordinate the activities of various bodies and organisations in China which had connections with Africa. The 'Chinese-African Peoples' Friendship Association' was formed in Peking in April 1960 on the initiative of seventeen national people's organisations:[1]

All China Federation of Trade Unions
All China Youth Federation
the Women's Federation of the P.R.C.
the China Peace Committee
the Chinese Committee for Afro-Asian Solidarity
the Chinese People's Association for Cultural Relations with Foreign Countries
the China Federation of Literary and Art Circles
the Union of Chinese Writers
the All China Journalists' Association
the China Council for the Promotion of International Trade
the All China Athletic Federation
the National Red Cross Society of China
the Political Science and Law Association of China
the Chinese People's Institute of Foreign Affairs
the China Islamic Association
the China Federation of Industry and Commerce
the All China Students' Federation.

All these had been responsible for issuing invitations to trade unionists, scientists, politicians, journalists and other African groups to visit China and had met their expenses.

A more important exercise, however, took place in April 1962 when the 'Asia Africa Society' was formed. It aimed to promote 'academic research into the political and economic affairs, history, philosophy, languages, literature, the arts, religion and social conditions'[2] of the Asian and African countries. It would also increase cultural and academic exchanges between China and these countries. It was said to have 500 members in various parts of China. The Chinese Government recognised the need for such a research body

[1] Hsinhua, 13 Apr. 1960.   [2] *Peking Review* No. 17, 27 Apr. 1962, p. 23.

and the Foreign Minister Chen Yi noted the increasingly important role which the Asian and African countries were playing in international affairs. 'It is essential for us in China to have a better knowledge of those countries with their ancient cultures, and to develop cultural and academic relations between China and the other lands on the two continents.'[1] The new Society was to be responsible for training Chinese in several African languages including Hausa, Arabic and Swahili.

6. Revolutionary Struggles in Africa

We pay special homage to the heroic Algerian People and their gallant National Liberation Army. They are standing at the forefront of the struggle against imperialism. They have won admiration and support from the Afro-Asian peoples and the whole world. . . . The imperialists dream they can crush the struggle of the Algerian people by 'superior weapons' and have their colonial empires by means of armed suppression. But they are digging their own graves for history has shown that justice always prevails over injustice, the weak over the strong and the newborn force over the decaying one. . . . The Chinese people entertain especially close warm feelings for the African people. . . . We were regarded by the imperialist aggressors as a so-called 'inferior race' and our people suffered the same bitterness of slaughter, plundering and enslavement at the hands of foreign colonialists.[2]

In the context of the Sino-Soviet debate over the desirability o aiding just wars of national liberation this speech in Conakry was supposed to place on record the unflinching support which the Chinese were giving to the Algerian people in their war with France. The Chinese urged the Algerians to carry on a protracted war until 'final and absolute victory' was achieved. They pointed to the decisive defeat inflicted on the French at Dien Bien Phu and urged that any peace moves, aimed at deceiving them and making them lower their revolutionary vigilance, be rejected. It was in this light that they rejected de Gaulle's proposal on October 1959.[3]

[1] *Peking Review*, No. 17, 27 Apr. 1962, p. 23.
[2] Liao Cheng-chih addressing the Second A.A.P.S. Conference in Conakry, N.C.N.A., 14 Apr. 1960.
[3] For a treatment of the domestic difficulties de Gaulle faced in his Algeria policy see Dorothy Pickles, *Algeria and France: From Colonialism to Co-operation*, Methuen, London, 1963. The author discusses the various restraints and internal pressures which for a long time limited the manoeuvreability of de Gaulle even when he had decided in principle on the policy of self-determination (in effect independent status). Conveniently, China chose to ignore these difficulties in her propaganda support for the Algerian nationalists.

On the other hand Khrushchev accepted de Gaulle's proposals for 'settling' the Algerian problem and claimed that 'even a tiny spark can cause a world conflagration'.[1] This he said as part of his efforts to dampen down local wars. He conveniently failed to distinguish between just wars of national liberation as in Algeria and unjust wars 'initiated by imperialism'. During his tour of the United States in September 1959 he had promised that 'we will work hard ... to put out the sparks that may set off the flames of war'.[2] He had refused to recognise the P.G.R.A. when China did so in 1958 and was prepared to continue with this policy. He visited France in March 1960 to prepare for the May Summit of the four great powers and did not want relations with the French to be affected by the Algerian issue. Moreover, the attitude of the French Communist Party was far from being in total sympathy with the Algerian nationalists.

Peking was not hampered by any similar desire to improve relations with the West and clearly distinguished between Khrushchev's attitudes and her own:

(1) There are two attitudes towards the national democratic revolutionary movement. The first is to maintain good relationships with the Western countries, giving no or little support to the national revolutionary movement as a general principle, with the possibility of having some contacts with the Western countries, but only for secondary reasons. Our country adopted the latter attitude, with firm resolution to support the national democratic revolutionary movement, and oppose colonialism and imperialism. While we may have some contacts with the Western countries, we shall never let those contacts gain the upper hand.[3]

It was therefore bent on making Khrushchev change his 'erroneous' attitudes, at least on the national liberation movements. This it would do through ideological arguments and statements which could prove embarrassing to Khrushchev's effort to gain widespread support in Africa while at the same time improving relations with the West. Addressing the Central Committee of the C.C.P. on 24 April, Lu Ting-yi[4] warned that the separation of the African people's struggles from those of the proletariat and working peoples in the capitalist countries could only serve the interest of the Western

[1] Report to the Session of the Supreme Soviet of the U.S.S.R. in Oct. 1959.
[2] Replies to questions by newsmen at the U.S. National Press Club in Washington, 16 Sept. 1959.
[3] Bulletin of Activities, *op. cit.*, p. 481.
[4] 'Unite Under Lenin's Revolutionary Banner!', *Peking Review* No. 17, 26 Apr. 1960.

countries and would be detrimental to Socialist interests. He called on all revolutionary Marxist-Leninists to support 'these just struggles, resolutely and without the slightest reservation'.[1]

The Chinese Government had already granted financial credits to the P.G.R.A. and was prepared to do more to keep the Algerian war going.[2] The P.G.R.A. was aware of the pressure that could be applied on France by the threat to accept Chinese volunteers and was therefore prepared to use Peking's outspoken support for its cause. During a cabinet meeting held in February, it decided to accept the offer 'of foreign volunteers irrespective of their origin, in accordance with the recommendations of the National Council of the Algerian Revolution. Priority will be given to technicians needed by the revolution.'[3] This was regarded as a rebuff for the moderates in the P.G.R.A. who were trying to limit contacts with China. 'Peking offered to send volunteers trained in guerilla warfare to North Africa to assist the F.L.N. and provide 20 or 25 fighter-bombers, automatic weapons and amunitions.'[4] In May a P.G.R.A. delegation arrived in Peking at the invitation of the Chinese Government; Vice Premier Ho Lung showered praise on 'the heroism of the Algerian people under extremely difficult conditions. The struggle has not only pinned down the main force of the French colonial army, thus constituting powerful aid to the independence fight of other peoples of Africa under French colonialist oppression, but also provides a brilliant example for the national liberation cause throughout Africa. . . .'[5] The Chinese urged on the Algerians the importance of protracted struggle till final victory and the need to beware of deceitful peace talks.

The Melun talks broke down, moreover, and the Algerian Premier Ferhat Abbas accepted an invitation to visit China. In his speech in Peking he pointed out that the war had been going on for more than six years, over one million had been killed and several thousand Algerians were suffering in torture camps. In spite of this the Algerian people were as determined as ever to fight till final victory and there could be no talk of 'peaceful co-existence'.[6] While Abbas'

[1] United Under Lenin's Revolutionary Banner!', *Peking Review* No. 17, 26 Apr. 1960.
[2] See above, pp. 52-3.
[3] B.B.C. *S.W.B.* Second Series, No. 309, Part IV, 13 Apr. 1960.
[4] Schatten, *op. cit.*, p. 199.   [5] *Peking Review*, No. 19, 10 May 1960.
[6] *Peking Review*, No. 40, 4 Oct. 1960. The exact number of Algerians killed during the fighting in Algeria will never be known, but after the war had ended the Algerian

tactics were designed to obtain a political victory, military aid from China began to take more practical forms. Back in North Africa, the P.G.R.A. encouraged press reports on the employment of Chinese volunteers.[1] Abbas denied this officially but at the same time confirmed that he would accept arms from China: 'China intends to help us in various ways – military, diplomatic and moral. Mao Tse-tung, with whom we carried on long discussions during our recent visit to Peking, knows well that we are not Communists. Despite this he has promised to help us unreservedly and without strings.'[2] The threat of direct Chinese interference in the Franco-Algerian war now seemed to be more than a remote possibility. In one sense it did hasten de Gaulle's acceptance of the principle of Algeria for the Algerians (rather than maintaining the old ideas of French Algeria). That acceptance led to new and direct contacts with the F.L.N. in 1961 and eventually to Algerian independence in 1962.

While congratulating the Algerian people on their hard-won independence, the Chinese wished them 'even more brilliant and greater successes in their just struggle to consolidate and safeguard national independence, build their own country and continue to fight against old and new colonialism'.[3]

Chou En-lai was to revert to this theme when he visited Algeria the following year and, by becoming a training centre for freedom fighters and a provider of arms, Algeria took up the call to continue the struggle in Africa.

While Algeria's struggles ended on a happy note, the Congo crisis had many frustrations in store for revolutionaries. This time, the United States did much to ensure that the Congo, with its

Government claimed that over one and a half million people died. See, for instance, President Ben Bella's speech of 28 Feb. 1965 (David and Marina Ottaway *Algeria: the Politics of a Socialist Revolution*, University of California Press, 1970, p. 182).

[1] French Colonial radio in Algiers noted that while the F.L.N. leadership had denied reports of military volunteers from China, it had become clear that pressure was being applied to Tunisia and Morocco to allow the passage of Chinese and Vietnamese volunteers through their territories to fight in Algeria. B.B.C. *S.W.B.* No. 484, Second Series, Part IV, 9 Nov. 1960. Whether or not China would send troops, such reports were also being encouraged by the Tunisian and Moroccan Governments, who meant in this way to soften de Gaulle's attitude to the P.G.R.A. and to restart negotiations.

[2] B.B.C. *S.W.B.* No. 482, Second Series, Part VI, 7 Nov. 1960.

[3] N.C.N.A., 3 July 1962. Message from Liu Shao-chi and Chou En-lai to the Algerian Premier declaring that the 'independence of Algeria is a great event in the contemporary national liberation movement in Africa'.

strategic materials, was not lost to world communism. Aided by Khrushchev's blunders, by effective propaganda among the African leaders and by control of the United Nations' operation in the Congo, the United States was eventually to frustrate the hopes of the Soviet Union and of China – though the latter would claim that this was only a temporary set-back normally expected in the zigzags of revolution.

The Congo crisis came as a surprise to many governments including China. Moreover the attitude of the new African states to the United Nations' activity in Africa and their acceptance of the U.N. as impartial was regarded by China as an illusion. The Soviet Union's initial support in the Security Council was viewed with dismay and regarded as unwise though the Chinese did not consider whether Khrushchev could at that point have gone against majority African opinion. His action on the Congo was declared to be naive, and he was to do even more 'harm' later on.[1] After four months of U.N. intervention in the Congo, the Chinese analysed the prospects for the revolution and the imponderables on the way. The analysis deserves to be fully quoted since it was at the time secret and throws light on Chinese activities throughout the next seven years. It was made in such a way as to explain any situations which might arise in future.

The Congo Situation and its development

Since the invasion of the Congo by the imperialist bloc under the aegis of American imperialism ... which used the name of the U.N. four months ago, the situation in the Congo, as seen from the surface, appears to be very confused and 'very rotten' but actually it is very good. It has tempered the Congolese people, made them realize who is enemy and who is friend, enabled them to differentiate right from wrong, so that they may further consolidate their strength and prepare to engage in new struggles for national liberation....

Favourable conditions for the struggles of the Congolese people against imperialism are manifested in:

(i) There is a steady raising of the Congolese people's awareness as well as a deepening of the struggle.

(ii) The United States is trying to use the U.N. as the 'prime instrument' for invading Africa, but the 'test point' has failed in the Congo....

(iii) The contradictions among the imperialists are getting deeper and deeper.

[1] *People's Daily*, 25 Nov. 1960. 'Some naive people originally were inclined to believe that the U.N. could help the Congolese people ... they did not realise ... that inviting in the U.N. means letting in U.S. imperialism.'

The U.S., Belgium and Britain are all fishing in troubled waters, striving earnestly to expand and conserve their own influence.

(iv) The capitalist nationalist elements and their party which led the independence movement of the Congo people have learned a lesson from the negative education of the U.N. ... They have slowly awakened.

But there are certain unfavourable factors in the struggle of the Congo people.

(I) At present the national liberation movement of the Congo is mainly led by the capitalist nationalist elements. Among them wavering and compromise prevail and so they cannot undertake correct and firm leadership. The strength of the nationalist party is also scattered and there is no single force to unite the whole country.

(II) As a result of long colonial control, there exist in various places of the Congo the comprador class and the reactionary, feudalistic tribal influence. They are in collusion with the imperialists to oppose the people and occupy different places to engage in secession activities.

(III) The struggle of the Congo people is extensive, severe and heroic, but at present there is no core guidance organized by the workers' class. ...

(IV) The Congolese people, in addition to the above unfavourable factors, also confront an enemy more ferocious, more crafty, than the Belgians, and that is the new Americal Colonialism. The Congolese people may need a process of struggle and tempering before they can understand clearly the real state of affairs of the new American Colonialism and before they can learn how to struggle against it.

According to the conditions described above, we estimate that there may be the following three possibilities in the development of the situation in the Congo:

First, the people's strength may be very quickly developed and organized to undertake armed struggle to sweep away the imperialist and unity. The concrete process of this struggle will be for the nationalist party headed by Lumumba and Gizenga to overcome continuously its own wavering and utilize correctly all internal and external revolutionary forces and the support of all the nationalist and democratic forces; then to use the Orientale Province as a base and to rely on the people to concentrate forces and to follow the correct policy, to start and persist in opposing external aggression and the internal armed struggle for splitting up the country; and then to fight back from Stanleyville to Leopoldville to unite the whole Congo.

Second, imperialism and comprador feudalistic influences may enjoy a certain period of superiority over the nationalist democratic forces in the Congo. They cannot exterminate the revolutionary forces of the Congo and the Congolese people cannot achieve national victory ... (attempts will be made at a grand coalition).

Third, the people's forces of the Congo will be in an inferior situation for a comparatively long period, the proportion of forces of the various reactionary influences within the country will be more or less equal for a certain period, the comprador feudalistic influences will individually rely on imperialist elements, each occupying a place and advocating independence so that there will be many factions in the whole country of the Congo. ...

No matter which possibility may materialise, the revolutionary forces of the Congolese people will achieve organization, refinement and growth. The road of struggle of the Congolese people is winding, but the future is bright. The key to achieve final victory is the further awakening of the Congolese people and the question whether the nationalist party which leads the struggle will follow a correct policy or not. The situation is favourable but the leadership is weak. This situation will add to the permanency of the revolutionary struggle of the Congo.[1]

In February 1961, after the assassination of Lumumba the Chinese Government recognised the Government of Premier Gizenga based in Stanleyville and later sent a resident ambassador.[2] Foreign Minister Chen Yi promised that 'The Chinese Government and people ... will extend all necessary and possible support and assistance to the Government of the Republic of the Congo and the Congolese people in their just patriotic struggle.'[3] However, the predicted attempts to achieve a grand coalition, which would be detrimental to Chinese aims, took place in the Congo. This was more galling because 'the leaders of the C.P.S.U. persuaded Gizenga to attend the Congolese Parliament, which had been convened under the "protection" of U.N. troops and to join the puppet government. The leadership of the C.P.S.U. feebly alleged that the convocation of the Congolese Parliament was "a success of the national forces".'[4] The new move led to the withdrawal of the Chinese representative from Stanleyville as well as those of other African and Socialist countries which recognised Gizenga. However, China was also aware of the role the new Kennedy administration was now playing and the influence it had on 'Compromising Countries in the Afro-Asian bloc' which it used to influence Gizenga.[5] In public, however, China simply blamed the Soviet Union for the 'catastrophe'. Defeat could not be accepted and the next phase was being prepared. 'The path of international struggle, naturally, is neither smooth nor straight. Dark clouds may appear in the skies and storms may suddenly rise on the sea. . . . It is, after all, a temporary phenomenon when the sun is overcast by a cloud. . . .'[6]

The situation in Cameroun illustrates clearly how China was

[1] *The Politics of the Chinese Red Army*, pp. 480–5.
[2] See above p. 74.
[3] *Peking Review* No. 824, 24 Feb. 1961.
[4] *People's Daily* and *Red Flag* editorial, 22 Oct. 1963. 'Apologists of New Colonialism: Fourth Comment on the open Letter of the Central Committee of the C.P.S.U.' See also *Pravda*, 18 July 1961.
[5] Bulletin of Activities, *op. cit.*, p. 399. Such 'compromising countries' were said to include the U.A.R., Ghana, etc.
[6] *People's Daily* Editorial, 'New Year Greetings', 1 Jan. 1962.

replacing the Soviet Union in supporting national revolutionary war. I have already mentioned the independence of Cameroun,[1] when Chou En-lai recognised the new state without the gesture being reciprocated. In October 1959 the Chinese had called attention to the number of French troops in Cameroun – which 'had risen from 14,000 to 84,000' – and to their attempts 'to combat the armed struggle of the Cameroun people who are determined to prevent the setting up of puppet parties and government in their country'.[2] Guerrilla warfare was being supported by the Soviet Union, but after independence in January 1960 this support waned drastically. The ban on the U.P.C. was lifted in February 1960 in an attempt to end the fighting. Some of the leaders of the U.P.C. returned but the fighting continued because of the conditions demanded by U.P.C. for its suspension. These included withdrawal of French forces, the release of all political detainees and the restoration of all democratic liberties including freedom of the press.[3] Félix Moumie and other leaders remained in exile to continue the armed struggle. As the Cameroun Government refused to recognise Peking and instead recognised Taiwan, China had no diplomatic qualms about sustaining this rebellion against a newly independent African state.

Moreover, as French troops were still fighting there, such support appealed to the more dynamic and 'progressive' sections of African opinion. Peking thus took over the training and part of the financing of the U.P.C. from the Soviet Union, accusing the Russians of dragging their feet and reneging on their internationalist duty.[4] Camerounians were sent by the U.P.C. to China for guerrilla training. Six students who were apprehended by the Cameroun Government on their return in July 1961 were caught with their arms, weapons, documents and lecture notes which showed that they had been trained in the handling of explosives, mines, incendiaries, grenades, and in sabotage, etc.[5] The students stated that while in China they had been kept apart from other groups of Africans who had also come for guerrilla training.[6] This was probably done in order to prevent leakage if some of these fighters were

[1] See above, p. 72.   [2] Hsinhua News Agency, 7 Oct. 1959.
[3] B.B.C. *S.W.B.* Second Series, Part IV, No. 272.
[4] Pieter Lessing, 'Moscow Fights Peking in Africa', *Sunday Telegraph*, 25 Mar. 1962.
[5] Photographs and photostatic copies of these appeared in *Sunday Telegraph*, 23 July 1961.
[6] *Ibid.*

arrested in their own countries. A significant number of Camerounian students continued to go to China on 'visits' and for study[1] and very soon they were to have better opportunities for training in Ghana.[2] The Chinese made use of the special Solidarity Fund Committee to help sustain the rebellion, and to offer scholarships to Camerounian students to study in China. The expulsion of thirty of the students from China in 1962 has already been mentioned. The case of Cameroun showed China's readiness to help in the violent overthrow of the government of a newly independent African state where such a government was regarded as reactionary. This was to cause a furore later on when at the end of his tour of African countries, Chou En-lai described the revolutionary situation in Africa as 'excellent'.[3]

While the struggles in Algeria, Congo and Cameroun continued, the Chinese were also carefully following developments in the Portuguese territories of Angola, Guinea and Mozambique which were soon to take over from Algeria the mantle of revolution. As the Chinese argued, the continued success of the Algerian nationalists through armed struggle gave impetus to the nationalists' struggle in the Portuguese territories. The people there should be shown how to embark on revolution in their own countries, relying entirely on their own resources. In Angola, the Soviets had the same influence as on the U.P.C. in Cameroun, but the Russians were not prepared for long and protracted struggles which would only validate Mao's theory of people's war in Africa.[4] In his stormy performance at the U.N. General Assembly debate in 1960, Khrushchev called for a resolution demanding the immediate independence of all colonies. The Chinese disregarded the propaganda aspect of this call and argued that no-one should be under any illusion about the U.N.'s ability to bestow independence on the oppressed peoples of Africa. The Peking Embassy in Guinea was already in contact with Angolians,[5] and in 1961 an Angolan delegation of freedom fighters visited China.[6] The relatively large-scale fighting which erupted in Angola in June 1961 drew the attention of the world to that neighbour of the Congo which was now undergoing

---

[1] In 1960-2 ten delegation groups paid such visits to China. See Table 2, Appendix I, on delegations.
[2] See below pp. 172-3.   [3] See below, p. 122.   [4] Pieter Lessing, *op. cit.*
[5] *Ibid.*   [6] See Table 2, Appendix I.

its own turmoil. The Portuguese authorities brutally suppressed the uprising, but only for a time. What the Chinese had been calling for was now beginning. They hailed the armed struggle of the Angolan people as 'a new important development of the African National Liberation Movement'.[1] There is no doubt that the Angolans were simply fighting in the interests of their own people and would only use Chinese and Soviet aid to achieve this, but at the same time their activities helped to justify China's arguments on revolutionary struggles in Africa.

During the years 1960–2 the nationalists in the Portuguese territory of Guinea sent four delegations to China to press for various forms of aid in their campaign against Portugal. The nationalists also visited other Socialist states and several African countries whose support was solidly behind the Africans resisting Portugal. The foundation was thus laid for widespread support for their armed struggle when it broke out.

China's attitude towards the struggles of the people in dependent territories won her much sympathy and support among progressive African opinion and was to play its part in October–November 1962 in damping down any anti-Chinese feeling aroused by the conflict with India. China's consistent support for armed struggle also made Khrushchev alter somewhat his unenthusiastic attitude towards such struggles in an attempt to show the Africans that the Soviet Union also supported 'just wars of national liberation' while at the same time opposing nuclear war.

7. The Sino-Indian Conflict (1962) – a Test Case

The attitude of the new African states towards the Sino-Indian border war of October–November 1962 is illuminating. Nehru had been regarded as one of the architects of non-alignment and India had been supporting African aspirations towards national independence. When the Congo crisis erupted, India was one of the countries which sent in a contingent, and it was very effective. She also had cordial diplomatic relations with the new African states, and the presence of large Indian communities in some of them (especially in East Africa) seemed to be a useful instrument for promoting good relations.

However, Nehru's ideas on world problems and the priority to be

[1] *People's Daily*, 24 June 1961.

given to the struggles in colonial territories were being drastically modified. He now seemed to be more concerned with world 'peace', claiming that only the Big Two could solve world problems – a point of view diametrically opposed to China's. During the Belgrade Conference of non-aligned states in September 1961 Nehru's reference to 'anti-colonialism, anti-imperialism, anti-racialism and all that' brought him into conflict with the ideas of such African leaders as Nkrumah, Nasser, Keita of Mali and the strongly nationalist leaders, who were more concerned about colonialism in Africa than with such problems as Berlin and Germany which they could not solve. Nehru's view that the classical colonialism was dead and gone was not accepted by those people who were still living in dependent territories and who sent observers to Belgrade.[1] Nehru's gradual shift away from the militant views of many non-aligned leaders on colonialism and imperialism was therefore to play a part in the lack of positive support from this quarter during the Sino-Indian conflict in 1962.

When large-scale fighting broke out between Chinese and Indian troops on 20 October 1962 the reaction of the Western countries was overwhelmingly anti-China and pro-India.[2] Within hours of the beginning of hostilities President Nasser sent a message to Nehru suggesting that he might be of help as a mediator between the two sides.[3] The immediate reaction from African countries was silence and the militant non-aligned countries were greatly concerned at the fighting between the two most important members of the Afro-Asian bloc. Most feared that the immediate offer of military aid for India from the United States and other Western countries might move Nehru away from his 'non-aligned stance' and into the imperialist camp.

It was this concern which led President Nkrumah to declare himself, in a letter to Macmillan, 'gravely distressed and saddened' at Britain's decision to offer India military aid. He argued that, whatever the merits and demerits of the case, the cause of peace

[1] See also G. H. Jansen, *Afro-Asia and Non-Alignment*, 1966.
[2] For the events leading to the war and the course of events see:
(1) Brigadier J. P. Dalvi, *Himalayan Blunder: The Curtain-raiser to the Sino-Indian war of 1962*, Thacker & Co. Ltd., Bombay, 1969. (2) D. R. Mankekar, *The Guilty Men of 1962*, The Tulsi Shah Enterprises, Bombay, 1968. (3) Neville Maxwell, *India's China War*, Cape, London, 1970.
[3] Jansen, *op. cit.*, p. 326.

could only be served by refraining from 'any action that may aggravate the unfortunate situation'.[1] On the receipt of a circular letter sent by Nehru to all governments asking for sympathy and support, the U.A.R. Presidential Council issued a statement expressing deep regret at the continuation of the fighting, urging acceptance of mediation by Afro-Asian states, an immediate ceasefire and withdrawal to the line of control of 8 September 1962.[2] The same attitude was adopted by President Abboud of the Sudan, who called for an end to the fighting on an Afro-Asian basis.[3]

Before the fighting broke out India had made arrangements with Egypt for the supply of small arms and ammunition. This arrangement was allowed to go through as a gesture of support for India, but the U.A.R. did in fact refuse to condemn Chinese action as aggression. Nasser's confidant, Muhammad Hasanayn Haykal, however, warned that China's 'stubborn' attitude might cause her friends to be disenchanted; they might be led to believe the Western propaganda that China wanted to dominate Asia. In the same article Haykal stated that Nasser had told the Chinese Ambassador he hoped the fighting would be over before the arms arrived in India. He had expressed fears that the Chinese action could drive the Indian Government into the hands of the reactionaries at home who had been clamouring for alliance with the West. Haykal called on China to explain her 'stubborn' attitude towards India and warned that continued fighting could lead to the alienation of her friends in the Afro-Asian world.[4]

On 20 November China declared a unilateral ceasefire and withdrawal of troops. Guinea's President Sekou Touré sent messages to Nehru and Chou En-lai which were broadcast by Conakry Radio. In his message to Nehru, he said he was convinced the Indian Government realised that the resolution of the conflict affected Afro-Asian solidarity and was liable to encourage neo-colonialist manoeuvres.[5] To Chou En-lai he expressed 'deep satisfaction and entire approval' of China's announcement of the ceasefire, 'considering that the unity of the third force countries of the world is the best bulwark against all imperialist schemes of domination and renewed colonisation as well as a decisive factor in reinforcing the

[1] Accra Radio, 31 Oct. 1962.
[2] Cairo Radio, 31 Oct. 1962.
[3] Omdurman Radio, 31 Oct. 1962.
[4] Al-Ahram, 8 Nov. 1962.
[5] Conakry Radio, 22 Nov. 1962.

conditions of world peace....'[1] This sense of working to preserve the Afro-Asian bloc and to safeguard non-alignment seemed to have been the overriding objective of the non-aligned African countries.

It was again echoed by the U.A.R. shortly before the Colombo conference of uncommitted countries in December 1962.[2] The Egyptian delegation was to be led by Ali Sabri, the Premier. Egypt's aim was said to be the preservation of world peace and of a non-aligned bloc: 'for the U.A.R. this interest overrode the merits of the Sino-Indian border dispute'.

On the wider African level, the French-speaking members of the U.A.M. sent messages of sympathy to India, but even then only Niger condemned 'Chinese aggression'. This could hardly compensate for the lack of support for India among the militant non-aligned African states who had been regarded as India's and China's friends. None of them condemned China's actions and they were greatly embarrassed by the possibility of being on the same side as all the imperialist countries supplying arms to India.

Furthermore, Chinese propaganda did much to discourage support for India. The African states had little adequate information on the issue other than what came in through Western propaganda. Of what they had the Chinese interpretation was the more persuasive. For instance when the Tanganyika Government called on the Chinese and Indian envoys to present information, the Chinese submitted well-documented evidence. Maps, photostatic copies of treaties, illustrations showing the territory disputed, the disposition of the Chinese and Indian troops as well as the lines of actual control by both sides prior to September 1962. The Indians could produce nothing to compare with it. This led Tanganyika to refraining from supporting either side. It was the same in Kenya.[3] In East Africa, the presence of unpopular Indian communities in those countries meant a rank-and-file welcome for the humiliation of India irrespective of who was in the right.[4]

The Indian Minister of State in the Ministry of External Affairs toured African countries in December 1962. During his tour he expressed disappointment at the 'lack of understanding' of the Indian position by the Afro-Asian nations. He attributed this to the

---
[1] *Peking Review*, Nos. 47 and 48, 30 Nov. 1962, p. 23.
[2] M.E.N.A. quoting *Al-Ahram*, 10 Dec. 1962.
[3] Interview with X.   [1] Interview with X.

superiority of China's propaganda.[1] India asked for condemnation of China as an aggressor or at least declared support for herself. This Nehru failed to receive.

China simply wished that she might not be condemned for aggression, and the cold silence of the Afro-Asian states on the Sino-Indian conflict was thus a phenomenal success, as she had also attained her military aim.

[1] B.B.C. *S.W.B*. Part III, No. 1133, 27 Dec. 1962.

4 1963-5 COMMITMENTS, CONSOLIDATION, REFLECTION

1. **The Dynamic International Situation**
The last period ended with two events which profoundly affected China's relations with the Soviet Union and which were to have great influence on Chinese tactics and strategy in the third world in the following years. The Cuban missile crisis had shown Khrushchev to be both an unpredictable 'adventurer' and a 'shameless capitulationist'. His ineptitude at crises management showed beyond doubt the 'bankruptcy' of the Soviet leadership in the world Communist movement; and his 'betrayal' of Cuba revealed to the whole world how far he could go in appeasing imperialism. A more deplorable and heinous crime in the eyes of the Chinese was his attitude in the Sino-Indian border war. To decide to back India against a fraternal country showed that he no longer cared about China. Even the 'despicable Chiang Kai-Shek clique' in Taiwan found it necessary to support China against India in that conflict.

These two events showed how futile were the imminent criticisms of and exhortations to the Soviet leadership to change its course. It now seemed that only a miracle could draw Khrushchev back from the doldrums of utter revisionism. If evidence was needed to show that he would not honour his obligation to aid China even with nuclear weapons, the Cuban crisis provided it, and the Sino-Indian war added to it by showing that he could even 'stab' China in the back. That he was 'lost' beyond redemption was proved by his signing the partial nuclear test ban treaty in July 1963 with the United States and Britain – the more so since it was widely believed that the treaty was primarily aimed at China and West Germany and constituted a direct attempt by Khrushchev to bind China by the Soviet Union's action. After this the Chinese accepted the unbridgeable gap in Sino-Soviet relations and moved to shape their strategy and tactics accordingly.

Whereas the struggle against imperialism had previously been conducted by the Socialist camp with the Soviet Union as its head, the whole international situation had now fundamentally changed. A fierce three-cornered struggle was now to be waged between the forces of (a) imperialism, old and new colonialism and reaction; (b) revisionism, capitulationism and defeatism; and (c) the genuine forces of proletarian revolutionaries led by China. An international united front must now be formed to unite all forces that could be united in the struggle against imperialism and revisionism. While the three-cornered struggle would take place in the first and second intermediate zones, the struggle in the first intermediate zone comprising Asia, Africa and Latin America would receive priority treatment. (Intermediate zones, in Communist phraseology, denote the phase preceding total world Communism. Khrushchev had earlier used the concept of 'the zone of peace' to include those new states which were non-aligned.)

It was in the context of changed strategic and tactical calculations that the policy towards Africa which was already gathering momentum attained new dimensions. Combined with the changing international situation was the improvement in the domestic economic situation following the disruption of the last period.[1] The new tasks would call for new commitments, economic, technical, material and political, which could be better sustained by a sounder economic base at home. The Chinese bid for the leadership of the world's revolutionary people was put in doctrinal form by Chou Yang in October 1963 when he addressed the fourth enlarged session of the Committee of the department of Philosophy and Social Sciences of the Chinese Academy of Sciences:

If... a proletarian party fails to stand in the forefront of the people's revolutionary struggle, discards the banner of revolution, renounces the revolutionary tradition of its own country and adopts a passive or even negative attitude towards the cause of the proletarian revolution, then it is bound to become an opportunist, revisionist party and forfeit its place in the ranks of the vanguards of the international proletariat.[2]

As the Soviet Union under Khrushchev had forfeited its leading role the Chinese were prepared to accept the noble obligation of leading the people of the world in their just struggle against

[1] During this period the Chinese completed the repayment on loans and interest charges to the Soviet Union. See Table 8 in Appendix I.
[2] *Peking Review* No. 1, 3 Jan. 1964.

imperialism. But if the struggle against imperialism demanded a united front of all the peoples of the world, the Soviet leadership could no longer enjoy the privilege of being in the vanguard of the people. Indeed, it would now be 'necessary for the people of the various countries to oppose modern revisionism'. To quote a joint statement by the Tanganyikan Trade Unions: '... imperialism, colonialism and the reactionaries of the various countries were the common enemies of the workers and people of the various countries in Asia, Africa and Latin America. In order to fight imperialism and colonialism effectively, it was necessary for the people of the various countries to oppose modern revisionism'. This would mean a general condemnation of the Soviet emphasis on collaboration with imperialism and on 'peace' rather than on revolution and freedom for the oppressed peoples of the world.

2. The Tactics of the New Situation

China sought to present herself as the model for the developing countries of Africa – politically, economically and revolutionarily. The instrumentalities of policy implementation developed earlier were now to be perfected and the competition for influence among Africans would take place on several levels – in the front organisations and trade unions, in the economic and diplomatic field and in the political and revolutionary sectors. The new tactics would be aimed not only at increasing Chinese influence but also at preventing the isolation of China by the combined diplomatic efforts of the United States and Russia. In 1955 it had been necessary to stem the tide of U.S. military alliances in Asia by embarking on peaceful coexistence with neighbouring Asian states, and so a new attempt to prevent a potentially greater isolation required cultivation of the new African states. In the new united front, everyone who was anti-imperialist would be welcome irrespective of his class affiliation. The Chinese had already noticed that the important element in Africa was anti-imperialism and not 'anti-feudalism'. (See above, p. 79.) Russian and United States propaganda to the effect that China wanted a nuclear war so that the surviving Chinese would 'inherit' the earth would be countered by getting as many Africans as possible to subscribe to the Chinese view that just wars of national liberation must be aided by all progressive forces.

In dealings with the Africans, China would also stress the kinship of the Asian and African peoples – a kinship cemented by the history of common suffering under colonialism and the continuing exploitation of their economic and natural resources. The solidarity of the Afro-Asian peoples would also be consolidated by a meeting of their leaders which would demand the cessation of all forms of exploitation, the dismantling of military bases by the imperialists and non-interference with the 'sacred right' of the people to move towards revolution.

The new tactics called for an intensification in depth and breadth of the revolutionary wars in Africa especially in Mozambique, Angola, Portuguese Guinea and the Congo to demonstrate that peace between the oppressors and the oppressed was impossible. Although revolution could neither be imported nor exported, China stood ready to make her experiences available to struggling patriots still under colonial rule. In this respect, the decision of the African Heads of State Conference in Addis Ababa in May 1963 to set up a Liberation Committee was of vital importance to the Africans and a vindication of the Chinese argument that colonialism was still flourishing in Africa.

3. Political Relations with African States
(i) *Diplomatic Relations*
By the end of 1962, China was represented by her ambassadors in ten African states, most of them belonging to the radical and progressive group of states who professed to be implementing one brand of Socialism or the other. The Democratic People's Republic of Algeria had now attained formal independence. This removed a major obstacle to diplomatic recognition of China on the part of the French-speaking African states, and also brought to an end suddenly Peking's virulent campaign against French colonial policy. In addition de Gaulle's increasing disenchantment with the N.A.T.O. alliance seemed to be moving France towards holding a common position with China. Both were vehemently opposed to the dualistic hegemony which the United States and the Soviet Union were enjoying. France was still conducting atmospheric nuclear tests and China was planning to do the same; they were therefore agreed on opposition to the partial nuclear test ban treaty of July 1963.

The identity of their views on this issue and the thaw in relations meant that France was no longer bitterly opposed to her friends in Africa offering China diplomatic recognition. Though there is no evidence to show that she went out of her way to encourage it. This was to bring a windfall for China in 1964, though one should also stress China's efforts in the new situation to obtain diplomatic recognition from these states whatever the political shade of their regimes.

Meanwhile other Chinese efforts paid dividends in three African states in 1963. Foreign Minister Chen Yi was invited to represent China at Kenya's independence celebrations in December 1963.[1] He made a courtesy call on Kenyatta and his deputy Oginga Odinga who had been a friend of China during the struggle for independence. During the visit, Oginga expressed Kenya's appreciation for China's help in the past and said that this support 'played a key role in the Kenyan people's struggle for independence'. Chen Yi expressed the hope that after the establishment of diplomatic relations there will be the necessary conditions to carry on closer economic and cultural exchange, a brotherly mutual assistance and co-operation, and to work for the common task of the Chinese and Kenyan people – to fight against the imperialist policies of war and aggression and defend world peace.[2] Diplomatic relations were established on 15 December.[3] With that, a sounder foundation was being established in East Africa than was ever the case in West Africa.

The new Chinese tactics of diplomatically welcoming any regime led to the establishment of diplomatic relations with the newly independent Zanzibar which was headed by a Sultan. A Chinese representative attended the independence celebrations of the Island State and diplomatic relations were established on 12 December.[4] This action took on a new dimension and significance when the Zanzibar revolution took place exactly a month after independence; China simply transferred recognition to the new regime.[5]

A significant development in diplomatic relations also occurred in Burundi. The Queen of Burundi visited China in March at the invitation of China's Women's Federation,[6] and China had supported

---

[1] N.C.N.A., 11 Dec. 1963.
[2] Peking Radio, 11 Dec. 1963. Chen Yi's Meeting on 10 Dec.
[3] S.C.M.P. No. 3123, 19 Dec. 1963.   [4] S.C.M.P. No. 3121, 17 Dec. 1963.
[5] See below, pp. 136–137.   [6] See Table 2, Appendix I, on delegations visiting China.

1963–5 Commitments, Consolidation, Reflection 117

the Burundi Government in the crisis over the 1962 massacre of Tutsis in Rwanda. China's action with regard to the Tutsi insurrectionary movement in Rwanda was indeed an irony. The Tutsis, who formed a minority in Rwanda, had ruled despotically over the Hutu peasant majority. The peasants had revolted in 1958 and overthrown the Tutsis, thus bringing into effect majority rule.[1] For China now to support the Tutsi attempt to regain power over the peasant majority contradicted the Chinese practice of supporting the revolutionary masses against aristocratic oppression. The most plausible explanation is that at this point China was interested in obtaining diplomatic recognition from Burundi, where the majority and the government were composed of Tutsis.

In December 1963 Ho Ying, China's Ambassador to Tanganyika, was invited to Burundi for talks at which it was decided to establish diplomatic relations.[2] In view of the current Congo crisis and Chinese aims in that region,[3] diplomatic recognition was more significant than the size of the country would seem to suggest, as Burundi has a border with the Orientale province of the Congo.[4] The establishment of diplomatic relations on 21 December thus set the stage for the activities of 1964 in connection with the Congo.

In January 1964 Tunisia joined the ranks of the North African states recognising China. Chou En-lai visited Tunisia on 9 and 10 January in the course of his famous tour of ten African countries.[5] While President Bourguiba was very 'frank' in pointing out the areas of disagreement between the two sides, the two parties agreed to strengthen friendship between the two peoples and to develop their economic relations and exchange of visits and to this end they decided to establish diplomatic relations between the two countries.[6] If this was the only achievement of Chou's visit, it was certainly worthwhile.

In February China and Congo-Brazzaville decided to establish diplomatic relations. A new regime in Congo-Brazzaville had replaced the right wing government of the Abbé Youlou after a popular revolution in 1963. The French recognition of China, which took place while Chou En-lai was in Africa, removed the

[1] See Colin Legum's article in *Policies Toward China* edited by A. M. Halpern, 1965 p. 429.
[2] S.C.M.P. No. 3128, 30 Dec. 1963.
[3] See above, p. 102.   [4] See below, p. 174.   [5] See below, p. 122.
[6] *Afro-Asian Solidarity Against Imperialism*, Peking (F.L.P.) 1964, p. 132.

obstacle in the path of Massemba Debat's Government and recognition was accorded on 22 February 1964.[1] This was to be followed by significant developments in the economic, political, technical and military fields.[2]

The President of Cameroun, however, held a different opinion, because of China's continued help to the U.P.C. guerilla movement. He said that China would not be recognised as long as she continued to interfere in Cameroun's internal affairs. If, however, the Chinese gave an indication that 'China will no longer interfere in our internal affairs, we will not find it inconvenient to recognise Communist China and vote for its admission to the U.N. . . .'[3] The Chinese were, however, already fully supporting the U.P.C. in their struggle and it would not be easy to withdraw that support, since such withdrawal was one of the accusations made against Khrushchev. Nevertheless in September 1964, they did send a trade and goodwill delegation to West African countries, including Cameroun.[4] This visit was not fruitful as the Camerounians were very 'frank' on the issue of Chinese support to the U.P.C. and no guarantee in this direction could be given by the visiting team.

The trade and goodwill delegation also visited Dahomey and the Central African Republic (C.A.R.), with better results. On 2 October China and the C.A.R. established diplomatic relations[5] and this was to be followed by economic assistance and help in militia formation.[6]

With Dahomey, diplomatic relations were established in November after talks with Huang Hua, Chinese Ambassador to Ghana.[7] This step was also to be followed by technical assistance in rice growing.

In central Africa, Zambia became an independent Republic in October 1964 and decided to establish diplomatic relations with China.[8] This was the southernmost recognition Peking received, and it was to become of great importance because of the wars of liberation in Southern Africa.

[1] N.C.N.A. 22 Feb. 1964; Sino-Congolese (B) relations.
[2] See below, pp. 156–158.
[3] Radio Cameroun, Yaounde Home Service, 10 Feb. 1964.
[4] See Table 1, Appendix I. The communiqué mentioned the talks being held in a very frank atmosphere.
[5] S.C.M.P. No. 3313, 7 Oct. 1964.
[6] See below p. 162.
[7] N.C.N.A., 12 Nov. 1964.
[8] N.C.N.A., 30 Oct. 1964.

China was apparently also prepared to offer economic assistance to Malawi if Dr Banda recognised Peking, though the Chinese Ambassador to Tanzania subsequently denied the offer as 'groundless fabrications and lies'.[1] There are strong reasons for believing that Malawi ministers passing through Dar Es Salaam in August 1964 did contact the Chinese, and they might have discussed such possibilities.[2]

Sino-Burundi relations received a setback in January 1965 following the assassination of Prime Minister Ngendandumwe.[3] The new Premier suspended diplomatic relations on 29 January, a move which gave rise to speculations of Chinese complicity in the assassination. This was denied by the Burundi Foreign Minister who said that the decision to suspend relations was taken in confusion and that resumption of relations would follow a clarification of the political situation. Earlier the new Burundi Premier had said that relations were suspended because the Chinese Embassy had interfered with internal affairs by sabotaging attempts to achieve internal unity in Burundi following a conference held in September 1964 for that purpose.[4]

A new addition was, however, made to the list of China's friends when Mauritania recognised Peking on 19 July 1965.[5] Chen Yi had discussions with the Mauritanian Foreign Minister in June during the preparatory meeting for the abortive Afro-Asian Conference in Algiers. This action was also to be followed by Chinese technical assistance.

By the end of the period, then, nineteen African states out of thirty-seven recognised China, though Burundi had suspended relations and Senegal was equivocal. This was reflected in the United Nations voting machine. In 1963 13 African states voted for the seating of the representatives of Peking in the Assembly, while 5 abstained. In the following year, no vote was taken. In 1965 the number of African votes for Peking had risen to 18 with 8 abstentions, while the number voting against had dropped from 16 in 1963 to 10.[6] On diplomatic relations with African States the period thus

[1] Radio Peking, 15 Sept. 1964. [2] Interview with X.
[3] N.C.N.A., 31 Jan. 1965.
[4] Burundi Radio; B.B.C. *S.W.B.* IV, Nos. 1777, 1785, 1797, 5, 15 Feb., 1 Mar. 1965.
[5] Peking Radio, 26 July 1965.
[6] Source: *Yearbook of the United Nations 1950–1964* and U.N. General Assembly. *Provisional Verbatim Record* (Plenary Meetings) 20th Session (1965).

ended on a higher note than the previous one. Out of the 51 U.N. members recognising China, 19 were in Africa, 17 in Europe, 14 in Asia and 1 (Cuba) in Latin America.

(ii) *Political Relations*

At a farewell banquet in Ghana on 15 January 1964, during his tour of ten African countries in 1963–4, Chou En-lai enumerated the principles on which China's relations with African countries were based. These, he said, were in accordance with the five principles of peaceful coexistence and the ten principles of the Bandung Conference. China (i) supports the African peoples in their struggle to fight imperialism and old and new colonialism, and to win and safeguard national independence; (ii) supports the pursuance of a policy of peace, neutrality and non-alignment by the governments of African countries; (iii) supports the desire of the African people to achieve unity and solidarity, in the manner of their own choice; (iv) supports the African countries in their efforts to settle their disputes through peaceful consultation; (v) holds that the sovereignty of African countries should be respected by all other countries and that aggression and interference from any quarter should be opposed. It should be noted that the first principle mentioned not only supports the liberation struggles in the remaining colonial territories but also the people's struggle to safeguard independence already won and to expel neo-colonialism. As the latter would involve support for operations in places like Cameroun, the Ivory Coast and Niger, African leaders might complain that this contradicted the fifth principle, which opposed interference in the affairs of African countries by any outside power, particularly when the leaders did not perceive it to be in their states' interests to fight neo-colonialism. From China's point of view, however, there was no internal contradiction or inconsistency in the principles. China was under an obligation to help people struggling against neo-colonialism and such support was not tantamount to political interference by an outside power. It was felt, however, that the current efforts to unite all shades of Afro-Asian opinion would help to submerge any differences which might exist between China and some African governments.

It was in the attempt to rally Afro-Asian support which began in earnest after the Moscow nuclear test ban treaty in July 1963, that Chairman Mao was 'persuaded' to make his famous speech on the plight of the American Negroes. While receiving a group of African visitors on 8 August, Mao declared total support for the black people in America and called for the unity of the world's peoples to defeat 'the United States ruling circles'.

The evil system of colonialism and imperialism grew up along with the enslavement of Negroes and trade in Negroes, it will surely come to its end with the thorough emancipation of the black people. [He emphasised however that:] The racial question is in essence a class question. Our unity is not one of race; it is the unity of comrades and friends.... In the fight for thorough emancipation, the oppressed peoples rely first of all on their own struggle and then, and only then, on international assistance.[1]

Mao's statement marked the official beginning of a drive to capture the leadership of the developing world and also a point of total cleavage in the Sino-Soviet conflict. The racial appeal had been used in Moshi, Tanganyika, in February, during the A.A.P.S.O. conference but this was the first open reference to it by the Chinese leader.[2] His statement was made at the very time when a Somali Government delegation led by the Prime Minister, Dr Sharmarke, was in Peking to sign an economic co-operation agreement.[3]

The Chinese increased the number of invitations extended to African delegations and also of their own delegations visiting African countries to promote improved political relations and 'similarity' of views. While the number of African delegations visiting China in 1962 had dropped to 34, in 1963 a record number of 113 came and these included trade unionists, journalists, members of parliament, women's organisations and government officials.[4] In September a K.A.N.U. (Kenya African National Union) delegation, led by Mr Kali, which had been badly treated in Moscow was accorded a warm and friendly reception in China.[5] In view of the Somali Prime Minister's visit and speculation over a reported Chinese promise to give military aid to Somalia, the Chinese Foreign Minister assured the Kenyan delegation that no weapons would be sent and that he had advised Dr Sharmarke to negotiate with Kenya over their territorial dispute.[6] This conformed with China's declared policy of non-involvement in inter-state conflicts especially where the two states concerned maintained cordial

[1] Peking Radio, 8 Aug. 1963.   [2] See below, p. 165.   [3] See below p. 153.
[4] See Table 2, Appendix I.   [5] Nairobi Radio, 10 Sept. 1963.   [6] Ibid.

relations with her. China was in the process of gaining a foothold in Somalia, following the visit of Dr Sharmarke, and the granting of more than $29m in aid: she would not have wished this relationship to be strained by Somalia's dispute with Kenya, or on the other hand that the relations she was building up with Kenyan politicians should be soured by her friendly relations with Somalia.

In 1964, the momentum was maintained and 104 African political, economic and military delegations visited China. These included visits by the Mali President, Modibo Keita[1] and the President of Congo Brazzaville, Massamba Debat, both of whom signed treaties of friendship with China. 1964 was a particularly hectic year in Africa with mutinies in East Africa, renewed rebellion in the Congo, the eruption of fighting in Mozambique, revolution in Zanzibar and the political preparation for a second Bandung. There was thus no lack of issues for propaganda and agitation.

In 1965, the year of the ill-fated Algiers Afro-Asian summit, the number of African delegations visiting China remained high at 113. Among the most important visitors were President Nyerere of Tanzania and Prime Minister Milton Obote of Uganda.[2]

During the same period 40 delegations from China came to Africa: in 1963, 87 in 1964 and 69 in 1965. These included high-ranking officials and Prime Minister Chou En-lai, whose visits I will discuss in the next section.

(iii) *Political Relations: China and the Second Bandung*
One of the paramount aims of Chinese policy after the nuclear test ban treaty was the convention of a second Afro-Asian conference. This, it was hoped, would naturally exclude the Soviet Union and would support Chinese views on international issues. It would, of course, mete out an all-round condemnation of colonialism and imperialism, and would crystallise Chinese efforts in leading the new States of the developing world. At the same time such a conference would prevent the isolation of China which U.S. and Soviet diplomacy was trying to achieve. Thus, Indonesia's suggestion for a Second Bandung which would increase the prestige of President Sukarno was now being fervently supported by China.

However, there was at the same time a Yugoslav–U.A.R. proposition for a second non-aligned conference to which China could not

[1] See below, p. 158.   [2] See Table 2, Appendix I.

of course be invited and which clashed with the Indonesian wish to have the second Bandung held before any second non-aligned conference.

It was partly to gather African support for a second Bandung that Chou En-lai undertook his extended tour of ten African states from December 1963 to February 1964.[1] Chou first visited the United Arab Republic where he was welcomed by Prime Minister Ali Sabri on 14 December. At a reception held in honour of Chou, President Nasser (who had now returned from a visit to President Bourguiba of Tunisia) expressed appreciation for Chinese support in the past and also invited Chou to visit the Aswan High Dam and other industrial projects.[2] (It will be remembered that China had originally opposed the 'squandering' of Soviet economic aid on bourgeois nationalist regimes.)[3] However, as Nasser in conjunction with Tito was one of the chief sponsors of a second non-aligned conference, Chou En-lai had to be content with a reference in the communiqué to the effect that 'Both parties held that the Bandung Conference marked an illustrious turning point in the Asian-African people's united struggle against imperialism [and that] the fundamental interests of the Asian and African peoples lie in the further strengthening of Asian-African Solidarity.'[4] There was no reference either to the desirability of summoning a second Bandung or to the priority of this conference over the non-aligned one. Moreover Nasser emphasised the need for 'good preparations' which in effect meant that he gave precedence to the latter.[5]

Next, Chou visited Algeria. Although the visit achieved other successes (which I will discuss later), on the question of a second Bandung Algeria was non-committal and the communiqué did not refer to it. However, both sides noted, 'with satisfaction that, since the Bandung conference, the cause of Afro-Asian Solidarity has developed tremendously ... [and that both] are determined to increase their efforts to develop the Bandung spirit and reinforce Afro-Asian Solidarity'.[6] This situation changed in the next few months, when Algiers was chosen as the site of the proposed meeting.

During Chou's visit to Morocco, the only reference to Bandung

[1] See Table on Chou's tour and results.
[2] *Afro-Asian Solidarity, op. cit.* p. 43.
[3] See above, p. 23.
[4] *Afro-Asian Solidarity,* p. 56.
[5] Chou's Press Conference in Cairo, 20 Dec. 1963.
[6] *Afro-Asian Solidarity,* p. 89.

was in connection with the formation of the Organisation of African Unity. In their communiqué both parties agreed that the 'creation of this organisation falls within the framework of the principles of the historic Bandung Conference which has never ceased to inspire the action of the African and Asian peoples for their complete liberation'.[1]

Chou's visit to Tunisia was significant both because diplomatic recognition was granted and because Bourguiba quite frankly and openly expressed his disagreement with various aspects of China's policy vis-à-vis the United States, India and the Soviet Union.[2] There was no reference at all to a second Bandung.

While Chou did not receive explicit support in North Africa for a second Bandung the response in all other states he visited was positive, though, as it afterwards turned out, this did not imply rejection of a second non-aligned conference. On his visit to Ghana, he and Nkrumah agreed that 'an Afro-Asian Conference was necessary and that active preparations should be made to convene it . . .' [also] 'that the convening of an Afro-Asian Latin American people's anti-imperialism conference was desirable'.[3] This was not surprising as the two sides had a 'community of views' on such issues as colonialism, imperialism and neo-colonialism and in the light of the co-operation between them on other fronts.[4]

On his visit to Mali, Chou and President Modibo Keita noted the effective contribution of the Bandung Conference to the liberation of Afro-Asian and Latin American peoples. Therefore they 'endorse[d] the idea of a second conference of the independent countries of Asia and Africa and are determined to work for its success'.[5] In militantly progressive Guinea Chou and Sekou Touré stated 'the conditions are ripe for the convocation of a second Asian-African conference and that active preparations should be made toward this end'.[6] Chou and the leaders of the three Western African States he visited agreed that the greatest danger facing mankind emanated from imperialism, colonialism and neo-colonialism. He was not told that none of these three would attend a non-aligned conference.

[1] *Afro-Asian Solidarity*, p. 104.
[2] *Afro-Asian Solidarity*, p. 122.
[3] *Ibid.* p. 160.
[4] See below, p. 142.
[5] Sino-Mali Communiqué, 21 Jan. 1964. *Afro-Asian Solidarity*, p. 184.
[6] Sino-Guinea Communiqué, 26 Jan. 1964. *Ibid.* p. 223.

1963–5 Commitments, Consolidation, Reflection

Chou's visit to the Sudan succeeded in eliciting General Abboud's support for a second Afro-Asian conference. Both sides praised the Bandung and Addis Ababa conferences, and 'held that the time was ripe for the convening of a second Afro-Asian conference, and that active preparations should be made for it'.[1] Chou of course expressed profound support for the Palestinians' struggle for the restoration of their homeland, and for Arab unity.

In Ethiopia, Emperor Haile Selassie expressed distress at China's refusal to sign the test ban treaty and at the continuing Sino-Indian conflict. He pointed out that Ethiopia resolutely supported all United Nations operations which China had condemned and called on Chou En-lai to be alive to his 'heavy responsibility not only to your own people but to all men everywhere'.[2] Chou stressed China's desire for peace and suggested that differences of opinion could be reserved while points of agreement should be recorded. During the visit, pressure was applied by the United States to prevent the signing of a joint communiqué.[3] However this was not successful and Chou was grateful that the communiqué foiled 'foreign attempts to undermine Sino-Ethiopian relations by concocting groundless rumours'.[4] On the question of a second Bandung both parties 'agreed that the time was ripe for convening a second Afro-Asian conference'.[5]

On his visit to friendly Somalia, Chou and Shermarke the Somali Prime Minister, surveyed developments on the international scene since the Bandung conference. They therefore 'agreed that the time was appropriate for the convening of a second conference of Afro-Asian countries and that active preparations should be made for its convocation'.[6]

Chou En-lai's proposed visits to Kenya, Uganda and Tanganyika were called off, because of army mutinies in the three countries and the revolution in Zanzibar. Of the ten African states visited, six expressed open support for a second Afro-Asian Conference

[1] Sino-Sudanese Communiqué, 30 Jan. 1964. *Ibid.* p. 242.
[2] Addis Ababa Radio, 2 Feb. 1964.
[3] In his press conference in Somalia, Chou said that 'Ethiopia is controlled by foreigners and a foreign hand is over her, pressing down very heavily upon her. The Ethiopian people therefore want and wish to escape from this and be free.' Somali Radio, 4 Feb. 1964.
[4] Addis Ababa Radio, 1 Feb. 1964.
[5] *Afro-Asian Solidarity*, p. 259.   [6] *Ibid.* p. 302.

and this at least justified such a visit. Chou left Africa to continue his tour of some Asian countries to obtain support for a second Bandung.

In April the Preparatory Meeting for an Asian-African Conference was held in Indonesia, with representatives from Algeria, Cameroun, Ghana, Ethiopia, Liberia, the U.A.R., Guinea, Morocco and some Asian countries attending.[1] Foreign Minister Chen Yi headed the Chinese delegation. Unfortunately for Indonesia, India proposed and convinced the meeting that the Summit Conference should take place in Africa. However, her other suggestion was rejected, when the sub-committee in charge of invitations 'decided not to invite the Soviet Union and neo-colonialist Malaysia'.[2] This was a tactical success for China, which was bent on keeping the Soviet Union out of the meeting.

On 25 April with this in view Chou En-lai declared in the report on his tour of fourteen Afro-Asian countries to the join session of the Standing Committee of the National People's Congress and the Plenary Meeting of the State Council, that

our visit was crowned with full success and attained the desired objectives . . we found everywhere that the Bandung spirit was deeply embedded in the people's hearts and that the Asian-African people's cause of unity against imperialism had developed greatly. Leaders of many Asian-African countries hold that the time is ripe for convening a second Asian-African conference and active preparations should be made for this purpose.[3]

The Soviet Government was naturally embittered by China's success and on 25 April sent out a letter to Asian and African countries expressing disappointment at the decision of the preparatory meeting not to invite the Soviet Union. The letter accused China of engineering that decision, of using racial arguments for the purpose, and asserted that it would lead to the 'isolation' of the Asian-African bloc and would divide the anti-imperialist forces. As two-thirds of Soviet territory was in Asia, non-participation at Bandung was an unfortunate omission. The letter further threatened to 'rebuff' those opposing Soviet participation in the proposed conference.[4] Thus, the African states as well as the Asians were drawn into the Sino-Soviet conflict more openly than before.

[1] Jakarta Radio, 10 Apr. 1964. B.B.C. *S.W.B.* III No. 1525, 11 Apr. 1964.
[2] Jakarta Radio, 15 Apr. 1964. B.B.C. *S.W.B.* III No. 1529, 16 Apr. 1964.
[3] S.C.M.P. 3208, 29 Apr. 1964.   [4] B.B.C. *S.W.B.* III No. 1568, 2 June 1964.

A well argued reply by the Chinese Government on 30 May, stated that the political centre of the Soviet Union was in Europe and more than 70% of its population lived there; that the Asian-African countries are not of one race as there are countries in the zone which are white; that the Chinese had never used the racial argument against the Soviet Union (this was incorrect); Russia had always been a European country and there was no objection to her exclusion from the first Bandung Conference in 1955; why the objection now? China had consistently tried to keep the Sino-Soviet dispute from embarrassing the Asian-African countries and it was unwise of the Soviet Union to drag them into it; to claim that the Jakarta decision was China's act was to call the other participating countries mere ciphers and therefore to insult them; Soviet talk about dividing the anti-imperialist forces could not be taken seriously, as the Soviet Union had long ceased to be anti-imperialist and had been preaching collaboration with the 'imperialist chieftain'; to threaten the Asian-African countries with a rebuff was misguided as these countries could no longer be ordered about: 'though they are poor, they nevertheless have backbone'.[1]

While the competition for Afro-Asian support went on, Nasser and Tito, now joined by India, succeeded in getting a second non-aligned conference convened before a new Afro-Asian one. Thus, the Indonesian and Chinese attempts to have the second Bandung before the second Belgrade conference were unsuccessful. This did not mean however that the non-aligned conference was itself a success for India and the Soviet Union. It was in fact the contrary. The conference took place in Cairo from 5 to 10 October, and though China was not present her point of view on the international situation was effectively expressed by the leaders of such states as Guinea, Mali, Ghana, Congo-Brazzaville, Burundi, Tanzania, Cambodia, Algeria and Cuba. The conference 'emphatically asserted the continuing and dangerous vitality'[2] of imperialism and colonialism. The communiqué condemned these, noting that, together with neo-colonialism, they formed the 'basic source of international tension and conflict' to be combated by force of arms if necessary. The Indian Prime Minister's attempt to have a mission sent to China to stop her making atomic weapons was rejected by the conference.

[1] N.C.N.A., 31 May 1964.   [2] Jansen, *op. cit.*, p. 389.

Thus the Chinese, who had opposed the holding of the non-aligned conference, now 'noted with complete satisfaction' its 'resolutions condemning imperialism, colonialism and neo-colonialism', and its declaration that 'peaceful co-existence cannot be fully achieved throughout the world without the abolition' of these three evils.[1] They also noted with delight the U.S. failure to have Moise Tshombe attend the conference as Prime Minister of the Congo.[2] He was not only prevented from attending, but also arrested on his arrival in Cairo. With the second non-aligned conference out of the way preparations for a second Afro-Asian conference went on with renewed vigour. The second Belgrade conference had, in fact, agreed with the Chinese emphasis on the primacy of anti-colonialism over 'disarmament and peace', and a second Bandung would be a crowning success.

After the Cairo conference, the Chinese upgraded the calibre of their delegations to African states. In late October Foreign Minister Chen Yi led a party and government delegation attending the anniversary of the Algerian revolution. During this visit plans for the forthcoming conference were discussed. In March and April 1965 a Chinese National People's Congress delegation toured Mali, Guinea, the Central African Republic and Ghana to generate goodwill for China and to solicit support for keeping the Soviet Union out of Algiers. Chou En-lai himself visited Algeria again in March 1965, and again discussed with Ben Bella the problems involved in the conference. While the Chinese had stated earlier on that they did not wish to embarrass African states with the Sino-Soviet dispute, they were in fact insisting that these states should take sides with them on the issue of keeping the Soviet Union out of the Afro-Asian conference. All the genuinely non-aligned African States friendly to both countries did not wish to be dragged into a conflict which could only embarrass them. Moreover a position equidistant from China and the Soviet Union would be preferable, and could mean competitive offers of aid from both sides as well as from the Western countries which wanted to undercut the Communist states. Such equidistance was, however, difficult to debate over the Afro-Asian conference.

In May and early June the Chinese Vice Foreign Minister visited Morocco, Guinea, Mali, Ghana, Congo-Brazzaville, and the Central

[1] *People's Daily*, 14 Oct. 1964.   [2] *Ibid.*

African Republic, while Chou En-lai himself paid a visit to Tanzania to compensate for the one he missed in 1964.[1] He was in the U.A.R. when an event took place in Algiers which was to rock the entire foundation of China's Afro-Asian aspirations.

The internal contradictions within the Algerian leadership were becoming more acute as the time for the conference drew near. Ben Bella was attempting to use the prestige that would accrue to him from its being held to deliver a coup de grace to his other colleagues in the government, notably Foreign Minister Abdul Boutifliqa and Defence Minister Houare Boumédienne.[2] To prevent their imminent purge, Boumédienne overthrew Ben Bella's government on 19 June in a seemingly bloodless coup.

Chou En-lai was already in Cairo and together with Nasser urged that the conference should take place as scheduled. Although this was Nasser's initial reaction too he was soon to favour a postponement, following pro Ben Bella demonstrations in Algiers. Many Afro-Asian countries also favoured this, but Chen Yi tried till the last moment to have the conference held as planned. In the hope that this would be possible China had joined some other states in extending early recognition to the new Algerian regime. It must be pointed out, of course, that Ben Bella was believed to be nearer to Moscow and the French Communist Party than to Peking, so that his deposition would make the representation of the Soviet Union more difficult.

Support for Soviet participation was evidently increasing, and a postponement of the conference would give the Soviets more time to canvass the African states. It was therefore imperative that it should be held as planned. China conveniently claimed to believe that a state's internal affairs were the business of the people concerned, though this argument was not extended to other cases where reactionary governments have been condemned.

Other African states, however, viewed the issue differently and China's insistence until the last moment on the holding of the conference only served to damage her reputation. Even her friends

[1] See below, pp. 140–142.
[2] For an excellent treatment of the internal politics and contradictions within Algeria see David and Marina Ottaway, *Algeria, the Politics of a Socialist Revolution*, University of California Press, Berkeley and Los Angeles, 1970. See also William B. Quandt *Revolution and Political Leadership: Algeria 1954–1968*, M.I.T. Press, Cambridge. Mass., 1969.

were worried by the somewhat cynical, opportunistic and unscrupulous attitude adopted towards the Algerian coup. Ghana, Guinea and Tanzania viewed the coup with disfavour, because of Ben Bella's marked contribution to the African revolution.[1] Of the thirty-six independent African states, only eleven had been represented in Algiers, and most of these were in favour of postponing the Foreign Ministers' meeting which was planned for 26 June. On that day, the eleven African states present announced that no African state would attend if the meeting were held.[2] This decision eventually led to a postponement of the conference.

This was a strategic setback for China and thereafter things were to turn sour. On leaving the Algerian capital, Chen Yi declared 'the conference has been postponed precisely in order that it may better succeed. The second Afro-Asian conference will still be held in Algeria. That is a unanimous decision. . . . Manoeuvres to impede and sabotage the conference cannot be tolerated.'[3]

Compare this with his subsequent attitude. China's behaviour showed a basic failure to understand African sensitivities in matters involving the overthrow of their governments. It also overestimated her own ability to make sure that the conference was held, in the teeth of widespread genuine opposition. A careful examination of what happened when President Olympio of Togo was overthrown in 1963 might have prompted the Chinese to act with caution in formally recognising the new Algerian regime and in being so insistent on holding the conference. Already some nine French-speaking African states had decided not to attend it because of Algeria's support for the nationalist revolutionaries in the Congo (L).[4] While this would have meant a more militant conference, Ben Bella's overthrow alienated the progressive militant states and this ensured the failure of the conference.

With the postponement of the conference until November, China's fears were realised. The Soviet Union gained increasing support among African states for her participation. As the issue was to be decided by the Foreign Ministers' meeting in October

[1] Algeria had trained more than 2,000 freedom fighters and was contributing handsomely to the O.A.U. liberation fund. See below, p. 170.
[2] Jansen, *op. cit.*, p. 395.
[3] N.C.N.A., 29 June 1965.
[4] African opinion was against Tshombe's use of mercenaries in the Congo. His opponents therefore were openly aided from outside.

there was a strong possibility that she would be admitted. Such a major defeat for the policy China had been pursuing in the previous twenty months could not be tolerated. Moreover two events occurred in Asia which affected China's fortunes. The abortive Communist coup d'etat in Indonesia resulted in a bloody backlash against the Communists and against China, thus removing the strong support Indonesia had been giving her in the Afro-Asian caucus. The Indo-Pakistani border war in September resulted in a partial victory for India and a relative defeat for China's friend, thus again lowering her prestige.

In the light of these adverse currents, China called for the postponement of the conference on 15 October, at a preparatory meeting of Ambassadors in Algiers, on the grounds that the prevailing circumstances were not suitable.[1] She was supported by Pakistan but opposed by the majority, including India and Indonesia.[2] On 23 October *People's Daily* set out the reasoning behind China's proposal.[3] Noting that of late 'more and more complicated factors unfavourable towards the convening of the conference have cropped up' the paper listed four obstacles:

(1) the existence of marked differences on whether or not the conference should condemn U.S. imperialism;
(2) the fact that the invitation to U.N. Secretary General U Thant had not been cancelled;
(3) the raising once again of the question of participation by the Soviet Union; and
(4) the new tensions and conflicts which had recently come to the fore among certain Asian and African countries, all of which could not fail to cast a gloomy shadow over the conference.

All these would damage the Bandung spirit instead of promoting it and would be a windfall for the imperialists. In spite of Chinese objections, however, it was announced on the 25 October that the conference would be held, and that the Foreign Ministers' meeting would take place on 28 October.[4] Chou En-lai wrote to Afro-Asian heads of state on the 26th, arguing that the holding of the meeting as planned would lead not to the 'natural' Afro-Asian unity against imperialism but to a split in that solidarity. He was, of course, aware of the immense preparations made by the Algerian people

[1] B.B.C. *S.W.B.* III No. 1987, 16 Oct. 1965. [2] *Ibid.*
[3] N.C.N.A., 24 Oct. 1965. [4] S.C.M.P. No. 3568, 29 Oct. 1965.

for the conference but one had to consider the pros and cons of holding such a conference in terms of Afro-Asian unity.[1] In view of this situation the 'Chinese Government solemnly declares that China will not take part in such an Afro-Asian Conference'.[2]

A similar position had already been taken up by Tanzania, whose President stated on 18 October that Tanzania 'felt unable' to send a representative to Algiers, because of her hostility to the overthrow of Ben Bella and the activities of Ho Ying the Chinese Ambassador.[3] Also, on his return from the O.A.U. conference in Accra, Sekou Touré had said that because of his attitude towards the overthrow of Ben Bella, Guinea would not attend. Congo-Brazzaville had also supported postponement.[4] Nevertheless it was reported that fifty countries had confirmed their intention to attend the conference and that the Foreign Ministers' meeting would open on the 28th as planned.[5]

In the event there was a two-day postponement to allow more delegations to arrive. Thus on 30 October, with forty-five delegations now attending, including some fifteen Foreign Ministers, the meeting began, and went into closed session after the opening speech by the Algerian Chairman Boutefliqa. In the closed session India formally proposed the immediate admission of Malaysia, Russia and Singapore. A clever counterattack came from Uganda, proposing the consideration of the report of the ambassadorial Standing Committee, a move which raised the question whether or not the Heads of State conference should be held in the absence of a substantial number of Afro-Asian states. The conference was thus confronted with two issues, that of representation and that of postponement.

About nineteen delegations were in favour of Soviet participation, including Nigeria, Malawi, the U.A.R., Tunisia, Somalia, Ruanda, Kenya, Mali, Morocco, Ethiopia and the Sudan,[6] but unfortunately for the Soviet Union and India there were still more who favoured postponing the conference itself. While most of the African delegations wanted postponement, Nigeria, Chad and Malawi spoke forcibly against it and Tunisia and Morocco also wanted the

[1] N.C.N.A., 26 Oct. 1965. [2] S.C.M.P. No. 3568, 29 Oct. 1965.
[3] Dar es Salaam Radio, 18 Oct. 1965, and interview with X.
[4] S.C.M.P. No. 3566, 27 Oct. 1965. [5] Jansen, *op. cit.*, p. 397.
[6] *El Moudjahid* of 3 November 1965 called the postponement a defeat for imperialism.

conference to be held. Because of the strength of opinion for postponement, the Algerian Revolutionary Council decided against the conference.[1] Militant and progressive Algeria could hardly be expected to relish the support of such conservative delegations as Malawi, Nigeria and Chad, while her more consistent friends in the progressive bloc were in favour of postponement. To antagonise China by pleasing the more conservative states would be detrimental to Algerian interests. After all, it was not so long ago that China had been the only major friend to the Algerians in their bleakest moment – at a time when Russia had hesitated at the prospect of antagonising de Gaulle. Moreover, even the Algerian government was not united in its enthusiasm for the conference. Foreign Minister Boutefliqa had been its most persistent sponsor and organiser, but this view was not at that time shared by President Boumédienne, who on 20 October had told Algerian journalists that 'spending 150 million dinars [$30m.] for a five-day invitation is not revolutionary.... This policy of prestige will not be followed any longer.'[2] It was thus easier for the Algerian Government to decide against holding the conference. Thus China's de facto veto on it was not as catastrophic for Sino–Algerian relations as could have been assumed. Against this background Algeria threw her decisive weight behind postponement and on 2 November the conference was postponed sine die.[3]

On 5 November, Haykal said in *Al-Ahram* that although the U.A.R. had pressed for the conference to be held as planned, its postponement was fortunate as it had prevented the idea of Afro–Asian solidarity from being destroyed. He referred to events since the 19 June coup in Algiers as a result of which several things had come to light.

(1) Obstacles to holding the conference had become more serious and all hopes of resolving them had disappeared.

(2) The balance had been tipped against China, particularly in view of the Soviet success in Africa and the dilemma of the Communist Party in Indonesia. As a result China turned against the idea of holding the conference and its refusal to attend if it were held became a possibility. With the absence of China the conference would have lost one of its most important mainstays.

[1] *El Moudjahid*, 3 November 1965.
[2] See also D. & M. Ottaway, *op. cit.* p. 202.   [3] *Ibid.*

The number of countries which would attend the conference was unimportant, because what mattered was the weight of the countries attending.
(3) Many Asian leaders could not come in the circumstances.
(4) It would be left mainly to African countries and as the O.A.U. had just met, a conference so composed was not necessary.
(5) The West, and the U.S. in particular, was encouraging the holding of the conference from behind the scenes. It was most paradoxical that the West had been urging its closest friends to adhere to the need to convene the conference. The purpose of course was for the conference to convene even without China, thus to fail, and to shatter the idea of Afro-Asian solidarity.[1]

In these circumstances the Foreign Ministers had no choice other than postponement. He concluded that the conference could not bear the consequences of isolating China at the request of the United States and the Soviet Union, and it could not therefore be held.[2]

Thus in effect China had successfully vetoed the conference. While its postponement in June had been a strategic set-back for her aims and the intervening events had confirmed her apprehensions, its indefinite postponement in November demonstrated her weight in the Afro-Asian world and the impossibility of holding the conference without her participation. Chinese efforts in Africa – economic, political, military and diplomatic – would have been in vain if the conference had taken place without her. She was still seen as militantly and materially anti-colonialist, and this by itself was enough to prevent her isolation at Algiers. The indefinite postponement of the second Afro-Asian conference was thus a tactical gain for China.

(iv) *Chinese–Tanzanian Relations: A Case Study in Chinese Diplomacy*
In the previous chapter, reference was made to Tanganyika's recognition of China in December 1961. However from that time till 1963 her foreign policy was more or less like Nigeria's, commonly described by the Western press as 'moderate' and 'realistic'. The Tanganyikan leader Julius Nyerere was one of those who were concerned about what was called the second scramble for Africa; this time a scramble not only by the imperialists but also by the

[1] *Al Ahram*, 5 Nov. 1965. [2] Quoted by Cairo Radio, 5 Nov. 1965.

Socialist giants themselves. At the Moshi A.A.P.S.O. Conference in February 1963, he declared 'I wish I could honestly say that the second scramble for Africa is going to be a scramble only between the capitalist powers.' He said that the Socialist countries seemed to be committing the same crime as the old capitalist ones – the acquisition of power and prestige. The open competition between China and the Soviet Union soon engulfed Africa and it was Nyerere's intention to prevent the East–West and the growing intra-East competition from disrupting African politics. Already within Tanganyika the Chinese were active in front organisations and the trade unions. The Tanganyika Federation of Labour was affiliated with the I.C.F.T.U. with headquarters in Brussels. The left-wing elements in the federation tried to sever this alliance, and urged affiliation with the W.F.T.U.[1] President Nyerere stepped in to resolve the internal conflict and decided that the T.F.L. should not be affiliated either to the I.C.F.T.U. or to the W.F.T.U. but rather should join the nationalist All Africa Trade Union Federation (A.A.T.U.F.).[2] This was done to reduce conflict and outside influence within the trade union movement and to bring the centralised unions under government control.[3] It did not, of course, mean that outside influence was removed, as the A.A.T.U.F. itself was moving left and the new decision was therefore favourable to the left-wing elements in the trade unions. The new move did not stop the visits to China by Tanganyikan trade unionists.[4]

As a concession to the left wing in Tanganyikan politics, Chou En-lai was invited to visit Tanganyika during his tour of Africa in 1963–4.[5] However, because of mutinies in Uganda, Kenya and Tanganyika he postponed his scheduled visits to these countries. Ironically the mutinies and the revolution in Zanzibar marked a turning-point in Chinese relations with East Africa.

Chou En-lai was in Ghana on 12 January 1964, when the Sultanate of Zanzibar was overthrown in a bloody revolution that shook the whole of East Africa.[6] Although China had no part in the revolution

[1] Interview with a progressive member of the T.F.L.
[2] Interview with X. Disaffiliation from I.C.F.T.U., Oct. 1963.
[3] Discussion with Government Officer.
[4] Talk with labour leader who visited China.   [5] Interview with X.
[6] On the prelude to and course of the revolution see Michael Lofchie *Zanzibar: Background to Revolution*, 1965, and Field Marshal John Okello, *Revolution in Zanzibar*, 1967.

it was a signal success for her advocacy of armed struggle rather than the illusory parliamentary road.[1] The immediate concern in the West was whether the new regime would remain friendly, or move into the 'Chinese orbit'.[2] On 17 January following Kenya, Uganda and Cuba, China recognised the Revolutionary Government of the People's Republic of Zanzibar.[3] Recognition was also granted by other Socialist states, including the German Democratic Republic. This swift action by the Socialist countries put them at an advantage vis-à-vis the Western countries, who were slow to accord recognition and gave the impression of wanting to restore the old government. The Zanzibar revolutionaries led by John Okello had no Communist leanings, but left-wing politicians were available who were ready and able to manipulate the revolutionary situation in their own favour.[4] One of these was the strongly nationalist Hanga, who had been educated in the Soviet Union. He now ensured Socialist aid and support for the tiny republic and was responsible for the first diplomatic recognition by an African country of East Germany.[5] The other was Abdul Rahman Mohammed Babu, a former correspondent of the New China News Agency who worked with the Chinese envoy Liu Kan to secure Chinese aid.[6]

In February 'Babu', now Minister for External Affairs, was able to announce the granting of £185,000 of Chinese aid to Zanzibar. It had also been indicated that gifts of tractors, irrigation machinery and technical help were soon to come.[7] At this stage apprehension increased in the West; it was feared that Zanzibar was becoming the African Cuba. This apprehension was not however confined to the West. Tanganyika viewed with alarm the prospect of Zanzibar becoming the successor to the Congo as the battlefield for the cold war. To remove the East–West conflict from her own doorstep the decision was taken in April 1964 to form the Union of Tanganyika and Zanzibar.[8]

It was at this stage that the shrewdness and efficacy of Chinese diplomacy came to the fore. The Soviet Union was angry at this

---

[1] Interview with Tanganyikan Minister.
[2] *New York Times*, 15 Jan. 1964; *The Times*, 15 Jan. 1964.
[3] N.C.N.A., 17 Jan. 1964. [4] Interview with Minister.
[5] Hanga was executed in Zanzibar in 1969.
[6] Liu Kan warned Western States to keep their hands off Zanzibar. Zanzibar Radio, 4 Feb. 1964.
[7] Zanzibar Radio, 19 Feb. 1964. [8] Interview with Minister.

1963–5 Commitments, Consolidation, Reflection 137

decision, not only because it aimed at reducing Soviet influence on the island but also because it would remove the first African recognition of East Germany. Efforts to block the merging of the two countries were therefore made.[1] While China too did not relish the idea of Zanzibar being taken over by Mainland Tanganyika, the Chinese Ambassador, Ho Ying, moved adroitly to assure President Nyerere of China's support for the Union.[2] China therefore began to work through the Union Government, and all her aid to Zanzibar was granted through President Nyerere while the Soviet Union and East Germany worked directly with Zanzibar.[3] This gave President Nyerere reason to believe that China was totally in favour of the Union and Ho Ying was able to prepare the ground for increased Chinese activity.[4]

A joint government delegation led by Second Vice President Rashidi Kawawa visited China in June 1964 and secured an interest-free loan of £5 million for Mainland Tanganyika.[5] China also gave a free grant of £1 million to Tanganyika.[6] The Zanzibar loan would be repayable over ten years from January 1975 in exports and cash.[7] In a communiqué issued jointly with the visiting Tanganyika-Zanzibar Government delegation, it was declared that:

> In order to lift themselves from poverty and backwardness, the Asian-African countries must first of all rely on their own people and resources for the work of national construction and secondly they also need mutual aid and economic co-operation among themselves on the basis of equality and mutual benefit. This is the reliable way for the Asian-African countries to attain economic independence and common prosperity.[8]

The signing of the aid agreement with China must be contrasted with the non-utilisation of a Soviet offer of $21 million because of the Soviet attitude to the Union of Tanganyika and Zanzibar.[9]

It would be wrong, however, to give the impression that the Chinese offer of aid to the Mainland went smoothly. In fact the Ministry of Economic Development in Dar Es Salaam was not prepared for the change, and implementation of aid projects was therefore slowed down.[10] While it was true that in 1960–2 China's

---

[1] Discussion with X. [2] Interview with X.
[3] Interview with Minister. [4] Interview with Minister.
[5] Zanzibar Radio, 9 June 1964; *Sunday Times*, London, 21 June 1964.
[6] *Sunday Times*, 21 June 1964. [7] Zanzibar Radio, 16 June 1964.
[8] Chinese Embassy in Afghanistan: News Bulletin, 24 June 1964.
[9] Interview with X.
[10] Interview with Government official. What was involved was the deliberately slow

economic difficulties had made it difficult for her to implement aid commitments, in this case the delay was caused by the recipient country.[1] Because of this delay attention was directed towards military aid.

In the military aid sector Chinese–Tanzanian relations reached a turning-point after the mutiny by Tanganyikan soldiers in January 1964 against their British officers and in support of pay claims. While the Socialist press in general berated the use of British troops to subdue the mutiny in East Africa, the Chinese showed an understanding of the situation and took steps to improve their position. The mutiny resulted in the 'destruction' of the British arms with which the Tanganyikan army was equipped.[2] They had to be replaced.

The Chinese Ambassador Ho Ying argued that a newly developing state should not use its scarce foreign exchange on arms and ammunition: all attention should be devoted to economic and social development. He offered to replace the British arms with up to date Chinese weapons – tanks, mortars, rockets, machine guns and other classes of weapon needed – free of charge.[3] Ho Ying was extremely shrewd. He made no mention of the British officers in the army; China's aid would be without strings and Tanganyika was free to run her army as she liked.[4] Already the Chinese, Russians and East Germans had been assigned to help train two battalions of the Zanzibar army and the implications of this had to be considered on the Mainland.[5]

The Chinese offer to replace the arms was accepted but no reference was made to training the Tanganyikan army in the use of the weapons.[6] Thus the supply of arms by China in 1964 preceded the invitation to China to help train the security forces.

In August 1964 it was announced that the Government of the United Republic of Tanganyika and Zanzibar had decided to invite a Chinese military mission to give instruction in the use of Chinese weapons. The mission would be eleven strong and would stay for a maximum of six months.[7] That a Chinese military mission stayed

process adopted in drawing up supplementary protocols with the Chinese on the specific projects the aid was to be used for.
[1] See above, pp. 85–93. [2] Interview with X.
[3] Discussion with Government Official. [4] Interview with X.
[5] See Colin Legum in *Observer*, 30 Aug. 1964. China was training about 300 Zanzibaris.
[6] Interview with X. [7] See Legum, *Observer*, 30 Aug. 1964.

years beyond that period is a commentary on Ho Ying's ability. There was great concern in the West when the decision was first announced, and fear that China would subvert the country's government.[1] This was, however, countered by well reasoned argument on the part of Tanzania (as the new Union was now called). The East African armies had been trained by Britain and they had mutinied. Other African armies trained by Britain and France had mutinied and even staged coups d'etat. A Chinese-instructed army could not possibly do anything worse than stage a coup. The new step did not therefore introduce a new element of danger. Moreover, as Tanzania had a policy of non-alignment, the government was not obliged to only accept Western military aid. Whereas Tanzania would have to pay for British arms, China was giving them free of charge.

The Chinese first helped to train a field force unit which was meant to deter the army from staging a coup. This was essential where the Sandhurst-trained officers could not be relied upon.[2] On 8 February 1965 the troops of the Fourth Battalion completed their training in the use of Chinese arms and staged a special public parade on Monduli Plains near Arusha in Northern Tanzania.[3] At the parade, Rashidi Kawawa, the Second Vice President who was also responsible for defence, said that the Chinese arms supplied to Tanzania, the use of which the Tanzanians had now mastered, were the same as the Chinese themselves were using. He contrasted China's policy of supplying the most modern weapons in their arsenal with the Mark 4 guns which the colonial government had left behind.[4] Some of the Chinese arms on display included tank guns, heavy machine guns, mortars and automatic rifles which had arrived in 1964.[5]

On the political and economic plane, the goodwill generated by the commitment of June 1964 was followed up in December with an offer to build two high-powered transmitters.[6] The Chinese Government would pay half the total cost calculated at more than

[1] The Western press was also concerned with the prospects of Chinese military aid to Congolese fighting against Tshombe and to nationalist forces in Southern Africa. These fears were justified, but Tanzania viewed the question from an African perspective.
[2] Interview with X.
[3] Dar Es Salaam Radio, 8 Feb. 1965.
[4] Ibid.
[5] Ibid., and The Times of 2 Sept. 1964.
[6] Dar Es Salaam Radio, 28 Dec. 1964, 11 Jan. 1965.

£350,000 and the other half would be an interest-free loan. Building started in 1965. Fourteen days later, an agreement was signed for the establishment of a 5,000 acre state farm at Ruvu, which would eventually employ 700 people including management and technicians. A total of about £450,000 would be invested. Until the farm was self-supporting China would meet the recurrent cost in the form of a loan. Tractors, trucks and farming equipment as well as staff to be understudied by Tanzanians would be provided by China. It was also decided in January that part of the £10 million loan would be used to build a fully integrated textile mill in Tanzania costing about £3 million, the largest of its kind in East Africa.[1]

With this as the background, President Nyerere visited China in February, accepting an invitation which Ho Ying had extended in 1964 when offering military aid. During the visit he thanked China for the gifts and interest-free loans made available.

> We are the more appreciative because we realise that this capital is not surplus to your own requirements, nor are your technicians otherwise unemployed. Certainly we on our side are anxious to learn what we can about China's development, in the hope that we shall, by its adaptation to our circumstances, be able to benefit from your experience.[2]

At the end of his visit on 20 February 1965, a Sino-Tanzanian treaty of friendship was signed on the same terms as the treaty with Congo-Brazzaville.[3]

Nyerere's visit to China had a profound impact upon him. Like other African leaders before him, he discovered the great similarity of the problems African States and China were trying to solve. He was impressed by the developmental model the Chinese adopted and considered its application to Tanzania's very similar situation — scarce foreign capital and labour resources in excess of other factors of production.[4] He noted the Chinese emphasis on frugality; they 'did not use private cars, they travelled by bus and bicycle'.[5] He was also much impressed by the discipline of the million people who turned out to welcome him. There was apparently no question

[1] Kampala Radio, 6 Jan. 1965.
[2] S.C.M.P. No. 3402. Nyerere's speech of 17 Feb. 1965.
[3] S.C.M.P. No. 3404, 25 Feb. 1965.
[4] Interview with a member of Nyerere's entourage.
[5] *East African Standard*, 27 Feb. 1965.

of police being used to keep the people back. What he saw of the health of the children in the Chinese cities he visited, influenced his subsequent decision to ask for Chinese medical teams.[1]

Although Nyerere's visit to China had partly taken place because of the insistence of the militants in his government, he was convinced while there of the efficacy of Chinese methods of development. He was also aware that if these methods were to be emulated, they needed to be applied creatively.[2]

In turn Chou En-lai visited Tanzania in June 1965 before the abortive Afro-Asian Conference in Algiers. During the visit Nyerere again spoke about the lesson of the Chinese revolution:

Courage, enthusiasm and endurance are not enough. There must also be discipline, and the intelligent application of policies to the needs and circumstances of the country and the time. There is no single answer which is applicable in all times and at all places. Each country and each generation has to deal with its own problems in its own way, exploiting to the greatest possible advantage such opportunities as are available to it.[3]

Chou's visit helped to cement the friendship that was already growing up between the two countries. He impressed Tanzanian Ministers with his knowledge of world history and current events, speaking for example to the Cabinet for six hours without notes. Although there was a divergence of views following the Algiers coup of 19 June 1965 and China's recognition of the new regime any ill feeling thus generated was quickly overcome as the two countries came to hold the same position on the postponement of the Afro-Asian Conference in October and November.[4]

Chinese-Tanzanian relations in this period showed the quality and calibre of the Chinese diplomats, and what could be achieved with limited resources and the skilful use of opportunities. In October Tanzania had to look for an external market for her tobacco surplus. A record 8m lb was produced of which the British-American Company bought 5m lb. China came to the rescue and bought 2m lb to save a serious situation. This naturally generated goodwill and increased Chinese purchases from Tanganyika to £4.31 million in 1965.[5] Tanzania could claim to have benefited from a relationship that provided economic aid on the most generous terms conceivable.

[1] Interview with member of entourage.   [2] *Ibid.*
[3] Nyerere's speech 4 June 1965. S.C.M.P. No. 3474, 10 June 1965.
[4] See above, p. 132.   [5] See Table on Trade.

(v) *Sino-Ghanaian Relations: A Second Case Study.*

Both sides unanimously recognised imperialism as the source of war and enemy of national liberation and world peace, and held that independence and peace can be won only when resolute struggle is waged against imperialism and colonialism. . . . Both sides expressed unanimous support for all oppressed nations and peoples in their struggle against imperialism and colonialism and for national liberation.[1] (Joint Statement of Chinese and Ghanaian Trade Unions in Peking, 27 October 1963.)

This statement contains in a nutshell the basis of the relations between China and Ghana – relations that became warmer and closer as China came to play a greater part in Ghanaian ideology. By omission it also reflects Ghana's determination to refrain from taking sides in the Sino-Soviet dispute. The statement made no mention of the need to combat revisionism in order to handle imperialism effectively. A similar statement made by the Chinese and Tanganyikan Trade Unions in the same period does mention this need.[2]

For Ghana, the struggle against colonialism and neo-colonialism in Africa was a task that demanded the militant solidarity of all progressive forces. Ghana therefore called for the resolution of the Sino-Soviet and Sino-Indian disputes which were weakening Afro-Asian solidarity. Reference has already been made to the role this frame of mind played in the Sino-Indian border war of 1962.[3] I have also mentioned President Nkrumah's anger at the behaviour of the Western powers in the Congo and that, as his disenchantment grew, Sino-Ghanaian relations became warmer.[4] At the same time he did not want the dispute within the 'progressive camp' to be openly exacerbated. It was this that led him to urge the postponement of the 3rd A.A.P.S.O. Conference in Moshi, Tanganyika, in February 1963. 'A meeting of the . . . Solidarity Conference at this time would be unfortunate and may weaken Afro-Asian solidarity (Sino-Indian negotiations are at a delicate state). Statements might be made which could seriously prejudice the chances of success.'[5] The meeting was of course held and was marked by

[1] S.C.M.P. No. 3091, 31 Oct. 1963.
[2] Peking 28 Nov. 1963. S.C.M.P. No. 3111, 3 Dec. 1963.
[3] See above p. 108.   [4] See above p. 102.
[5] W. Scott-Thompson, *op. cit.*, p. 283.

1963–5 Commitments, Consolidation, Reflection 143

Sino-Soviet and Sino-Indian conflicts.[1] Again in September 1963, by which time the Sino-Soviet conflict had reached the point of no return, Nkrumah cabled to the Executive Meeting of the A.A.P.S.O. in Nicosia: 'Our goal should be to seek the unity of the socialist countries, for it is only through this unity that they can support us in our struggle against imperialism and colonialism. It should be our concern at this conference to appeal to China and the Soviet Union most strongly to eliminate their differences.'[2] The Sino-Soviet dispute had of course gone beyond the point where even powerful Communist parties could do anything to resolve it, and it was no surprise that Nkrumah could not perform such a feat.

Nevertheless, in the years 1963–4 Ghana's relations with China grew more cordial and the Chinese Ambassador Huang Hua was said to be after the Soviet envoy the most influential diplomat in Accra.[3] Chou En-lai arrived in Ghana on 11 January 1964. He was warmly welcomed by the Ghanaians, but an article in the government newspaper reminded him that Ghana did not intend to take sides in the Sino-Soviet ideological dispute.[4] Chou's visit came when questions were being asked about the implementation of the economic and technical co-operation agreement signed in 1961 on the occasion of Nkrumah's visit to China. This agreement had stated that the loan of £7 million was to be used in instalments between July 1962 and June 1967 and earlier implementation had been held up by economic difficulties in China.[5] By January 1964 only a very small part of the loan had been disbursed. It should be pointed out, however, that the delay in implementing the agreement was not a one-sided affair. Ghana too had economic difficulties which made it difficult to undertake certain projects. One of the three projects in the protocol of 1962 was a textile factory. For the project to succeed, Ghana needed supplies of raw cotton which the country did not grow. This meant that cotton had to be imported at a period when Ghana's external reserves were depleted and when there were other imports demanding higher priority. Chou En-lai pointed out this weakness to Nkrumah and suggested that

[1] See below, p. 165. At one stage China threatened to walk out of the conference if her view was not accepted: interview with participant on the Tanganyika delegation.
[2] Radio Ghana, 30 Sept. 1963.
[3] Scott Thompson, *op. cit.*, p. 297 and interview with Z.
[4] See *New York Times*, 13 Jan. 1964.
[5] China completed repayment of her debts to Russia in 1964.

Ghana was laying the 'wrong' emphasis on industrial development and neglecting the agricultural side.[1] Thus Chou explained China's position and offered aid in another direction.

China's economic aid to Ghana did not play a significant role in the latter's economy; Ghana herself had offered Guinea £10m in 1958 at the latter's independence and Ghana's rich economy was not modelled on China's. Their close relations emanated from a congruence of ideological viewpoints. Nkrumah acknowledged this when he said at the farewell banquet to Chou: 'We have learned with interest the methods by which the people of China have mobilised their resources for the reconstruction of their country and the improvement of their living conditions... the example of China's determination, organisation, discipline and unity cannot be lost on Africa at this time.'[2] At the conclusion of Chou's visit, the two leaders noted

with satisfaction, that significant achievements had been made in the promotion of mutual friendly relations between their two countries. Contributory to this achievement was the satisfactory implementation of the various agreements – Treaty of Friendship, Agreement on Economic and Technical Co-operation, a Trade and Payments Agreement and an Agreement on Cultural Co-operation – which were signed between the two countries during the Ghanaian leader's visit to China in 1961.[3]

This was issued despite the fact that so far the promised economic aid had not been given.

From Chou's point of view, Nkrumah's support of the second Bandung, and their common views on imperialism contained in the joint communiqué, made his visit to Ghana a success.[4]

The following February, Ambassador Huang Hua offered to second Chinese agricultural experts to help increase Ghana's rice production, the aim being to achieve self-sufficiency within two years.[5] The experts arrived in August 1964.[6]

Meanwhile, as the competitive aid-giving between China and the Soviet Union was intensified in 1964, Ghana was offered another long-term interest-free loan of £8 million to be utilised within

[1] Interview with Michael Dei Arang, former Secretary General, of Ghana's Ministry of Foreign Affairs and Head of the African Affairs Secretariat at Flagstaff House.
[2] *Afro-Asian Solidarity, op. cit.*, p. 156.   [3] *Ibid.* p. 164.
[4] Nkrumah also suggested Afro-Asian/Latin-American People's Solidarity.
[5] Ghana Radio: B.B.C. *S.W.B.* Weekly Supplement IV No. 250, 13 Feb. 1964.
[6] N.C.N.A., 15 Aug. 1964.

the period of Ghana's first Seven Year Development Plan (1963-4 to 1969-70).[1] However, serious utilisation of China's pledged loans did not begin until 1965. The construction of the integrated cotton textile and knitwear factory at Juapong began in the second half of that year. In October intensive work began on the nine principal workshops of the proposed mill, and more than 7,000 tons of material and equipment arrived before the coup of February 1966.[2] The personnel for the construction of the pencil factory arrived in December 1965 with some material and equipment. By the time of the coup the Chinese had brought in 1,000 tons of material and equipment for this second factory. According to the arrangement, the Chinese had paid the local expenses of its construction.[3]

If the Chinese were far behind Russia in aid pledged to Ghana, they at least impressed Ghanaian officials with the easy terms of their aid and the unpretentiousness of their personnel. 'When the Chinese say they will give you a glass, they will not change their word. The Russians are not like that, they can change their minds. By the way they behaved, you would think they were building the whole of Ghana.'[4] Chinese discipline, enthusiasm and devotion to work became proverbial.

While China played a minor role in economic matters in Ghana, this was partly compensated by the political and revolutionary unity existing between the two states. Chinese prospects in Ghana rose with the increasing radicalisation of Ghana's foreign policy in Africa. This, of course, was a function of Nkrumah's Pan-African diplomacy and the promotion by all possible means of what he considered Africa's genuine interests. Ghana, he had said, could not be regarded as free until *all* Africa was free.[5] The so-called political independence granted to many African states merely camouflaged the continuing stranglehold of colonialism.[6] The new situation described as neo-colonialism could not co-exist peacefully with a genuinely free Africa, as attempts were made and would

[1] N.C.N.A., 16 July 1964 and *Financial Times*, London, 17 July 1964.
[2] N.C.N.A., 6 March 1966, giving details of Chinese aid.   [3] *Ibid.*
[4] Interview with Z. This view was confirmed by Michael Dei Arang who said that the Chinese were very frank about what they could and what they could not do for Ghana. It was more difficult to decipher Russian diplomacy, with the result that even when the Russians were being frank, one could still entertain an element of doubt. Interview with Dei Arang.
[5] Kwame Nkrumah, *I Speak of Freedom*, 1961.
[6] This is restated in his *Neo-Colonialism, The Last Stage of Imperialism*, 1965.

continue to be made to subvert the governments of the progressive and militant African states. Ghana was therefore prepared to help freedom fighters from various areas of Africa to gain independence for both colonial and so-called independent states. The insistence on maintaining borders imposed on Africa by imperialism was an attempt to hinder the salvaging activities of progressive Africans in all parts of the continent. For the purposes of the revolution interference in the internal affairs of other states was essential, although openly, the opposite view would be expressed.

China's persistent emphasis on the need for revolutionary activity meant that her diplomatic relations benefited from crises which needed a revolutionary great power. On the revolutionary side, she favoured Ghana's wish to train African freedom fighters even if this was to serve Ghanaian aims. A secret camp had been established in Mankrong, Ghana, in December 1961 with two Russian instructors, but little had come of it, and Ghanaians had complained about the patronising behaviour and overbearing manner of the Russians.[1] They left in June 1962 and the Ghanaians were glad to see them leave.[2]

When Chou En-lai visited Ghana in January 1964 he was aware of Ghana's needs on the revolutionary side. He offered assistance in training of freedom fighters but apparently Nkrumah discreetly turned it down at that time.[3] While Nkrumah's ideological views agreed with China's on the issue of liberation movements, he was said to be still suspicious of the Chinese.

Nkrumah believed that China had to have a conspicuous position in the world of Ghanaian ideology, because he suspected that in the final analysis they were right in their view of the liberation movement.
But basically he feared them. He instinctively trusted Russians, he instinctively distrusted Chinese. He was, simply, scared that the Chinese did not have his own best interests at heart, and I had clear instructions to watch their movements closely.[4]

However, this initial rejection of Chou's offer was reversed in September 1964, when Nkrumah approved the recommendation of the Director of the Bureau of African Affairs as regards Chinese aid in that field.[5] The first group of five Chinese experts in guerrilla

[1] Ghana Ministry of Information, *Nkrumah's Subversion of Africa*, Accra 1966.
[2] *Ibid.* [3] Scott-Thompson, *op. cit.*, p. 297.
[4] Officer in charge of surveillance of Chinese activities: in Scott-Thompson, p. 297.
[5] *Nkrumah's Subversion, op. cit.*, p. 7.

warfare arrived in Ghana in October 1964, though their arrival was kept secret at the request of the Chinese Embassy in Accra.[1] It was said that, before they arrived, conditions at the Half Assini training camp had been steadily deteriorating and the students were demoralised because of the ineffective training they received.[2] This situation changed with the arrival of the Chinese. 'The presence of the Chinese has given an added impetus to the aspirations of the freedom fighters. The instructors are happy and have been doing their work expertly. The camp command is very fatherly and with this contingent there is no complaint.'[3] The Chinese instructors remained in Ghana until the coup in February 1966 although training was suspended for a short time in 1965 while preparations were made for the meeting of the O.A.U. in Accra.[4] Some of the Chinese instructors spent their leave in Accra while others remained in the camp.[5]

Apart from the Chinese guerrilla instructors, some employees of the Bureau of African Affairs were also sent to China in October 1964 for four months' intensive training in guerrilla warfare.[6] Thus Sino-Ghanaian relations on the revolutionary side were very warm indeed. One could argue that this was a time when Ghana made use of Chinese capabilities to further her own African aims, but it must be remembered that these aims, in so far as guerrilla warfare was concerned, were not incompatible with China's emphasis on revolutionary warfare. For their part the Chinese were glad to make use of this great opportunity to promote their revolutionary interests in Africa. China and Ghana thus drew closer together.

In spite of Nkrumah's great reluctance to take sides in the Sino-Soviet dispute it became clear that on ideological issues he generally agreed with China, especially over the need for national liberation wars and the role and subterfuges of imperialism. In time Chinese influence grew and late in 1965 they successfully advised him to

[1] *Ibid.* pp. 7 and 8.   [2] *Ibid.* p. 8.
[3] *Ibid.* p. 9. Bureau Officer stationed at the camp.
[4] The activities of the Chinese instructors in Ghana had received adverse publicity in 1965, when a number of French-speaking African states accused Nkrumah of attempting to subvert their governments by violent means. Led by Ivory Coast, Niger and Cameroun, they threatened to boycott the O.A.U. meeting scheduled for Accra later in the year unless all the nationals from those countries who were being trained in Ghana were expelled.
[5] *Ibid.* p. 20. See also below, p. 172.   [6] *Ibid.* p. 39.

form a people's militia whose effective organisation might have prevented a coup d'etat.[1] The Militia was created but its organisation could not proceed for lack of funds: it was also delayed by the army's resistance to a second force.[2] The officer corps' attitude was understandable in that an effectively organised people's militia would encroach on the army's powers. It could have formed an alternative source of military power for the President in a crisis in which the army considered it to be its duty to intervene.[3]

It would be wrong to give the impression that Sino-Ghanaian political relations continued perfectly smoothly after Chou's visit to Ghana in January 1964. Nkrumah was one of the very few non-aligned leaders who disapproved publicly of the Chinese detonation of an atomic bomb in October 1964. Unlike China he had supported the partial test ban treaty of 1963, and now said that Chou's call for a summit conference to discuss nuclear disarmament would have carried more conviction if China had not accompanied it with an atomic test. 'As it is now, those who are anxious to consolidate their own programme of nuclear stockpiling will be only too ready to show scepticism about the sincerity of your wise appeal.'[4] Nkrumah was to change his mind later and to support China.

I have already referred to the reaction of African leaders to the Algiers coup of 19 June 1965.[5] Nkrumah was also angered by the speed with which China recognised the new regime. He received an intelligence report, apparently from a Russian source, of Chinese complicity in the coup, and after this he placed their activities at the training camps under the supervision of the trusted General Barwah.[6] Nor was he pleased by China's refusal to help in his attempt to mediate in the Vietnam war. Perhaps Nkrumah failed to realise that the Vietnam war was more important to China than was the wish to please an African leader by allowing him to act as 'peacemaker' – especially since he had refused to take sides openly in the Sino-Soviet dispute. Perhaps the irony of it all was that Sino-Ghanaian relations were becoming warmer just when China's concentration was being shifted to East and Southern Africa.

Though, as has been seen, Nkrumah remained suspicious of the Chinese, it was never alleged that Chinese military personnel

[1] Scott-Thompson, *op. cit.*, p. 401.
[2] Interview with Michael Dei Arang.
[3] *Ibid.*
[4] N.C.N.A., 4 Nov. 1964.
[5] See above, p. 130.
[6] Scott-Thompson, *op. cit.*, p. 398.

contravened the protocol on military aid between the two countries either during this period or after the coup. Article 5 of that protocol stated that 'During their working period in Ghana, the Chinese experts should observe Ghana's laws and regulations, habits and customs, and shall not interfere in Ghana's internal affairs, nor ask for any privileges or special treatment.'[1] If other African states had reason to complain of subversion, Ghana had not.

4. Economic and Trade Relations

The period 1963–5 witnessed a Chinese economic and trade offensive in some African countries. In the first place, the intensification of the rivalry between China and the Soviet Union produced competitive offers of aid both to African states who asked for it and those who did not or who hesitated.[2] For the African states concerned, competitive offers of aid increased their political importance and gave them additional scope in their relations with the big powers. This was therefore a situation to be welcomed in so far as such aid did not distort their priorities of economic growth. For China, political and revolutionary interests seemed to dictate a greater commitment than would have been prudent for a newly recovered Chinese economy which had just succeeded in paying off its debt to the Soviet Union. Chinese economic involvement with African states, however, took place on two levels: bilateral trade relations, and economic and technical assistance.

(i) *Trade Relations*

Political considerations influenced Chinese trade relations less than it did her economic aid policy, although there were obvious examples of political considerations in trade matters. Nigeria, for instance, remained the third largest market for Chinese goods in Africa (after the U.A.R. and Morocco) though no diplomatic relations existed with Peking. China also continued to buy from South Africa and this brought some reaction from her African friends. In June 1963 the Ghanaian Embassy in China asked the Chinese Foreign Ministry to refute the B.B.C's allegations of orders being placed for South African grain. There was at first no reply

[1] *Nkrumah's Subversion*, Appendix B, p. 56. For text of the protocol, see below, p. 283.
[2] The Chinese, for instance, reported that an offer of aid to Malawi was rejected. So also was a negotiated $18 million to Kenya in 1964.

to this request.¹ On 15 July the N.C.N.A. issued a government statement:

> the Chinese Government has since July 1960 discontinued all its economic and trade ties with the South African colonial authorities. . . . The Chinese Government . . . solemnly declares that . . . [it] will in future continue to have no economic and trade ties, direct or indirect, with the South African colonial authorities. This stand of the Chinese Government is unswerving.²

This official denial was reiterated by Chen Yi during Ghana's Republic Day celebrations; he spoke as usual of the Chinese people's love for the Africans 'in their just struggle against the South African fascists'. Ghanaian officials, however, did not accept the denial of economic dealings with South Africa, stating that China 'is not unaware of the effective role which hypocrisy plays in international affairs'.³ The Chinese statement was, of course, incorrect as can be seen from the African trade figures. However, after March 1963 South Africa stopped publishing trade figures with China though this did not mean that trade had now been suspended. In fact, a year later (July 1964) the President of the Durban Chamber of Commerce, Mr Todd, revealed that China had trebled her trade with South Africa since 1963 and that the Soviet Union had also increased hers.⁴

The other attempt to disregard political considerations was with regard to trade with Cameroun. Even though supporting the U.P.C. guerrilla struggle China wanted to have trade relations and in September 1964 sent a trade and goodwill delegation to Cameroun. Of course the Camerounian officials did not mince words in their discussions and they sought to obtain Chinese withdrawal of aid from the U.P.C. The Chinese delegation explained that it did not control the U.P.C., as this was based in Accra. The talks were said to have 'proceeded in an atmosphere of great frankness and mutual understanding'.⁵ In fact Chinese involvement with the U.P.C. continued and trade relations with Cameroun did not materialise.⁶

As stated earlier,⁷ Chou En-lai's African tour also had economic repercussions, particularly in North Africa and above all in Morocco, which was China's second largest trading partner. China was inter-

---
¹ Scott-Thompson, *op. cit.*, p. 278. ² S.C.M.P. No. 3021, 18 July 1963.
³ Scott-Thompson, *op. cit.*, p. 279. ⁴ Johannesburg Radio, 14 July 1964.
⁵ S.C.M.P. No. 3308, 30 Sept. 1964. ⁶ See below, p. 173.
⁷ See above, p. 124.

ested in Morocco's cobalt, a strategic material, and Berliet lorries, while Morocco purchased green tea from China. Sino-Moroccan relations were questioned by the United States Government in February 1964 as the issue of strategic material to China was raised.[1] The U.S. Government wanted to stop Sino-Moroccan and Cuban-Moroccan trade relations or alternatively to cut off American aid to Morocco. This of course called into question the Moroccan policy of non-alignment, which would be affected by her acceptance of U.S. conditions. Recognising the delicate situation, the Moroccan Minister of Trade argued that

If we stop selling cobalt to the C.P.R. our economic relations with the C.P.R. would be out of balance – these relations are regarded of great importance to our country. The U.S.A. did not give serious consideration to Morocco's need for the tea which she imports from the C.P.R. On the other hand we may not be able to sell our cobalt to any other country than the C.P.R. The U.S.A. does not buy this material.[2]

Sino-Moroccan trade did not stop however. In fact, in 1964 exports to China were double those of 1963, while Chinese exports to Morocco had also nearly doubled. For Morocco to have backed down at that time would have been regarded as compromising her political independence.

In 1964 and 1965 Chinese exports to Africa rose steeply, to £23.31 million and to £39.76 million respectively, while imports also rose markedly to £20.85 million and £39.72 million respectively. Exports were to rise even higher in 1966. The Chinese were not averse to undercutting Western trade markets in African states. Here there were both political and economic aims. In 1964, there was a general shortage in the world sugar market, with the price soaring to £80 per ton. The Sudan was in great need of sugar, and China stepped in to sell the commodity at only £51 per ton, thus demonstrating to the Sudan that profit was not her main aim in trade relations. Thus she could achieve political gain, while paving the way for the sale of more Chinese goods in the Sudanese market.

As yet, Chinese trade with countries receiving economic and technical assistance was still unimportant compared with trade

---

[1] The United States, since the Korean war, has sought to discourage other states from selling strategic goods to China and there was nothing spectacular about the application of the policy to Morocco.
[2] Rabat Radio: in B.B.C. *S.W.B.* No. 1486, Part IV, 22 Feb. 1964.

with other African states.[1] Ghana was the only country with which appreciable trade was being conducted. This was because the states in receipt of aid were poorer and had less to sell: Chinese supplies were simply aid. (The U.A.R. was in a different category.)[2]

(ii) *Economic Aid and Technical Assistance*

The aid China offers to all friendly new emerging countries is based on socialist principles and the principle of respecting the sovereignty of the countries concerned. It never takes the form of the export of capital, direct investment and profit seeking. It consists of providing economic and technical assistance to the governments of these countries and helping these countries develop their own independent national economies.[3]

This was Chou En-lai's rendering in Ghana of China's philosophy of aid. The emphasis is on self-reliance and the development of an independent national economy. In Somalia, he elaborated on the philosophy and form of aid as follows.

In providing economic aid to other countries, the Chinese Government has always strictly abided by the following eight principles:

(1) The Chinese Government always bases itself on the principle of equality and mutual benefit in providing aid to other countries. It never regards such aid as a kind of unilateral alms but as something mutual and helpful to economic co-operation.
(2) In providing aid to other countries, the Chinese Government strictly respects the sovereignty and independence of the recipient countries, and never attaches any conditions or asks for privileges.
(3) China provides economic aid in the form of interest-free or low-interest loans and extends the time limit for the repayment when necessary so as to lighten the burden on the recipient countries as far as possible.
(4) In providing aid to other countries, the purpose of the Chinese Government is not to make the recipient countries dependent on China but to help them embark step by step on the road of self-reliance and independent economic development.
(5) The Chinese Government tries its best to help the recipient countries build projects which require less investment while yielding quicker results so that the recipient governments may increase their income and accumulate capital.
(6) The Chinese Government provides the best quality equipment and material of its own manufacture at international market prices. If the equipment and material provided by the Chinese Government are not up to the agreed specifications and quality, the Chinese Government undertakes to replace them.
(7) In giving any particular technical assistance, the Chinese Government will see to it that the personnel of the recipient country fully master such technique.

[1] Aid extended to Guinea, Mali, Congo (B), Tanzania, Somalia, C.A.R.
[2] U.A.R.-China trade in 1965 amounted to £29.2 million.
[3] *Afro-Asian Solidarity Against Imperialism*, p. 148.

(8) The experts and technical personnel dispatched by China to help in construction in the recipient countries will have the same standard of living as the experts and technical personnel of the recipient country. The Chinese experts and technical personnel are not allowed to make any special demands or enjoy any special amenities.

At present, the mutual aid and economic co-operation between Asian-African countries are still limited in scale. However, inasmuch as we share the same experience and are in similar positions and so best understand each other's needs, our mutual aid and economic co-operation are dependable, conformable to actual needs, equitable and of mutual benefit, and helpful to the independent development of various countries. . . .[1]

The only omission was the political influence China would obtain by offering economic aid to African states. Expressed in another way, the recipients would have greater consideration for Chinese views on international issues. The logic of the Chinese argument makes this inevitable. The continued domination and exploitation of the economies of the new states by neo-colonialism greatly hampered their manoeuvreability in the international arena. Their actions, instead of being genuinely progressive, must inevitably cater to the needs of imperialism. A reduction of imperialist influence would give the new states more independence but it would also improve Chinese relations with them. In spite of the claim that dependence on China would not arise, a relationship akin to that between China and Albania could hardly be described by any other word. So far, however, no such relationship had yet developed in Africa.

(a) *Sino-Somali Economic Relations*. Like that of all other aid-giving countries, Chinese aid to African countries was decisively influenced by political considerations. This was so in 1963 when the Somali Republic rejected British aid and announced plans to increase exports in order to earn foreign exchange. The Chinese Government signed a trade agreement with Somalia in May and invited the Prime Minister to visit China.[2] During his visit in August, China instantly made available £1.05 million to help balance the budget, and promised to offer £7 million repayable in seventeen years with seven years' grace.[3] The Chinese told the Somali Prime Minister: 'Although we have internal difficulties and are shut off from most parts of the world, we are prepared and willing to give you whatever

---
[1] *Ibid.* pp. 280 and 281.　　　　　　　　　[2] N.C.N.A., 15 May 1963.
[3] Mogadishu Radio: Prime Minister's Speech to National Assembly, 5 Sept. 1963.

is possible.'[1] They promised to establish whatever industrial or technical projects the Somalis decided upon. The Somali Prime Minister also discussed the possibility of Chinese military aid, details of which he did not wish to divulge. He told the National Assembly on 5 September: 'There are other aid programmes... although I regret that it is not possible for me to mention these.'[2] This was taken to mean that military aid by China would be forthcoming, and here, Russia, till then reluctant to grant Somalia's request for fear of offending Kenya, now jumped in to outbid China in economic aid pledged and to supply military hardware and equipment. In this competition Somalia was the winner.

In September 1964 the Somali Finance Minister, Abdulahi Said, went to Peking for talks. It was agreed that China would complete the construction of a highway in Somalia, set up a textile mill to produce fifteen varieties of textiles, and establish a state rice-growing farm which would end rice imports by 1976.[3] Work on these projects began in 1965 with the arrival of Chinese engineers and prospectors and rice-growing experts. A medical team was also sent. In February 1965, following a long drought in Somalia, China sent 1,200 tons of rice and 438 cases of medicines and medical equipment. All this aid was granted to reinforce Somalia's 'struggles to safeguard state sovereignty and consolidate national independence against control and interference by old and new colonialists'.[4]

(b) *Sino-Algerian Economic Relations.* On formally attaining independence in 1962, Algeria received some $1.8 million from China. (The Soviet Union and other Socialist countries also offered aid.) In 1963, Algeria was the only other African state besides Somalia to which China promised a loan. In October of that year, the Chinese Government agreed to grant a long-term interest-free loan of 250 million French francs ($50 million).[5] This was given in order 'to further the relations of friendship and co-operation

---

[1] Mogadishu Radio: Prime Minister's Speech to National Assembly, 5 Sept. 1963.
[2] *Ibid.* 5 Sept. 1963. On Chen Yi's assurance to Kenya that China would not give military aid to Somalia, see above p. 121–2.
[3] Mogadishu Radio, 11 Oct. 1964. See B.B.C. *S.W.B.* No. 1682, Part IV of 14 Oct. 1964.
[4] Chou's report on his African tour, 24 Apr. 1964, *op. cit.*
[5] N.C.N.A., 11 Oct. 1963.

between the two countries and to assist the Algerian Government and people in their efforts to develop their national economy'.[1]

Algeria had already established her credentials as a revolutionary state. She had embarked on a land reform programme, taken over almost 3 million hectares from former owners, and was one of the main suppliers of aid to African liberation movements. Earlier, in September 1963, Premier Ben Bella opened a Chinese exhibition in Algiers and expressed great appreciation for 'the just value of the experience of that country, that just as we had learned from its experience during our liberation struggle, we would likewise learn with firmness and foresight from it in the building of our country'.[2] In other words Algeria was ready to learn from China in solving the problems of economic development. China's offer of $50 million was the largest single offer made to date to an African country, though she was definitely under no illusions about the degree to which Algerian economic development would follow the Chinese model. The offer of $50 million was her counter-bid to Russia's offer of $100 million in September 1963. Moreover, when Ben Bella visited the Soviet Union in April–May 1964 Russia promised an additional $127.6 million loan. East European countries were also entering the scene.[3] Apart from this, the Algerian Government maintained strong economic ties with France, which both countries saw as indispensable to their interests. (In fact French aid to Algeria during the first three years of independence amounted to some $800 million.)[4]

During Chou's visit to Algeria in 1963 Chinese officials had discussions with the Algerians on the utilisation of the Chinese loan and on mutual trade. As in Morocco, China was interested in Berliet lorries and it was agreed that 400 of these would be shipped to China.[5] The first batch of 40 was sent in April 1965.[6] The building of trans-Saharan roads linking Mali and Algeria was also discussed, but they did not materialise.[7]

Before the coup d'etat in June 1965, the Chinese had donated a 13,000 ton freighter, the Shu Guang, to the Algerian National Navigation Company and four transport aircraft as gifts to the

[1] S.C.M.P. No. 3081, 16 Oct. 1963.
[2] *Ibid.* No. 3055, 9 Sept. 1963.
[3] See Ottaway, *op. cit.*, pp. 158 and 160.
[4] *Ibid.*, p. 150.
[5] Algiers Radio, 13 Apr. 1965.
[6] B.B.C. *S.W.B.* Weekly Supplement No. 311, 23 April 1965.
[7] *Far Eastern Economic Review*, Vol. XLIII, 6 Feb. 1964.

Algerian Government.[1] One thousand tons of school equipment were also given to the Algerian Ministry of Education, and Chinese equipment to the Algerian militia.[2] This latter was provided under a protocol signed in Algiers. Although Sino-Algerian militant solidarity was considerable in matters relating to liberation movements in Africa, it was difficult not to see the spate of gifts in June 1965 in the light of the Chinese effort to keep the Soviet Union out of the Second Afro-Asian Conference scheduled for that month. Apart from the exchanges on the abortive conference, the coup against Ben Bella did not affect Chinese aid programmes. In December a Chinese medical team of 35 arrived to replace an earlier one which had spent some one and a half years in Algeria; their diligence and simple living had been commended by the Algerians.[3] I will consider the fulfilment of the Chinese economic aid pledge to Algeria in the next chapter. By the end of 1965 however not much of the aid had been disbursed.

(c) *Sino-Congolese Brazzaville Economic Relations*. The popular revolution in Congo-Brazzaville which overthrew the Abbe Fulbert Youlou was not immediately followed by formal recognition of Peking. This came in February 1964 after General de Gaulle had given the lead. Since then close Sino-Congolese relations had developed in several directions.[4] In the first place the proximity of the country to the troubled Congo-Kinshasa in which China was helping to promote revolution, meant that she considered the development of close relations very important. A bridgehead in Brazzaville would allow revolutionaries from the other Congo to receive direct Chinese aid and could even facilitate the establishment of guerrilla training camps.[5] On the other hand, Congo-Brazzaville being a small and poor country (population less than one million), Chinese economic aid would be better appreciated and more visible than in the rich economies of Ghana or the U.A.R.

[1] The transport planes Boumédienne received just four days before he staged the coup. N.C.N.A., 15 June 1965.
[2] B.B.C. *S.W.B.* Weekly Supplement No. 319, 18 June 1965.
[3] The first team had left in Oct. 1964 after reportedly treating some 4,500 hospital cases and 60,000 out-patients. S.C.M.P. No. 3317, 14 Oct. 1964.
[4] Communist influence in the Congo (B) reached its zenith in December 1969 when the country was decreed to be the first Communist state in Africa governed by a Marxist-Leninist Congolese Labour Party.
[5] On the training of Congolese (K) by Chinese military personnel. See below, p. 175.

Congo-Brazzaville had depended all along on French subsidies and this dependence was not altered by the 1963 revolution. For the Congolese regime this was compatible with its growing relations with China, the Soviet Union and other Socialist states which had not been able to take the place of France.

In July 1964 a government delegation from Congo-Brazzaville visited China and signed an economic co-operation agreement.[1] This provided for an immediate disbursement by China of some $5.2 million to help balance the Congolese budget.[2] Another agreement, providing for a long-term interest-free loan of $20 million to be used in establishing consumer-goods industries was signed when President Alphonse Mazzamba-Debat visited Peking in September–October 1964. During his visit the two countries also signed a treaty of friendship on similar lines to the Guinea and Ghana treaties.[3] This came into effect on 9 January 1965 and was to last for ten years with automatic renewal, unless one party indicated within a year of the date of expiry, its intention to terminate it.[4]

In November the Congolese Prime Minister indicated the role Chinese aid was already playing: 'We will continue to rely, for a long time to come, on the bilateral aid of all the countries of the world, particularly France, whose cultural and technical assistance we appreciate and the Chinese People's Republic, whose material aid has already proved *as effective.*'[5]

In 1965 a protocol to the economic co-operation agreement was signed, whereby China would set up a textile mill capable of producing some 3½ million metres of fabric each year and employing about 2,000 Congolese. Work on the project would begin in 1966.[6] Here again could be seen the Chinese direction of aid to labour-intensive rather than capital-intensive projects. In the first place, China's lack of heavy capital precluded the export of such sophisticated machinery to African states, and if it were exported Chinese personnel would need to stay a long time to man such complexes, when they were also needed at home. On the other hand this practice could be said to help the recipient country by utilising

[1] N.C.N.A., 13 July 1964.   [2] Brazzaville Radio, 13 Oct. 1964.
[3] See Table on Economic Aid and N.C.N.A., 2 Oct 1964.
[4] N.C.N.A., 9 Jan. 1965.
[5] Brazzaville Radio in B.B.C. *S.W.B.* Part IV, No. 1703, 7 Nov. 1964.
[6] Brazzaville Radio, 13 Sept. 1965.

labour as its most abundant factor of production. By helping to reduce unemployment China also helped to reduce that volatile section of the urban population which had played an important role in overthrowing Fulbert Youlou.[1] She thus became interested in promoting the stability of a friendly government when she would otherwise have wished to help generate unrest and revolution.

(*d*) *Sino-Mali and Sino-Guinean Economic Relations.* I have already discussed the promise of loans of $26 million to Guinea in 1960 and $19.6 million to Mali in 1961.[2] In the period under consideration, the implementation of the agreements went ahead though no new loans were announced for either country. Chinese agricultural experts were working in Guinea on rice cultivation and other crops, and technical experts worked on the construction of a cigarette and match factory, which was expected to make Guinea self-sufficient in both items when it was completed in 1964.[3] In July 1964 the Chinese began to construct a hydro-electric station some 400 kilometres north-east of Conakry. It was a difficult undertaking.[4] China also seemed to appreciate the difficulties Guinea faced because of her lack of foreign exchange. As part of the $26 million promised in 1960, $7 million in convertible currency was made available during this period. If, as was reported, the Guinean Government did not use this amount wisely, the Chinese could hardly be held responsible.[5]

During Chou En-lai's visit to Guinea in January 1964 he was able to remark that 'the relations of friendship and co-operation between our two countries have steadily developed, and economic and cultural exchanges have daily increased',[6] and he did not forget to praise Guinea's emphasis on self-reliance. Sekou Touré for his part, expressed appreciation of Chinese experience in economic development and noted that the people of Guinea were mobilising their resources in the same way and relying on themselves. 'If it is true that revolution can be neither imported nor exported, it is just as true that revolutions, born in similar historic conditions, based on the same principles, directed towards similar goals,

[1] On the performance of the Chinese personnel and utilisation of the pledged aid see below p. 222.
[2] See above, p. 90.   [3] N.C.N.A., 27 Sept. 1963.
[4] N.C.N.A., 31 Jan. 1967.   [5] See M. Goldman, *Soviet Foreign Aid*, 1967, p. 173.
[6] *Afro-Asian Solidarity*, p. 192.

necessarily partake of the same nature, are under the same banner and in one and the same historical current, determining the nature of universal evolution. It is through joining their awakened material and human forces that the Solidarity, uniting the P.R.C. and the Republic of Guinea is established, independently of the feelings of deep and true friendship which bring together the peoples of China and of Guinea within the framework of Afro-Asian relations.'[1] He thanked Chou En-lai for 'the important and disinterested help which your Party and Government have given the Republic of Guinea in its fight of consolidation of our independence and the rapid development of our economy'.[2] Again, the relative poverty of Guinea gave the Chinese economic and technical contribution a greater impact than would have been the case in a richer economy.

In Mali, Chinese agricultural experts were working on rice-growing projects and sugar-cane plantations. A sugar refinery, which was being built with Chinese aid and by Chinese technicians, was expected to come into operation at the end of 1966.[3] Located in the Segou region, it would be capable, at full capacity, of producing thirty tons of sugar a day.[4] The Mali Government noted the differences of approach between China and 'other' countries in the carrying out of aid projects. While other countries limited their activity to supplying the equipment with which Mali was supposed to embark on economic development, China undertook to build factories herself and only handed them over when completed.[5] This ensured that lack of local personnel did not hamper construction, and removed the opportunities for pilfering and wasting of the aid provided by the foreign country – many governments suffered greatly from their officers indulging in this practice. At the same time, however, it meant that Chinese equipment would be used in those projects and this constituted an indirect condition of the loan as well as serving as a form of export promotion for China.

By the time Chou En-lai visited Mali in January 1964, much of the Chinese aid pledged was already being implemented, and he was able to hear President Modibo Keita pay

warm homage to the P.R.C. for the low cost of its technical assistance, for the

[1] *Ibid.*, p. 212. [2] *Ibid.*
[3] N.C.N.A., 13 Apr. 1964. [4] *Ibid.*
[5] Mali Minister of Development, Seydou Kouyate on Sino-Mali Protocol on Economic Co-operation, N.C.N.A., 30 Dec. 1963.

readiness of its technicians to adapt themselves to the life of our people, for the speed and competence with which the projects undertaken by People's China are carried out one by one, and all these things are done without the slightest intention of interfering in our internal affairs.[1]

Chou was, however, aware that the aid China was providing was 'very limited'. At a mass rally of welcome at Koulikovo, he offered to change any Chinese equipment or machinery that might malfunction.[2] In a joint communiqué at the end of the visit, the two sides stated that they

exchanged views extensively on the experiences acquired by the two countries in national construction and the prospects for the economic development of the African and Asian countries ... considering that ... to consolidate national independence, the young countries must, first and foremost, count on their own strength, rely on their own people and fully tap their own natural resources, while foreign aid is only an auxiliary means.[3]

Modibo Keita accepted an invitation to visit China. He set off in September 1964, heading a delegation of fifty-one, in an extended tour of the Far East including North Korea and North Vietnam as well as China herself. During his visit to China a Sino-Mali treaty of friendship was signed on 3 November.[4] He and his Chinese hosts were also able to note with 'pleasure that the situation is most favourable for revolution *throughout* the continent of Africa'.[5] The treaty of friendship similar to that with Congo-Brazzaville came into effect on 20 April 1965.[6] The economic negotiations begun during Keita's visit bore fruit in the following year. In September 1965, three agreements were signed in Bamako, Mali: China would help to construct a radio transmitter, a cinema and a hotel, bearing three-quarters of the cost herself.[7] Chinese technicians would instruct Malian counterparts in how to handle the projects.[8] Thus on the economic front the period ended with increasing Chinese involvement in Mali's developmental efforts.

(e) *China and the U.A.R.* The U.A.R., the first African state to recognise China in 1956, has been China's largest trading partner in

[1] *Afro-Asian Solidarity*, p. 179.
[2] N.C.N.A. 17 Jan. 1964. See also *Afro-Asian Solidarity*, p. 172.
[3] N.C.N.A., 21 Jan. 1964. [4] S.C.M.P. No. 3333, 6 Nov. 1964.
[5] S.C.M.P. No. 3334, 8 Nov. 1964. [6] N.C.N.A., 20 Apr. 1965.
[7] The Mali Minister of Information and Tourism announced the new agreements. Bamako Radio, 1 Sept. 1965.
[8] Brazzaville Radio, 2 Sept. 1965.

1963–5 Commitments, Consolidation, Reflection 161

Africa. Apart from the $4.7 million hard-currency grant to Egypt at the time of the Suez crisis, China did not extend any loan to her. The granting of such a loan by Khrushchev had, in fact been one of the issues in dispute between him and China at that time.[1] When Chou En-lai visited the U.A.R. in 1964 he was able to see the 'relatively' advanced state of the Egyptian economy as well as the fruits of Soviet economic aid. He was no doubt touched by Nasser's mention of the Aswan High Dam as one of the projects he should visit in Egypt, and the message sank in.[2]

Later in the year Chinese officials began to negotiate about possible aid. In December the U.A.R. Deputy Premier for Industry, Dr Aziz Sidqi, announced the signing of an economic and technical co-operation agreement.[3] China would help to implement Egypt's Second Five Year Plan by supplying industrial equipment and machinery worth $80 million. This would be delivered between 1965 and 1968. Repayment would be spread over ten years from 1972, and would bear no interest.[4]

If this was export promotion on China's part, the terms were very generous considering the already advanced state of the Egyptian economy compared with other African States. It was the greatest single commitment in Africa to date, but it had to be big if it was to match the impact Soviet aid was already having in Egypt. In fact it was only to be surpassed by the sum involved in the Tan-Zam railway project. President Nasser had, however, shown himself to be a master of practical non-alignment, with an uncanny ability to make use of economic aid from both East and West. Thus the Chinese had no illusions as to the amount of influence over the Egyptian economy their aid would bring. Why therefore did China assume a commitment which departed from her practice in other African States. She had tended to confine her aid to those projects which were labour- rather than capital-intensive, since unemployed and underemployed labour had always been the more available resource. Moreover, there was a limit to what she herself could export in terms of industrial machinery and equipment – these items were being imported. Critics were therefore likely to interpret China's promise in the context of Sino-Soviet competition pre-

---

[1] See above, p. 23.
[3] Cairo Radio, 28 Dec. 1964.
[2] *Afro-Asian Solidarity*, p. 43.
[4] *Al-Ahram* of 31 Dec. 1964.

ceding the second Bandung and to cast doubts on her ability to fulfil it.

(*f*) *Dahomey, Central African Republic and China.* In October 1964, after the visit of a Chinese trade and goodwill delegation to the C.A.R., diplomatic relations were established between the two countries.[1] In November Dahomey formally recognised Peking.[2] Both moves were in turn followed by the dispatch of Chinese agronomists to help in rice cultivation. In 1965 the Central African Republic received a loan of $4 million, half of it in the form of supplies and the other half in foreign currency.[3] The C.A.R. President David Dacko was also interested in other forms of aid, in particular Chinese help in setting up a militia. No decision about this was announced, although in 1965 Chinese weapons were in fact brought into the country and kept in the State House.[4] This was, however, being done by China at the request of a lawfully constituted government and could not be described as subversion. Chinese influence increased in this poor African state, and remained until the coup d'etat which toppled the President in January 1966.[5] The same fate was to befall Chinese prospects in Dahomey, where a coup in the same month resulted in the severance of diplomatic ties and expulsion of Chinese agronomists.[6] In 1965, both countries voted for the admission of Peking to the United Nations. They were also in favour of the indefinite postponement of the second Afro-Asian Conference in Algiers in accordance with the Chinese argument.

(*g*) *Sino-Kenyan Economic Relations.* I have already mentioned the attendance of Chen Yi, the Chinese Foreign Minister, at the Kenyan independence celebrations in December 1963;[7] and that Kenyans were among the African students in China. The Chinese attached importance to Kenya and had a most influential supporter in the person of Oginga Odinga, who became Home Minister and later Vice President. A visit to Kenya had been planned during Chou's tour of Africa in 1963–4, but this had to be cancelled after the

[1] S.C.M.P. No. 3313, 7 Oct. 1964.   [2] N.C.N.A., 12 Nov. 1964.
[3] Alex Blake, 'Peking's African Adventures', *Current Scene*, Vol. 15, 15 Sept. 1967.
[4] B.B.C. *S.W.B.* Part IV, No. 2069, 24 Jan. 1966.   [5] See p. 185.
[6] See p. 184.   [7] See above, p. 116.

mutiny in East Africa in January. Having consistently supported Kenya's independence struggles the Chinese were eager to increase the goodwill which that support had generated for them.

In May 1964, in a move aimed at gaining political capital, China made an immediate cash grant of $2.8 million to help subsidise the budget.[1] This naturally made a good impression. In June a long-term economic agreement was concluded in Peking, under which China would provide, over five years, complete sets of equipment and individual machines worth $18 million. These would be accompanied by Chinese technicians who would service the machines and train Kenyan personnel in handling the equipment.[2] Repayment of the loan, without interest, in goods and convertible currency would start in 1975.[3] This agreement was similar to those China had made with Mali, Guinea and Ghana. Up to the end of 1965, however, no disbursement had yet been made to meet the promised aid. This was mainly due to the suspicion which Chinese activities aroused in Kenya.

Contrary to frequent Chinese declarations, China was in fact interfering in the internal affairs of Kenya and in so doing backed the wrong man. Kenyan politics revolved around the personalities of Kenyatta, Oginga Odinga and Tom Mboya. Although it was true that Oginga was receiving financial support from the Communists, he had his own political ambition, which was to be seen as Kenyatta's right-hand man and successor. The politics of Kenya in this period and the involvement of the Chinese have been well treated elsewhere and will not be retold here.[4] But in backing Oginga Odinga, China burnt her fingers in a fire which also destroyed Soviet prestige and influence. In his bid for power, Oginga had arranged for military training in China and Bulgaria for more than a hundred Kenyan students. This activity was known to the Kenyan security police who were following his moves.[5] Moreover, Chinese and Soviet funds were still being made available to Oginga after Kenya's independence, and this was disliked by Kenyatta, who also called for a stop to American funds being paid to Tom

---

[1] *Current Scene*, Vol. 15, 15 Sept. 1967.   [2] *Ibid*.   [3] *Ibid*.
[4] See W. Attwood, *The Reds and the Blacks: a Personal Adventure*, 1967. Attwood was the former United States Ambassador to Guinea and Kenya in the Kennedy and Johnson Administrations.
[5] Attwood, *op. cit.*, p. 241.

Mboya.[1] Unfortunately for China, Oginga's supporters within the ruling Kenya African National Union (K.A.N.U.) were outmanoeuvred by Tom Mboya and his men. In the event, the acceptance of Chinese technicians in the country became impossible. China's hopes of gaining influence were thus dashed, but only because she deliberately interfered in Kenyan politics and aroused suspicion of her long-term objectives. Chou En-lai's declaration in Tanzania in June 1965 that Africa was ripe for revolution[2] cost the Chinese dear, especially in a situation where their activities and intentions were already suspect. Revolution against whom? was the question asked by the elite, who could hardly be expected to cherish the prospect of being overthrown. Chou was pointedly not invited to visit Kenya.

On 5 June 1965, while Chou was still in Tanzania, Kenyatta delivered a speech which was in effect a coup de grâce to any hopes the Chinese might have of increasing their influence. Obviously referring to Oginga's claim that communism meant food for the people, Kenyatta declared

It is naive to think that there is no danger of imperialism from the East. In world power politics the East has as much designs upon us as the West and would like us to serve their own interests.

This is why we reject Communism. It is in fact the reason why we have chosen for ourselves the policy of non-alignment and African Socialism. To us Communism is as bad as imperialism.[3]

On 22 July, following investigation into his activities, a Chinese N.C.N.A. correspondent was expelled from Kenya and given twenty-four hours to leave the country.[4] The Chinese protested at the dismissal but they could not genuinely claim to be unaware of his activities in connection with Odinga.

Although diplomatic relations between the two countries were maintained, there was no longer any hope of generating goodwill by supplying Chinese equipment and having Chinese experts working in Kenya.[5] Each government is surely the judge of what is advantageous or inimical to national interest, and Kenyatta's

[1] *Ibid*. The Chinese Embassy in Dar Es Salaam was stated to have secretly made funds available to Oginga to help in his bid for power within K.A.N.U. This is corroborated by interview with X.
[2] This was only a repetition of his 1964 statement.
[3] Full text in Attwood, *op. cit.*, p. 252.   [4] N.C.N.A., 4 Aug. 1965.
[5] On further developments see below p. 188.

1963–5 Commitments, Consolidation, Reflection

action in keeping a close watch on Chinese and Soviet activities was in accordance with that legitimate duty. This duty is increasingly necessary in a world where great-power diplomacy has become little more than competitive interference in the internal affairs of other states.

5. People's Organisations

Beginning with the close of 1961, Chinese representatives in international democratic organisations have been openly imposing their erroneous views. . . . They opposed participation of representatives of the Afro-Asian Solidarity Committees of the European Socialist countries in the third Afro-Asian People's Solidarity Conference in Moshi. The leader of the Chinese delegation told the Soviet representatives that 'whites have no business here'. At the journalists' conference in Djakarta, the Chinese representatives followed a line designed to deprive Soviet journalists full-fledged delegate status on the plea that the Soviet Union . . . is not an Asian country.[1]

In the field of propaganda and agitation, Marxist-Leninists have always resorted to the use of 'front' organisations in their struggle against imperialism. In 1963–5, however, the main energy and attention of such organisations seemed to have been dissipated by the Sino-Soviet conflict and the struggle to control their own organisations. This struggle was extended to the activities of the A.A.P.S.O. and its affiliates in such a way as to distort the original aims of that body.

I have already mentioned the second A.A.P.S. conference which took place in Guinea in April 1960.[2] The third was held in Moshi, Tanganyika from 4 to 11 February 1963. (It will be recalled that it was during this conference that Julius Nyerere uttered his warning about a second scramble for Africa which included the Communist powers.)[3] The conference took place against a background of increasing Sino-Soviet rivalry and began with a tactical success for the Chinese. The heads of delegations, meeting on 3 April, agreed on an agenda which conformed with the Chinese view. The first item to be discussed was the 'struggle against imperialism and colonialism and for national liberation'. 'World peace' was to come after that, and even then it was to include 'the struggle against

---

[1] Open letter of the Central Committee of the C.P.S.U. to all Party Organisations, to all Communists of the Soviet Union. 14 July 1963. *The Polemics on the General Line of the International Communist Movement*, Peking, 1965, p. 537.
[2] See above, p. 94.   [3] See above, p. 135.

foreign bases and aggressive blocs'.[1] This was in opposition to the Soviet view which gave priority to the struggle for 'disarmament and world peace', anti-colonialism coming later. This divergence of views was carried into the conference itself, and great pressure was applied on the Chairman.[2] The issue was complicated by the Sino-Indian and Kenyan-Somali border disputes. On the second day of the conference, the Tanganyika Minister for National Culture and Youth told the delegates frankly to get down to business; 'We have heard much abuse and many slogans, but the question is what can we do – I repeat, do – for our brothers not yet free.'[3] His appeal, however, went unheeded and at one point the Indian delegation walked out, although its leader, Chaman Lal, returned later to accept a watered-down recommendation concerning the non-aligned states' efforts to settle the Sino-Indian conflict. Behind the scenes, great pressure was brought to bear on the Chairman by the Chinese and Soviet delegates, who absolutely refused to compromise.[4] They were reminded that Africa's interest lay in the liberation of the remaining colonial territories and not in taking sides in the Sino-Soviet conflict. At this stage the Chinese threatened to walk out if they did not have their way.[5] They did not need to do this, however, since the majority of the delegates supported them and sympathised with the view that colonialism was the main enemy. In lobbying for support the Chinese made use of the race issue in appealing to the Afro-Asian delegates and were to a great extent successful – hence the bitterness expressed in the Soviet open letter.[6]

Although most of the sessions were held behind closed doors, journalists attending the conference protested against the favouritism shown to Chinese journalists who forced their way into those sessions. This was one reason why they found it easier to lobby support. For the chairman of the conference it was the 'most difficult and hellish'[7] assembly he had ever chaired; it was like being between the devil and the deep blue sea.

[1] B.B.C. *S.W.B.* Part IV, No. 1167, 5 Feb. 1963.
[2] Extended discussion with the chairman of the third A.A.P.S. Conference.
[3] Dar Es Salaam Radio, 6 Feb. 1963.
[4] Interview with chairman of the Conference. [5] *Ibid.*
[6] This Soviet allegation is confirmed by a participant and by the writer's personal experience.
[7] Discussion with chairman of the Conference.

For the Chinese, however, the conference was a great success. It has 'urged the use of force to meet force and called on the Afro-Asian peoples to give warm support for the oppressed nations' armed struggle'. This was a frontal blow at the revisionists who persistently advocated that the people should not fight, but should wait for the bestowal of independence by imperialism.[1] It was made use of to show that the Chinese view held sway among the struggling masses of the world – an additional reason why China's success was galling to the Soviet Union. This was hardly any exhibition of Afro-Asian solidarity.

In April, at the Afro-Asian Journalists' Conference in Djakarta, Indonesia, another blow was dealt to Soviet prestige in the front organisations. Before the conference began, huge banners saying 'We Love Peace but We Love Freedom More', and showing Asians, Africans and Latin Americans struggling against U.S. imperialism had been put up.[2] This made clear to the arriving Soviet delegates that there would be no place for them at such a conference. The Soviet delegates were not in fact recognised as full and equal members and they naturally criticised the 'undemocratic' methods of the conference's chairman.[3] This criticism was also voiced by the leader of the South West African delegation, whose travelling expenses incidentally had been met by the Soviet Union, when he reached Mongolia.

In Moscow two months later the Chinese were pointedly isolated during the World Congress of Women. The Chinese chief delegate was attacked by women delegates from India and Eastern Europe, and 'those other organisations controlled by Moscow'.[4] According to the C.P.S.U. letter partly quoted above, only China and Albania, out of the 110 delegations present, voted against the Congress's 'Appeal to Women of all Countries'.[5] Clashes in the front organisations continued, and the Soviet Union made particular use of the nuclear test ban treaty both at the August Hiroshima meeting of the world conference on hydrogen bombs (which refused to endorse the treaty), and at the A.A.P.S.O. Executive meeting in Nicosia

[1] N.C.N.A., 8 Mar. 1963. Liu Ning-yi addressing Peking Rally to celebrate the success of the conference.
[2] B.B.C. *S.W.B.* Part III, No. 1261, 29 May 1963.   [3] *Ibid.*
[4] N.C.N.A., 14 July 1963, reporting on the statements by women leaders from Zanzibar, Comoro Islands, Brazil and Mozambique.
[5] C.P.S.U. Central Committee letter of 14 July 1963.

in September 1963 (which endorsed the treaty despite Chinese objections),[1] and the World Peace Council which met in Warsaw in November.[2] Throughout 1964 clashes continued, thus dividing the ranks of the Afro-Asians. Generally, African delegates resented Chinese and Russian attempts to force them to take one or other side in these international conferences. It was a wasteful dissipation of energy at a time when all efforts should have been directed towards securing freedom for the remaining colonial peoples.

Because of African objections to Soviet and Chinese tactics, the A.A.P.S.O. permanent secretariat decided that ideological quarrels should be kept out of future meetings. The fourth A.A.P.S. conference was held from 9 to 16 May 1965, at the Winneba Ideological Institute in Ghana. Before it began Accra Radio stated that its theme was to be resistance by the peoples of Africa, Asia and Latin America and all progressive forces to imperialism, colonialism and neo-colonialism.[3] In spite of Ghanaian efforts, the atmosphere was poisoned two days before the conference opened by a Soviet exhibition of literature in the conference hall. This depicted the divisive activities of Chinese leaders. The Chinese persuaded some Ghanaian officials to close the exhibition on the evening of 7 May, but it re-opened the following morning with even more pungent accusations against China.[4] Messages to the conference came from many leaders, including Brezhnev, who had now replaced the deposed Khrushchev, and Chou En-lai.

In his opening address to the conference's 400 delegates, Nkrumah stressed that the struggle was against the colonialist system and was not racist. He then referred to the success of the non-aligned conference to show that the oppressed peoples had friends in Europe and America.[5] He was opposed to the use of the racial solidarity issue by the Chinese, since it was quite conceivable that the Soviet Union might withdraw material support from those liberation movements she was still, even if reluctantly, supporting.[6] Despite attempts to prevent virulent polemics breaking out, thus

[1] It will be recalled that Nkrumah sent a message to the conference calling for Sino-Soviet reconciliation.
[2] The W.P.C. was never out of Soviet control.
[3] B.B.C. *S.W.B.* Part IV, No. 1855, 11 May 1965.
[4] N.C.N.A., 9 May 1965.   [5] Accra Radio, 9 May 1965.
[6] Nkrumah was disquieted by Chinese tactics at the conference – see Scott-Thompson, *op. cit.*, p. 398.

making the American delegations more independent, the Indonesian delegates attacked the Malaysian delegates and the Chinese delegation was said to have attacked Soviet and Yugoslav views. The conflict however was not as virulent as at Moshi. The general political resolution of the conference stated that 'It is the legitimate right of the Afro-Asian peoples to answer imperialist violence by revolutionary violence in their struggle for national liberation and for safeguarding national independence.'[1] Even though this agreed with Chinese formulations during the period, Moscow Radio was nevertheless able to say that on the whole the conference was a success for the unity of nations. It was decided to hold the next conference in China; this however was to lead to a formal split in the organisation.[2]

6. Revolutionary Situations and Activities

The African people who have suffered for centuries from endless enslavement, oppression, plunder and humiliation have stood up today to speak for themselves and become independent. This is a great cataclysmic event in the second half of the 20th century. *That is why we say that an excellent revolutionary situation exists in Africa*.... The main content of what we refer to as the revolutionary situation in Africa is that the African peoples are demanding complete destruction of *colonial rule* and thorough elimination of the colonial forces.... *The people of many African countries that have won independence are pushing the revolution forward*, with the aim of carrying through the national democratic revolution and building up their countries.[3]

Thus said Premier Chou En-lai at the end of his famous tour of ten African states in 1964. It is obvious that he was referring to the whole continent when he spoke of the excellent situation for revolutionary activities. What was conveniently omitted in the wide publicity given to the statement in the world press was that Chou was *not* advocating the violent overthrow of the African states *friendly* to China. This is clear from the report on his tour in which he said that 'Leaders of many new emerging African states indicated that they would continue to push to revolution forward',[4] and by what he described as the features of the anti-imperialist national revolution in Africa. This included Egyptian nationalisation of the

---

[1] S.C.M.P. No. 3463, 24 May 1965. [2] See below, p. 230.
[3] Chou's Press Conference in Somalia, 3 Feb. 1964. N.C.N.A., 5 Feb. 1964.
[4] Speech on 25 Apr. 1964 to the joint session of the State Council and the Standing Committee of the N.P.C.

Suez Canal; Algerian expropriation of farmland 'occupied by the colonialists'; Tunisia's recovery of the French military base at Bizerta; the dismantling of U.S. military bases in Morocco; Malian and Guinean nationalisation of foreign companies, and such acts by African governments as directly or indirectly hurt the Western powers.[1]

These activities could not of course be attributed to Chinese influence, though they could rightly be described as setbacks for Western interests. But there are also other factors in a revolutionary situation – national liberation, wars and subversion of 'the reactionary lackeys of imperialism'. I will now turn to this latter feature.

Between 1963 and 1965 revolutionary activities continued in Angola, Cameroun, Congo Kinshasa, Portuguese Guinea and spread to Mozambique, and Zanzibar. I would not suggest that all these activities had Chinese support and financial help. This would give undue credit to China's obviously limited ability to foment and sustain revolution. However, it is fair to point out that in the shaky and unstable state of socio-political relations in Africa relatively few resources were needed to cause great damage to the regimes concerned. Other militant African states were particularly interested in the liberation wars going on in the Portuguese territories, and China capitalised on this interest.

In January 1963 Ben Bella announced, for instance, that Algeria had sent arms to Angola and would soon send a military mission; freedom fighters were also receiving training in Algeria.[2] By the end of that year, the Chinese N.C.N.A. correspondent in Algiers reported that Algeria had trained over 1,000 military personnel from the colonial territories in Africa.[3] Algeria allowed the two liberation movements in Angola to open offices in Algiers and the personnel of Holden Roberto's group made contacts with the Chinese embassy.[4] These contacts bore fruit later in the year (1963)

[1] *Ibid.* 'Ko-ming', the Chinese word for revolution, means literally a change of fate. When the Chinese refer to a revolutionary upsurge in Socialist education or in China's construction they obviously do not mean an armed struggle. In this sense the use is nearer to the English expression of industrial or scientific revolution or computer revolution. But the Chinese do use the same word to apply to armed struggle and violent overthrow of what they describe as reactionary regimes, and hence there is a confusion of meanings when it is used in reference to Africa. In fact both meanings are applicable to Africa.
[2] Algiers Radio, 18 Jan. 1963.   [3] N.C.N.A., 30 Dec. 1963.
[4] Holden Roberto's U.P.A. (Popular Union of Angola) had initially turned to the United

when Roberto met Chen Yi, who was attending the Kenya independence celebrations in Nairobi.[1] Chen Yi offered to supply military aid to the Angolan nationalists and this was accepted and implemented. Subsequently Angolan nationalist fighters went to China for advanced training while others were trained in Ghana by Chinese instructors.[2] Factions, however, did exist in the liberation movement in Angola; this pattern was repeated in other colonial territories and the division proved difficult for the O.A.U. to heal.[3]

In May 1963 the various groupings of African states came together in Addis Ababa to establish the O.A.U. (Organisation of African Unity). As far as China was concerned the most important achievement of the summit conference was the establishment of a Liberation Committee. This showed the determination of the independent states to free the remaining colonial territories. Replying to a letter from Sekou Touré informing him of the O.A.U's decision and calling for Chinese support, the Chinese Head of State Liu Shao-chi stated that China considered it her bounden duty to support the just struggles of the Africans.[4] He did not, however, state that such aid would only be channelled through the O.A.U. Liberation Committee at Dar Es Salaam. The O.A.U. Liberation Committee was particularly concerned with the unity of the various nationalist parties in the colonial territories and with the co-ordination of their activities. Its aim was to increase the efficacy of the movements, to encourage African unity, and to remove the external influences which might result from dependence on Communist countries for aid and which exacerbated western Opposition to nationalist struggles.

As Sino-Soviet rivalry had by now spread to gain control of the African Liberation movements this venture received no cooperation from the Communist states. The Chinese and Russians even brought pressure to bear on the Liberation Committee.[5] At this stage they were advised to keep their ideological dispute out of the liberation struggles. What was needed most was unity among

States and enjoyed considerable American sympathy. His government in exile, G.R.A.E., did not receive the O.A.U. Liberation Committee's recognition in 1963 and he thus turned to China for aid. As China was interested in continued fighting the aid was forthcoming.
[1] *New York Times*, 5 Feb. 1964.   [2] *Nkrumah's Subversion, op. cit.*
[3] See below, p. 173.   [4] N.C.N.A., 19 July 1963. Liu's letter of 10 July 1963.
[5] Interview with member of Liberation Committee.

the African nationalists and their energy and efforts should not be dissipated. Sino-Soviet rivalry should be kept to the independent states where it could do less harm; its extension to the liberation struggles was inimical to the very success of those struggles. The Chinese in particular were reminded that in their own revolutionary war against Japan, all movements united to face the common aggressor.[1] Sino-Soviet rivalry did not subside with such appeals but the damage it had caused so far was not great.

The Chinese did achieve major successes in Tanzania, Ghana and Congo-Brazzaville. President Nyerere gave the Chinese permission to train freedom fighters on Tanzanian soil. This meant increased Chinese influence in the movements as well as increased adoption of Chinese tactics of guerrilla warfare.[2] The freedom fighters were also supplied with Chinese arms and weapons free of charge. Obviously the struggle in Mozambique received considerable support from Africans and from progressive quarters in the West, and the leaders tried to maintain a 'non-aligned' stand, but as China was providing aid their influence could not be negligible. Until the end of 1962 no Mozambique delegation visited China, but in 1963 alone five delegations, including one headed by Eduardo Mondlane,[3] did so. In 1964, the armed struggle in Mozambique began, thus opening another front against the Portuguese in Africa.

I have already referred to the Sino-Ghanaian military agreement under which Chinese arms experts trained Africans in the strategy and tactics of guerrilla warfare.[4] Those trained in Ghana included nationalists from the Portuguese territories as well as from independent states such as Cameroun, Congo-Kinshasa, Ivory Coast and Niger.[5] The presence of the Chinese experts in Ghana was kept secret and so were their activities. It was intended that as far as possible revolutionary activities should appear to be spontaneous; this effect would be spoiled by the disclosure of outside help. Before their entry into Ghana late in 1964, the Chinese had continued to help the Cameroun U.P.C. based in Accra. Their aid had partly been channelled through the Afro-Asian Solidarity Fund and

[1] Discussion with X.
[2] Training was carried on in the Southern region of the country and naturally Chinese weapons were used. Interview with member of Cabinet.
[3] Mondlane was a former professor in America who left his job to take over active leadership of the Mozambique Liberation Front (FRELIMO).
[4] See above, p. 147.   [5] *Nkrumah's Subversion in Africa, op. cit.*

partly had consisted of the training of Camerounians in guerrilla tactics in China.

The Camerounian Government was aware of this. In July 1963 President Ahidjo said that China was one of the states 'supporting terrorism in Cameroun. We have proof, for Cameroun terrorists are in Communist China. As long as that situation exists, we shall vote against Communist China's admission to the U.N.'[1] But the Cameroun Government could do nothing except continue to fight the guerrillas. The split which occurred in the U.P.C. movement in Accra later in 1964 did not stop the fighting in Cameroun, though the split did involve Chinese support for some elements within the movement.[2] Although the Cameroun Government also tried to give little publicity to the guerrilla activities in the country in 1965, the President had to say that China was still interfering in Cameroun's internal affairs.[3] Chinese support for the fighting in Cameroun long after independence shows how far she would go in helping to overthrow governments considered reactionary. Unlike the Congolese Nationalists the U.P.C. did not enjoy popular support in African circles, and consequently Chinese activity could only be described as subversion. It could not be said that she was simply giving unselfish aid to revolutionaries in Africa, as the same view was not taken of other cases in Africa.

In the Sudan the S.A.N.U. (Sudan African National Union) had been waging war against the central government since 1955.[4] The Southern Sudanese were struggling for autonomy and independence, and these efforts might have been described by China as a people's war meriting support. The Sudanese Government, however, had diplomatic relations with China and both countries were on friendly terms. Chinese support for the war would have had implications for Chinese interests in other parts of Africa. Her position in Egypt, Algeria, Morocco and the Arab world would in general have been jeopardised. Even if China had wanted to support the guerrilla fighters in the south, a rational calculation of the interests involved

[1] B.B.C. *S.W.B.* Part IV, No. 1292. 5 July 1963.
[2] In Sept. 1964 the U.P.C. Revolutionary Committee declared in Accra that China had interfered in the internal affairs of the movement by supporting 'opportunist' elements which opposed the leadership.
[3] Cameroun Radio, 14 Sept. 1965.
[4] The African Southern Sudanese were fighting against the Arab north. I had a discussion with a member of S.A.N.U. in Dar Es Salaam.

in other areas would have weighed against such support, especially as there was no guarantee of success for the fighters. That the Sudanese Government supported the Congo nationalists fighting against Tshombe in 1964 was perhaps also important as it accorded with China's own policy.[1] When as a result of Sudanese support, the Congo threatened to help the Southern Sudanese, the Chinese Government expressed its great concern. It hoped that the problem would be solved within the framework of Sudanese unity and announced *its readiness to help the Sudan* against any foreign intervention aiming at undermining this.[2]

Understandably the Chinese also failed to pay attention to the Tuareg's struggles against the Mali Government. Mali was very friendly with China and had received Chinese aid. China could not support revolutionary activity. This is one situation in which China developed a vested interest in the stability of a friendly African state. Such is, after all, normal practice for other states, and the easy conclusion is that, for the African state concerned, friendship with China removed a potentially dangerous and powerful external source of inspiration for rebellious and discontented elements. In these cases 'co-operation' with China serves as a security insurance for the regime concerned, especially where relatively few resources are needed to cause considerable anxiety. The perfect example, perhaps, is Samdech Norodom Sihanouk's Cambodia, where an otherwise dangerous insurgent group was kept under control by the Prince's skilful diplomacy. China's participation in this kind of game removed some of the sting from her attacks on Khrushchev for retiring from the struggle in Cameroun. That country after all established diplomatic relations with the Soviet Union and the two countries signed economic, scientific and technical agreements.

Congo-Kinshasa

After U.S. imperialism and its followers murdered Lumumba, smothered the Congolese independence, and swallowed the Congo, they clinked their glasses in 'congratulation'.... How could they know that their 'throne' is built upon the volcano of the Congolese people's indignation. Blood debts must be paid back in blood. Now a people's armed struggle has broken out again in the Congo. The unyielding people have arisen again.[3]

[1] See below, p. 175.   [2] Omdurman Radio, 18 Aug. 1965.
[3] *People's Daily*, 28 Jan. 1964 – 'Flames That Can Never Be Put Out'.

Thus proclaimed the *People's Daily* on 28 January 1964 hailing the renewed outbreak of rebellion in the Kwilu Province of Congo-Kinshasa. The new revolt was led by Pierre Mulele in a way reminiscent of Chinese Communist revolutionary tactics during the civil war.[1]

The eight instructions on conduct Mulele issued to his guerrilla fighters showed the influence of Mao's writings on people's war on the whole operation. These instructions included:

(1) Respect all men, even bad ones. (2) Buy the goods of the villagers in all honesty and without stealing. (3) Return borrowed things in good time and without trouble. (4) Pay for things which you have broken and in good spirit. (5) Do not harm or hurt others. (6) Do not destroy or trample on other people's land. (7) Respect women and do not amuse yourselves with them as you would like to. (8) Do not make your prisoners of war suffer.

This attempt to adapt Chinese practice to African conditions also extended to Mulele's use of the peasants as the mainstay of revolution. It was not merely an attempt to seize power by military coup in Leopoldville. Such a step would have been so easily crushed. Nevertheless, by the end of April 1964 Mulele's rebellion had been rendered less dangerous. The Soviet Union, with an embassy in Leopoldville, did not support the Mulele revolt and had had no part in its preparation: lack of support from this quarter was in the first place responsible for Mulele turning to China. This was revealed in a document found on Soviet diplomats returning from a meeting in Brazzaville with members of the Congo National Liberation Committee.[2]

---

[1] Pierre Mulele was a former Minister of Education in the Lumumba Government. With the assassination of Lumumba and the later arrest of his recognised deputy, Antoine Gizenga, Mulele became one of the top Lumumbists determined to continue the struggle. He went to Cairo as the representative of the Congo National Liberation Committee based in Brazzaville. From Cairo he proceeded to China in 1963 to receive military training and also took Congolese youth with him who received training in guerrilla tactics. With the renewed rebellion in the Congo, the revolution in Zanzibar and the mutinies of East Africa coupled with the visible revolution of rising frustrations in African states, it would have been surprising if Chou En-lai had not said at the end of his tour that the prospects for revolution were excellent.

[2] The diplomats were forcibly searched and accused of subversive activities. The *African Mail* of Lusaka in what was then Northern Rhodesia reported the document as saying 'We have done everything to get our Russian comrades to help us, but they have never comprehended our difficulties. That is the reason Comrade Mulele left for China. China gave him a course to enter a Military School... We do not wish to offend our Russian friends, but we judge it best to address ourselves to China... China has aided Mulele.' (*African Mail*, 10 Jan. 1964.)

Though Mulele's revolt was effectively rendered impotent, it was soon succeeded by more extensive and intensive struggles in two provinces. The new fighting led by Gaston Soumialot, operating from Burundi, and Christophe Gbenye from Congo Brazzaville, received Chinese propaganda, financial and military support.[1] Initially the Soviet Union was silent on these developments, and it was criticised by China for having 'played the role of accomplice in the U.S. imperialist crime of repressing the national independence movement in the Congo . . .' as a consequence of which 'advanced revolutionaries there had learned to distinguish between true and false friends'.[2] Although the situation in the Congo appeared to be developing in the way predicted in China's secret document of 1961,[3] hazards in the revolutionary path and fluctuations in the people's movement were to be expected. Earlier, superficial setbacks, were now being succeeded by ones of profound importance.

> The Congolese people's struggle for national independence is continuing to develop. The popular armed struggle which broke out in Kwilu in the Western part of the Congo in the latter part of last January, has extended to the eastern provinces of Kivu and North Katanga. . . . The flames of armed struggle have also spread to Kwango Province, south of Kwilu. An excellent revolutionary situation is emerging on the vast expanse of the Congo.
>
> The triumphant revolutionary developments in the Congo prove that a radical change will take place in the revolutionary situation once the revolutionary people take up arms to meet the armed suppression by the imperialists and their flunkeys.[4]

The Chinese referred to Western reports that China was helping the rebellion by supplying funds and arms, but pointedly *did not* deny any of these charges, merely claiming that revolution cannot be exported and that the Congolese people were waging their own heroic struggles.[5]

At this juncture, in July 1964, the Congolese Premier Cyril Adoula resigned and was replaced by Tshombe, whose name had become synonymous in African circles with treachery and

---

[1] Weapons and arms were passed through Tanzania and Uganda as well as through Congo Brazzaville. Interview with X.
[2] N.C.N.A., 5 May 1964.
[3] 'Bulletin of Activities', *op. cit.*, see above p. 82.
[4] *People's Daily* – 'Triumphant Revolutionary Developments in the Congo'. 24 June 1964.
[5] *Ibid.* The *Sunday Telegraph* of 31 May went out of its way to publicise that the Chinese are 'stepping up their efforts to foment revolution in the Congo' and are supplying arms to the Congolese people.

imperialist intrigue. Many African states, the Soviet Union and progressive African opinion now openly supported the Lumumbists with arms funds and propaganda. On 4 August Soamialot's troops operating in the Orientale Province captured the city of Stanleyville which was under the command of General Nicolas Olenga and remained in control until the Belgian–American operation in November.[1] Tshombe's use of South African and Rhodesian mercenaries added to the support received by the Lumumbists (from Algeria, the U.A.R., the Sudan, Congo-Brazzaville, Ghana, Guinea, Tanzania, Mali and Somalia) and led to his exclusion from the Non-Aligned Conference in Cairo in October.[2]

The troops fighting under Soumialot and Gbenye were routed in November after intensive drives by central government troops officered by mercenaries and the landing of Belgian paratroopers in Stanleyville.[3] The latter move made the United States very unpopular in Africa. The action was even criticised by Ethiopia and Senegal, normally friends of the United States. The Congolese revolution again suffered a set-back, but in the process proved a vital point which China had stressed in the past. Without expatriate officers and backing, the Congolese central government would have been defeated. In a way, this would have enhanced Chinese prospects in the heartland of Africa, which the Chinese themselves described as possessing enormous mineral and strategic resources.[4] Sporadic fighting, however, continued in the Orientale Province in 1965, and Soumialot, now President of the Supreme Council of Revolution of the Congo-Kinshasa was invited to visit China.[5] He arrived with a large delegation as guest of the Chinese People's Institute of Foreign Affairs, apparently to discuss the next phase of the struggle.[6] By the end of 1965, however, Tshombe had himself been removed by Kasavubu in a power struggle and the Congo was placed under the military rule of General Mobutu. Thus it remains.

[1] Stanleyville Radio, 4 Aug. 1964. See also Leopoldville Radio of the same date accusing China of using her embassy in Burundi to distribute arms and uniforms to Soamialot's troops. The Leopoldville accusation was justified, and this was not denied by China.
[2] See above, p. 128.
[3] The Belgian paratroopers were dropped by American planes taking off from Ascension Island – a British colony. Their professed mission was to save American and European citizens held hostage by the Stanleyville authorities.
[4] See above, p. 87.   [5] N.C.N.A., 19 Aug. 1965.
[6] B.B.C. *S.W.B.* Part III, No. 1942, 21 Aug. 1965.

Towards the end of 1965, the well-known essay by Lin Piao, the Chinese Defence Minister, 'Long Live the Victory of People's War', which called for the unity of the poor countryside of the world against the cities, had appeared. However, events were taking place in Vietnam and China which were to shift Chinese attention away from Africa in the next period.[1] In the next chapter I will discuss the significance of this shift.

By 1963, therefore, the international situation took on a more challenging shape for Chinese policy, particularly in the third world. The Sino-Soviet conflict, which had been further aggravated by the Cuban missile crisis and the Sino-Indian border war in late 1962, went beyond the point of no return with the signing of the partial nuclear test ban treaty. The three-cornered struggle between China, the United States and the Soviet Union in the second intermediate zone of the third world was intensified.

China thus tried to strengthen relations with African states and the third world in general in an attempt to form an international united front of the poor people of the world. She also aimed at obtaining African support for a second Bandung Conference from which the Soviet Union would be excluded and which would serve her own interests.

At the same time, China increasingly presented her experience as a developmental and revolutionary model for African states, who were urged to rely on themselves alone in their effort to develop and to scorn Western aid. Her developmental model appealed to Guinea, Mali and Tanzania, relatively poor countries whose leadership adopted a philosophy more in tune with Chinese urgings. In no country, however, was the rejection of Western aid accepted in principle.

Chinese economic aid commitments in this period (1963–5) increased to the unprecedented level of about $269 million. Apart from some direct grants, all the commitments were in the form of long-term interest-free loans and the supply of Chinese technicians. Although the shipment of industrial equipment and machinery could be interpreted as promotion in relatively new markets, the terms of the agreements were nevertheless generous and designed to have great political impact. This was particularly so in poor

[1] See below, p. 180.

economies such as those of Mali, Congo-Brazzaville, Guinea and Tanzania.

Even though China's share of African trade was still relatively small, her trade relations showed a rising trend throughout the period. Trade relations, however, followed a more pragmatic line than aid commitment which was based on political decisions.

In the people's organisations, Sino-Soviet rivalry continued, especially in the A.A.P.S.O., which held two conferences during the period in Moshi, Tanganyika and Ghana. The Russians accused China of using the race question to engender support among the Afro-Asians and of imposing her will on the organisations.

The armed struggles in Mozambique, Angola and Portuguese Guinea received ample support from China, and the revolutionary situation on the continent was fuelled by the Zanzibar revolution, the East African mutinies and renewed rebellion in the Congo, which became very important in 1964. These situations were by no means created by China, though she did play a part in supporting anti-colonial struggles and the rebellions in Cameroun and the Congo.

5 DARKENING CLOUDS: THE CULTURAL REVOLUTION

1. The International Situation

Towards the end of 1965, ominous clouds began to appear on the horizon of Chinese diplomacy. While the 1963–5 period witnessed a rapid increase in economic, political, diplomatic and revolutionary activities accompanied by rising influence in the developing world, certain events during the latter part of the period called for reflection on the part of Chinese policy-makers. The much-wanted second Afro-Asian Conference could not be convened under conditions the Chinese would approve. While its indefinite postponement implied a Chinese veto and hence negative power, the fact that it could not meet in circumstances favourable to China made the Peking leadership aware of the limitations of their influence in the developing world. In general the African states had chosen a position midway between the two Communist giants at a time when neutrality and non-alignment were not welcome to the Chinese.

In Asia, the abortive Communist-inspired coup d'etat in Indonesia decimated the Indonesian Communist Party (P.K.I.). The P.K.I. had stood staunchly by China in her ideological polemics with the Soviet Union and was highly instrumental in the militant nationalist posture adopted by Indonesia in this period. The destruction of the party was a great blow to China, and brought Chinese–Indonesian relations to a new low.

The Indo-Pakistani war in the autumn of 1965 called into question China's willingness to help Pakistan effectively in times of crisis. China did ship some MIG fighters to Pakistan, but nevertheless it was India's prestige which rose as a result of the encounter, while China was shown to be unable to implement the 'ultimatum' she had delivered to India at the height of the crisis.[1] To make the

[1] During the Indo-Pakistani clash, China referred to the fact that Indian troops were still stationed on territory claimed by her and that, in some sectors of the Sino-Indian border, Indian troops were making fresh incursions into Chinese territory. On 17

affair even more unpalatable to China, the United States and Soviet Union appeared in the role of peacemakers bringing pressure to bear on India and Pakistan to halt the fighting.

On the ideological front, the fall of Khrushchev had seemed at first to indicate that the Soviet leadership would move towards the Chinese position, but in fact it soon became clear that 'Khrushchevism without Khrushchev' would continue, and that Russia's state and ideological interests would conflict with China's, irrespective of Khrushchev's successor. During this period the Chinese leadership was debating the correct position to take in foreign policy in view of the increasing danger posed by American military activity in Vietnam. It was in the course of this debate that Defence Minister Lin Piao wrote his famous 'Long Live the Victory of People's War' in September 1965 in effect advocating a defensive and most unhawkish posture for China which would not necessitate a degrading rapprochement with the Soviet Union.[1] The other posture supporting China's entry into the Vietnam war to avoid being herself invaded by America meant that she would have to depend on the Soviet Union for military aid. This would mean a loss of face in the world.

These events were taking place in the international arena just as preparations for the launching of the Great Proletarian Cultural Revolution (G.P.C.R.), which was to engulf China from the middle of 1966 to 1968 were nearing their completion. This effectively turned China inwards, and resulted in less activity in some parts of the world. During this period, a Soviet suggestion for joint action by the Communist states on the Vietnam war was turned down by China as a fraud. The new policy called for self-help in achieving revolution, though did not rule out material and political help from fraternal countries. Chinese experience in the Korean war, when she had to bear the burden (financial and military) of the fighting,

---

September the Chinese Foreign Ministry delivered a Note to India 'demanding that India dismantle within three days its aggressive military works' built on Chinese territory. India did not comply with the demand but instead issued a Note professing peaceful intentions and claiming that the Chinese demand was a pretext for waging war against India. The Chinese government issued another Note on 19 September in which the time-limit was extended. However, no Chinese military action followed the expiry of the ultimatum. See *Peking Review*, No. 37, 10 Sept. 1965, p. 5; No. 39, 25 Sept. 1965, pp. 8-16.

[1] When this first appeared, it was taken instead as a blueprint for a Chinese revolutionary takeover of the world.

made her suspect that the Soviet Union would stay safely in the background and allow China to be devastated by American strategic bombing.[1] A militant posture and strategic boldness were matched with tactical caution and a realistic assessment of Chinese capabilities.

The international situation at the beginning of this period thus contained disturbing factors which called for deep reflection from the Chinese leaders. Their anxiety was increased by the adverse currents in Africa which endangered Chinese positions.[2] The changing world scene, however, had to be explained in ideological terms – effectively rationalisations of what had happened. Writing in the *People's Daily* of 7 March 1966,[3] Hiang Tung-Lui pointed out that

> On the path of revolutionary development, it is unavoidable that zigzags of this or that kind will appear. The revolution twists and turns as it rolls forward . . .
> Marxist-Leninists and consistent revolutionaries are not confounded when twists and turns appear. They adopt the correct strategy and tactics to persist in the revolution . . .
> Why must the revolution encounter twists and turns of this or that kind on its way forward? It is because the newborn forces of the revolution have to wrestle with the decadent forces at all times. Sometimes because the balance of power is temporarily unfavourable to the revolutionary side or because the revolutionary leaders have made subjective mistakes of this or that kind, some twists and turns would be brought to the revolution on its way forward. . . . The revolutionary struggles in some places have encountered some temporary setbacks. Reverses have also occurred in the political situation of some countries.[4]

The best attitude was therefore to consider what had happened as temporary isolated deviations from the revolutionary path which must not be allowed to mar the clear vision of the essential phenomenon. Chou En-lai made the same point on 30 April 1966, when he welcomed Mehmet Shehu and Hysni Kapo of Albania (a country which in ideological verbiage was far left of China).[5] He stated that the revolutionary peoples of the world were now carrying on an intense struggle against U.S. imperialism. The different contradictions in the world were growing sharper, while drastic division

---

[1] In the Korean war, China had to pay for all military supplies from Russia, though the war had in fact been started without the Chinese being consulted. If Soviet planes flew sorties from Chinese bases, U.S. retaliation would be against China and not the Soviet Union, and this was naturally not acceptable to China.
[2] See below, p. 184.
[3] Current Background No. 789, 24 May 1966.
[4] *Ibid.*
[5] *People's Daily*, 1 May 1966.

Darkening Clouds: The Cultural Revolution 183

and regrouping were taking place among the various political forces.

The situation is an inevitable result of the deepening of the people's revolutionary struggle and is the prelude to a new revolutionary storm of the people of the world. . . . Although imperialism and reactionaries have recently staged counter revolutionary coups and embarked on rabid campaigns of vilification against China, these will not deter the Chinese people from supporting the revolutionary peoples of the world. We will unswervingly carry on with what we have been doing. Although the desperate struggles of the imperialists and reactionaries of various countries may make a lot of noise for a time, they cannot in any way change the course of development of world history.[1]

From Chou's point of view then, the great upheaval, division and reorganisation taking place in the international arena would result in new groupings of political forces which would go forward together into the battle with imperialism. However, the outbreak of Cultural Revolution diverted the Chinese leaders' attention to internal affairs. The rest of the world looked on uncomprehending.

In Africa, the first days of January 1966 brought a bad omen. Military coups in Dahomey and the Central African Republic resulted in the expulsion of their Chinese missions.[2] This was followed in February by a more important setback in Ghana. Dr Nkrumah's Government was overthrown while he himself was in China en route to Vietnam.[3] While the Chinese had no illusions about Nkrumah's efforts to bring about peace in Vietnam and did not sympathise with them, nevertheless China's influence in Ghana had been growing. The government's overthrow therefore came as a great blow. On 15 April 1966, 'Africa Freedom Day', the *People's Daily* examined the series of adverse events in Africa and the difficulties facing the progressive forces there. The paper observed that successive military coups d'etat had taken place, particularly south of the Sahara. Six coups had been staged within four months in Congo-Leopoldville, Dahomey, the Central African Republic, Upper Volta, Nigeria and Ghana. In a few cases the Chinese recognised that government changes were the result of patriotic and democratic forces overthrowing the reactionary regimes of imperialist lackeys, or of factional strife among the ruling circles. But, in most cases they were attributed to counter-revolutionary military

---
[1] B.B.C. *S.W.B.* Part III, No. 2151 of 3 May 1966.
[2] See below, p. 185.   [3] See below, p. 186.

coups d'etat stage-managed or engineered by imperialism. These were classified under three headings.

(1) One type is that in which imperialism instigates the reactionary army men to overthrow those nationalist governments which stick fast to an independent policy, or those leaders with nationalist inclinations.
(2) Another type is that in which, when the imperialist puppets can no longer maintain their rule as a result of dissatisfaction and resistance of the masses of the people, imperialism plays the trick of swapping horses to deceive the people and at the same time strengthen suppression.
(3) A third type is that in which the agents of one imperialist country are replaced by those of another as a result of the rivalry between the old and new colonialists for spheres of influence.

These circumstances fully testify to the acuteness and complexity of the struggle between the African people on the one hand and colonialism and neo-colonialism on the other.[1]

To prevent the situation deteriorating further, other African states must completely eradicate all imperialist, colonialist and neo-colonialist influences in the political, economic, military and cultural fields. Only by so doing could the fruits of revolution be safeguarded and complete independence won. Welcoming a Tanzanian economic delegation in June, Finance Minister Li Hsien-nien made the same point: the series of counter-attacks launched in Africa by the imperialists must serve as 'lessons by negative example and stimulate the vigilance and awakening of the African people'.[2] It was essential to wage massive campaigns against subversion.

At the end of 1966, a Chinese survey of the African scene was able to note that 'many countries have in the past year stepped up the Africanisation of their armies and cadres, taken over colonialist enterprises and adopted other positive measures, and dealt further blows at colonial influence'.[3] The governments of Tanzania, Mali and Guinea were in the forefront of this struggle. They must not relax their vigilance: the imperialists would always try to achieve their counter-revolutionary aims.

2. Sino-African Political Relations

(i) *Diplomatic Relations*

At the end of 1965 eighteen African states recognised China, though the degree of reciprocal diplomatic warmth varied. The new

[1] Hsinhua News Agency.
[2] B.B.C. *S.W.B.* Part III, No. 2180, 7 June 1966.
[3] S.C.M.P. No. 3851, 3 Jan. 1967.

period began badly for China on the diplomatic front. After the coup d'etat in Dahomey in the last days of 1965, the new government decided to terminate Sino-Dahomeyan relations. On 3 January 1966 the Foreign Minister delivered a note to the Chinese Ambassador breaking off diplomatic relations and withdrawing recognition.[1] No reason was given for this action. The Dahomey Government also requested the departure of Chinese agricultural experts (mainly rice-growing technicians) who had been sent under an agreement with the former government. The Chinese had scarcely had time to digest the implications of this move when another African state took the same action.

A coup d'etat in the Central African Republic brought the overthrow of President David Dacko and his replacement by Colonel Bokasa. On 6 January the new military government decided to sever diplomatic relations with China.[2] This was coupled with the expulsion of Chinese personnel. As in Dahomey, these included Chinese agronomists sent under an economic co-operation agreement.[3] In addition there were Chinese personnel attached to a Chinese exhibition on economic construction and an N.C.N.A. correspondent.[4] Unlike that of Dahomey, however, the Government of the C.A.R. explained their action. They mentioned the deposed president's plans to set up a private people's army with China's aid, and the discovery of arms caches in the State House together with documents on the formation of a people's army and the conduct of guerrilla warfare.[5] While it is possible that a people's army would have endangered the position of the Officer Corps in the regular army, it is difficult to see how such activity could be described as subversion. The Chinese could not have sent in the military hardware without the knowledge of the government and though doubts could have been expressed on the secrecy surrounding delivery, the discovery of the arms in the State House confirmed that Chinese action was not subversive.

In their reaction to the Dahomeyan and C.A.R. actions, the Chinese saw the hand of the United States. They suspected that a new and sinister campaign to discredit China had begun:

The two incidents in the wake of military coups d'etat in both countries were by no means accidental. Imperialism headed by the United States is trying to stir

[1] S.C.M.P. No. 3613, 10 Jan. 1966.   [2] S.C.M.P. No. 3615, 12 Jan. 1966.
[3] S.C.M.P. No. 3624, 26 Jan. 1966.   [4] Ibid.   [5] Dakar Radio, 21 Jan. 1966.

up an adverse anti-China current in Africa so as to bring about a breach in the normal relations between China and the African countries and undermine the militant friendship and solidarity between these peoples. Dahomey's ending and C.A.R.'s severance of diplomatic relations with China under the manipulation of imperialism are part of this adverse anti-China current.[1]

The C.A.R.'s decision was the more painful as China had earlier given the country a grant. It implied that other African states with whom China had cordial relations could take similar steps to sever relations if military regimes took over. Though this had not happened after the Algerian coup of June 1965, the new situation was obviously unpredictable. China now had to reckon not only with the possibility of a decline in diplomatic influence but also with the loss of any economic aid given before the overthrow of an African government. Chinese apprehension at the new turn of events was to be fully justified by events in Ghana in the following month.

Argument will, I think, continue on whether or not the coup which overthrew Dr Nkrumah in February 1966 would have taken place if the President had not gone abroad. Here, however, I wish to consider the events as they affected Sino-Ghanaian relations and Chinese influence in Ghana. Nkrumah accepted an invitation from President Ho Chi Minh to visit North Vietnam, and left Ghana for Hanoi in February 1966. He and his delegation were in transit through China when the bad news was delivered. 'Mr President, we are in trouble. There is a coup d'etat in Ghana.'[2] These were the words of the Chinese Ambassador to Ghana, who had gone on to Peking to prepare for Nkrumah's stay there. Although they had learned of events in Ghana before the arrival of Nkrumah on 24 February, the Chinese did not fail to show the characteristic courtesy which they accord to all visiting dignitaries. The whole diplomatic corps came to welcome him, while Liu Shao-chi the President and Prime Minister Chou En-lai, at the airport to welcome him, behaved as though nothing had happened.[3]

[1] *People's Daily*, 9 Jan. 1966.
[2] This is the quotation related to me by a very senior member of the Cabinet present at the meeting with the Chinese Ambassador to Ghana. Nkrumah himself uses slightly different words; 'Mr. President, I have bad news. There has been a coup d'etat in Ghana.' See Nkrumah, *Dark Days in Ghana*, 1968, p. 9.
[3] A senior member of the presidential delegation pointed out that the diplomatic corps in Peking seemed to have learnt the Chinese art of courtesy befitting such occasions; none of them showed any awareness of events in Ghana. Witness also Norodom-Sihanouk's welcome by envoys for forty-two countries in Peking after the coup in Cambodia.

The Chinese Ambassador's somewhat laconic statement was pregnant with meaning. Obviously, everyone was now in trouble including the Chinese. On 28 February the new military regime in Ghana demanded the immediate withdrawal of the Chinese technical experts and the pruning of the Embassy establishment down to eighteen.[1] The Chinese experts were engaged in the construction of the integrated cotton textile and knitwear factory at Juapong and the pencil factory at Kumasi.[2] The Chinese protested against the demand for immediate withdrawal, stating that this would lead to economic losses. They made suggestions for handing over the factories under construction and transferring the thousands of tons of material and equipment to responsible Ghanaian officials.[3] They also agreed to cut down Embassy staff to the required eighteen. Having paid the local costs of constructing the two factories, the Chinese were naturally anxious to see that the change of government did not adversely affect prospects for the repayment of the loan.[4] Thus, like the Russians, the Chinese did not break off diplomatic relations with Ghana simply because Nkrumah had been overthrown. It could be argued, of course, that the presence of their diplomatic mission could serve as a source of intelligence for the deposed President in his efforts to return to Ghana.

At the request of the new government about 430 Chinese personnel left for China. These included thirteen guerrillla warfare instructors who were training freedom fighters in Ghanaian military camps.[5] International attention was centred on these guerrilla warfare experts and on the accusations of subversion against Ghana launched at them. Referring to various Ghanaian statements on Chinese subversion, a Chinese Embassy note of 19 March rightly pointed out that

the military experts as well as the economic and technical experts sent by the Chinese Government to work in Ghana were dispatched at the request of the Government of the Republic of Ghana in pursuance of the relevant agreements signed by the two countries. They always worked in accordance with the arrangements made by the Ghanaian Government.[6]

Essentially, however, Ghanaian statements after the coup alleged

[1] S.C.M.P. No. 3653, 9 Mar. 1966. [2] See above, p. 143.
[3] S.C.M.P. No. 3653, 9 Mar. 1966. [4] B.B.C. *S.W.B.* Part III, No. 2105, 8 Mar. 1966.
[5] *Nkrumah's Subversion*, Ghana Information Ministry, Accra, 1966, p. iv.
[6] B.B.C. *S.W.B.* Part III, No. 2118 of 22 Mar. 1966.

that China was sending arms and finance to Guinea to help reinstate President Nkrumah, who had taken refuge there. The Chinese note of 19 March naturally denied the Ghanaian charges.[1] In February 1967 the Ghanaian Government alleged further subversion by China, the Soviet Union and Cuba. The Vice Chairman of the ruling council stated that a few weeks after the 1966 coup the Soviet Ambassador in Conakry had given Nkrumah £71,400, and the Chinese Ambassador had given him £500,000, to enable him to plan his return to Ghana.[2]

As I have already mentioned, China did not recall her mission from Ghana of her own accord. On 20 October 1966, however, following a deterioration in Sino-Ghanaian relations, the Ghanaian Government suspended diplomatic relations between the two states. The new Ghanaian regime did not immediately transfer recognition to the Taiwan Government. In fact, the formal rupture in relations was an anticlimax. It was much less important than the actual overthrow of Nkrumah, which took place at a time when relations between the two states were growing more cordial. Nkrumah's downfall had released information on the subversive activities he and China were carrying out together on the continent. This revelation had been effectively used by the United States to discredit China in Africa and to draw the attention of several states to the 'Chinese threat'. The fall of Nkrumah also meant the loss of a strongly militant ideological ally who, though sometimes critical of some aspects of Chinese policy, was none the less sympathetic on several important issues.

Dahomey, the C.A.R. and Ghana were not the only states causing China diplomatic headaches during this period. In the last chapter, I mentioned China's role in Kenya's internal political struggle as well as her declining influence in the government. In 1966 the political opponents of Oginga Odinga took advantage of Chinese setbacks in some African states to demand the severence of relations with China. A motion was tabled in the Senate stating that since Chou En-lai made his speech in 1964 about Africa being

[1] B.B.C. *S.W.B.* Part III, No. 2118 of 22 Mar. 1966.
[2] *The Times* and *Daily Telegraph* of 27 February 1967. There is no way of verifying such statements, but considering the blow Nkrumah's overthrow was to Russia and China, it is not unlikely that the two countries wanted to help him regain power. The amount of money involved may have been exaggerated.

ripe for revolution, a number of coups, crises and assassinations had actually taken place. The motion inferred that these occurrences were linked with Chinese activities on the continent.[1] Although the motion calling on the government to sever diplomatic relations with China was altered by the Defence Minister to advocate the severence of relations with any government found participating in subversion in Africa, it was unanimously adopted.[2] In a Note handed to the Kenyan Government on 17 March, the Chinese Embassy in Nairobi protested against the motion, 'which arbitrarily linked up Premier Chou En-lai's remarks about the excellent revolutionary situation in Africa with the recent series of reactionary coups d'etat, assassinations and other incidents engineered by imperialism in Africa. This can only be deemed a premeditated scheme to poison the normal relations between the two countries.'[3] The Chinese argument was that Chou's statement referred to the upsurge in anti-imperialist and anti-colonialist revolution and that his conclusion 'completely tallies with the realities of the African situation'.[4]

Nevertheless, Chinese influence in Kenya declined commensurately with the deterioration of Oginga Odinga's political fortunes. The situation was not helped by the events of the Cultural Revolution which soon erupted in China, and which led to violent and undiplomatic language being used by the Foreign Minister in Peking.[5] On 29 June 1967 the Kenyan Government declared the Chinese Chargé d'Affaires ad interim persona non grata and gave him 48 hours to leave the country because of his 'interference' in Kenya's internal affairs. China thereupon took identical action against Kenya's Chargé d'Affaires in Peking.[6] Both countries, however, stopped short of formally breaking off diplomatic relations.

In the previous chapter I discussed Chou En-lai's visit to Tunisia and the diplomatic recognition accorded to Peking which resulted from it. This was a good omen for China's efforts to obtain maximum diplomatic support for her views on the continent. In effect, however, for a long time Chinese–Tunisian relations only operated on a formal level, as Tunisia could not possibly be defined as one

[1] B.B.C. *S.W.B.* Part IV, No. 2102, 3 Mar. 1966.   [2] *Ibid.*
[3] B.B.C. *S.W.B.* Part III, No. 2127, 1 Apr. 1966.   [4] *People's Daily*, 31 Mar. 1966.
[5] On the effects of the Cultural Revolution see below pp. 192–6.
[6] S.C.M.P. No. 3973, 5 July 1967.

of the militantly progressive states. The onset of the Cultural Revolution in China, moreover, made the relationship between Tunis and Peking even more unstable. China alleged that this was because the reports of events in China by Tunisian information media were 'tendentious and slanderous'.[1]

Like all other Chinese Ambassadors except the one in Cairo, China's envoy to Tunisia was recalled to Peking for re-education early in 1967.[2] It is fair to point out, however, that the deterioration in Sino-Tunisian relations was perhaps more the result of the Tunisian Government's changing views than of events in China. China had all along opposed the policy of 'two Chinas' which the Tunisian Government was now beginning to favour. In February 1967 Habib Bourguiba Jr, the Tunisian Foreign Minister, declared the need to be realistic and to accept that 'there are two Chinas'.[3] China could not accept this view without undermining the whole basis of her policy since 1950. Indeed she had refused to take up the diplomatic recognition offered earlier by Senegal, because the concept of two Chinas was implied in the Senegalese conditions.[4] Following Bourguiba's statement, the Tunisian Government sent an economic delegation to Taiwan to conclude an 'agreement on agro-technical co-operation', which meant Nationalist Chinese agricultural experts would come to Tunisia.

Sino-Tunisian relations worsened after the Arab-Israeli war of June 1967. In the aftermath of Arab defeat and allegations of American and British military support for Israel, widespread demonstrations took place in Arab cities and towns, including Tunis. In these demonstrations Communist involvement, especially Chinese, was detected by the Tunisian Government.[5] This took the form of 'news bulletins' distributed and compiled by Chinese personnel, which the government regarded as subversive and likely to incite people to riot. The Tunisian Government imposed restrictions on the activities of the Chinese Embassy staff. Thus film receptions for Tunisian citizens and the distribution of news bulletins was for-

[1] Tunisia's reports were not unique, as very often the International News Agencies were quoted as the source of information.
[2] See below, p. 192.
[3] S.C.M.P. No. 4031, 29 Sept. 1967.
[4] See above, p. 119.
[5] China could hardly be held responsible for the widespread demonstrations which took place in the Arab world at this time.

bidden and mail addressed to the Embassy was held up.[1] In July, two Chinese, a table-tennis coach, Hua Cheng-te, and a staff member of the Embassy, Chang Chia-hsiang, were detained by the Tunisian authorities.[2] In August President Bourguiba made a statement in which he attacked China 'and slandered Chairman Mao, the great leader of the Chinese people and the other peoples of the world'.[3]

In a note dated 14 September, the Chinese responded by withdrawing immediately the four Chinese coaches who had been sent to Tunisia under a physical education agreement and 'categorically rejecting' the restrictions placed on the activities of their diplomatic staff.[4] In a statement typical of those made during the Cultural Revolution, but which no government could have accepted without the strongest protest, the Chinese predicted the fall of the Tunisian Government. 'By attempting to use its opposition to China to divert the attention of its people and cover up its own crime of entering further into the service of U.S. imperialism and Soviet revisionism and selling out the interests of the Tunisian and other Arab peoples, the Tunisian government will certainly come to no good end.'[5] The Tunisian Government demanded an unreserved apology for this statement failing which all Chinese diplomatic personnel would be declared personae non gratae.[6] The Chinese note was not of course meant to improve relations between the two governments, and the possibility of a formal rupture had probably already been considered. It was not thought that the disadvantages outweighed the benefit of diplomatic recognition. Moreover the Cultural Revolution had made the Chinese less interested in maintaining diplomatic relations with other nations at all costs. Consequently they refused to apologise and withdraw their diplomatic personnel. Relations were formally severed on 26 September 1967.

In a review of the international situation at the end of 1967, after a series of diplomatic ruptures – Feng Piao, Director of the Infornation Department of the *People's Daily*, asserted that 'severance of relations can do us no harm. We have no diplomatic relations with the United States, but we carry on just the same. . . . Severance of relations will only make a mess of things politically and economi-

[1] S.C.M.P. No. 4025, 21 Sept. 1967.
[3] *Ibid.*
[5] *Ibid.*
[2] S.C.M.P. No. 4031, 29 Sept. 1967.
[4] S.C.M.P. 4025, 21 Sept. 1967.
[6] S.C.M.P. No. 4031, 29 Sept. 1967.

cally for a given country, since we can then support the people of that country to make revolution.'[1] While it is certainly not true that severance of diplomatic relations did not worry the Chinese, this statement nevertheless highlights the inherent contradiction in the need to obtain diplomatic recognition and at the same time to support revolution. Thus the extension of diplomatic recognition to China by some governments in the developing countries could help to forestall Chinese support for local insurgents and opposition groups.[2]

By the end of 1968 the number of independent states in Africa had increased to forty-one and China maintained diplomatic relations with thirteen of them.[3] Even with these thirteen relations varied from formally correct to very friendly. This does not mean that Chinese interest in Africa declined steeply. On the contrary her curtailed sphere of activity was more than compensated by the increased cordiality of relations with some selected states. This I will consider later.

(ii) *The Cultural Revolution and Sino-African Relations*

Chairman Mao commands very high prestige among the revolutionary people of the world because he has developed Marxism-Leninism in a brilliant, creative, comprehensive, integral and systematic way. Mao Tse-tung's thought is the integration of the universal truth of Marxism-Leninism with the concrete practice not only of the Chinese revolution but also of world revolution. It is the summing up of the experience of the contemporary world revolution as well as the Chinese revolution. It is the encyclopaedia both of the Chinese revolution and of world revolution. It is the acme of Marxist-Leninism in our epoch, it is living Marxism-Leninism at its highest.[4]

Thus *Jen Min Jih Pao* at the beginning of the Great Proletarian Cultural Revolution in 1966. This statement was preceded by reports from various parts of the world, in particular Afro-Asian and Latin American countries, on the universal acknowledgement of Chairman Mao's works and China's role in world revolution. Although greater claims for Mao's thoughts were to be made in the course of the Cultural Revolution, this statement marked the beginning of a

[1] *Current Background* No. 850, 24 Jan. 1968, citing *People's Daily*, 13 Dec. 1967.
[2] The case of the Sudan was considered on p. 174 above. On Nigeria see below, p. 233.
[3] Viz the U.A.R., Morocco, Sudan, Guinea, Mali, Somali Republic, Tanzania, Algeria, Uganda, Kenya, Congo (B), Mauretania and Zambia.
[4] *People's Daily*, 1 June 1966. 'Mao Tse-tung's Thought Is the Beacon Light for World's Revolutionary Peoples', S.C.M.P. No. 3712, 6 June 1966.

systematic campaign to present Chairman Mao as *the* leader of the world.[1] While it is easy for the cynic to disregard such reports in the Chinese press during this period, it is nevertheless true that they played an important part in the propaganda of the Cultural Revolution. They served to reinforce in the Chinese masses the belief that Chairman Mao was indeed the world leader. Proof was to be found in statements by representatives of the various peoples of the world.[2] That most poor people abroad had probably never heard of Chairman Mao or what he represented was immaterial as far as propaganda for internal consumption was concerned. To the Chinese masses, the following poem, written by a member of the Cameroun General Confederation of Labour, meant more than statements in imperialist newspapers.

> Mao Tse-tung is seventy years old
> In the Yangtse he swam once again.
> Happy news that is, that rejoices
> The hearts of the peoples and the revolutionaries.
> To know that you are in good health
> As vigorous as a green pine,
> Is a joy ineffable for the peoples.
> High is the sea,
> And white are the waves;
> The sky is aglow with
> Clouds gold rimmed;
> A strong wind is filling the sails
> The boat of hope is forging ahead in the foam,
> At its helm standing erect is a giant,
> Mao Tse-tung, successor to Marx, Lenin, Stalin,
> Helmsman of the new era,
> Who guides the revolution of the peoples.
> In the Yangtse you swam again,
> Against the winds and waves together with your people.
> What a happy precept it is.
> As your students, we will
> For ever be loyal to your teachings,

[1] At a diplomatic reception held in Dar Es Salaam by the Chinese in 1967, a film of some of the events of the Cultural Revolution was shown. At the end of the film a Chinese official was reported to have asked one of the Tanzanians what he thought of Chairman Mao. He replied that Mao was the great leader of the Chinese people just as Nyerere was the great leader of the Tanzanian people. The Chinese official quickly 'corrected' him by saying that Nyerere was the leader of Tanzania but Chairman Mao was the leader of the whole world. There was to be no misunderstanding (Interview with participant at the reception).
[2] The reports usually quoted workers, freedom fighters, peasants and other poor people who 'formed the vast majority of the world's population'.

And like the sunflower, follow
The sun which is your thought.
Once again let's wish Mao Tse-tung a long life.[1]

It would be wrong, however, to give the impression that statements made during the Cultural Revolution were *only* meant for internal consumption. In fact the Chinese took great pains to disseminate the works of Chairman Mao in African countries.[2] This was followed up by reports of revolutionary African people 'eagerly studying the brilliant works' of Mao Tse-tung in the quest of truth about revolution.[3] However, in keeping with previous Chinese exhortations to the developing countries, 'the people' of the countries concerned were still expected to carry out their own revolution, which was now, like China's, to be mainly in the cultural field. Thus, reports from Moscow in April 1967 suggesting that Chou En-lai and Chiang Ching (Mao's wife) had given orders for Red Guards to be sent to Chinese Embassies in Africa were vehemently denounced by the Chinese. They regarded such reports as attempts to sabotage China's 'good' relations with African states by suggesting interference in their internal affairs.[4]

The Cultural Revolution did not, however, affect only the 'people's diplomacy' aspect of Chinese activities. In 1967 all Chinese Ambassadors, except the Ambassador to the United Arab Republic, were recalled to Peking, nominally to 'participate' in the Cultural Revolution but in fact to answer various charges which were being levied against the Foreign Ministry and its top personnel by the youthful Red Guards.[5] As Cairo had been China's first

[1] Poem by Ekwalla Robert in Commemoration of Chairman Mao's Famous Swim in the Yangtse. B.B.C. *S.W.B.* Part III No. 2240, 16 Aug. 1966.
[2] Volumes I to IV of Mao's *Selected Works* and the *Selected Military Writings* now became available in European bookshops. In many African countries however, these were given away free of charge. I obtained my own copies in Lagos in 1967 from a twelve year old boy making a shilling on each copy, though he ought to have been distributing them free of charge.
[3] Such reports in N.C.N.A. dispatches from African states, see for instance S.C.M.P. No. 3947, 26 May 1967.
[4] With the Chinese campaign against the Soviet Union, it could hardly be expected that the latter would not capitalise on the rather chaotic situation in the Foreign Ministry in Peking. It was curious, however, that Chou En-lai was lumped with Chiang Ching as ordering Red Guards to go abroad, since Chou was the moderating influence throughout the Cultural Revolution.
[5] Foreign Minister Chen Yi was already under attack before his Ambassadors were recalled from their posts. The Red Guards in the Foreign Ministry attacked top diplomats, their 'huge' salaries, mode of living in foreign countries and other privileges.

diplomatic seat in Africa as well as the post from which Chinese policy had been, for a long time, co-ordinated, the decision to leave the Ambassador there was no doubt made so that he could continue to oversee the work of other diplomatic personnel in Africa and in the Middle East as a whole. Moreover, the Ambassador Huang Hua who replaced Chen Chia-kang in Cairo in December 1965, had performed brilliantly in Ghana, his previous post.

The attacks on the Foreign Ministry, diplomats and the leaders of people's organisations (including the indomitable Kuo Mo-jo and Burhan Shahidi of the Afro-Asian Solidarity Committee), led to a significant decline in the number of African delegations invited to China. Although in 1966 the number of African delegations visiting China for one reason or another reached a record level of 116, this was only so because the invitations had been issued and arrangements completed before the more violent forms of the Cultural Revolution took place.[1] In 1967 the number dropped to 53 and in 1968 to an all-time low of 12.[2] On the Chinese side the figure for 1966 was 48, dropping to 17 in 1967 and to 14 in 1968.[3] The Africans who did visit China tended to be high government delegations intent on furthering relations with her.[4] One of these delegations was that headed by Prime Minister Ambroise Noumazalay of Congo-Brazzaville in September and October 1967. (He was met by Chou En-lai but not by Foreign Minister Chen Yi, who had been under vigorous attack by the Red Guards, whose place was taken by Finance Minister Li Hsien-nien.)

In his speech at the airport, the Congolese Prime Minister referred to slanders and tendentious statements in imperialist

---

They were accused of living a bourgeois life and were said to be unwilling to study Chairman Mao's works or take part in labour. It is difficult to see how Ambassadors could have taken part in labour in foreign capitals. Normally the envoys needed more finances than they would have received at home if they were to perform their diplomatic tasks in a manner befitting a great country like China. The Red Guards called for a thorough revolutionary overhaul of the Chinese Foreign Ministry, turning it into a forward post for carrying out world revolution. That this would have involved undiplomatic interference in other countries' affairs was overlooked. See S.C.M.P. No. 4002, 16 Aug. 1967; No. 4004, 18 Aug. 1967 for some of the attacks on diplomats. The articles were written by the 'Proletarian Revolutionaries Liaison Committee of the Foreign Affairs System of Peking'.

[1] See Appendix I, Table 2 on African delegations visiting China.
[2] *Ibid.*
[3] *Ibid.*
[4] See also below, pp. 270.

reports on the events of the Cultural Revolution. These, he said, he did not believe. His Chinese hosts, however, did not deny the reports of violent outbreaks in the country; indeed Chairman Mao invited the Prime Minister to visit the East China city of Huainan to see the difficulties which had existed among the revolutionary masses, how they had divided into warring factions and how they had then brought about the revolutionary great alliance.[1] During his visit there the Congolese Prime Minister expressed pleasure at the reconciliation of the warring factions, stating that he could not conceive of proletarian revolutionaries being divided into two big factions.

In fact, if proletarians are divided into two big factions, they will forget their historical mission which is not only to emancipate themselves but also to emancipate the whole of mankind.... If there are any good wishes we may offer we would like to say we hope that the proletarian revolutionaries of Huainan will not only reach but surpass the level attained before the great proletarian cultural revolution in all fields of production.[2]

This was a clear reference to the economic and industrial dislocation which was accompanying the Cultural Revolution in many areas. Obviously if it continued unchecked, it would not only affect China internally but would hamper her ability to meet her commitments abroad, particularly to her friends in Africa. As I will show later, in fact the Cultural Revolution and the withdrawal of Ambassadors from their posts did not check Chinese commitments and initiative in Africa, though these were no doubt limited to states which already had good relations with China. Perhaps the degree of continuity in China's African policy during the period, despite the withdrawal of Ambassadors, prompted decision-makers in the Foreign Ministry to consider whether or not the envoys were actually achieving more than officials of lower level could have done. For a long time after this period no Ambassador was sent back to his African post. His functions were performed on the one hand by a Chargé d'Affaires and on the other by instant diplomacy, by high-powered African delegations going down to Peking to present their requests.

[1] Li Hsien-nien accompanied the delegation to Huainan. S.C.M.P. No. 4039, 11 Oct. 1967.
[2] S.C.M.P. No. 4039, 11 Oct. 1967. The Congolese delegation visited some factories whose production had been disrupted by the events of the Cultural Revolution.

(iii) *Sino-Tanzanian Relations – A Continuation of the Case Study*
In Chapter 4, I examined the development of Sino-Tanzanian relations and the growing cordial relations resulting from similar ideological positions, economic co-operation and Ambassador Ho Ying's shrewd moves. As decisions were made on specific projects to implement the Chinese loan, more Chinese personnel were needed on a short-term basis to help in the work of construction. The Chinese therefore began to press for the establishment of an economic mission,[1] and a large mission, headed by Chiang Ta, was opened in Dar Es-Salaam to cope with the increasing economic activities. This meant that closer co-operation and better working relationships could now develop between the government ministries and the Chinese economic mission on the spot. Any misunderstanding between the two sides could also be cleared up before it affected activities in other fields.

By June 1966, China had advanced a considerable proportion of the loan promised in 1964. In that year she had pledged some $45.5 million in aid to the new union of Tanganyika and Zanzibar, On 16 June 1966 Tanzania's Economic Affairs Minister, Bomani. announced that $14 million of this had been received by the Zanzibar Government for various development projects, while the mainland had received some $3 million. At the same time $11 million was being spent on the integrated textile mill in Dar es-Salaam. The balance of $17 million had not yet been committed to specific projects.[2] Considering the reluctance of the Ministry of Economic Development in 1964 when the loan was first pledged, the fulfilment of the promise showed how far suspicions and obstacles had been overcome. It also confirmed China's determination to maintain the goodwill which had been generated and to increase mutual co-operation.

Solidarity between the two countries increased after Rhodesia's illegal unilateral declaration of independence and the breaking off of diplomatic relations between Tanzania and Britain, in accordance with a recommendation by the Ministerial Council of the Organisation of African Unity.[3] The Tanzanian Cabinet did consider the

[1] Interview with X.
[2] *Far Eastern Economic Review*, Vol. LIII, 15 Sept. 1966.
[3] In those African states where the Foreign Ministers' recommendation was not followed, it was not regarded as binding on member states of the Organisation.

possibility of Britain freezing proposed aid to Tanzania if the recommendation were acted upon. By December 1965, however, projected British aid not yet in the pipeline was only about £2 million.[1] Apart from the low figure, Tanzania considered that the principle involved – African independence – was such that no amount of projected British aid should prevent the government breaking off diplomatic relations. Being realistic, of course, the government did consider alternative sources of aid.

In June 1966 a Tanzanian Government economic delegation visited China and discussed additional aid. The Chinese granted a new interest-free loan of £3 million, designed to 'initiate or bring to completion a number of development projects, most of which the British Government had promised to help build'.[2] This compensated for financial loss the government sustained when diplomatic relations with Britain were severed. At the same time it showed China was a valuable friend in time of need and increased her standing in the country. Apart from this, the aid would increase economic ties between the two countries.

Already mutual trade was increasing, with China using part of the trade to finance local projects in Tanzania. Proceeds from Chinese goods sold in the country were not taken out but used to meet the cost of Chinese-sponsored projects. In 1966 Chinese exports increased by more than 100% over the 1965 figure.[3] Chinese imports from Tanzania also remained high in 1966. They were only slightly less than in 1965 when cotton purchases had pushed the figure up. To cope with increasing trade, the Chinese proposed the establishment of a joint China–Tanzania shipping line. They argued convincingly that this would increase the invisible earnings of the two countries, reduce imperialist control of shipping and hence reduce arbitrary charges.[4] On 22 April 1966 the governments of China and Tanzania 'with a view to further strengthening relations of friendship and economic co-operation between the two countries,

[1] The total amount of financial aid Britain promised to Tanzania was £15 million. Out of this sum £9 million would be used to meet the cost of paying retired British Civil Servants who had worked in the country before independence. This amount could obviously not be regarded as a contribution to Tanzania's development. This meant that effective British aid promised amounted to only £6 million. See statement by Mr Jamal, Tanzania's Finance Minister, to Parliament on 10 May 1968.
[2] Tanzania's Economic Affairs Minister quoted by N.C.N.A., 18 June 1966.
[3] See Appendix I, Table 6 on Chinese exports to African states.
[4] Interview with X.

have reached an agreement to establish a Chinese-Tanzania Joint Shipping Company... the two governments will each provide to the joint company one vessel of similar tonnage'.[1] The arrangement was finalised when China agreed to lend Tanzania the sum of £750,000, half the initial capital of the joint company. £700,000 was used to buy a ship and £50,000 deposited with the Bank of Tanzania as working capital. The loan would be repaid gradually from the profits of the company and it was hoped that the line would in due course expand beyond the initial two ships which started it. (It should also be pointed out that a joint shipping company would reduce the adverse publicity abroad accompanying any Chinese delivery of goods and weapons to Tanzania, something which was not always possible in the past.) Tanzanian seamen would also be trained under the agreement so that they could participate fully in operating the new company. This was an opportunity Tanzanians would not have had if the joint shipping line had not been established.

The Friendship Textile Mill. On the industrial side, one Chinese-aided project needs to be examined for its contribution to Tanzanian development. On 29 July 1966 President Nyerere laid the foundation stone of the £2.5 million integrated textile mill at Ubungo near Dar Es-Salaam.[2] It was to be completed within two and a half years. In fact the mill was inaugurated in less than two, on 6 July 1968.[3] This project, apart from being the largest fully-integrated textile mill in East Africa (producing 24 million square yards of cloth and 2 million pounds of thread for use by smaller textile mills), illustrated the main elements of Chinese aid-giving to African states.

The initial Chinese approach was welcomed by Tanzanian Government officials.[4] With the textile mill as with all other projects, the training of the required personnel was made the priority task. The Chinese did not ask for university graduates or even school-certificate holders. They simply asked for primary school leavers or simply literate people. They then turned Tanzanians into skilled men in a short time through intensive on-the-job training – an

---

[1] N.C.N.A., 7 July 1966.   [2] Dar Es-Salaam Radio, 29 July 1966.
[3] S.C.M.P. No. 4216, 12 July 1968.
[4] Discussions with Tanzanian Government officials and Chinese personnel.

approach which they had used effectively in their own country. In fact, they did not simply present the government with a new factory or project: they did something more important – they equipped Tanzanians with technical skills which the country, like most African countries, was short of. In a situation where technicians are scarce, this approach has been extremely advantageous. I have been told that, in contrast, other aid-givers would present Tanzania with a list of personnel required, most of whom had to be trained in the donor country.

The training of Tanzanian citizens to man the project from the beginning means that, as soon as a project is completed, the Chinese personnel leave Tanzania, having ensured that the local citizens have mastered the operation. Some of course stay in an advisory capacity, but only at the specific request of the Tanzanian Government. This approach ensures that both management and staff are from the start under Tanzanian control. The Chinese are said to have insisted that no European should be employed in any Chinese-aided project. Even the suggestion of bringing in Pakistanis was opposed. The Chinese preferred that if any misunderstanding arose this should not happen because of sabotage or manipulation by foreigners, who could not be as committed to the success of a project as Tanzanians.

Moreover, by insisting on Africans operating the project, the Chinese meant to prove that Africans and Asians were not backward, as suggested by Europeans, but could be taught to handle complicated machinery just like people in the technologically advanced states.[1]

Chinese determination, discipline and wholehearted devotion to work, their sense of urgency and awareness of the speed needed in development, coupled with Tanzanian co-operation, often led to projects being completed well ahead of schedule. Tanzanians were also impressed that many of the Chinese personnel who came to the country did not ask to be put up in expensive hotels the cost of which would siphon away the better part of the loan involved. In fact they lived in cheap hostels and in many cases erected makeshift houses of wood and tin without cost to the host government.[2] This practice which only the Chinese adopt inevitably makes a favourable

[1] Interview with official of Chinese Embassy in Dar Es-Salaam.
[2] I visited some of these makeshift houses at Ubungo near Dar Es-Salaam.

impression in countries where people are accustomed to seeing foreign officials living in luxurious houses.

Critics could of course point out that since Chinese personnel only stayed for relatively short periods they could well put up with the hard living conditions, and that they had to go back to China so soon because China needed them. This however ignores the contribution the Chinese have made by their personnel practice, and inadvertently recognises the disinterestedness of the Chinese aid. If China was prepared to spare much-needed technicians, they were making a great sacrifice to help a friendly country.

The Friendship Textile Mill has been criticised in some quarters as outmoded and inferior to the most up-to-date mills in the field. This criticism ignores some fundamental factors of developing economies. In the first place, urban unemployment is the main scourge of new African states and a highly sophisticated textile mill employing a hundred people would do little to alleviate the problems. The Friendship Textile Mill gives employment to 3,000 Tanzanians and thus helps to solve the urban unemployment problem. There is everything in favour of a country making use of the resources most available to it. In African states, labour, in many cases unskilled labour, is most freely available. A project that turns literate people into skilled workmen is therefore most advantageous. Moreover donors for sophisticated capital-intensive projects are hard to come by, especially when many developing countries compete for aid from the few technologically advanced ones. For Tanzania with a policy of self-reliance and self-help, a start therefore had to be made with projects requiring less foreign capital and more local resources. (The fact that the mill uses Tanzanian cotton as raw material is also a strong point in its favour.) The Tanzanians working in the mill have not complained of breakdowns in the machines which they have not been able to rectify. (Since the Chinese had no vested interest in staying and making personal profit on the mill, the training of Tanzanians was most thorough.)

A second line of criticism, however, is more serious. Obviously at the present level of Tanzanian development the textile mill is much appreciated, but one has to look forward to a time when more sophisticated machinery will be needed. Since the Chinese gave the Tanzanian personnel only on-the-job training they will not be able to handle the new machines to which they will be introduced in the future. It would have been better if theory had also been taught. This point was raised with Tanzanian officials who acknowledged it as a mistake but pointed out that it was being rectified with other projects. The Chinese now combine theory with practice and draw up syllabuses in accordance with Tanzanian wishes. This was specifically taking place in the Farm Implements and Tools Factory built near the textile mill with Chinese aid and by Chinese and Tanzanian personnel.[1]

Although still having teething troubles in 1969, the textile mill was already producing various grades of material, including specialised products such as combat uniforms for the Tanzania People's Defence Forces and the National Service uniforms. The mill's products have also been exported to Zambia, Kenya, Canada, Sweden and the United States. On balance then, the textile mill has been a positive contribution to Tanzania's economic and technical goals. It may not yet be making profits but this element cannot be regarded as the sole criterion of a project's success. In February 1968 Chiang Ta, China's economic representative in Tanzania, declared in connection with the textile mill that 'Chinese assistance is designed to help the recipient country embark on the road of independent development and self-reliance.'[2] That declaration can hardly be disputed.

Other samples of Chinese aid and assistance included the 100 KW short-wave transmitter completed in December 1966, three months ahead of schedule;[3] printing works supplied to the Tanzanian Government free of charge (the printing press used in the production of *The Nationalist*, the ruling Tanganyika African National Union newspaper); the headquarters of the T.A.N.U. Youth League; the Economic Exhibition Pavilion at Nazi Moja in Dar Es-Salaam and

[1] This factory is expected to eliminate the need to import agricultural implements from abroad. The training programme for the Tanzanian personnel had three phases; (1) two months theoretical training followed by (2) demonstrations, drawings and practical operations on the machines, lectures by personnel from various Ministries on the position of the factory in society and the economy; and (3) practical training concerning production. The General Manager of the project, which was started in 1967, who had himself twice visited China spoke highly of Chinese help in the agricultural sector. When I visited the factory there were only 26 Chinese experts left, who were helping to train Tanzanians. I met the head of the Technical Assistance team, Comrade Li, who was earning not more than £30 a month and was the highest paid of the Chinese personnel.
[2] N.C.N.A., 7 Feb. 1968.
[3] Dar Es-Salaam Radio, 7 Dec. 1966.

other forms of aid under the cultural co-operation agreement of May 1966.[1]

Chinese aid to Zanzibar also continued. This included the training of Zanzibar youths in China and a six months' course sponsored by the Department of Works, Communications and Power;[2] the building of a printing press at Saateni in 1967;[3] the completion of a leather and shoe factory in February 1968;[4] the building of a factory for the manufacture of small implements and tools requested by the Zanzibar Minister of Agriculture as well as the construction of residential quarters for workers at Kisongoni;[5] the training of some three hundred tractor drivers,[6] together with the construction of a tractor and farm implements repair plant completed in 1968.[7] A Chinese medical team working in the country built the island's first pharmaceutical workshop at the Lenin Hospital which was opened by Tanzania's first National Vice President Hamani Karume.[8]

The Chinese were also responsible for the establishment of the Upenja State Farm. This involved clearing 1,300 acres of wilderness and turning it into Zanzibar's first mechanised farm. The first group of Chinese agro-technicians arrived in 1965 and set about the difficult task of converting the land and at the same time training Zanzibari technicians – harvester operators, machine repairmen, tractor drivers, etc.[9] At the end of the period the farm, producing rice and expected to produce large quantities of grain, beans and vegetables, was completed. It was handed over to the Zanzibar Government on 11 January 1969, the eve of the 5th anniversary of the Zanzibar revolution.[10]

All in all, then, Chinese technical and economic aid to Tanzania continued during this period despite the events of the Cultural Revolution. By May 1968 some £12.5 million of the £16 million interest-free loan pledged in 1964 had been utilised, thus making China Tanzania's main source of development aid since independ-

[1] Hsinhua News Agency, 22 May 1966.
[2] Zanzibar Radio, 19 May 1966.
[3] B.B.C. *S.W.B.* Weekly Supplement Part IV, No. 438, 13 Oct. 1967.
[4] *Ibid.* No. 456, 23 Feb. 1968.   [5] *Ibid.* No. 374, 15 July 1966.
[6] Peking Radio, 23 Feb. 1967.   [7] N.C.N.A., 18 Sept. 1968.
[8] S.C.M.P. No. 4248, 30 Aug. 1968.
[9] S.C.M.P. No. 4339, 16 Jan. 1969.
[10] B.B.C. *S.W.B.* Weekly Supplement Part IV, No. 502, 17 Jan. 1969.

ence in 1961.[1] This figure did not include other forms of cultural and military aid which were non-refundable; an example of such aid was the building in 1967 of an extension to the Tanzanian Police Training School at Moshi in northern Tanzania.[2] When President Nyerere visited China in June 1968 another agreement provided for a further £100,000 for agricultural projects – irrigated farms, small scale hydro-electric plants and flood control measures.[3] It is, however, true to say that new Chinese commitments during the period of the Cultural Revolution were undertaken mainly on the initiative of the Tanzanians who continued to send high-powered government delegations to China – delegations which included the President and Vice President. These delegations could hold effective discussions with responsible Chinese authorities in Peking after preliminary discussion with the Chinese diplomatic and economic missions in Dar Es-Salaam.[4] By far the most important decision taken during this period was in connection with the construction of the Tanzania–Zambia Railroad – the largest single foreign-aid project China has embarked upon anywhere in the world.[5]

The Tanzania–Zambia Railroad Project. As the Tan-Zam railroad project was the responsibility of Zambia as well as China and Tanzania the decision making process had to go on in three different capitals. It was complicated and slow because initially Zambia had no experience of Chinese-aided projects. On achieving independence in 1964 Zambia recognised China and a Chinese envoy arrived in Lusaka in 1965. This was a time when the political situation in Southern Rhodesia was deteriorating from the African point of view. It was becoming clear that the minority regime in that country was bent on proclaiming independence on the basis of white minority rule. If that step were taken, Zambia would be one of the African states to react in such a way as to help the African nationalists in Rhodesia. Zambia's position was, however, delicate. Having no

[1] Figure given by Mr Jamal, Tanzania's Finance Minister in a speech to Parliament on 10 May 1968.
[2] N.C.N.A., 13 Jan. 1967. Nyerere laid the foundation stone on 12 Jan. 1967.
[3] *Africa Contemporary Record*, 1968, p. 222.
[4] In 1966 13 Tanzanian delegations visited China and in 1967 eight important delegations visited the country, with the number only dropping to three in 1968.
[5] The final agreement signed in 1970 put the cost of the railroad project at £167,067,055, with repayments beginning in 1983 and spread over 30 years. Repayments will be in third party currency or export proceeds from Zambia and Tanzania.

outlet to the sea, she depended on Portuguese-controlled Angola and Mozambique and on Rhodesian railways to get her exports to the outside world. Moreover, her economy was interwoven with that of Southern Africa as a whole rather than with the north. If decisions were to be taken against Rhodesia and the Portuguese in the interests of African nationalists, then Zambia needed an alternative outlet to the sea which would bypass Portugal's authority and Rhodesia's railways. The need to build a railway between Tanzania and Zambia was therefore at first primarily political. This does not mean that the economic reason for undertaking such an ambitious project were inconsequential. Apart from the reorientation of Zambia's economic links which would result from the new project, Tanzania would also benefit. The country's southern region, which is poorly served with roads and more under-developed than the other parts, will benefit from the arterial roads constructed to join the railway. The servicing of the region with rail and road links will also help in the eventual exploitation of substantial coal deposits which have been discovered as well as of other mineral resources whose commercial viability is at the moment in doubt.[1]

In 1965, having decided to build the railway, Zambia and Tanzania approached Western countries.[2] A joint British–Canadian team of experts considered the project and reported that it was not viable, and would not contribute to the social and economic development of the two countries.[3] On the basis of this report the World Bank turned down a request to finance the project. After this rejection a joint delegation went to the Soviet Union; the Soviet Government turned down the project.[4] No doubt the U.S.S.R. still supporting the Aswan High Dam project in Egypt did not relish the idea of being saddled with another huge project in Africa while the dam was not yet fully completed. There could be no question of tactically agreeing to build the railway in order to goad the West into changing its view. An open undertaking by a super-power

[1] The existence of coal deposits in the southern region of Tanzania was known earlier. However, in the course of their survey work the Chinese have discovered what are described as deposits of coal far greater than what was known to the Tanzanian Government before.
[2] Interview with Tanzanian Government official.
[3] Short discussion with the Chief Executive Officer of the Tan-Zam Railroad Authority in Dar Es-Salaam.
[4] Interview with X.

could not be reneged upon without loss of prestige, if the West should call the Soviet Union's bluff.

At this stage it seemed that the project would have to be dropped for lack of finance and technical knowhow. However, a joint approach was made to China, though there was little serious hope that it would succeed.[1] The two governments concerned took rather different views of the approach to China. Zambian officials were prone to consider it as a tactical move to get the Western powers interested in the railway and secure World Bank aid.[2] The Tanzanian officials took a more serious view having now had experience of Chinese activity. The approach to China was successful and a Chinese team was to be sent out in 1966 for a preliminary examination of the proposed route. Zambian officials still thought that the West could be goaded into backing the project for fear of a Chinese 'take-over'. This view, however, proved counter-productive in that the West could easily 'see through' the Chinese decision and thus regard it as a bluff aimed at obtaining Western finance.[3]

In the second half of 1966 the Chinese team submitted its report to the two governments. Contrary to the earlier British–Canadian report, it came down in favour of the rail-link.[4] The Chinese also stated that they would be prepared to build and finance the project. At this stage the most difficult obstacle to the projected Chinese aid was not imperialist machinations but Zambian officials who still considered that the Chinese announcement would rouse the West from its lack of interest. They therefore stalled hoping by so doing to get the West round to their point of view.[5] Zambian opposition was gradually overcome as relations between Zambia and China grew warmer. Zambia's Vice-President visited China in August 1966 and later in the year a trade delegation and a goodwill delegation followed.

In June 1967 President Kaunda himself visited China during a tour of Asian countries,[6] and on 23 June an agreement on economic and technical co-operation was signed.[7] This provided for an interest-free loan from China of some $16.8 million to be used in

[1] Interview with X. [2] Interview with X.
[3] The West regarded these tactics as a form of 'blackmail'.
[4] Tanzania's Minister for Economic Affairs announced the imminent submission of the report in June 1966.
[5] Interview with X.
[6] S.C.M.P. No. 3967, 26 June 1967. [7] B.B.C. *S.W.B.* Part III, No. 2502, 28 June 1967.

financing projects mutually agreed upon. The first part of the loan was to be used to meet the cost of tarring a road from Lusaka to the Barotse Province, and Chinese technicians were expected to survey this project before the end of the year.[1] Kaunda also discussed the proposed Tan–Zam rail-link and at the end of the visit he announced a Chinese offer to build the one thousand mile railroad, noting that the Western countries and Japan had earlier refused to help.[2]

President Kaunda's visit confirmed the close and cordial relations developing between China and Zambia, although it was made at a time when factional violence among various Red Guard groups had broken out and when the Foreign Ministry had come under severe attack. It also marked the end of opposition by some Zambian officials to accepting Chinese financial and technical aid for the railway.

From August to September 1967, a joint Ministerial economic delegation from Zambia and Tanzania visited China and on 5 September signed an agreement on the construction of the railway,[3] for which the Chinese Government undertook to extend to the Governments of Tanzania and Zambia an interest-free loan.[4] Although no hard and fast figure was as yet agreed upon the venture was expected to cost about £100 million, and the agreement was to be implemented by the signing of protocols.[5] Western observers, viewing the rather chaotic situation caused by the Cultural Revolution, doubted whether China could ever fulfil her commitment. These doubts proved unfounded, however, as Chinese engineers and technicians arrived in Zambia, at the beginning of January 1968, less than four months after the signing of the agreement in Peking. On 19 January, a team of Chinese railway engineers and road construction experts working in Zambia had an informal meeting with President Kaunda. The President stressed the mission's importance for Zambia's economic revolution, and also to free Zambia 'from dependence on an oppressive goverment whose— policies China has continually condemned'. The leader of the

[1] Rhodesia Radio, 26 June 1967.
[2] He also noted that China did not, at that moment, want to join the United Nations as she felt it was an organisation run entirely by big nations.
[3] B.B.C. *S.W.B.* Part III, No. 2561, 6 Sept. 1967.
[4] See S.C.M.P. No. 4017, 8 Sept. 1967.
[5] Interview with Executive Officer of the Railroad Authority.

Chinese railway team said that 'Chou En-lai had personally stressed the importance of the project for Zambia and has been continually pressing for its implementation'.[1] Already study maps and blueprints had been completed and ground work began at the end of January.[2] The seriousness of the Chinese approach was no longer in doubt. In February President Kaunda announced the appointment of an ambassador of cabinet rank to China.[3] He believed it was necessary to send Zambia's highest ranking ambassador to Peking, not just because of the size of China's population but because she was helping to build a railway line in East Africa.

On 8 April China's Chargé d'Affaires in Dar Es-Salaam, Chou Poping, and the competent Zambian and Tanzanian officials, signed three protocols implementing the 1967 agreement. The protocols covered forms of loans to be provided for the railway; the dispatch of technical personnel by China, their treatment and working conditions; and physical survey and design work for the railway.[4] In May Chinese engineers and technicians, together with Tanzanian workers, began the actual survey and design work on the Tanzania section of the route and, by October 1968, 80% of the preliminary surveying had been completed well ahead of schedule.[5] The head of the Chinese team, Chin Hui, accompanied Tanzanian, Zambian and Chinese Government representatives on a tour of inspection of the work being done on the Tanzanian side.[6] After praising the hard work of the Chinese technicians, the Tanzanian Minister of Communications pointed out that when completed the railway would not only expedite the economic development of Tanzania and Zambia, but would also help the African people in their struggle against imperialism and colonialism. '... the construction of the railway is a contribution to the total liberation of Africa. That is why it has evoked hatred and sabotage from the imperialists and colonialists.'[7] The Zambian High Commissioner to Tanzania spoke of the importance of the railway to Zambia and dispelled 'imperialist rumours' that she was still reluctant to undertake the project.[8] He then predicted that all the imperialist machinations aimed at sabotaging the project would collapse in the face of

[1] Lusaka Radio, 19 Jan. 1968.   [2] B.B.C. *S.W.B.* Part IV, No. 2675, 22 Jan. 1968.
[3] The appointment was made on 14 Feb. 1968.
[4] *Peking Review*, No. 16, 19 Apr. 1968.   [5] S.C.M.P. No. 4285, 24 Oct. 1968.
[6] *Peking Review*, No. 45, 8 Nov. 1968.   [7] *Ibid.*   [8] *Ibid.*

the determination of the three countries to build the railway.[1] Later in October the Zambian Minister of Transport inspected the construction camp of the Chinese team working on the Zambian section.[2] By the end of this period, survey work by the Chinese was already well advanced.

This leaves us to consider why China undertook so huge a project in Africa, one that would certainly stretch her own resources. Is she merely altruistic, contributing to the development of two countries without expecting political gains, or is it an attempt to secure a permanent foothold in a part of Africa which is bound to become the focus of the African struggle against the minority regimes in Southern Africa? Or by strengthening economic ties and by the method of financing the project does she aim to gain paramount control of the economies of the two states and thus create a neo-colonial situation where important decisions cannot be made without her fiat? Or is she trying to create a fortress north of the Zambesi river whence future military expeditions can be launched against Southern Africa? Or could one see the project in the context of the great-power struggle for Africa: as the Soviet Union is so strong in North Africa is China countering in the only way possible – by gaining control of East and Central Africa? Or could it be that the Chinese wish to leave in that part of Africa, an indelible mark, a symbol of China's status as a great power? Or is there a connection between the Tan–Zam project and the less ambitious Guinea–Mali railway project for which China promised aid at the same time.[3]

These questions have been answered very differently by various interested parties. To the regimes of Southern Africa, China is bent on spreading communism by violence and military control. Her support for national liberation movements in these areas and the supply of weapons and ammunition free of charge form part of a great plan to eradicate Western civilisation in Southern Africa. The railway when completed, together with its infrastructure, would provide an excellent communication system for Chinese military 'aggression'. To the fact that China is the only great power that does not have troops stationed in foreign territories, and that she has consistently stressed the responsibility of each people to carry out revolution, it is replied that when China is well entrenched

[1] *Peking Review*, No. 45, 8 Nov. 1968.   [2] S.C.M.P. No. 4293, 6 Nov. 1968.
[3] See below, p. 215.

in that part of Africa all this will change – Chinese troops will come in. Moreover the minority regimes argue that in the struggle to come the Zambian and Tanzanian Governments will be mere ciphers, their economies and decision-making systems will have been taken over by the Chinese. The minority regimes will therefore go to great lengths to ensure the Chinese 'advance' is stemmed. Their concern is not allayed by the Tanzanian Government's statement referring to the projected railway as a 'contribution to the total liberation of Africa'.[1]

Apprehension about Chinese motivations is, however, not limited to the minority regimes of Southern Africa. Western commercial concerns with interests in that part of Africa never tire of asking how Chinese activities will affect their interests. They point out that they will be damaged by the Chinese method of financing the local costs of the project. If Zambia and Tanzania received some £20 million worth of Chinese goods for sale, so that the proceeds could be used to meet the local costs this would mean a gradual erosion of their trading position, especially as there is a trend towards the nationalisation of wholesale import and export and a greater control of retail trade. There is also concern that the relatively free movement of merchandise between Tanzania, Kenya and Uganda would help spread the market for Chinese goods to those other countries. While not willing to concede that Chinese goods are superior to their own products and would thus drive these out of the market, it is thought that the Chinese could take a political decision to cut prices and thus make Western goods uncompetitive. Paradoxically, it is Western observers who are always pointing to the paucity of consumer goods in China and the Soviet Union! The fears of the Western commercial interests are now, however, totally preposterous. One only argues that there is no reason why these interests should dominate the markets of these new African states which are struggling to maintain a non-aligned posture.

This having been said, the problems resulting from the ways of using the loan must be examined. Obvious problems are involved in a loan indirectly tied to imports. Tanzania was already importing goods worth £3m–£4m from China each year, and there were indications that not all the goods imported for sale in Tanzanian

[1] See for instance the Tanzanian Minister of Labour's statement of 19 Oct. 1968. Mr J. M. Lusinde referred to the sabotage of the project by colonialists.

markets were being sold.¹ As the loan for the railway will require annual imports of some £8 million, this will present the Tanzanian Government with great difficulties. There is definitely a limit to the absorptive capacity of the internal market. To fulfil its obligations the government must increase its control of retail trade. (It has now done this by nationalising wholesale trade, thus reducing the difficulties presented by the previous unwillingness of retailers to receive Chinese goods.) This action inevitably portends ill for Western interests. This will be even more the case if the experiment spreads to Zambia, where these interests have more at stake. As they see it, it will mean an economic link with China and give that country greater influence and control.

As for the attitude of the parties directly involved in the construction of the railway, the Tanzanians and Zambians argue that accepting aid from China does not mean that their interests are being subordinated to hers; that they retain and intend to retain the sovereign right to make independent decisions in the interest of their peoples; that they have with equal willingness accepted aid from the Western and Scandinavian countries when no unacceptable political strings have been attached; that, moreover, the Western countries were first approached for help in building the railway and that only when they rejected this appeal was an approach made to China; after all, as independent States Tanzania and Zambia are entitled to accept aid from a country which has shown interest in their socio-economic development; rejection of Chinese help

[1] This was alleged to be due to the domination of the retail trade by Asians who were accustomed to importing their products from the Western countries. This view seem to be confirmed by two experiments reported to the writer. A Kenyan student surveying Chinese influence in Tanzanian markets in 1968 discovered that the shops in Independence Avenue and its environments (the main shopping centre in Dar Es-Salaam) rejected Chinese goods. He went along with Chinese-made clocks to see whether the shops would be interested in importing them. He was told that it would be impossible to sell them as they were inferior and no spare parts were available in the country. He then went to the Kariakoo Market (where the poorer people do their shopping) and discovered that the African petty traders were quite prepared to buy clocks and asked him for more. The traders said the clocks were cheaper than those they had previously sold and nothing was said about their inferiority. (Interview with P.) There was also the case of an African importer of goods from some Western and Communist states who encountered the same difficulty with the big shops in Dar Es-Salaam. He was given the same reasons – impossible to sell Chinese goods, no spare parts available, inferior quality. (Discussion with the importer.) It seems that those who controlled the retail trade were deliberately trying to undermine the import of Chinese goods.

would involve Zambia's continued dependence on the goodwill of the minority regimes which Africans are bent on overthrowing, and this would postpone the fulfilment of the aspirations of the peoples of Southern Africa; that whatever the motivation of China in offering to build the railway, the important issue is that the project is needed by Tanzania and Zambia, and as long as the two countries have a clear idea of their interests and objectives and have everything under control, the motives of China, even if they are unhealthy, are irrelevant. After all, President Nkrumah of Ghana accepted American aid for the Volta Dam project without being subservient to America and President Nasser accepted considerable American aid and still maintained his independent policy.

Chinese help for Tanzania during the years 1966–8 was not confined to the technical, economic and cultural fields. The military aid embarked upon in 1963–5 continued with the delivery of various grades of Chinese weapons and equipment to the Tanzania People's Defence Force (T.P.D.F.). These weapons included semi-automatic and automatic rifles as well as machine guns and long range field guns. The scope of the Chinese military mission was also expanded, as Chinese weapons were supplied to the Police Force and the National Youth Service, thus gradually replacing the old British weapons left behind at independence. With China helping to construct the expanded Police Training School at Moshi and with the Police Force being equipped with Chinese weapons, training was gradually transferred to the Chinese.[1] Critics may point out that this was the use of salami tactics to 'take over' the area of security in the country, but, in fact, Tanzanian officers still control security.

Canadians were helping to train the air wing of the T.P.D.F. and Tanzanians were sent to Canada to be trained as pilots. There were, however, reports of clashes between Chinese military advisers and Canadian air force experts working in Tanzania.[2] These clashes may have been one of the reasons why the air-training agreement with Canada was not renewed.[3] It is reliably reported that the Tanzanian goodwill military delegation which visited China

[1] Interview with X.   [2] Discussion with Officer of the T.P.D.F.
[3] President Nyerere said that the Canadian team had successfully completed its task and there was therefore no need to renew the contract. It is known, however, that some of the Tanzanians sent to Canada returned home without completing their training.

in August 1966 reached an understanding with Peking about the future construction of a Navy and Air Force by China and that naval officers were sent to China for training without any publicity.[1] It was thought that Canadian economic and technical aid was welcome, but that in the military field, the loyalty of Canadian officers in an air force would be in doubt in the event of a showdown with Portuguese forces in Mozambique, since both Portugal and Canada belonged to N.A.T.O. It was therefore possible that Tanzania's military secrets would be passed on to Portugal.

By the end of the period a closer working relationship existed between the T.P.D.F. and the Chinese military experts attached to the forces. This was a reflection of the general status of Sino-Tanzanian relations at that time.

In concluding this discussion of Sino-Tanzanian relations, it is appropriate to refer to President Nyerere's visit to China in June 1968. He told the Chinese that he had not come to ask China to declare Tanzania a nuclear protectorate as this would be a new form of colonialism. China's friendship with Tanzania was based on respect and equality and did not stop Tanzania from being friendly with states hostile to China – this was an assertion of the country's independence. The friendship, the President said, at the farewell banquet he gave in Peking on 21 June:

is not an exclusive thing, and we do not interfere in each other's affairs. When we feel able to co-operate we do so; if either of us feels reluctant, then we move on to some other matter. I can state quite categorically that Tanzania is enriched by this friendship, and we value it. No outside nation will be able to interfere with it; only we ourselves, by our own actions to one another, could destroy it. I have therefore no reason to believe that friendship between Tanzania and China will not continue indefinitely, and grow stronger as time passes.[2]

I think the Chinese too cherish the same hope.

(iv) *Sino-Guinean and Sino-Mali Relations.*

Sino-Guinean Relations. Guinea was one of the few African countries China remained on friendly terms with during the period of the Cultural Revolution. In the first place the militant solidarity and friendship which existed between the two states in 1963–5 con-

---
[1] Interview with X. China is now building a base for Tanzania's Navy. There is also a concerted attempt to turn the T.P.D.F. into a People's Army closer and more useful to the people.
[2] *Peking Review*, No. 26, 28 June 1968.

tinued in 1966–8. Political solidarity was further promoted by the vehement hostility shown by the two states to the overthrow of President Nkrumah of Ghana in February 1966. President Sekou Touré welcomed Nkrumah from China and declared him a co-President of Guinea.

Sino-Guinean relations also remained warm because the events of the Cultural Revolution did not stop Chinese technical personnel working in Guinea nor delay the implementation of the Chinese added projects which had already begun in 1963–5. In January 1966, Guinea's Minister of Economic Development laid the foundation stone of the 'Palais du Peuple' which was to be built with Chinese aid.[1] The plan for the building was drawn up by Chinese architects; it was expected to be completed in 1967 and to be capable of holding 2,500 people. The building stands today, the most magnificent edifice south of the Sahara.[2] At its inauguration in September 1967 Sekou Touré paid tribute to the 'selfless and worthy behaviour of the Chinese representatives and experts who have always enjoyed the high respect and admiration of our people, our working class in particular. We salute the political, economic and moral significance of this disinterested aid given us by the People's Republic of China.'[3]

In November 1966 a Guinean economic delegation visited China and signed a further agreement on economic and technical cooperation. The delegation also signed an agreement on the provision of trade loans to Guinea.[4] The amount involved was about $6 million. Chinese goods and products were to be delivered to Guinea but the latter was not required to pay for them with exports from her slender resources of foreign exchange.[5] Premier Chou En-lai got away from the preoccupations of the Cultural Revolution to attend the ceremony.[6]

In January 1967 a Chinese Government delegation led by a Vice Foreign Minister visited Guinea in connection with the opening of the Kinkon hydro-electric power station, built with Chinese aid and by Chinese technicians in co-operation with Guinean workers.[7] The power station, situated some 400 kilometres north-

[1] Conakry Radio, 21 Jan. 1966. [2] The comment of an O.A.U. official.
[3] N.C.N.A., 26 Sept. 1967. [4] B.B.C. S.W.B. Part III No. 2320, 18 Nov. 1966.
[5] Goldman, op. cit., p. 206. [6] B.B.C. S.W.B. Part III No. 2320, 18 Nov. 1966.
[7] S.C.M.P. No. 3870, 30 Jan. 1967.

east of Conakry, supplies electricity to the main cities and agricultural areas of central Guinea.[1] The Guinean Government commended the achievements of the Chinese team, especially as the project was constructed on a most difficult site, and, more important, because it raised the Guinean's enthusiasm for work.[2]

In February 1967 Sekou Touré referred to the invaluable work the Chinese agricultural teams were doing and stated that their approach was proving successful because their methods suited Guinea's conditions:

At present Guinea does not need big technical measures in her agriculture because our peasants have not reached such a level. We want small technical measures that are suitable to their level, to raise agricultural production. China has rich experiences in developing agriculture, so we want to profit by the Chinese presence in Guinea to find such measures as are suitable for the farming and rural conditions of our country to develop our agriculture.[3]

Chinese agricultural experts were not only working on various agricultural projects throughout the country; they were also helping to build a tea factory and a tea plantation in Macenta; both these were opened in February 1968 in the presence of the Guinean President and the visiting Tanzanian President Nyerere.[4] Later in the year the Chinese embarked on yet another factory dealing with Guinean agricultural products. A groundnut oil factory capable of producing 3,500 tons a year was begun in Dabola city.[5] Expected to be completed in some fifteen months, it is now in operation.

In the following year, China agreed to embark on major new projects including a 200,000 ton cement factory, the modernisation of the Conakry–Karkan railway line and the port of Conakry and a 'vast agricultural development programme'.[6]

The projected Guinea–Mali Railway. After China had signed the agreement to build the Tan–Zam railway in September 1967, Guinea and Mali also decided to approach China. Their aim was a less ambitious rail-link between Bamako, the capital of Mali, and Guinea. Although both Mali and Senegal belonged to the Organisation of Senegal River States, to which Guinea and Mauri-

[1] B.B.C. *S.W.B.* Weekly Supplement No. 402, Part IV, 3 Feb. 1967.
[2] Hsinhua News Agency, 1 Feb. 1967. [3] *Current Scene*, Vol. 15, 15 Sept. 1968.
[4] B.B.C. *S.W.B.* Weekly Supplement No. 458, Part IV, 8 Mar. 1968.
[5] Conakry Radio, 10 Dec. 1968.
[6] B.B.C. *S.W.B.* Part IV, No. 3220, 4 Nov. 1969.

tania also belong, the ruling party in Mali had a long-standing dispute with Senegal's President Senghor. However, Mali is a landlocked state like Zambia and desired an outlet to the sea through neighbouring Guinea which was ideologically compatible. As the two countries maintained close relations with China they decided to seek Chinese aid and finance.

Since China's Ambassadors to Mali and Guinea, Lai Ya-li and Ko Hua, were recalled in 1967, as part of the general withdrawal of Chinese envoys, negotiations were mainly conducted by Mali and Guinean delegations visiting China.[1] In May 1968 a joint delegation headed by Ousman Ba and Lansana Beavogui, the Malian and Guinean Foreign Ministers, signed an agreement providing for the construction of a Guinea–Mali railway to be financed and built by China. Finance Minister Li Hsien-nien signed for China in the presence of Chou En-lai.[2]

In August 1968 a Chinese team arrived in Conakry and proceeded to Mali to survey the Mali section of the railway which would be only 150 kilometres long. Their work was completed in the first half of November and they flew out of Bamako to Guinea on 15 November.[3] Four days later a military coup overthrew the government of Mali's President Modibo Keita.[4] Relations between Guinea and Mali consequently deteriorated and nothing was done for the rest of the year on the joint railway project. Some improvement in relations with Senegal lessened the need for the railway.

Sino–Mali Relations. Common anti-imperialist ideology which in 1963–5 had kept Sino–Mali relations warm maintained them thus in 1966–8. The presence of Chinese agricultural and technical personnel remained the symbol of Chinese commitment. Mali was, however, also receiving considerable amounts of aid from the Soviet Union. The army was completely equipped with Soviet weapons and so was the air force. Mali therefore, like Congo-

[1] The envoys were recalled in the process of the general withdrawal of Chinese envoys in 1967.
[2] Bamako Radio, 28 May 1968. *Peking Review*, No. 22, 31 May 1968. The railway project was expected to cost some $50 million. This was a minor project compared with the Tan–Zam railroad. See W. A. Nielsen, *The Great Powers and Africa*, Pall Mall Press, London, 1969, p. 234.
[3] N.C.N.A. dispatch from Bamako, 15 Nov. 1968.
[4] For the implications of the coup for Sino–Malian relations. See below, p. 218.

Brazzaville and indeed all other African states with which China maintained cordial relations, shrewdly refused to take an open stand in the Sino-Soviet wranglings. Although, in their welcoming speeches to Mali and other government delegations, the Chinese continually referred to the 'Soviet revisionists as the appendage of imperialism', African government delegations astutely avoided any reference to the Soviet Union in their responses. It was, as it were, a practical application of the non-alignment principle developed in the period of the cold war. Now it was prudently applied to avoid incurring the wrath of the Soviet Union in the interest of China. By strict adherence to those issues of interest to Mali and Africa much could be gained from both sides.

However, during the period an event occurred which forced many African states to declare their position. The Soviet invasion of Czechoslovakia in August 1968 put the Mali Government in an embarrassing situation. Soviet action had been condemned by China and most African states, others maintained an embarrassed silence. But the Mali Government approved the action and thus showed the extent of Soviet influence in the country. China noted this but wisely did not allow it to interfere with Sino-Mali relations. It must have been clear how little she could as yet influence Mali. Mali's approval of Soviet action was reversed in less than four months when the military government which overthrew President Keita in November stated that it could not condone the invasion.

On the economic front, relations with Mali remained good. Chinese exports to Mali in 1966 exceeded the 1965 mark, reaching £3.68 million. In 1967 the figure climbed further to £4.14 million as China increased exports to help pay for local projects being set up by Chinese technical personnel. In June 1966 a Mali Ministerial delegation led by Madeira Keita signed an agreement in Peking under which China was to furnish additional loans.[1] The agreement involved a credit of $3 million to Mali's Central Bank. This was another example of an initiative on the part of an African state to seek Chinese financial help at a time when competitive aid-giving by China, the Soviet Union and the United States had lost momentum.

[1] B.B.C. *S.W.B.* Part III, No. 2184, 11 June 1966. Mali, facing a shortage of hard currency, was obviously in need of this loan. See W. A. Nielsen *The Great Powers and Africa*, p. 232.

Chinese technical personnel working in Mali completed the 'Lightning' match factory; it was inaugurated in Bamako in February 1967, and was expected to obviate the need for imports.[1] During the same month the sugar refinery begun in 1964 was completed and began processing some 400 tons of sugar-cane daily.[2] Chinese technicians had worked extensively on sugar-planting and made it a going concern. At the opening of a Chinese exhibition in Mali, on 27 January 1968, President Keita paid tribute to the Chinese personnel for helping his country to develop an independent national economy, without which political independence was only a chimera. He pointed out that 'Chinese aid has never required us to give an account of what we did at home and abroad and Chinese technical assistance is practical... No word can qualify such an economic assistance which is adapted to our local conditions.'[3] In May 1968 an integrated textile mill built in Segou with Chinese aid was completed.[4] Other Chinese-aided projects included a hotel, a cinema, tea planting, irrigation projects and cement works, apart from gifts of radio transmitters. At the same time a Chinese medical team was working in Mali, as in neighbouring Mauritania and Guinea. Taken together with the agreement to help construct the Mali–Guinea railway, Sino-Mali relations seemed set for a new and warmer period.

That prospect was dampened when on 19 November the Mali Government was overthrown by a coup d'etat staged by junior army officers. Before the coup, the government had decided to set up a people's militia which appeared to have more in common with Chinese ideas than the concept of a well-equipped standing army and air force. China helped to supply uniforms for this militia, which was more than twice the size of the army, and would, when effectively trained, stand as a formidable obstacle to an army takeover of the government.[5] After the overthrow of President Nkrumah the possibilities or such a takeover could not be taken lightly. Mali military delegations visited China in October 1966, August 1967 and finally in June 1968. However, it was not until 1968 that the establishment of the militia became a concrete proposal. China agreed to help with the supply of arms.

[1] N.C.N.A., 3 Feb. 1967.   [2] See above, p. 59.
[3] S.C.M.P. No. 4111, 5 Feb. 1968.   [4] S.C.M.P. No. 4188, 29 May 1968.
[5] Congo-Brazzaville and Guinea have tried the same method.

It would be inaccurate, however, to suggest that the establishment of a people's militia was the reason for the coup. Political struggles within the ruling party seemed to be the main reason, but the prospect of the consolidation of a militia no doubt affected the timing of the coup by the junior officers. There was never any question of personal corruption or aggrandisement on the part of the President, and Franco-Mali relations had improved since the decision of Keita's Government to return to the franc zone. The militia was effectively disarmed by the seizure of the armoury by junior officers, and the army left unopposed.

It was not immediately clear how far the coup would affect Sino-Mali relations. The Chinese did not, in fact, react publicly against the new regime, as it took no action to close either Chinese or Russian missions in Bamako. The rail project with Guinea remained suspended, as Guinea's reaction to the coup was very uncompromising. A few Chinese technicians left Mali for Guinea but many others remained, working on the projects China was helping to construct. This would seem to follow the practice in Algeria in 1965 when Ben Bella was overthrown.[1] Thus by the end of the period Sino-Mali relations were in what might be called a state of suspended animation. Political relations were obviously cool and only the future would tell how the relationship would develop.

3. Economic and Trade Relations

During the previous period there was a considerable increase in Chinese commitments to the economic and technical development of African states, as well as an upward trend in Sino-African trade. Towards the end of the period, however, darkening clouds were beginning to appear on the horizon for China. The situation required reassessment, especially as competitive aid commitments with the Soviet Union and the United States did not seem to have produced a situation totally to the liking of Chinese leaders. African states still sought to act on the practicalities of non-alignment. Moreover, costly pledges had been made to a number of states and these would have to be fulfilled. One would therefore expect that, unless

[1] Though enthusiasm for the rail project on the part of Mali did wane, it was in fact announced in 1969 that the radio station the Chinese were helping to build would be completed at the end of that year. *Africa Research Bulletin* No. 1436, July–August 1969.

absolutely essential, no new Chinese aid commitment would be made to a country where none existed before, and that if any were made then it would be the result of an initiative from the African state concerned. The new policy would be one of intensive commitment to a selected number of states to increase the impact rather than the expensive spreading of China's limited resources. Whereas such a policy was dictated by the international situation, the events of the Cultural Revolution also gave China no alternative, as she turned her primary attention to the bourgeoisification of many of her leaders and the degenerating bureaucratisation of the Communist Party. In fact though trade with Africa seemed to have been little affected her expansive aid commitments declined.

(i) *Trade Relations*
The groundwork for Sino-African trade relations had been laid by Chinese delegations before 1966. Thus it was not now necessary to repeat the elaborate efforts made in the past to promote mutual trade. Chinese entry into hitherto Western-dominated markets no longer met with strong hostility experienced in the late fifties and early sixties. As in the previous periods, the four biggest markets for Chinese goods were in those states – the U.A.R., Morocco, Nigeria and the Sudan – which could by no stretch of imagination be thought to be under Chinese influence. (Nigeria for one did not offer diplomatic recognition to China and in fact accused her of helping the rebel insurgents in the Nigerian civil war.)[1]

Chinese exports to African states, which in 1965 had risen to £39.76 million, rose further in 1966 to £51.75 million. On the other hand imports from Africa fell from the 1965 figure of £39.72 million to £26.57 million in 1966. This might seem to represent a surplus in China's favour but in some cases the sharp increase in exports simply provide a way for China to finance local development projects. In the case of Libya and Nigeria China acquired foreign exchange, as she had no aid programmes in either country. Chinese exports in 1966 could have been still higher if the change in Ghana had not resulted in a 50% decline which continued in 1967. During 1967 the total amount of Chinese exports to Africa decreased, mainly because Sino-Egyptian trade decreased after the June war which closed the Suez Canal, and because exports to

[1] See below, p. 233.

Darkening Clouds: The Cultural Revolution 221

Ghana dropped further to only £0.28 million. Yet Chinese exports, at £44.30 million, still surpassed the 1965 figure. Chinese imports for the same year fell from the £26.57 million of 1966 to £19.17 million, less than half of total exports.

Generally, the importance at first attached to breaking into Western-dominated markets in Africa no longer prevailed, as Chinese trade sought to settle down to the normal commercial practice, and as attention was diverted more and more to the politically more important task of economic and technical aid to the narrowing circle of China's friends.

(ii) *Economic Aid and Technical assistance*
Rather than extending her economic commitments to African states during 1966–8 China attempted to concentrate attention on a selected number of states and to implement the earlier pledges made during the competitive aid giving of the early sixties. I have already referred to the cases of Tanzania and Zambia and the growing importance of East and Central Africa in China's policy.[1]

(*a*) *Congo-Brazzaville and China.* Sino-Congolese relations were not ruffled by the Cultural Revolution throughout 1966 and 1967.[2] Arriving when the campaign was at its most hectic the delegations paid the customary homage to the Cultural Revolution 'personally led by Chairman Mao', indicating the 'indissoluble' solidarity between the two countries. In Congo-Brazzaville Chinese technicians continued their work on projects already underway.

In January 1966 the two governments signed a protocol on the construction of a broadcasting station by Chinese technicians and using Chinese equipment. It would also be used to send out programmes to the Portuguese-controlled territories and to South Africa. Work began in June 1966 and was completed in March 1967.[3] Inaugurated in April, it was the first project to involve China in providing complete sets of equipment and to be completed under the technical co-operation agreement.[4]

A more important project which the Chinese embarked upon in

[1] See above, p. 197.
[2] In those two years 24 Congolese delegations, governmental and non-governmental, went to China including one led by the Prime Minister.
[3] Peking Radio, 20 Jan. 1966. S.C.M.P. No. 3907, 29 Mar. 1967.
[4] Brazzaville Radio, 8 Apr. 1967.

1966 was the textile complex which I referred to in Chapter 4. In November twenty-three Congolese who were expected to take over the administration of the mill were sent to China for a nine months' course in textile technology.[1] At the same time the foundation stone of the factory was laid by President Massamba-Debat and completion was scheduled for the end of 1968.[2] The factory was completed in May 1969 and handed over to the Congolese Government as a symbol of the 'crystalisation of the friendship' between the two countries.[3]

In 1968 the Chinese began to construct a shipyard in the Congo under an agreement signed in February of that year.[4] A Technical School was set up at Port Rousset for the training of Congolese technicians. In August another agreement was signed in Brazzaville. China was to finance two projects costing 250 million CFA francs ($1 million). This would cover the establishment of state farms.[5] In September yet another agreement was signed: Chinese personnel were to be sent to Congo to help construct a radio transmitting station at Edone and to train Congolese radio technicians.[6] In various parts of the country Chinese agricultural experts were also working on sites and helping to set up state farms. A Chinese medical team of 20 doctors was also in the field under an agreement signed in January 1967 and they had brought with them the bulk of medicine and medical equipment used.[7]

All these activities seem to have been little hampered by the change of government in Congo-Brazzaville which resulted from clashes between the army and the militia in August 1968. A people's defence corps or militia was set up late in 1967. Cuban experts helped to train the young Congolese, but the militia were trained and armed with Chinese weapons and equipment which arrived in January 1968.[8] The militia or the Jeunesse, as they were called, openly professed admiration for Chairman Mao and seemed to constitute an ultra-left-wing force in the country. In August clashes broke out between the army and the militia and the army gained the upper hand thanks to its superior organisation and weaponry.

[1] S.C.M.P. No. 3980, 14 July 1967.
[2] B.B.C. *S.W.B.* Part IV, Weekly Supplement No. 394, 2 Dec. 1966.
[3] *Peking Review* No. 39, 26 Sept. 1969.   [4] N.C.N.A., 9 Feb. 1968.
[5] Brazzaville Radio, 12 Aug. 1968.   [6] Brazzaville Radio, 27 Sept. 1968.
[7] Hsinhua, 27 Jan. 1967.
[8] Minister of the Interior's announcement. Brazzaville Radio, 23 Jan. 1968.

These events led eventually to the resignation of President Massamba-Debat and the replacement of the government. These changes, however, did not have any marked effect on Sino-Congolese relations.

As the period ended therefore relations between the Congo and China were gradually improving. In fact the new Congolese Government moved further left in its declarations and rhetoric, until at the end of 1969 Congo-Brazzaville was declared a People's Republic ruled by a Marxist-Leninist party – the Congolese Party of Labour with Marien Ngouabi as the Chairman and Alfred Raoul as Vice Chairman. In denunciation of imperialism, Congolese pronouncements can stand even with the Albanians in violence of language. When the change of government occurred in 1968, Marien Ngouabi was reputedly the most leftist of the militants and he was in charge of the paratroop force.

(b) *Sino-Algerian relations.* In Chapter 4 it was shown that, apart from Chinese medical and agricultural personnel, and gifts of aircraft, ocean-going freighters and other items, little of the $50 million promised in 1963 had been disbursed. In September 1965, however, Chinese experts arrived in Algiers to begin work on the first major project directly to come under the economic and technical co-operation agreement of 1963. In association with Algerian specialists, the Chinese prepared a plan for building a 'palace of exhibitions' which would cover an area of 37,000 square metres. The Algerian Cabinet approved the plan in June 1966 and China was expected to finance the building from the interest-free loan already promised to Algeria.[1] Actual work on the project was expected to begin in the early months of 1967, but it seems this particular project was a victim of the unsettled situation in China. Work did not begin as planned and the foundation stone was not laid until November 1968.[2] It was started only after pressure from the Algerian authorities for the implementation of the long promised aid. One of the problems was scarcity of hard currency. China preferred to finance projects by exporting Chinese goods and using the proceeds to meet the local cost of projects.

In April 1967, Algiers radio stated that China had announced an

[1] B.B.C. *S.W.B.* Weekly Supplement Part IV, No. 372, 1 July 1966.
[2] N.C.N.A., 20 Nov. 1968.

offer of 10 million francs ($2½ million) in hard currency to the Algerian Government as part of the 200 million francs ($50 million) interest-free loan promised in 1963. The Algerian statement noted (incorrectly) that this was the first time a Socialist country had offered this form of assistance to a developing country, and urged other states to follow China's example.[1] (China had of course offered hard currency to Egypt in 1956 and helped Congo-Brazzaville in a similar way in 1964.)

China also undertook under a protocol signed in September 1966 to build a ceramics factory near Guelma as one of the projects to be financed from the 1963 loan. By the end of the period the ceramics factory had not, however, been completed.[2] Obviously the Chinese attached less importance to relations with Algeria than to relations with their friends south of the Sahara, where the events of the Cultural Revolution were not allowed to slow down implementation of aid projects. The militant solidarity of the war of independence days, which had continued during the Ben Bella period, was no longer an over-riding consideration. The focus of attention had turned to Southern Africa especially as the Soviet Union gained more ground militarily and otherwise in North Africa. True in August 1968 a new Chinese medical team with more than fifty members arrived in Algeria for a second tour of duty, but this could not make up for the decline in enthusiasm in other fields.

(c) *Mauritania and China*. Mauritania recognised the Peking Government in 1965. Recognition was followed by the development of friendly relations involving the exchange of delegations and leading to the request that China should assist in Mauritania's development, particularly in agriculture. In 1966 one of the Chinese delegations visiting the country was a team of agricultural experts. An agreement was signed in August under which Chinese agronomists would help develop rice cultivation in the Senegal river valley.[3] This was followed in February 1967 by a Mauritanian Government delegation, led by the Finance Minister, which negotiated an interest-free loan of $4.043 million to be repaid in

[1] B.B.C. *S.W.B.* Part IV, No. 2447, 24 Apr. 1967.
[2] B.B.C. *S.W.B.* Weekly Supplement Part IV, No. 385, 30 Aug. 1966.
[3] B.B.C. *S.W.B.* Weekly Supplement Part IV, No. 381, 2 Sept. 1966.

twenty years.[1] The loan was to be partly used in the development of rice cultivation, land reclamation and the building of a 13 kilometres long dam in the Rosso region. The President inspected this in May 1968.

To consolidate closer relations the Mauritanian President visited China in October 1967, when the Cultural Revolution was still at its peak, and had discussions with Chairman Mao and other Chinese leaders. The visit was most important for the Mauritanian President. He was in the process of developing strong ties with militant and revolutionary Mali and Guinea in an effort to counter Moroccan propaganda which described him as a French stooge.[2] Chinese experts working in the country and improved relations with Guinea and Mali could hardly lend support to the allegations of left-wing critics at home or to those of the Moroccans. After all, Congo-Brazzaville had a defence pact with France and was more dependent economically on France than Mauritania. It could thus be argued that the latter's courting of China was a rational and logical calculation to improve the standing of the government.

Quite apart from this, Chinese agricultural experts were contributing to Mauritania's development without interfering in her internal affairs. Moreover in April 1968 the Chinese sent in a medical team to work for some two years under the health agreement of November 1967.[3]

(*d*) *Somali Republic, Uganda and China.* In Somalia, China continued the relations which had taken on momentum following the granting of a £7 million interest-free loan in 1963.[4] Though the Soviet Union had stepped in to supply equipment and weapons to the Somali Army and MIG fighters to the Air Force, and had provided other forms of aid, Chinese aid to Somalia did not become

---

[1] Algiers Radio, 23 Mar. 1967, reporting interview with Mauritanian Finance and Trade Minister.
[2] The dispute with Morocco was long-standing. Morocco claimed Mauritania as part of its national territory usurped by the French colonialists who had seen it wise to impose a 'reactionary' as the President in the guise of granting political independence to the country. Though Mauritania was economically tied to France, she was no more dependent than many other French-speaking states in Africa. Curiously enough the Moroccan Communist Party supported the claim on Mauritania.
[3] Nouakchott Radio, 8 Nov. 1967.
[4] See above, p. 153.

unwelcome.[1] In the context of Sino-Soviet rivalry, however, the Soviet Union had the upper hand. However, Chinese experts continued to work on agricultural projects, mainly rice growing and tobacco planting.[2] Somali delegations, including a Ministerial one in September 1968, continued to visit China[3] (seven in 1966 and five in 1967). Earlier on, China had agreed to provide an interest-free loan of 8 million Swiss francs ($1.83m) repayable over ten years from 1971.[4] This was an indication that at least relations between the two countries were still warm, though China was not in any way the major donor of aid, and the Soviet Union retained the favourable position.

In Uganda there was no previous Chinese aid commitment although China was buying quite a lot from the country, £6.24 million worth in 1965. In 1968, however, the Ugandan Government invited a team of Chinese agricultural experts to examine the possibility of cultivating rice on a commercial scale. The team arrived in the last months of 1968, and in January 1969 after experiments in the Busoga swamp areas submitted a plan to the government.[5] The plan involved setting up a 17,000 acre state farm which would produce some 3.3 million pounds of rice per year. It would give employment to 400 people and would yield a profit of £25,000 a year from an initial investment of £500,000.[6] This was the first time technical assistance was obtained from China in such a form. There was, however, no public announcement that China had been requested to provide funds for the rice project.[7] Perhaps this is one reason why nothing was done about the report up to the end of 1971.

(e) *China and the U.A.R.* During the period 1966–8 the U.A.R[7] remained China's most important trading partner on the African continent. I pointed out in Chapter 4 that in terms of great-power competition, the Soviet Union was in a very favourable position

[1] Army equipped with about 150 T-34 medium tanks and Soviet made 100mm. field guns.
[2] N.C.N.A. 20 Aug. 1967 and S.C.M.P. No. 4302, 20 Nov. 1968.
[3] See Table on African delegations visiting China.
[4] Mogadishu Radio, 30 May 1968.
[5] *Africa Research Bulletin* No. 1261, Jan./Feb. 1969. [6] *Ibid.*
[7] It would be interesting to follow developments, but these fall outside the period under consideration.

here as she had decided to participate heavily in the U.A.R.'s industrial and economic development. I also showed that Nasser's practical non-alignment, and his skill in making use of aid from the East as well as from the West, meant the U.A.R. could resist undue pressure from either side. Although in 1956 Egypt was the first country to recognise China, the two countries nevertheless had quarrels, which at times led to open Press attacks on each other. Nor was this element totally absent in Soviet–U.A.R. relations, as Nasser based his decisions solely on whether or not a proposal was favourable to Egyptian interests.

In December 1964 it was announced that under an economic agreement China would deliver industrial equipment and machinery costing $80 million to the U.A.R.[1] This was in addition to the trade agreement between the two countries which was set at $15 million each way. Given the time when it was pledged, it was difficult not to see this said in the context of Sino–Soviet rivalry on the issue of Soviet participation in the proposed Second Bandung Conference, and therefore to doubt whether it would be fulfilled. I have already suggested that if China really wanted to make an impact on the Egyptian economy her aid had to be substantial because the relatively advanced stage of the economy and heavy Soviet commitment. Delivery of the industrial machinery was supposed to take place between 1965 and 1968 with repayment beginning in 1972.[2] This obligation was not carried out. Some industrial equipment was delivered but this was under the trade agreement with the U.A.R. by which Egypt exported goods to China in return.[3] There was no record of the aid being disbursed during the period.[4]

In the first place, from the Chinese point of view, the U.A.R. was no longer as important as when China was desperately looking for an opening into Africa. The U.A.R's attitude to Soviet participation in the abortive second Bandung further reduced China's interest in fulfilling its promise. The focus of China's attention in Africa had long shifted to the area south of the Sahara and a heavy commitment to Egypt would only impede her ability to fulfil promises in the south. Moreover, the Chinese were quite aware that they could not influence Egyptian policies: they would therefore

[1] *Al-Ahram*, 31 Dec. 1964 quoting the Minister for Industry, Dr Aziz Sidqi.
[2] *Ibid*. [3] Interview with U.A.R. diplomat in London.
[4] I was unable to trace any record of fulfilment during this period.

not hurry to fulfil their promise. Furthermore, the Soviet Union was delivering substantial stocks of military hardware to the Egyptian armed forces, and there could be no question of emulating her in the foreseeable future. This did not of course rule out political gestures at opportune moments, as for example, immediately after the 1967 June war.[1]

China's policy was influenced by the effects of Cultural Revolution. Although her ambassador to the U.A.R. was the only envoy not recalled during this period, this was only because of the co-ordinating role of that Mission for the whole of China's activities in the Middle East and North Africa. It was no indication of the 'excellent, state of relations between China and the U.A.R. I have shown that despite the Cultural Revolution, China did fulfil her obligations to many other African states and in fact entered into new commitments. One can only conclude therefore that the Cultural Revolution was not responsible for China's failure to produce the aid promised. It could only have had a marginal effect, in that industrial production was disrupted and industrial equipment and machinery were the items the U.A.R. needed.

A political gesture to the U.A.R. was made at the time of the June war – a particularly difficult moment for the Soviet Union. Before the outbreak of hostilities, the Chinese Government had in various statements expressed unconditional support for the Arabs' cause in their struggle against 'U.S.-instigated Zionism', and accused the Soviet Union of collusion with imperialism while 'feigning support' for the Arabs. The end of the war brought a great loss of prestige to the Soviet Union, China made a political gesture by offering the U.A.R. Government 150,000 tons of wheat and a loan of $10 million in hard currency, without conditions and with no date set for repayment.[2] This was said to be a token of admiration and appreciation for the 'Egyptian people's stand in face of a mighty imperialist conspiracy . . .'[3] In fact China was trying to undercut the Soviet position and to capitalise on the momentary Arab disillusionment with the Soviet Union. She could not step in with supplies of the military equipment needed by the U.A.R. but she could exploit the Soviet predicament in other ways. Predictably China denounced imperialist support for Israel; she also

[1] See below, p. 229.   [2] Cairo Radio, 11 June 1967.   [3] Ibid.

launched heavy attacks on the Soviet Union.[1] She was also no doubt pleased to see demonstrations in Arab cities directed not just at the imperialists but also against the Soviet Union. China claimed that the Arabs at least understood Soviet 'perfidy'.

It was with malicious intent that the Soviet revisionists had given aid to the Arabs in the past in order to reap huge profits in their political schemes. Now that they had been unmasked they were again feigning support for the Arabs in order to betray them again. The Arabs had not forgotten that during his visit to Cairo last year Kosygin pledged that the Soviet Union would defend its friends with all the weapons in its hands and that the Arab people could always look for assistance from the Soviet Union. Facts had proved that all the gallant Soviet promises were sheer lies.[2]

Although the Soviet Union did suffer a setback in prestige, this was to be recovered later on, when the Soviet leaders undertook to replace the military hardware lost by the U.A.R. in the June war and actually proceeded to do so. At the same time, however, China successfully portrayed herself as the unshakeable champion of the Arab people, with little cost to herself and without expecting to be called upon to send in troops to confirm that support.

4. People's Organisations

The fissiparous tendencies which were beginning to have a telling effect on the activities of the various people's organisations during the period 1963-5 were exacerbated from 1966 onwards by Chinese and Russian attempts neither to dominate each of these bodies completely or to sponsor the emergence of new ones. This trend was accelerated by the totally uncompromising stand taken by both parties. This divisiveness which also produced rival Communist parties in many countries, involved these bodies more in the Sino-Soviet conflict than in the struggle against imperialism, their original raison d'etre. As the central organisations were often composed of many national groups, the formal split at central level was carried into the individual committees in many countries and rival bodies were set up. Where Soviet control was secure and absolute, as in the World Federation of Trade Unions and the World Council of Peace, and there was no prospect of setting up rival bodies, China simply withdrew from participation after a series of attacks.

[1] e.g. *People's Daily* of 15 June 1967 – Commentator's article: 'Poisonous Snakes Can Never be Made into Charming Women'.
[2] B.B.C. *S.W.B.* Part III, No. 2492, 16 June 1967.

At the World Council of Peace meeting in Geneva in June 1966 Chinese views were 'resolutely rebuffed' as a result of what the Chinese called a 'gang-up against China'. It was the last meeting of the body the Chinese attended.

The first formal split occurred in the Afro-Asian Writers' Organisation in June 1966. The permanent Bureau of the Organisation was based in Colombo, Ceylon, where the Russians believed it was under Chinese control. They attempted to have the headquarters moved to Cairo so as to be under the permanent secretariat of the A.A.P.S.O. in which they now had the upper hand. A meeting was convened in Cairo in June which under Soviet pressure called for a general meeting of the Organisation to take place in Baku, a Soviet city. This attempt resulted in complete fiasco, partly because of Chinese counteraction.[1] The Writers' Bureau met in Peking on 20 June and after condemning the Soviet action went on to make preparations for an emergency General Conference which took place from 27 June to 6 July.[2] Unlike the rival Soviet meeting taking place at the same time, the emergency meeting in Peking was attended by 161 delegates and observers from 53 countries and regions, including those from 26 African states.[3] It was attended by Kuo Mo-jo and delegates were received by Chou En-lai. It was decided to hold another conference in China in 1967, though the events of that year did not allow it to take place.[4] Nevertheless the Soviet Union's limitations in that organisation had been clearly revealed.

The atmosphere was more congenial for the Russians at the 6th Congress of the International Organisation of Journalists, which took place in Berlin in October 1966. Because of the method of selecting the delegates the Soviet Union was in an unassailable position. China therefore refused to attend. The same attitude was adopted towards the meeting of the International Association of Democratic Lawyers which was held in Paris in January 1967.

A more ominous development concerned the A.A.P.S.O. In

---

[1] Observer Foreign News Service, 8 Dec. 1966. See Richard Hall's piece.
[2] S.C.M.P. No. 3725, 24 June 1966.
[3] From Africa delegates came from Cameroun, Ghana, Congo (K), the Sudan, Botswana, Lesotho, Tanzania, Angola, Swaziland, South-West Africa, South Africa, Niger, Malagasy, Portuguese Guinea, Mali, Rhodesia, Algeria, Rwanda, Ivory Coast, Morocco, Sierra Leone, Congo (B), Guinea, Mozambique, Somalia and Uganda.
[4] S.C.M.P. No. 3737, 13 July 1966.

1965 the A.A.P.S.O. Meeting at Winneba, Ghana, decided to hold the next general session in Peking in 1967. This decision was not, however, approved by the Soviet Union, who pressed to have the venue shifted. The Council of the Organisation meeting in Nicosia in February 1967 decided, as a result of Russian pressure, to hold the meeting in Algiers. The Chinese objected and declared the decision to be illegal: 'the Soviet revisionists had openly split the Afro-Asian People's movement for solidarity against imperialism'.[1] The Chinese Committee for Afro-Asian Solidarity declared that preparations would go ahead for the meeting to take place in China as planned and that, as the permanent secretariat of the A.A.P.S.O. in Cairo 'has already degenerated into a tool of the Soviet revisionists for implementing their counter-revolutionary lines ... [China] shall henceforth have nothing to do with this organ'.[2] This marked the formal split in the A.A.P.S.O. central organisation and led to the establishment of two rival Afro-Asian Solidarity Committees in many countries. The meeting scheduled for China in 1967 never took place, nor did that which the Soviets arranged for Algiers. There was insufficient support for the Russian plan to hold the meeting in Algiers while China was too deeply absorbed in the Cultural Revolution to convene a meeting. Until the end of 1968 no A.A.P.S.O. general meeting was held, though the Russians planned to hold one in the Sudan in 1969 in order to rejuvenate the torn central organisation. The fact that the Chinese did not try to set up a rival central A.A.P.S.O., but only limited factional activities to the national committees in many states, suggested that in future they could still consider taking part in the central organ. A parallel situation existed with the W.F.T.U., the World Peace Council and the World Federation of Democratic Youth.

5. Revolutionary Activities

In Chapter 4, I indicated that the threatening events in Vietnam, and the massive entry of American troops into the war tended to draw Chinese attention towards Asia and away from other parts of the world. The events of the Cultural Revolution also reduced

[1] B.B.C. *S.W.B.* Part III, No. 2422, 22 Mar. 1967.
[2] Committee statement of 17 Mar. 1967.

interest in revolutionary activity in Africa. On one level, Chinese introversion affected the attention they paid to revolutionary activities in Africa. Leaders of the national liberation movements in Mozambique, Angola and Portuguese Guinea did not lead or send any delegations to China from September 1966 to the end of 1968.[1] This, no doubt, was a result of the unsettling situation in China, though leaders might simply have been paying more attention to the developing situation in their respective areas of operation.

This, however, does not mean that the Chinese stopped supporting national liberation movements during this period. In fact, Chinese propaganda support continued and positive steps were taken to disseminate the military writings of Chairman Mao within the movements. The flow of military aid to guerrillas via Tanzania Congo-Brazzaville continued, while Chinese personnel helping to train the guerrillas at bases in these countries continued their work in spite of the Cultural Revolution.[2] They were, of course, taking part in that revolution by persuading their students to learn more of Chairman Mao's writings and apply the lesson in their theatre of operations.[3] In response to the O.A.U. Liberation Committee's appeal to channel foreign aid to freedom fighters through the Organisation, the Chinese began to do so. But they also continued to give direct aid to those liberation movements they supported.[4]

By the end of 1968, the three liberation movements fighting in Mozambique, Angola and Portuguese Guinea and especially the P.A.I.C.C. had made considerable progress in their struggles. Their success could not however be in any way attributed to Chinese assistance. In the first place the movements received arms, ammunition and finance from African sources as well as from the Soviet Union and East European countries. More important, the freedom fighters were using their own personnel and adapting guerrilla

[1] In 1966 six delegations went from these movements but mostly on political duties.
[2] Pointe Noire in Congo-Brazzaville and Mtwara in Tanzania were the entry points for Chinese arms for the liberation movements in Mozambique and Angola. Chinese instructors trained guerrilla fighters at a camp in Dolisie in Congo-Brazzaville. I have already pointed out that Tanzania allowed Chinese personnel in 1965 to train freedom fighters for Southern Africa, in particular for Mozambique.
[3] Various pictorial reports in the Chinese press showed African freedom fighters studying and applying Mao's strategy and tactics of people's war, e.g. *Peking Review* No. 31, 2 Aug. 1968.
[4] Interview with X.

warfare tactics to their own local conditions: they were in no way committed to following the Chinese blueprint for success. Nevertheless Chinese military aid was much appreciated, and in Mozambique Chinese technical assistance contributed to the pace of success.

Revolutionary prospects in Congo-Kinshasa during this period were bleak as General Mobutu's Government established firm control over the whole country. Diplomatic relations were re-established with the Soviet Union on 3 December 1967, but not with China. Naturally, the Soviet action was vehemently attacked by China especially as the Soviet Union had tried to persuade Congo-Kinshasa dissidents with headquarters in Congo-Brazzaville to reach a rapprochement with Mobutu.[1] The only sizeable violent uprising in the Congo involved the former Katangese gendarmes led by South African, Rhodesian and European mercenaries, who attempted to restore the deposed Moise Tshombe to power in June 1967.[2] This was unanimously condemned in Africa and was the exact opposite of what the Chinese advocated: it was reactionary in nature and if successful would have been worse for the Congolese people and for Africa.

One African issue on which China was reluctant for a long time to take a stand was the Nigerian Civil War which began on 6 July 1967.[3] The first Nigerian coup d'etat in January 1966 fell into the category of 'anti-reactionary coups' and was therefore welcomed by the Chinese. Recognition of China did not follow however.[4] The counter-coup of July 1966 was for that reason not welcomed, it was not mentioned in the Chinese press and a discreet silence was maintained on Nigerian events. This silence continued even when the rebels declared secession in May 1967 and renamed the former Eastern Nigeria 'Biafra'. When fighting began between the federal troops and rebel forces in July, again no mention was made in the Chinese press or in Chinese broadcasts to Africa.

[1] This persuasion eventually succeeded in Oct. 1968 with the help of the Congolese-Brazzaville authorities, and Pierre Mulele who had led the revolt in 1964 returned to Kinshasa under a guarantee of safe conduct and amnesty, but he was in fact executed within a few days of his return.
[2] Tshombe was detained in Algeria in June 1967 when his personal jet plane was hijacked to Algiers.
[3] It is outside the scope of this book to discuss the war as a whole. I concentrate only simply on Chinese involvement in it.
[4] See above, p. 184.

In the first place, the Chinese realised that the situation was very complicated and that openly taking a stand would be unhelpful. Before the first coup they had connections with the two parties: with the Northern Elements Progressive Union (N.E.P.U.), whose leader was Aminu Kano and whose delegations had visited Peking in the past; and with the Dynamic Party in the old Eastern Region whose leader Dr Chike Obi, had visited China on more than one occasion, the latest being in July 1966 to attend a science conference; and with several trade unionists including Tanko, Yakasai and Saka Bashorun. In short China had friends in the north, east and west of the country and it was therefore sensible for her not to make any move until everything sorted itself out. Moreover Nigeria was the third largest market for Chinese goods on the continent and trade was in China's favour.[1] This could easily be cut off as a retaliatory measure if she took the wrong step. These factors counselled caution on China's part.

In August 1967, after the Western governments had refused to sell military planes and anti-aircraft guns to counter the rebel bombing, the Nigerian Government turned to the Soviet Union and Czechoslovakia. They promptly agreed to sell the required planes. China saw this move as an attempt by the Soviet Union to cultivate the Nigerian authorities and increase her influence. Still no public statement on the matter issued from Peking, and China's assessment of the situation cannot have been helped by the openly pro-Western stand of the leadership in 'Biafra': they accused Nigeria of being a beach-head for Communism in West Africa.[2] Moreover no African state had yet formally recognised 'Biafra', and the Chinese did not want to be seen as openly supporting the fragmentation of Nigeria, simply because the Soviet Union (now an enemy) was supporting the Federal Government.

However, in October 1967 the radical wing in 'Biafra' sent a delegation to China to explore the possibility of obtaining military assistance. China is reported to have promised help. From this time Federal Nigerian radio broadcasts spoke of Chinese personnel fighting with the 'Biafran' troops, while propaganda broadcasts from 'Biafra' condemned the 'Soviet revisionists' for 'trying to

[1] The figures for 1966 and 1967 were £5.03 million and £6.26 million respectively.
[2] The U.S. State Department at this time expressed concern at the Nigerian decision to purchase Soviet planes.

crush by the vilest slanders and lies the thoroughgoing revolutionary Marxist-Leninist policy of the P.R.C.'.

The Nigerian Ministry of External Affairs in Lagos weighed the advantages of recognising Peking in order to forestall any recognition or open support China might wish to accord the rebels. It was thought that recognising her in 1968 when she had not yet declared her position, would further antagonise the United States already disquieted by apparent Soviet 'gains' in Nigeria, and would give more impetus to the private organisations in America which were helping the rebels in the guise of fighting 'Communism'. If China recognised 'Biafra' she could not fly in arms as the French Government and other Western private agencies were already doing, and Chinese propaganda for 'Biafra' would not do much harm.[1] It was thus decided that Nigeria should not forestall Peking's recognition of 'Biafra' by simply extending diplomatic recognition to China.

On 18 September 1968 the Chinese broke their long silence on the Nigerian Civil War with a statement which, though falling short of recognising 'Biafra', called on the dissidents to persevere in the struggle and wage a people's war till victory was achieved. The unlikely occasion for the statement was the banquet held for the visiting Foreign Minister of the People's Republic of Southern Yemen,[2] unlikely because Southern Yemen staunchly supported the Nigerian Federal Government and the statement was not made when Nyerere visited China in June of the same year. Speaking at the banquet, Chen Yi said that 'In Africa, Soviet revisionism, in league with U.S. and British imperialism, is even openly supporting the military government of Federal Nigeria in massacring the Biafran people in a vain attempt to squeeze into Nigeria and enjoy an equal share with imperialism there.'[3] The Chinese were thus taking issue not so much with the Federal Nigerian Government as with the Soviet Union, which they saw had already increased her popularity in Nigeria. They could not have been unaware of the pressures brought to bear on the Nigerian Government by the United States to settle the conflict at the conference table, or of American uneasiness over Soviet 'gains' in Nigeria. No doubt the Chinese were also aware that what was going on was a con-

[1] Briefing by Nigerian diplomats.
[2] B.B.C. *S.W.B.* Part III No. 2878, 20 Sept. 1968.
[3] N.C.N.A., 20 Sept. 1968.

frontation of two armies fighting in a conventional way and not a 'Biafran' people's war which the 'Biafran' Officer Corps was not trained to conduct. Though only Tanzania and Zambia were openly mentioned in the press, the Chinese must also have known of the Portuguese, South African, Rhodesian and Israeli support for 'Biafra'. While Tanzania and Zambia were firm friends of China, so too were Mali, Guinea, Congo-Brazzaville and Algeria which stood firmly behind the Federal Nigerian cause.[1] One must conclude that China finally decided to see the war in the context of the triangular competition with Russia and America. If 'Biafra' succeeded then China would gain a friend. If it was eventually crushed then her position could not become worse: the Nigerian Government had not accorded recognition, which could be withdrawn. The Chinese at this point chose to discount their favourable trade balance with Nigeria.[2]

On several occasions the Nigerian Government accused China of financial and military involvement on the rebel side, and Chinese weapons supplied through Tanzania were among those captured by Federal Nigerian troops during the fighting. Open Chinese support for the rebels was unwise, and their example was not followed by their more radical allies in North Korea, North Vietnam and Albania, who simply kept the news out of their press and radio reports.[3] The Chinese did not take a similar attitude towards the Southern Sudanese rebellion which had been going on since 1955. They did have and still do have an embassy in the Sudan, and thus support for the Southern rebels would have had impossible reper-

[1] When Chen Yi's speech was first reported in the *Financial Times* in London, an official of the Chinese Legation in London, Comrade Wang, said that he had not received any information from China to that effect and that very often imperialist newspapers chose to distort Chinese views and policies and this could be one such occasion. When the N.C.N.A finally issued the statement and it happened to confirm the British press reports, Comrade Wang tried for an hour to argue that the Chinese statement was correct and that the United States was supplying arms to the Nigerian Government! This of course was false. Indeed, the C.I.A. was being attacked in Nigeria for ferrying arms to 'Biafra'. To be fair, however, he could hardly be expected to contradict his government's statement and could have argued otherwise if China had come out in support of the Nigerian Government.
[2] The smaller figure for 1968 was the result of a general damp-down on imports by Nigeria to save foreign exchange needed for arms, but in the following year the volume of trade was deliberately reduced.
[3] The collapse of the rebellion in January 1970 without an attempt by the rebel regime to order guerrilla warfare and refuse to surrender must have been a source of great embarrassment to China, as it was a rejection of the plea to persevere in struggle.

cussions on Chinese interests in the Middle East and North Africa. In the Nigerian case, the Chinese could not justly claim to have been supporting a revolutionary struggle in the interests of Africa, since in the event of a successful rebellion, many African States would have faced fissiparous uprisings which would only distract African attention from the struggle going on in the remaining colonial territories in Southern Africa. This was why Rhodesia, South Africa and Portugal initially supported the rebel secessionists, and China should have thought carefully before taking a public stand. Basing her decision solely on the narrow perspective of Soviet 'gain' in Nigeria tended to blur the wider aspects and ramifications of the conflict, which China should otherwise have taken seriously.

Chinese support for the rebels also amounted to a direct contradiction of one of the declared principles governing her relations with African states. It involved interference in the internal affairs of an African state – something China had repeatedly asserted she could not do. Formal diplomatic recognition was not granted to 'Biafra' by China so she could not argue that it was being given to another African state. Even if diplomatic recognition had been granted, Chinese support for that 'state' in the war contradicted another declared principle of her policy – that she supported the settlement of disputes between African states by peaceful means. In the past this was done by not openly supporting any party in the Somali–Ethiopian, Somali–Kenyan and Algerian–Moroccan disputes. The Nigerian case appears therefore to have been a departure from previous Chinese practice in this direction. A more realistic analysis of the situation would have prevented Chinese support for the rebels.[1]

From 1966–8, then, revolutionary activities in Africa were intensified particularly in the Portuguese colonial territories of Angola, Mozambique and Guinea Bissau. At the same time China was rent internally by the Cultural Revolution though this did not stop military aid being given to the liberation movements through friendly African countries. It must be stressed, however, that the progress made by the movements in their struggle during this period resulted entirely from their own self-reliance, self-sacrifice

[1] Perhaps the outcome of the Civil War and the capitulation of the rebels would persuade China that her open support was an error that should not be repeated.

and the application of well known guerrilla warfare strategy and tactics to local conditions.

At the end of 1965, prospects for Chinese diplomacy and aspirations in the developing world were gloomy. The conflict with the Soviet Union and the insistence on African states taking a clear stand with or against China had resulted in the indefinite postponement of the second Afro-Asian Conference. This had shown the limitations of Chinese influence and, more important, the reluctance of the African states to be dragged into a conflict which was at most of merely peripheral interest. The abortive coup d'etat in Indonesia had led to the decimation of its Communist Party, a staunch ally of China. The Indo-Pakistan War increased Indian prestige and cast the Soviet Union and the United States in the role of peacemakers. Moreover the situation in Vietnam was becoming more serious and the threat of possible American incursion into China intensified.

As if this was not ominous enough, Chinese aspirations in Africa began to receive diplomatic setbacks in the very first days of 1966. After military coups Dahomey and the Central African Republic severed relations with China and expelled Chinese technical personnel. A more serious blow fell in February, when President Nkrumah was overthrown in Ghana by a military coup while he was on his way through China to Vietnam. The existence of camps where African freedom fighters were being trained by Chinese army personnel became known and the new Ghanaian administration expelled the Chinese technical and military personnel working in the country. Diplomatic relations were broken off later in the year and were not renewed until 1972.

Chinese relations with Kenya also deteriorated, as political struggles in Kenya sharpened and opponents of Oginga Odinga strove to have relations suspended. Further north, Sino-Tunisian relations soured in the course of 1967, as the Tunisian Government attempted to implement a 'two Chinas policy'. In the aftermath of the Six Day War, the dispute reached its peak with the severance of diplomatic relations. By the end of 1968, although the number of independent African states had risen to 41, the number recognising China had fallen to 14.

Moreover the events of the Cultural Revolution in China gave the impression of internal chaos and caused anxiety among China's few friends in Africa. As the Cultural Revolution resulted in the withdrawal of all Chinese ambassadors abroad (except for the envoy to Egypt), the number of African delegations visiting China fell drastically and those which occurred were confined to highly essential government delegations.

With setbacks in some parts of Africa and the events of the Cultural Revolution directing Chinese energies to internal politics, attention in Africa was centred on the few states where Chinese commitments were growing rather than decreasing. Further economic and technical commitments were made to Tanzania and Zambia, and to Guinea, Mali and Congo-Brazzaville. Here the projects embarked upon in the previous period were completed and new ones were undertaken. Relations with Algeria, the Somali Republic and Mauritania also improved, and in the case of Algeria China was called on to fulfil her earlier pledges of economic aid. In the U.A.R. on the other hand there was as yet no evidence of the $80 million worth of industrial equipment and machinery promised in December 1964. This resulted from China's disenchantment with the U.A.R. because of the latter's support for Soviet participation in the abortive second Afro-Asian Conference and the increasingly favourable position of the Soviet Union in that country's economy. Although a political gesture involving $10 million hard-currency loan was made after the Six Day War this did not dramatically alter relations.

Sino-Soviet rivalry in the various people's organisations led to formal splits in several of these, to the establishment of a few rival ones by China when control of the central body could not be gained, or simply to her withdrawal from participation. The A.A.P.S.O. secretariat in Cairo came under the effective control of the Soviet Union and China pulled out of that central body. This resulted in formal splits in the Afro-Asian Solidarity Committees of many African states and inevitably in the dissipation of their energies.

Chinese propaganda and military aid to the national liberation movements in Mozambique, Angola and Portuguese Guinea continued and arms were delivered through Congo-Brazzaville and Tanzania. These liberation movements made gains during 1966-8 though these should not be solely attributed to Chinese support. In a more controversial way, China voiced her open support for the rebel secessionists in Nigeria after more than a year of discreet silence over the civil war. This move was strictly motivated by Soviet support for the Federal Military Government, and it would seem to have been uninhibited by the lack of diplomatic relations. This decision was of course contrary to previously declared principles governing Chinese policy towards Africa, and also contrasted with China's lack of support for the rebellion in the Southern Sudan, where the central government was on friendly terms with China. Chinese support for the rebellion in Nigeria was unfortunate, and its failure may discourage future Chinese support for similar uprisings in African states.

6 AFTER THE CULTURAL REVOLUTION

At the close of 1968 the Chinese authorities began to intensify their efforts to bring the tumults of the Great Proletarian Cultural Revolution under control. Plans were far advanced for convening the long-overdue Ninth Congress of the C.C.P., which was expected to set the seal of approval on that revolution's achievements. It was hoped that after the Congress China would re-enter the main stream of the 'civilised' diplomatic community and put an end to the xenophobic behaviour of some of the Red Guards, and that the recalled diplomats would now be allowed to return to their posts. As we saw in the last chapter, their withdrawal had no very adverse effect on China's operations in Africa, except that no new initiatives were taken towards states that did not already have diplomatic relations with her. Fewer delegations crossed the sea in either direction but economic commitments to old friends increased. Now that the Chinese internal situation was stabilised, and the 'ugly head' of bureaucratic elitism in the C.C.P. was smashed, the development of relations was expected to be more rapid.

Diplomatic Relations

One sign of the new trend was the growing number of states recognizing China and agreeing to establish diplomatic relations. Up to the end of 1969 only fourteen maintained diplomatic relations; in addition four others, Ghana, Tunisia, Burundi and Mauritius, had recognised the Peking Government.[1] In 1970-1, however, no less than eight states took action. An agreement with Equatorial Guinea (the former Spanish possessions of Fernando Po and Rio Muni), on recognition and the exchange of envoys, was announced in October 1970, after a visit from the Chinese envoy to Congo-Brazzaville. It was followed by economic and technical assistance

[1] See App. I, Table 7, p. 274.

in January 1971.[1] Following the renewal of diplomatic relations with Burundi in October 1971, the neighbouring state of Rwanda also established diplomatic relations with Peking in November. On the west coast of the continent Senegal finally agreed in principle to recognise Peking in October 1971. All these events took place at a time when China was actively campaigning for support among the United Nations members. Earlier in the year, events in Sierra Leone had led to the arrival of troops from neighbouring Guinea. The new radical outlook of the Sierra Leone Government led it to recognise Peking in July 1971.

Ethiopia, visited by Chou En-lai in 1964, had for a number of years voted in favour of China's admission to the U.N. On the other hand, though the Chinese did not openly support the insurgents of the Eritrean Liberation Front, who were (and still are) active in Ethiopia, the fact that Syria was passing on Chinese weaponry to the Front suggested that they did not oppose it. As late as June 1969 they themselves were reported to be giving the insurgents covert aid through this channel.[2] Looking across its north-west frontier, however, the Ethiopian government must have noticed that China did not help the rebels in the Southern Sudan, and maintained cordial relations with the Government at Khartoum. Apart from the need to adopt a realistic attitude towards a nation of 750 million people, these considerations provided a strong motive for extending recognition. In November 1970 a joint Sino-Ethiopian communique announced the establishment of diplomatic relations on the basis of the five principles of peaceful coexistence.[3] This was followed almost a year later by Emperor Haile Sellassie's one-week visit to China beginning on 6 October 1971. In 1936, Chairman Mao had commented on the Ethiopian Government's strategy during the invasion of that country by Musolini's Italy. Now in 1971, he was able to meet the Emperor in person.

During this visit, the Emperor signed an economic co-operation agreement whereby Peking would provide an interest-free loan of £33.5 million for agricultural development which Ethiopia would repay over a long period. Apart from the Tan–Zam Rail Project agreement covering £169 million, this was the largest single loan

[1] S.C.M.P. 4764, 23 Oct. 1970; B.B.C. S.W.B. (WS) IV, 607, 2 Feb. 1971.
[2] *Observer* (London), 22 June 1969.
[3] B.B.C. S.W.B. III, 3549, 2 Dec. 1970.

agreement to date. The two countries also agreed to extend to each other most-favoured-nation treatment. Commenting on the agreement, an Ethiopian official described it as the most favourable Ethiopia had signed with any nation.

The position taken up by China during the Nigerian Civil War has already been referred to. The end of the war in January 1970 was not reported in the Chinese press. The Chinese hoped, however, that given time, they could re-establish their position with the Nigerian Government given the considerable support they enjoyed in Nigerian progressive circles. With the reconciliation between Nigeria and the four African states which had recognized 'Biafra', the way seemed clear for a Chinese move. Nigeria had consistently supported Peking's admission to the U.N. That support had proved helpful in the 1970 General Assembly debate which resulted in the first simple majority in China's favour. Moreover Nigeria had remained a good market even during the civil war, her imports rising to over £5.4 million in 1969 as against £3.72 million in 1968. In 1970, the figure rose to £7.03 million and was to rise further to £10 million in 1971. Apart from this the Nigerian Government was coming to the forefront of the struggle against continued colonial oppression in Africa. This completely agreed with the stand China had taken in the past against Portuguese oppression. When establishing diplomatic relations the two governments pledged themselves 'to the struggle against imperialism and reactionary forces in the world', and Nigeria recognised the People's Republic as the 'sole legal government representing the entire Chinese people'. It was a sign of support for China in Nigeria that all the newspapers welcomed the establishment of diplomatic relations and not one referred to China's attitude during the civil war.

In April 1971, diplomatic relations were established with Nigeria's neighbour, the Federal Republic of Cameroun. Commenting upon this, in an editorial of 4 April, the *People's Daily* quoted Chairman Mao:

We must endeavour to establish normal diplomatic relations, on the basis of mutual respect for territorial integrity and sovereignty, and of equality and mutual benefit, with all countries willing to live together with us in peace.[1]

As I have already shown[2] the Camerounian government had withheld recognition because China had given material support

[1] *Peking Review*, no. 8, 19 Feb. 1971. [2] See p. 150.

to the U.P.C. movement, but had nevertheless stated that the position could change if she stopped interfering in Cameroun's internal affairs. Late in 1970 the government finally crushed the insurgents. Their leaders, including Ernest Ouambi who had visited China several times, were arrested, sentenced to death, and executed early in 1971. An embarrassing stumbling-block was thus conveniently removed at a time when improved diplomatic relations with African states were becoming very important for China. With the help of Mauritania, talks took place in March 1971 in an atmosphere of frankness (obviously on the Camerounian side) during which China promised not to interfere in internal affairs.[1] The establishment of diplomatic relations on 26 March made Cameroun the twenty-first state to accord recognition. In September, the first Chinese Ambassador, Chao Hsing Chih, arrived in the Cameroun.

Libya became the twenty-second when President Moamer Gadafi announced, early in June 1971, that diplomatic relations would soon be established. After carrying out a popular and progressive revolution against King Idris in September 1969 his government had been in the forefront of the anti-imperialist movement and had received several congratulatory messages from Chou En-lai. At the same time he had remained an anti-Communist Muslim puritan, and was in no hurry to accord recognition. However, China's support for the Arab states and the Palestinians against Israel helped him to make up his mind.

Trade and Economic Relations

I pointed out in Chapter 5[2] that the triangular competition in aid-giving by the Soviet Union, China, and the U.S.A., declined as the donors came to realise the limitations imposed on their influence by the non-aligned posture of their beneficiaries. Further, I illustrated the effects of the Cultural Revolution on increasing economic commitments in Africa. After 1968, however, the numerous Chinese economic and technical assistance teams continued their work with renewed vigour.

Relations with Mali had cooled after the coup d'état of November 1968. Only one Mali delegation visited China in 1969 and another

[1] *Peking Review*, no. 15, 9 Apr. 1971.   [2] See pp. 180.

in 1970; Chinese exports declined slightly from the £1.43 million of 1968 to £0.42 in 1970; and the Guinea–Mali railway had been shelved. Chinese teams nevertheless continued work on other projects. A newly-completed tannery and a radio transmitting station were handed over in August 1970; and in December an economic delegation led by the Foreign Minister signed a new economic and technical co-operation agreement in the presence of Chou En-lai.[1] A Chinese team was already helping to set up a tea factory at Sikasso.[2]

On the other side of the continent, in the Somali Republic, the Chinese as well as the Russians continued to render technical assistance. In March 1969 a protocol was signed about a hydrogeological survey and prospecting teams.[3] A medical team arrived in April and another in December. In 1970 the Jowhar rice and tobacco experimental station was completed and handed over; and when the Somali Vice-President visited China in June of that year agreement was reached about expanding it.[4] This agreement also provided for the construction of factories to supply all Somalia's requirements of cigarettes and matches (thus saving £0.6 million of scarce foreign exchange), of a meat-processing plant, and for technical assistance in building 2,000 km of roads.[5] The Somalis thus seemed to be doing well out of their connection with China. Not far away, relations with the Sudan continued cordial. The civilian government in Khartoum was overthrown in May 1969 and the new revolutionary regime co-opted prominent members of the Communist Party. Though understood to be pro-Moscow, the Sudanese Communist Party was the largest in Africa, and for a long time after the coup it enjoyed pride of place with the young military rulers of the country. Trade relations with China were healthy (exports from the Sudan of £6.4m in 1969 and £6.8m in 1970; imports into the Sudan of £4.8m and £3.1m). The first Sino-Sudanese economic-aid agreement, signed by a Sudanese delegation visiting China in June 1970, granted an interest-free loan of £14.5m repayable over fifteen years by the export of Sudanese

[1] B.B.C. *S.W.B.* IV, 589, 22 Sept. 1970; HNA, 22 Dec. 1970.
[2] B.B.C. *S.W.B.* IV, 607, 2 Feb. 1971.
[3] S.C.M.P., 4384, 26 Mar. 1969.
[4] *Ibid.* 4635, 14 Apr. 1970, B.B.C. *S.W.B.* IV, 3414, 26 June 1970.
[5] B.B.C. *S.W.B.* IV, 613, 16 Mar. 1971; III, 3410, 22 June 1970; IV, 3543, 25 Nov. 1970.

crops.[1] When President Jaafar Nimeiry paid a goodwill visit in August, Mao paid tribute to his staunch opposition to imperialism and racial discrimination. Three Chinese survey teams arrived in December and a road construction team in March 1971. At the same time General Nimeiry's regime continued to maintain very good relations, both economic and military, with the Soviet Union, and, like other African governments, declined to align itself openly with either of the Communist giants. However there was an abortive coup d'etat in the Sudan late in July 1971. Undoubtedly the coup was left wing oriented and involved the Sudanese Communist Party – the largest and best organised in Africa. Its leader was the Vice President of the Communist dominated World Federation of Trade Unions (W.F.T.U.) who was held in high respect in world communist circles.

However, the coup failed and the return of General Jaafar Nimeiry to power led to a witchhunt against left-wing elements and the decimation if not total annihilation of the Sudanese Communist Party. The Party chief, and some of his lieutenants were tried for treason and executed on the order of General Nimeiry. A well-orchestrated outcry from the Soviet Union and the East European countries against what was called the 'barbarity and savagery' of the Sudanese Government followed. The Soviet Union had helped to build up the Sudanese armed forces and did have several advisers working in the country. This does not imply Soviet involvement in the abortive coup, but the acrimonious protestations from that quarter gave grounds for supicion. The Sudanese Government accordingly rebuked the Soviet and East European press for interfering in the Sudan's internal affairs – friendship with Socialist states was one thing, toleration of Sudanese Communists quite another.

This may be compared with a similar occurrence in Indonesia in 1965 which resulted in the decimation of the P.K.I. and for which the Russians blamed Chinese adventurism. In the Sudanese case however, if an accusation of adventurism can be made, it should probably be against the Moscow-oriented Sudan Communist Party. In contrast to the comments of the European and Soviet Communist press about the Sudanese Government's action, the Chinese leaders sent a letter of congratulations and encouragement to

[1] Omdurman Radio, 30 June 1970.

General Nimeiry for crushing the abortive coup. If one recalls the vehement criticism China launched against President Nasser's Egypt in 1958–9, for persecuting local Communists, one cannot but call into question the consistency of Chinese views. Proletarian internationalism would demand Chinese sympathy for the Sudanese Communists and, at the least silence might have been expected from China. Chinese action can only be interpreted as an attempt to cultivate the Sudanese Government and to prevent any anti-Communist backlash in Africa against China – especially when the Communist Party concerned was not on particularly good terms with Peking.

Looked at from another perspective, Chinese action can be said to have helped the general cause of Communism. If China had not come to Nimeiry's support, then it is just possible that anti-Communist feeling in the Sudan following the coup would have been absolute and that the country could have gone over to imperialism. As it was, anti-Communist feeling was tempered as the people realised that a giant Communist state like China had stood by the regime in time of need and that perhaps the Soviet-East European reaction was after all an aberration.

Needless to say the Soviet press attacked China for the way it reported events in the Sudan and described Chinese action as opportunistic. On the other hand the Sudanese leader expressed his profound gratitude to Chairman Mao and the other Chinese leaders for their support. Undoubtedly, Soviet-Sudanese relations have begun to improve but disquiet was undoubtedly engendered by the abortive coup.

In North and West Africa, the Chinese continued to help Algeria and Mauritania. In February 1969 some twenty-six Algerians left for eighteen-months' training in China, to prepare for work at the Chinese-built Guelma factory. In December 1970 Algeria entered into a contract for the export of 40,000 tons of cast-iron, and a second contract, in March 1971, for 80,000 tons made China the main purchaser of this product.[1] The Mauritanian Government received a gift of 3,000 tons of cereals in April 1969 and in December an agreement was signed on the construction of boreholes for civilian use. Since then the Chinese have succeeded in bringing more piped water to the capital, a problem that the French had never been able

[1] B.B.C. *S.W.B.* III, 615, 30 Mar. 1971.

to solve satisfactorily. In February 1970 President Daddah, when opening a modern hospital completely equipped by China, warmly praised the Chinese who were working in Mauritania. A newly-constructed Youth Centre was handed over in November of that year.[1] In April 1971, it was announced that China had agreed to finance the construction of a deep water port at Nouakchott. The cost to China would be around £8 million.

As regards the whole field of Sino-African trade, the figures so far available show an upward trend in the volume of Chinese exports. In 1969 Nigeria was still a larger market for these than Tanzania, but by 1970 the latter, with imports of over £15.5 million, moved rapidly ahead, and probably now takes more Chinese goods than the U.A.R., formerly China's largest market.[2] This is because work has now begun on the Tan–Zam railway project, the local costs of which are being financed by imports.

Guinea and Congo-Brazzaville

In 1969–71 Sino-Guinean and Sino-Congolese relations remained as close as before, completely undisturbed by the Cultural Revolution. In February 1969 a Guinean delegation signed an agreement on Chinese loans in the form of commodities.[3] Another agreement, signed in October 1969 at the same time as the Sino-Congolese agreement already mentioned[4] involved a 200,000-ton cement plant; the complete repair of the Conakry–Kankan railway; the launching of a large-scale agricultural development programme; 15,000 uniforms for the Guinean militia; and thirty landrovers for the P.D.G. A Chinese team arrived in May 1969 to set up a sugar refinery, a building factory delegation in October, and, in December, a team to study the project planned for the Timkisso region. China also undertook the construction of another hydro-electric power station. The Dabola oil-pressing plant built under the technical co-operation agreement was handed over in May 1970, and a high-tension transmission and distribution project to supply power to five cities of Central Guinea was inaugurated. President Sekou Touré praised the sincerity and hard work of the Chinese personnel when he

[1] S.C.M.P., 4552, 8 Dec. 1969; B.B.C. *S.W.B.* (WS) III, 559, 600, 27 Feb., 9 Dec. 1970.
[2] See Appendix I, Table 6, p. 273.
[3] S.C.M.P. 4370, 6 Mar. 1969.
[4] See p. 250.

visited the aid projects in June. Next month, another medical team, 33 strong arrived.[1]

When, in November 1970, a Portuguese-led military force invaded Guinea – an action which was universally condemned – China, together with some African states which offered material and financial aid, made a strong gesture of solidarity by pledging $10m as a contribution to military aid.[2] This was the largest promise of aid made by any country. In his message of thanks to Chairman Mao of 27 November Sekou Touré declared:

> I have the honour to extend to you my sincere, militant gratitude for your courageous taking of an unequivocal stand showing solidarity and support to the Guinean people in their fierce war of resistance against the Portuguese fascist bandits. I assure you of the consciousness and total preparedness of the people of Guinea who are fully mobilized with a view to carrying on the struggle against the international imperialist hydra until its last strongholds are battered down.... As concrete proof of your sincerity and solidarity, I am convinced that our peoples will emerge from the present severe trials with their relations of mutual understanding, mutual respect and true militant cooperation ever more consolidated.[3]

At the end of that year, China arranged additional budgetary aid for Guinea – this involved £3.5 million.

One state which was on the best of terms with both China and France was Congo-Brazzaville. In July 1969 President Ngouabi expressed to President Pompidou the hope that 'the century-old bonds of friendship and co-operation so firmly established between our two countries will develop day by day'. In the same month, when receiving the credentials of the new Chinese Ambassador, Ngouabi spoke of the excellent state of relations between China and Congo-Brazzaville, the high regard that the Congolese people had for the Chinese people and their leader, Mao Tse-tung, and of how Congo-Brazzaville had chosen Socialism as its path to progress.[4] This was a symbol of the non-aligned stance taken up by Congo-Brazzaville and of that revolutionary state's ability to maintain cordial relations with a conservative France. Nor did relations deteriorate when, at the end of 1969, the People's Republic of the Congo was born, ruled by a Marxist-Leninist Party of Labour and the first Communist state in Africa.

[1] B.B.C. *S.W.B.* IV, 3320, 4 Nov. 1969; S.C.M.P., 4550, 4668, and 4681, 4 Dec. 1969 2, 22 June 1970.
[2] B.B.C. *S.W.B.* IV, 3543, 25 Nov. 1970.
[3] Hsinhua New Agency, 1 Dec. 1970.   [4] B.B.C. *S.W.B.* IV, 3125, 15 July 1969.

In August 1969 the textile combine at Kinsundi – a crystallisation of Sino-Congolese co-operation – was transferred to the Congolese Government and within a fortnight of its completion, ahead of schedule, the Chinese work team returned home. In October Prime Ministers Alfred Raoul and Chou En-lai signed yet another economic and technical co-operation agreement in Peking.[1] More medical and technical assistance teams arrived during 1969, the foundation stone of the state farm at Kembe was laid in May 1970, and in August work began on a boat-building yard at Brazzaville.[2] In 1969–70 seven Chinese delegations went to the Congo and five Congolese economic and military delegations to China. Their friendly relations with China are highly beneficial to these two African states, for though the agreements between them have always referred to economic and technical co-operation, China has done virtually all the giving. During 1971 there were other developments. In March an agreement was signed providing for the construction of a hydro-electric power station in Southern Congo and, in the previous month, the Chinese had completed a survey at Fort Rousset for a large hospital. In September, a military aid agreement was signed covering the sending of Chinese military training teams to the Congo and of Congolese soldiers and sailors to China.

Zambia and Tanzania

Since 1968 more attention has been given to Chinese activities in Tanzania and Zambia than to those in any other part of Africa. This is because of the implications of the Tan–Zam railroad for the African nationalist confrontation with the minority regimes in Southern Africa. Chinese activity is not, however, limited to the railway. In Zambia, besides lending £6m free of interest for building the Lusaka–Mankoya–Miemba road, they have promised a free gift of radio transmitters and other auxiliary equipment.[3] The Zambians have, of course, been sensitive to any Western suggestion that their country might be dragged into the Chinese orbit. Their most persistent critics are the South African and Rhodesian regimes, which consider themselves threatened by the use of Zambia as a springboard for subversive agents, and also by the drawing away

[1] S.C.M.P. 4479, 20 Aug. 1969; B.B.C. *S.W.B.* III, 3201, 13 Oct. 1969.
[2] S.C.M.P. 4660, 4711, 20 May, 5 Aug. 1970.
[3] B.B.C. *S.W.B.* (WS) III, 308, 26 Feb. 1969. S.C.M.P. 4574, 12 Jan. 1970.

of her economy to the north to the detriment of their own future expansion. This is why the South African government objects so strongly to the method of financing the local costs of the Tan–Zam project.

In Tanzania the Chinese work teams have continued to render useful service wherever employed. In June 1969 the second of five water projects in Zanzibar was completed; and aid was extended for enlarging the Dar Es-Salaam stadium. Army barracks in Nachingwea, Southern Tanganyika, another Chinese-aided project, were opened by President Nyerere in December, and the army took up positions in the south to prepare for any Portuguese aggression from Mozambique.[1] When the agreement on the employment of the Canadian military instructors who had been working in Tanzania for five years expired on 31 December 1969 it was not renewed; Chinese instructors took over some of their functions. On 6 May 1970 Nyerere laid the foundation stone of a naval base which was being constructed near Dar Es-Salaam with Chinese assistance.[2] Another project on the Mainland, the Ubungo Farm Implements and Tools Factory, was inaugurated in July. In Zanzibar a large sports stadium was opened in January and a hospital in July.[3] By May 1971, as a result of the merits of the Chinese personnel – their ability to live and work like the local population and their behaviour – China had become the dominant aid donor in Zanzibar, outdistancing the Russians and East Germans who had rivalled the Chinese in the mid-1960s.[4] Tanzania is undoubtedly China's most influential friend in Africa today, and large commitments of financial aid have been made to her. The Tanzanian Government nevertheless continues to pursue its declared policy of non-alignment. During the past three years it has received from the United States, Sweden, the World Bank and other Western sources loans and grants for such projects as road-building, agricultural development and sugar-refining.[5] Nor did Tanzania or Zambia make any statement supporting China when in March 1969 Soviet and Chinese troops clashed along the Ussuri River, an incident of great importance to both China and the Soviet Union.

[1] B.B.C. *S.W.B.* (WS) IV, 526, 4 July 1969; S.C.M.P. 4447, 2 July 1969.
[2] B.B.C. *S.W.B.* IV, 3247, 3269, 3373, 5 Dec. 1969, 3 Jan., 8 May 1970.
[3] S.C.M.P. 4678, 4579, 4705, 17 June, 19 Jan., 28 July 1970.
[4] See article by David Martin in *The Guardian*, 13 May 1971.
[5] *Financial Times*, 11 Mar. 1971; B.B.C. *S.W.B.* (WS) IV, 609, 16 Feb. 1971.

The most important event during this period was the official beginning of the Tan-Zam railway project. In July 1970 a joint Tanzanian-Zambian finance delegation went to China to sign the final agreement. Under this China provides an interest-free loan of over £169m, repayable over thirty years, from 1983. Construction officially started on 26 October; completion is expected in 1975. By the end of 1971 the first 300-mile section had been opened for traffic.

In terms of finance, Chinese commitments to Africa since the Suez crisis of 1956 have been heavy. From that time to 1971 some £406 million credit was pledged, about £240m of which had been utilised by 1970. Tanzania had received over £106 million since 1964, no small amount considering China's limited capability.[1]

One significant event should be dealt with here – the October 1971 debate in the General Assembly on the representation of China and the consequent admission of Peking to the U.N. by an overwhelming majority. It will be recalled that one condition demanded by Peking was the expulsion of the representatives of Taiwan from the United Nations before Peking could agree to join. Another condition, which was quietly dropped in the early sixties, was that the General Assembly rescind the resolution of 1950 which labelled China as an aggressor during the Korean war. Since the beginning of 1970, Peking had shown a new willingness to join the world body by systematically thanking in turn all those states which had supported the restoration of the rights of the People's Republic of China. That this culminated in October 1971 in a resounding victory at the United Nations marks a major success for Chinese ability to signal a new direction in foreign policy and to have this signal accepted by many other countries.

The efforts of the Chinese Government first achieved a major breakthrough in 1970, when for the first time there was a simple majority of United Nations members in favour of Peking's admission. (See Table 11, p. 277). That breakthrough prompted the United States to embark on a review of her China policy in the U.N. to see whether Taiwan could be allowed to retain a seat in the General Assembly even if Peking entered and took over the Security Council seat. However, both Taiwan and Peking rejected this sugges-

[1] Martin, *The Guardian*, 13 May 1971. Credits pledged by China for the whole Tan-Zam project have been put at over $400m the largest lump sum of aid ever promised by the Communist countries for any project (*The Economist*, 7 Nov. 1971).

tion; they are both agreed that Taiwan is an inalienable part of China. The American policy was therefore doomed from the beginning.

After the 1970 vote, Peking intensified its efforts to seek closer co-operation from many states and these resulted in the extension of diplomatic recognition by several states including Cameroun, Nigeria, Senegal, Sierra Leone. The announcement in July 1971 by President Nixon of his proposed visit to Peking before May 1972 encouraged Chinese efforts. It also called into question the policy of hostility to Peking adopted by the small 'allies' of the United States. They became more susceptible to Peking's overtures and from that time it seemed that Peking's entry into the U.N. was only a matter of time.

However, the American and the Taiwan Governments did not take this lying down. The Taiwan Foreign Minister went round some 22 African states and claimed that 19 of them supported Peking's exclusion. The Americans too embarked on a monumental diplomatic offensive to obtain support for the dual representation of China. The American Secretary of State personally received and talked to more than ninety Foreign Ministers and leaders of delegations to the United Nations while President Nixon telephoned several Heads of State to ask for support. American efforts did not stop there as U.S. diplomats threatened to cut off aid from those countries which refused to co-operate. At the same time, paradoxically, President Nixon's National Security Adviser was in Peking discussing his proposed visit with the Chinese authorities. It was not surprising therefore that the smaller countries should see the United States threats in New York as insincere. Up to the last moment however, the United States delegates at the U.N. were convinced that their procedural device to keep Taiwan in the organisation would succeed.

But when the first vote on the United States motion, calling for the expulsion of Taiwan to be regarded as an important question, was taken on Monday 25 October, the narrow majority claimed by the United States disappeared. The result was 59 votes against the motion, 55 in favour and 15 abstentions. Of the 59 contrary votes, 19 came from African states, while Morocco, Tunisia and Senegal which had earlier promised to vote with the United States, joined, to her great discomfiture, the camp of the abstainers.[1]

See Appendix 2, p. 285.

With the American effort defeated, the adoption of the Albanian resolution calling for the admission of Peking and the expulsion of Taiwan was a foregone conclusion. Nevertheless even Peking must have been surprised by the overwhelming vote in favour of the Albanian resolution – more than the two-thirds majority that the earlier United States resolution would have required. Seventy-six votes were cast in favour of Peking including this time twenty-six African states. To the consternation of the United States delegation Israel and Portugal supported China and were applauded by the Arab and African states for so doing. Thirty-five states voted against the Albanian resolution including some 15 African states.

The result was generally welcomed, though the great elation displayed by many delegates to the U.N. angered President Nixon. For once the small states had administered a resolute rebuff to the wealthiest and most powerful nation on earth. The American delegate described the decision as a 'moment of infamy' while the Albanian Deputy Foreign Minister (who with the Tanzanian and Pakistani delegates had stage-managed the resolution) described the decision as a victory for the peoples of the world and for reason, and a great defeat for the United States policy of foisting a two-China policy on the United Nations. The French Foreign Minister described the decision as sounding the death knell for the era of super-power collusion to divide the world.

In welcoming the decision of the United Nations, the Chinese Government called it a victory for the world and for Chairman Mao's proletarian line on foreign policy, and said that China would not play the role of a super power in the organisation but would strive to work with the underprivileged nations to see justice done and to prevent a Soviet–American division of the world. On 2 November 1971, Huang Hua, the veteran Chinese Ambassador to Canada (earlier to Ghana and the U.A.R.), was named Peking's Permanent Representative to the United Nations.

One issue, of which the critics of the U.N. decision were not conscious, was the role it played in the debate on foreign policy going on in the top echelons of the Chinese hierarchy. The favourable decision in fact strengthened the position of Chou En-lai, the revolutionary pragmatist and his followers. It vindicated their argument in favour of the new outward policy.

At the United Nations itself the African group of nations can presumably now count on the constant support of a great power and a permanent member of the Security Council. I think it can safely be predicted that China will try as much as possible to work with the Afro-Asian group in the organisation. This is of course far from saying that, with China now in the United Nations, all major international problems can now be solved. Even the Chinese agree with this view. Indeed the continued impotence of the Organisation was dramatically demonstrated in December 1971 when, in the face of a Soviet veto, it proved unhelpful in the Indo-Pakistan war. However, the U.N. decision represents for Chou En-lai, the architect of Chinese foreign policy, a fitting crown for twenty-two years of tireless diplomatic effort.

These diplomatic developments in Africa were however tied in with the general trend of Chinese diplomacy – in Europe and the Americas. The Chinese leadership was becoming increasingly apprehensive over Soviet intentions since the border clashes with the Soviet Union in March and June 1969. The Soviet Union was heavily reinforcing her troops on the long border with China to the extent where the force level reached some forty-four divisions many of these armed with nuclear weapons. She was also trying to promote a relaxation of tension in Europe in order specifically to be more able to face China in the east. This reality accelerated the process of China seeking out new friends all over the world.

A culmination of that process was the announcement by President Nixon on 15 July 1971 that his National Security Adviser, Henry Kissinger, had just paid a secret visit to Peking in consequence of which the United States President had accepted an invitation to visit China before May 1972. The Nixon announcement was a stunning surprise to the diplomatic world though one might argue that it was the culmination of gradual but steady efforts which the President had been making from even before his formal accession to the Presidency in January 1969.

Naturally, the Nationalist Government in Taiwan and its friends abroad viewed the announcement with grave misgivings: the long held, though entirely mythical, legitimacy of the regime's rule over the whole of China was being called in question and Nixon's example might lead to a stampede of smaller states into the Peking camp – a move which could result in the isolation of Taiwan. It could also affect the chances of Nationalist China retaining the

China seat at the United Nations. Outside Nationalist China, however, the announcement was generally welcomed, especially in progressive circles in the United States. Coming so soon after the Supreme Court decision on the Pentagon Papers, President Nixon was able to draw the attention of the nation once more to presidential activity and thus increase his popularity. The announcement was not enthusiastically welcomed by the Soviet Union which had reason to fear that this could result in Sino-American collusion against her, and this in spite of Nixon's protestations to the contrary.

In Europe and Africa generally, it was greeted with elation and with satisfaction: the United States was at last coming to grips with reality by moving to deal with a government that controlled about one-fourth of humanity. There was of course some question as to how the changing outward look of China would affect her hitherto undaunted support for liberation movements in Africa, seeing that the United States administration is basically anti-revolutionary. Would it for instance lead to cuts in the aid Peking offers to those movements if America presses for it? Or will Peking now urge these movements to resort to peaceful settlement, always hitherto regarded as a fraudulent solution? I can only say here that Peking is not likely to reverse its policy in this way, but only time will tell if this prognostication is correct.

From 22 to 28 February 1972 Nixon visited China and had useful discussions with the Chinese leaders. In the communique issued after the talks, both sides agreed to work for a normalisation of relations and to oppose any move by any major power to impose domination on Asia. For his part, Nixon recognised the existence of one China and promised to withdraw American troops from Taiwan as tension in the area was reduced. One area that was not discussed during the visit was Africa. Nevertheless, it is relevant to ask again after Nixon's visit to China, how far the thaw in Sino-American relations may be expected to affect China's willingness to give generous aid to African states to prevent them being swallowed up by imperialism?

After all, the increasing Soviet-American understanding in the late sixties led to a decline in their competitive aid-giving to African states. Yet another dimension of the question is the expected windfall that the detente may have in Africa. As most African states now formally recognise Peking, would China's resources not be

After the Cultural Revolution 257

overstrained if she attempts to extend aid to her friends or will she be forced to refuse requests for economic aid for lack of resources? These questions will probably have to remain partly unanswered, though it should be patently apparent from our discussion in the rest of the book that there is obviously a limit to the resources China can expend. Perhaps a partial answer may be found in the fact that after the President's intended visit had been announced in July 1971, Ethiopia (as discussed above) was still able to obtain an aid commitment of £33.5 million from China. Also in April 1972, Prime Minister Dom Mintoff of Malta obtained a commitment of £17 million from Peking. Though not within Africa, Malta's success would tend to confirm the suggestion that China's aid would continue. Indeed, Nigeria is at present (May 1972) negotiating a loan agreement with China.

CONCLUSION

In the period covered by this book, China's policy in Africa went through a process of change and adaptation; a metamorphosis largely caused by the realities of the African situation and by the realisation of the Chinese leaders that shifts in emphasis had to be made if China was to take part in the triangular competition with the Soviet Union and the United States.

From the time when Chinese domestic policy shifted drastically to the left, when most African territories were still under direct colonial rule, China would have preferred competition with imperialism to take place on the ideological and revolutionary level. The weaknesses of the Chinese economy placed a definite limit on the regime's ability to compete with other major aid donors. The Chinese also realised, of course, that the West might well outstrip the Socialist bloc in an economic competition in the third world. Coupled with this, the debate with Khrushchev questioned the wisdom of Russia granting substantial economic aid to bourgeois governments when there were other fraternal states in dire need of such aid.

Yet, as the number of independent African states increased and the politics of development propelled these states to seek external aid, the Chinese view on such foreign aid changed to conform with the new realities. This is not to say that the 'political independence' granted to the African states did not present China with a dilemma; she would have preferred to see these states carry out armed struggles before achieving independence.

The new flood of independent African states in 1960 and 1961 was accepted, and China initially expected that her chances of regaining the United Nations seat would be improved as Afro-Asian states came to constitute a significant force in that organisation. This hope was, however, shortlived, as the United States successfully introduced a procedural device in the General Assembly in 1961 which made the China question an 'important' one, requiring a two-thirds majority.

Nevertheless, China sought the friendship of the new African states as a counter to the United States' efforts begun in the fifties to isolate her. This became more necessary in the sixties as Khrushchev joined the United States in trying to isolate China diplomatically. A breakthrough had been made in Egypt in 1956, to be followed in 1958 by Morocco and the Sudan, all of which had growing trade relations with China.

This success in North Africa occurred just when the Algerian war of independence was becoming the main issue in North African politics. China's support – financial, diplomatic and material – for the National Liberation Front and her recognition of the P.G.R.A. gained her considerable goodwill at a time when even Khrushchev demurred at granting formal recognition to the latter. No doubt Khrushchev was more concerned with Soviet policies in Europe and what he saw as the need to preserve cordial diplomatic relations with France. He also had to consider the attitude of the leaders of the French Communist Party, whose support for the Algerian nationalists only came at the last moment. Nevertheless, China used her support for the Algerian revolutionaries to advantage in showing the unpalatable side of Khrushchev's 'reckless' policy of detente with the West.

The Chinese, however, tended to over-simplify Khrushchev's position on national liberation movements in the third world and his 'relentless' pursuit of detente. Indeed, the West would have wished him to be as 'moderate' and 'reasonable' as the Chinese tried to paint him. The Soviet Union, of course, also distorted the Chinese view, claiming, contrary to all evidence, that China was advocating a general nuclear war.

The fire of revolutionary war which the Algerians had lit spread in time to other colonial areas in Africa. This development conformed with China's advocacy of armed struggle, but this does not mean that the Chinese were directly responsible for it.

While the Algerian struggle continued, however, there was little chance of China making headway in most French-speaking states, for they conformed with French policy. A satisfactory settlement of the war in 1962 ended the virulent propaganda campaign which China had launched against France. President de Gaulle's growing disenchantment with United States' hegemonic control of N.A.T.O. and what he saw as a developing Soviet-U.S. condominium in the world led him to recognise China in January 1964, a decision which had repercussions for her in Africa.

Before that China's policy in Africa had already made advances. African leaders, in their dealings with her, had to consider their own interests and the extent to which these would be served by relations with Peking. In most cases China seemed to support African aspirations, especially in respect of the liberation of the African territories still under colonial rule. Her advice to the new African states was to continue the struggle to attain economic independence, without which political independence was only a chimera. A concomitant of this advice was the need to reject Western aid, which was designed to maintain economic control of the new states. At a later stage even Soviet aid to the new states was bracketed with Western aid as predatory. This latter attitude was adopted after the Soviet Union had abruptly withdrawn her assistance from China and had urged other East European countries to follow suit.

No African state, however, accepted China's advice to reject Western aid in principle as well as aid from other Socialist States, and to depend solely on self-reliance. Indeed, some saw the triangular competition as a favourable situation, enabling them to secure economic and technical assistance from all sources, thereby improving their chances of development and enhancing their political independence.

However, Chinese economic and technical assistance had more impact in states such as Guinea, Tanzania, Congo-Brazzaville and Mali where the philosophy of the ruling parties laid emphasis on self-reliance and on state direction of economic development. Significantly, these states also tended to be relatively poor in natural resources and thus to offer less attraction for the 'imperialist vultures' China wanted to keep out. Their relative poverty also tended to maximise the impact of Chinese economic and technical assistance, whereas in countries such as Nigeria it seemed small indeed.

I have shown that the implementation of Chinese aid did not proceed without difficulty. In the first place, the disastrous economic years of 1959–61 placed considerable limitations on her ability to meet any commitment abroad, the more so as she was forced to enter the economic aid war with the Soviet Union and the United States in order to maintain any influence in Africa. Like the Soviet Union and other East European countries, she was embarking on new ground in Africa and communications with the continent were not easy. Some of the machinery which had been tested in Europe and the Soviet Union could not operate in tropical conditions like those of Guinea. In such cases, China's concentration on those projects which were labour-intensive considerably reduced the chances of failure which the Soviet Union had earlier faced.

The shortage of hard currency experienced by states like Ghana also impeded the implementation of Chinese-aided projects, and in Mali for example China had to send the raw materials needed for a match factory. In Tanzania, as in Ghana, the initial opposition of some government officials had first to be overcome.

It can be argued that China's method of financing the projects she helped to set up was a method of trade promotion in that it involved importing Chinese goods and using the proceeds to finance the projects locally. This is to some extent valid, but one must also consider the terms of the loan agreements which China signed with African states. In all cases, when the aid was not in the form of direct grant, it was an interest-free loan repayable after a long gestation period. On another level, Chinese concentration on those projects which were labour- rather than capital-intensive helped to reduce urban unemployment – the scourge of most developing countries. Obviously China's lack of highly sophisticated machinery for export largely determined the form of her aid; at the same time, however, the advantage of the method to the African recipients was that it concentrated on the internal resources which they had in abundance – labour.

Initial delay in implementing promised Chinese aid was compensated for in the latter part of the sixties and by the end of the period many projects had been completed. This was in spite of the disruptive activities of the Cultural Revolution. Indeed, new commitments to old friends were undertaken in these years, the most significant of which was the Tan–Zam railway agreement in September 1967. By the end of 1968 most of the promised aid to Guinea and Mali had been disbursed and all of Mauritania's. Much of that to Tanzania had also been utilised, and China had become the main source of external aid for that country. Congo-Brazzaville and the

Somali Republic had also utilised much of their Chinese aid. The United Arab Republic was, however, an exception as political differences and the great Soviet inroads into the Egyptian economy made China's fulfilment of her promised aid less urgent. Indeed, until the end of 1968 the $80 million promised in 1964 had not been utilised at all. Although Algeria had received some $10 million during the liberation war, the $50 million promised in 1963 was slow in coming and the Algerian Government had to press for fulfilment in 1966 and 1967 before China took positive action. There was thus a marked difference in China's implementation of promised aid in states south of the Sahara. One reason for this was probably China's realisation that North Africa was already 'lost' to the Soviet Union and economic competition there would be more expensive. After the Cultural Revolution, a new impetus was given to the aid-giving activity of the Chinese. In 1970 budgetary and military assistance worth nearly $20 million was pledged to Guinea. In the same year Sudan received a £14.5 million interest-free loan and a year after that, succeeded in receiving another £14 million loan, at a time when Soviet–Sudanese relations were at their lowest level and President Nimeiry had threatened to look somewhere else for arms. There was also of course the most important agreement on the Tan-Zam railway, the first three hundred miles of which the Chinese completed in November 1971. Chinese commitment to Ethiopia of nearly $94 million in 1971 confirmed the return to the aid-giving role and this was maintained in 1972. It is significant that these new loans were not given to North African countries.

On the trade level, Chinese exports to African states rose from insignificance in the early fifties to more than £51 million in 1966, though falling to £37 million in 1968. On the other hand Chinese imports from Africa had reached a record level in 1965 when the figure was just over £39 million. In some cases the surplus in China's favour was used to finance local projects, and in others she gained much needed external reserves. Although in absolute terms her share of Africa's market was still very small, by the end of 1970, it had shown a significant expansion, which could be expected to continue in future.

China's policy was by no means limited to offering economic and technical assistance and improving trade relations. In fact political relations and objectives were often interwoven with economic

Conclusion 263

relations, though China was quite capable of maintaining commercial relations where no diplomatic relations existed. China set out to develop political relations with African states and people's movements on the basis of a common solidarity against imperialism based on common experiences of imperialist exploitation. In doing this she consistently supported liberation movements in Africa and rendered material and propaganda help where possible. Her anti-colonial stand won much respect, as her views reflected those of militantly nationalist African states and movements. This respect and goodwill paid dividends during the Sino-India border war in 1962. Not one of the non-aligned African states, whose support India and China cherished, condemned China as an aggressor or declared their support for India. By adopting a non-aligned stand in the dispute, those African states effectively gave a diplomatic cold shoulder to India.

The same attitude, however, undermined Chinese objectives when the Sino-Soviet conflict found its way into Africa. African leaders on good terms with both China and the Soviet Union refused to take a stand in the conflict, and indeed detested being pressurised by both sides to 'stand up and be counted'. The practicalities of non-alignment as applied to the East-West confrontation were now applied to the Sino-Soviet dispute, and China did not like the outcome. While Chinese views conformed ideologically with those of many African leaders, especially with regard to the liberation struggle, those leaders were reluctant to come out overtly on China's side. Instead, they urged a solution of the Sino-Soviet dispute in the interests of anti-imperialist solidarity.

The African stand was particularly galling to the Chinese as the abortive second Bandung approached. China had expended considerable energy on calling the conference, but failed to have it convened in circumstances acceptable to her. Its postponement in June 1965 was a great setback for Chinese diplomacy, and the negative veto cast in November of the same year was scarcely a compensation. China's friends in Africa had been greatly displeased by her premature recognition of the Algerian regime which overthrew Ben Bella – a staunch supporter of the African revolution. China was not aware of the deep sensitivity of African leaders to the military overthrow of another government. Other setbacks were suffered in January 1966, as Dahomey and the Central African

Conclusion

Republic severed relations with China and expelled Chinese technicians working in those countries. A much greater blow was the overthrow of President Kwame Nkrumah of Ghana in February while he was in Peking on his way to Hanoi. In him China lost a significant ideological ally. Further, the Chinese position in Kenya deteriorated rapidly when Vice President Oginga Odinga lost ground in the internal political struggle, though diplomatic relations were not severed.

China thus suffered a series of setbacks in her African policy, and political relations deteriorated further during the Cultural Revolution. It would be a gross misrepresentation, however, to think that the record was a catalogue of failure. Indeed China's relations with such countries as Congo-Brazzaville, Tanzania, Guinea, Mali, Somalia, the Sudan, Algeria, Mauritania and Zambia bore witness to successes in policy. Taking into consideration the resources *actually* expended by China during the period, the achievement was disproportionate to the efforts.

This was more so on the revolutionary level. The Algerian war of liberation, which China supported financially and politically, helped to vindicate the thesis that armed struggle by the oppressed peoples would lead to independence. The successful conclusion of that war gave a great fillip to the other liberation movements in Portuguese Guinea, Angola and Mozambique. The leaders of these movements adopted the strategy of protracted armed struggle advocated by China, though taking care to adapt Chinese tactics of guerrilla warfare to local conditions. Here too, the leaders strove to keep clear of the vagaries of the Sino-Soviet dispute. In the first place, in order to prove that China was distorting the Soviet position on national liberation movements, Khrushchev and other Soviet leaders had to make available to these movements weapons and other forms of aid. As a result those movements had varied sources of military supply, although the Sino-Soviet conflict introduced in these movements tended to divert their attention and dissipate their energy. This was harmful to them at a time when strong solidarity was needed.

China had a significant success in Tanzania when the government allowed Chinese experts to train freedom fighters from Mozambique. Her influence also increased in this field when her experts trained freedom fighters in Ghana under a Sino-Ghanaian military agreement. This was one reason why Nhrumah's fall was unfortunate.

From China's point of view however, revolutionary activities were not limited to the remaining colonial territories. Her support for these revolutionary groups elsewhere often accompanied her intention to develop normal relations with some of the African states. In Cameroun, she continued to finance the U.P.C.'s armed struggle after the country had been granted political independence in 1960. This was one reason why Cameroun refused for a long time to recognise Peking. China's help in training nationals of Niger, the Ivory Coast and Cameroun in Ghana did not endear her to the leaders of those states. There was no doubt that Cameroun could have recognised China before 1971 if Peking had not stepped in to be the main supporter of the U.P.C. after independence in 1960. It was a difficult situation for China since she had just been criticising Khrushchev for sacrificing revolutionary interests in pursuit of a detente with the West.

The Congo crisis of 1960 and subsequent years supported Chinese arguments that colonial states would not grant political independence unless they knew they could maintain control afterwards. Rebellions and uprisings up to 1965 also vindicated the Chinese viewpoint, especially as little effort was needed to disrupt and damage a country like Congo-Kinshasa. The net result, however, was negative as far as China was concerned. Many African states had supported Lumumba and his successors, and progressive opinion in Africa had been against Tshombe's return to power. However, after General Mobutu's coup d'etat in November 1965, there was a change in African opinion. The new government moved to the left and the mining interests were nationalised. Moreover, Mobutu now allowed freedom fighters from Angola to use his country as a base, which had not been the case when Tshombe was there. These at least were noteworthy steps which China should have taken into consideration before expressing personal hostility to Mobutu. The continued exclusion of China from a state she considered to be the heart of Africa was a failure of policy.

The prospects of continued revolution also had to be considered in those states which recognised China and those to which she offered economic and technical assistance. While stating that steps taken by these governments to bring their foreign-dominated economy under state control constituted a contribution to the anti-imperialist struggle, China developed a vested interest in the stability of these regimes. She could not favour any destabilising factors, no matter how revolutionary these could otherwise have been considered objectively. The instability of these regimes could more easily result in 'right-wing' successor regimes which would endanger her position in these countries. In this way she was simply behaving like other great powers in the world, putting state interest above the need for revolutionary advance. Here the emphasis was on her unwillingness to export revolution and the often-stated principle of non-interference in the internal affairs of other states. This, of course, was pragmatism in operation. Thus China refused to support the protracted Southern Sudanese rebellion against a government friendly to her. Such support would in any case have had adverse repercussions in the rest of the Arab world. The decision was taken after a rational calculation of state interests and did not differ from the way the United States or Russia would have behaved in similar circumstances. That the Southern rebellion has now ended is a timely relief for the Chinese.

From the African standpoint, relations with China helped to construct a progressive aura of respectability and independence. Thus, Mauritania recognised Peking in 1965, and received economic and technical assistance, mainly to prove that the President was not an imperialist stooge set up by the French to frustrate Morocco's 'just' demands on Mauritania. Moroccan propaganda had done much to give Mauritania that image and the only way to combat it appeared to be to move left. The President's visit to Peking in 1967 and the pictures showing him waving the *Thoughts of Chairman Mao* put the final seal on the new image.

One means of policy implementation in Africa was direct people's diplomacy. Solidarity committees and other 'democratic' groups were responsible for generating goodwill for China in many countries. At one stage, Sino-Soviet rivalry tended to tear apart these useful organisations. Indeed, in 1967 China found herself compelled to withdraw from the central organisation of the most famous of these bodies – the Afro-Asian People's Solidarity Organisation. However, the various African delegations visiting China during the period ensured that some degree of goodwill remained even in countries where diplomatic relations had been severed. From 1958 to 1970 some 827 delegations were reported to

Conclusion 267

have visited China, while about 473 Chinese delegations went to Africa. These visits, official and unofficial, helped to generate interest. It is noteworthy that during the Nigerian Civil War when China came out in support of the rebels and was being accused by Federal Nigeria of sending 'mercenaries' to fight with them, something curious was going on. The pro-China Afro-Asia Solidarity Committee in Federal Nigeria continued to operate openly while the left-wing section of the trade unions produced one pro-China body, though this was not recognised by the government. Indeed, in January 1969 the pro-China Solidarity Committee was allowed to attend the A.A.P.S.O. meeting in Khartoum, while the pro-Soviet group was not allowed to leave the country! The Chinese must have been satisfied with that performance.

It was seen that in 1967 all Chinese envoys except the Ambassador to Egypt were recalled to Peking to 'take part' in the Cultural Revolution. None returned to his post before 1969 and, after that, new envoys were posted to African capitals. However, some of those ambassadors, such as Ho Ying, the shrewd envoy to Tanzania, have been put in charge of, or assigned to, the West Asia and Africa Desks in China's Foreign Ministry, and Huang Hua is now at the United Nations. Perhaps the control of these desks by personnel with first-hand experience of African affairs will produce more realistic and consistent policies in future. This will be the result of the efforts of Chou En-lai, the 'revolutionary pragmatist' who in the past years shaped the Chinese foreign policy examined in this book. It has combined pragmatism essentially dictated by the state interests of China with 'revolutionism' emanating from the ideological foundation and infrastructure of the Chinese Government. In the course of time tension did arise between the two aspects but fortunately for China the result was not disintegration but what I have called 'revolutionary pragmatism'.

APPENDIX I

Table 1: Chinese Delegations visiting African countries 1958-70

Country visited	58	59	60	61	62	63	64	65	66	67	68	69	70
United Arab Republic	11	3	5	10	5	6	7	8	8	–	–	–	1
Morocco	3	2	3	3	3	6	2	3	–	–	–	–	–
Tunisia	2	2	3	1	–	–	1	–	–	–	–	–	–
Sudan	2	1	1	1	3	–	2	2	2	–	–	–	2
Ghana	2	–	1	5	8	5	7	8	–	–	–	–	–
Guinea	–	2	7	4	9	3	6	8	6	3	4	2	4
Algeria	–	–	1	–	5	15	17	11	2	–	1	1	3
Congo-Kinshasa	–	–	1	1	1	–	–	–	–	–	–	–	–
Ethiopia	–	–	1	1	2	–	2	–	1	–	–	–	1
Mali	–	–	1	3	8	7	9	8	7	1	2	–	2
Somali Republic	–	–	1	1	1	–	2	3	3	2	1	2	2
Dahomey	–	–	–	1	1	–	3	–	–	–	–	–	–
Niger	–	–	–	1	–	–	1	–	–	–	–	–	–
Nigeria	–	–	–	1	–	–	2	–	–	–	–	–	–
Senegal	–	–	–	2	–	1	–	–	–	–	–	–	–
Sierra Leone	–	–	–	1	–	–	–	–	–	–	–	–	–
Tanganyika	–	–	–	1	1	2 } 14	6	7	6	2	8	7
Zanzibar	–	–	–	–	–	1						
Togo	–	–	–	1	1	–	–	–	–	–	–	–	–
Upper Volta	–	–	–	1	–	–	1	–	–	–	–	–	–
Burundi	–	–	–	–	1	1	–	–	–	–	–	–	–
Gabon	–	–	–	–	1	–	–	–	–	–	–	–	–
Ivory Coast	–	–	–	–	1	–	–	–	–	–	–	–	–
Uganda	–	–	–	–	1	1	–	–	–	–	–	–	–
Kenya	–	–	–	–	–	2	4	–	–	–	–	–	1
Cameroun	–	–	–	–	–	–	1	–	–	–	–	–	–
Central African Republic	–	–	–	–	–	–	1	4	–	–	–	–	–
Congo-Brazzaville	–	–	–	–	–	–	4	8	7	3	1	3	4
Zambia	–	–	–	–	–	–	1	–	1	2	1	3	2
Mauritania	–	–	–	–	–	–	–	–	3	–	1	–	2
Mauritius	–	–	–	–	–	–	–	–	–	–	1	–	–
Equatorial Guinea	–	–	–	–	–	–	–	–	–	–	–	–	1
Libya	–	–	–	–	–	–	–	–	–	–	–	–	1
Annual total	20	10	25	39	52	50	87	69	47	17	14	19	33

Source: Radio and Press reports of China and the African states in S.C.M.P., N.C.N.A., and B.B.C. Summary of World Broadcasts 1958-70.

Note: China made use of the device of sending a mission to visit two, three or four African states in one stretch. Thus the total number of delegations does not reflect the number actually setting out from Peking.

Appendix I

Table 2: African Delegations visiting China 1958–70

Country of origin	58	59	60	61	62	63	64	65	66	67	68	69	70
Algeria	5	6	6	3	2	8	9	4	6	1	–	2	–
Angola	1	1	–	1	–	1	2	2	3	–	–	–	–
Botswana	–	–	–	–	–	–	–	1	2	1	–	–	–
Burundi	–	–	–	–	–	2	2	–	–	1	–	–	–
Cameroun	1	6	6	3	1	2	2	–	1	–	–	–	–
Congo-Brazzaville	–	–	–	1	–	–	3	11	16	8	1	1	4
Congo Kinshasa	2	1	11	2	1	3	–	2	1	2	–	–	–
Central African Republic	1	1	1	–	–	–	1	4	–	–	–	–	–
Chad	–	1	1	–	–	–	–	–	–	–	–	–	–
Dahomey	–	–	–	–	1	–	1	1	1	–	–	–	–
Ethiopia	–	–	–	1	–	1	–	–	–	–	–	–	–
Gabon	–	–	1	–	–	–	–	–	–	–	–	–	–
Gambia	–	–	–	–	–	2	3	–	–	–	–	–	–
Ghana	1	3	6	3	2	6	4	8	2	–	–	–	–
Guinea	–	3	7	5	4	6	5	8	7	2	4	2	1
Guinea (Bissau)	–	–	2	1	1	1	–	1	2	–	–	–	–
Ivory Coast	–	–	3	–	–	1	–	–	1	–	–	–	–
Kenya	1	2	3	1	5	11	7	5	–	–	–	–	–
Lesotho	–	–	1	–	–	3	1	2	2	–	–	–	–
Libya	1	–	–	–	–	–	–	–	–	–	–	–	–
Malawi	–	–	1	–	–	–	1	–	–	–	–	–	–
Mali	1	1	5	4	2	7	10	8	10	6	3	1	1
Mauritania	1	1	1	–	–	–	–	–	2	3	–	1	–
Mauritius	–	1	1	–	–	1	1	1	–	–	–	–	–
Malagasy	1	2	1	–	–	2	1	–	1	–	–	–	–
Mozambique	–	–	–	–	–	5	1	2	1	–	–	–	–
Morocco	2	4	6	2	–	4	3	3	5	1	–	1	–
Niger	–	–	–	–	–	–	1	–	1	1	–	–	–
Nigeria	1	1	4	4	2	4	1	–	1	1	–	–	–
Rhodesia	–	–	–	1	–	2	3	–	2	–	–	–	–
Rwanda	–	–	–	–	–	1	1	–	1	–	–	–	–
South Africa	1	1	–	1	–	5	2	3	3	3	–	–	–
Senegal	3	1	–	7	–	1	1	2	–	2	–	–	–
Sierra Leone	1	1	4	1	–	–	2	–	2	–	–	–	–
Somali Republic	1	–	6	3	3	6	3	6	7	5	1	–	2
Sudan	2	3	4	7	1	2	4	4	7	3	–	–	2
South West Africa	–	–	1	–	–	3	1	2	1	1	–	–	–
Swaziland	–	–	–	–	–	–	–	–	1	1	–	–	–
Tanganyika	1	–	1	1	3	9	5 } 16	13	8	3	1	3
Zanibar	–	–	5	–	4	8	10						
Tunisia	1	2	2	1	1	–	1	1	–	–	–	–	–
Uganda	1	2	2	1	1	3	3	2	3	–	–	–	–
United Arab Republic	9	1	1	1	2	2	5	10	2	1	–	1	–
Togo	1	–	3	–	1	–	–	–	1	–	–	–	–
Zambia	–	–	–	–	–	–	3	1	3	5	–	2	2
Blk. African Youth	3	3	2	2	–	3	1	1	1	1	–	–	–
Blk. African Trade Un.	1	2	–	1	–	–	1	–	1	–	–	–	–
Annual total	44	50	98	58	37	113	103	114	114	57	12	12	15

Source: Radio and Press reports of China and the African States in S.C.M.P., N.C.N.A.. and B.B.C. Summary of World Broadcasts 1958–70.

Appendix I   271

Table 3: Chou En-Lai's African tour and responses to proposed second Bandung

Country visited	Date	Response
United Arab Republic	14-21 Dec. 1963	No reference
Algeria	21-7 Dec. 1963	No reference
Morocco	27-30 Dec. 1963	No reference
Albania visit		
Tunisia	9-10 Jan. 1964	No reference
Ghana	11-16 Jan. 1964	Yes – strongly
Mali	16-21 Jan. 1964	Yes – very strongly
Guinea	21-6 Jan. 1964	Yes – strongly
Sudan	27-30 Jan. 1964	Yes – strongly
Ethiopia	30 Jan.-1 Feb. 1964	Yes
Somali Republic	1-4 Feb. 1964	Yes – strongly

Table 4: The Afro-Asian People's Solidarity Organisation. Member countries represented on permanent Secretariat and Executive committee up till 1967

Secretariat	Executive Committee	
Ghana	Ghana	
Guinea	Guinea	
India	Algeria	
Algeria	Cameroun	
Angola	China	
China	Ceylon	
Soviet Union	Congo (K)	
Tanzania	Indonesia	
South Africa	India	
Indonesia	Iran	
Iraq	Iraq	
Kenya	Japan	
Japan	Kenya	
North Vietnam	Lebanon	
U.A.R.	Mongolia	South West Africa
	Basutoland	South Africa
	Liberia	South Vietnam
	Tunisia	Morocco
	Soviet Union	Mozambique
	U.A.R.	Somalia
	Uganda	North Vietnam
	Yemen	North Korea
	Tanzania	Pakistan
	Zambia	

Table 5: Chinese imports from selected African states (in £ millions) – £1 = $2.8

year	58	59	60	61	62	63	64	65	66	67	68
State											
U.A.R.	12.46	11.76	16.75	5.21	6.89	5.86	6.4	16.1	11.6	6.79	6
Morocco	1.11	2.21	2.36	1.32	1.11	2.25	5.04	3.3	3.25	2.96	2.64
Nigeria	–	–	0.44	1.36	–	0.36	0.59	0.7	Neg.	0.94	0.25
Sudan	0.72	1.03	3.36	1.43	3.35	4.5	1.75	5.5	4.04	2.71	3.53
Ghana	–	–	c.5	0.07	0.06	0.18	1	2.04	1.86	0.29	0.21
Tanganyika	0.25	0.12	0.27	Neg.	–	3.71	2.32	4.31	3.39	2.76	2.74
Uganda	–	Neg.	1.82	3.35	–	3.99	3.25	6.24	1.21	1.42	1.74
Kenya	0.21	0.23	0.35	0.05	0.17	0.36	0.39	0.63	0.93	1.09	0.44
Tunisia	–	0.27	–	0.18	0.07	–	0.11	0.89	0.29	0.21	0.07
S. Africa	2.5	–	3.32	–	0.54	1.89*+	+	+	+	+	+
Total	17.25	15.62	29.17	12.97	12.19	23.10	20.85	39.71	26.57	19.17	17.62

Neg. = Below £9,000
– = Nothing
+ = Not Available
* = Figure for January – March 1963. After that date, South African statistics ceased to show figures of trade with China.
Sources:
(1) U.N. Economic Commission for Africa – Foreign Trade Statistics of Africa Series A.
(2) East Africa Trade and Revenue Report. Common Services Organisation, Mombasa, Kenya.
(3) Republic of Sudan: Foreign Trade Statistics, Khartoum.
(4) External Trade Statistics of Ghana, Accra.
(5) U.A.R. Annual Statement of Foreign Trade, Cairo.
(6) Nigeria Trade Summary, Lagos.
Note: £1 = $2.8 This has been retained, as most of the period covered was before the November 1967 devaluation of the £. The old figure has been used to convert all the values for all the years to £ Sterling.

Table 6: Chinese exports to selected African states (in £ millions) –
£1 = $2.8

year ▶ State	58	59	60	61	62	63	64	65	66	67	68
U.A.R.	8.96	8.26	7.42	6.75	6.89	7.1	6.37	13.1	14.39	8.32	8.00
Morocco	5.71	2.64	2.53	3.07	3.14	2.46	4.28	4.26	6.26	4.71	4.36
Nigeria	1.45	1.87	1.8	2.28	1.57	1.57	3.13	4.86	5.03	6.26	3.72
Sudan	0.52	0.9	0.79	1.68	1.36	1.1	2.36	2.32	4.5	6.12	3.42
Ghana	0.25	0.79	1.07	0.86	1.36	0.75	0.96	5.25	2.68	0.28	0.60
Tanganyika	–	Neg.	Neg.	Neg.	0.01	0.09	0.31	1.75	3.71	3.1	4.31
Uganda	–	Neg.	Neg.	Neg.	Neg.	0.31	0.26	0.97	1.71	0.79	1.03
Kenya	0.04	0.05	0.03	Neg.	0.04	0.09	0.69	0.95	1.94	0.88	1.59
Mali	–	–	+	0.02	0.28	0.43	1	3.64	3.68	4.14	1.43
Senegal	–	–	+	1.14	1.86	0.82	1.18	1.07	2.55	4.21	1.84
Tunisia	0.13	0.51	0.32	0.46	0.21	0.32	0.07	0.57	0.61	0.43	0.05
Sierra Leone	–	–	1	0.15	0.17	0.11	0.28	0.46	0.52	0.67	0.97
Libya	–	–	0.11	0.23	0.35	0.68	0.54	1.71	2.82	3.61	4.39
Niger	–	–	+	0.03	0.06	0.07	0.18	0.64	0.89	0.96	0.99
Togo	–	–	+	Neg.	0.07	0.11	0.21	0.21	0.46	0.82	0.73
South Africa	1.43	0.71	0.82	0.32	0.46	*0.39	+	+	+	+	+
Algeria	0.86	0.71	+	+	–	–	1.49	–	–	–	–
Total	19.35	16.44	15.89	16.99	17.83	16.40	23.31	41.76	51.75	45.30	37.43

All notes on the table of Chinese imports from Africa also apply to this table.

Appendix I

Table 7: African states recognising Peking as at 31 December each year

year▶	58	59	60	61	62	63	64	65	66	67	68	69	70	71
United Arab Republic	Y	Y	Y	Y	Y	Y	Y	Y	Y	Y	Y	Y	Y	Y
Morocco		Y	Y	Y	Y	Y	Y	Y	Y	Y	Y	Y	Y	Y
Sudan		Y	Y	Y	Y	Y	Y	Y	Y	Y	Y	Y	Y	Y
Guinea			Y	Y	Y	Y	Y	Y	Y	Y	Y	Y	Y	Y
Ghana				Y	Y	Y	Y	Y	S	S	S	S	S	S
Mali				Y	Y	Y	Y	Y	Y	Y	Y	Y	Y	Y
Somali Republic				Y	Y	Y	Y	Y	Y	Y	Y	Y	Y	Y
Tanganyika					Y	Y	Y	} Y	Y	Y	Y	Y	Y	Y
Zanzibar							Y							
Algeria						Y	Y	Y	Y	Y	Y	Y	Y	Y
Uganda						Y	Y	Y	Y	Y	Y	Y	Y	Y
Kenya							Y	Y	Y	Y	Y	Y	Y	Y
Burundi							Y	Y	S	S	S	S	S	Y
Tunisia								Y	Y	Y	R	R	R	R	–
Congo Brazzaville								Y	Y	Y	Y	Y	Y	Y
Central African Republic								Y	Y	R	R	R	R	R	R
Zambia								Y	Y	Y	Y	Y	Y	Y
Dahomey									Y	Y	R	R	R	R	R
Mauritania									Y	Y	Y	Y	Y	Y
Mauritius												Y	Y	Y
Equatorial Guinea												Y	Y
Rwanda														Y
Nigeria														Y
Cameroun														Y
Sierra Leone														Y
Senegal														Y
Ethiopia													Y	Y
+Libya														Y
Annual Total	3	4	7	8	10	13	17	17	14	13	13	14	16	23
Annual Total of Independent States	9	9	26	29	33	35	36	37	39	39	41	42	42	42

S = Suspension of relations.
R = Rupture of relations and transfer of recognition to Taiwan.
+ Libya recognises Peking but does not maintain diplomatic relations.
Source: Joint Communiques published by the New China News Agency.

Table 8: Estimates of Soviet loans, repayment and interest charges 1950–64 (million new roubles)

	year▶50	51	52	53	54	55	56
Outstanding Debts	54	108	162	359	756.9	1453.8	1298.6
Of which loans received in the year	54	54	54	197	397.9	745.8	52.8
Interest Charges	0.5	1.1	1.6	3.6	7.6	14.5	13
Repayment (Including Interest)	−0.5	−1.1	−1.6	−3.6	−56.5	−222.5	−266.6
Balance to be Carried Forward	54	108	162	359	708	1245.8	1045

	year▶57	58	59	60	61	62–4	50–64 Total
Outstanding Debts	1871.8	1613.3	1346.9	1082	1009.5	809.4	–
Of which loans received in the year	826.8	–	–	–	–	–	2382.3
Interest charges	18.7	16.1	13.5	10.8	7.2	12.6	120.8
Repayment (Including Interest)	−277.2	−282.5	−278.4	−83.3	−207.3	−82.2	−2503.1
Balance to be Carried Forward	1613.3	1346.9	1082	1009.5	809.4	–	–

Source: *China Mainland Review*, Vol. 1, p. 7, June 1965, University of Hong Kong Institute of Modern Asian Studies.

Table 9: Chinese aid pledges to African states 1958–71 (in $ million)

year▶	58	59	60	61	62	63	64	65	66	67	68	69	70	71
United Arab Republic	4.7 (1956)						80			10§				
Guinea			0.5	26					6		‡		19.8	
Ghana					19.6		22.4							
Mali					19.6				3		‡			
Somali Republic						21.6					1.83			
Algeria		++	++		1.8	50								
Congo-Brazzaville						25.2								
Kenya						18*								
Tanzania+						45.5	1.75	10.5		0.28 ⎱				
Zambia									16.8	⎰	474†			
Central African Republic							4							
Mauritania										4.04			19.5	
Sudan												40.2	39.2	
Ethiopia														93.8
Uganda						14.8								

Notes:
§   – This was a hard currency loan with no date set for repayment plus 150,000 tons of wheat.
++ – Algeria received more than $10 million during the liberation war.
*   – Excluding $2.8 million grant for the budget.
+   – Excluding free deliveries of weapons and military equipment.
†   – In September 1967, China signed an agreement to finance and build the Tan-Zam Railroad. Final agreement in 1970 put the figure at about $474 million.
‡   – In 1968 China signed an agreement to finance and construct the Mali–Guinea Railway expected to cost $50 million. Survey work was completed on the Mali side in November 1968 just before the coup against President Modibo Keita.

Table 10: Chinese guerrilla warfare experts in Ghana

Rank	Name	Position or Speciality	Date Arrived	Date Departed
Col.	Yen Len	Leader	Oct. 64	Aug. 65
Col.	Sun Hung-wen	Deputy Leader	Oct. 64	Feb. 66
Sr Capt.	Li Fu-k'un	Explosives Expert	Oct. 64	Feb. 66
1st Lt	Chang Chuan-shih		Oct. 64	Aug. 65
1st Lt	Yang Te-yeh	Interpreter	Oct. 64	Feb. 66
Col.	Pien Chih-hai	Tactics Expert	Dec. 64	Feb. 66
Major	Chu Chang-fa	Military Doctor	Dec. 64	Aug. 65
Sr Capt.	Sun Chun-yueh	Unit Commander	Dec. 64	Feb. 66
Capt.	Wang Hsien-chen	Interpreter	Dec. 64	Feb. 66
Capt.	Shen Kuang-wu	Interpreter	Dec. 64	
Capt.	Chao Tsung-huan	Machinist	Dec. 64	Feb. 66
1st Lt	Wu Meng-ch'un	Communication Expert	Dec. 64	Aug. 65
1st Lt	Chen Shu-yu	Interpreter		Feb. 66

Mai Ch'ihua, Hsiao Hsin-yu, Wang Ken-fa and Huang Hung-sheng all arrived in December 1964, but their positions and specialities are not known. They may have departed in April 1965.
Source: *Nkrumah's Subversion in Africa*, Ghana Ministry of Information, Accra, 1966.

Table 11: General Assembly voting on the China question

Year	For Peking	Against Peking	Abstentions
51	11	37	4
52	7	42	11
53	10	44	2
54	11	43	6
55	12	42	8
56	24	47	8
57	27	47	7
58	28	44	9
59	29	44	9
60	34	42	22
61	36	48	20
62	42	56	12
63	41	57	12
65	47	47	20
66	46	57	17
67	45	58	17
68	44	58	23
69	48	56	21
70	51	49	25
*71	76	35	17

* The substantial voting was in fact more than two-thirds majority in favour of Peking though that requirement had been earlier rejected by the General Assembly.

APPENDIX II

Treaty of Friendship Between the People's Republic of China and the Republic of Guinea.

The Chairman of the P.R.C. and the President of the Republic of Guinea,

Desiring to consolidate and further develop the profound friendship between the P.R.C. and the Republic of Guinea,

Convinced that the strengthening of friendly co-operation between the P.R.C. and the Republic of Guinea conforms to the fundamental interests of the two peoples of the two countries, conduces to strengthening the friendship and solidarity between the peoples of China and Guinea as well as among Asian and African peoples, and in the interest of world peace,

Have decided for this purpose to conclude the present Treaty.

Article I

The Contracting Parties will maintain and develop peaceful and friendly relations between the P.R.C. and the Republic of Guinea.

Article II

The Contracting Parties decide to take the Five Principles of mutual respect for sovereignty and territorial integrity, mutual non-aggression, non-interference in each other's internal affairs, equality and mutual benefit and peaceful co-existence as the principles guiding the relations between the two countries. The Contracting Parties will settle all disputes between them by means of peaceful negotiation.

Article III

The Contracting Parties agree to develop the economic and cultural relations between the two countries in the spirit of equality, mutual benefit and friendly co-operation.

Article IV

The present Treaty is subject to ratification and the instruments of ratification shall be exchanged in Conakry as soon as possible.

The present Treaty will come into force immediately on the exchange of the instruments of ratification and will remain in force for a period of ten years.

Unless either of the Contracting Parties gives to the other notice in writing to terminate it one year before the expiration of this period, it will remain in force indefinitely, subject to the right of either Party to terminate it by giving to the other notice in writing of its intention to do so one year in advance.

Done in duplicate in Peking on the thirteenth day of September, nineteen sixty, in the Chinese and French languages, both texts being equally authentic.

(Signed)
Chou En-lai
Plenipotentiary of the People's
Republic of China

(Signed)
Sekou Touré
Plentipotentiary of the Republic of Guinea

Source: *Peking Review* No. 37, 14 Sept. 1960.

Agreement Between the Government of the People's Republic of China and the Government of the Republic of Guinea on Economic and Technical Co-operation

The Government of the People's Republic of China and the Government of the Republic of Guinea, for the purpose of promoting the friendly relations and of developing the economic and technical co-operation between the two countries, and in accordance with the Treaty of Friendship Between the P.R.C. and the Republic of Guinea, have concluded the present Agreement, the articles of which are as follows:

Article I

With a view to helping the Government of the Republic of Guinea to develop its economy, the Government of the P.R.C. is willing to grant the Government of the Republic of Guinea within the period from September 13, 1960 to June 30, 1963, a non-interest bearing loan without any conditions or privileges attached. The amount of the loan is 100,000,000 (One Hundred Million) Rubles.

This loan shall be utilised in instalments during the period of validity of the present Agreement by the Government of the Republic of Guinea in accordance with the items of economic construction to be agreed upon by both sides. The above loan shall be repaid within a period of ten years from 1970 to 1979 by the Government of the Republic of Guinea in instalments either with export goods of Guinea or with currency of a third country agreed by China. The repayment of the loan shall be completed in ten years with one-tenth of the above loan each year.

Article II

According to the capability of the P.R.C. and the requirement of the Republic of Guinea, the Government of the P.R.C. will supply the Government of the Republic of Guinea techniques and materials within the amount of the above loan and within the following scope:
1. The supply of technical assistance by dispatching of experts, technicians and skilled workers;
2. The supply of complete set equipment, machinery and materials, techniques and other goods;
3. Assistance in the training of technicians and skilled workers of the Republic of Guinea.

Article III

The travelling expenses, going and coming, of the Chinese experts, technicians and skilled workers to be dispatched in accordance with items 1 and 3 of Article II of this Agreement to the Republic of Guinea and their salaries during the period of working in the Republic of Guinea shall be borne by the Government of the P.R.C. The living expenses of the Chinese experts, technicians and skilled workers during the period of working in the Republic of Guinea shall be paid out of the loan, and their standard of living shall not exceed that of personnel of the same rank in the Republic of Guinea. The living expenses of the trainees to be sent to China by the Government of the Republic of Guinea to learn techniques shall be paid from the amount of the loan.

Article IV

For the entries of drawing the loan and its repayment, the People's Bank of China and the Bank of the Republic of Guinea shall discuss and make separately the technical agreement.

Article V

In accordance with item 2 of Article II, the Governments of both countries shall appoint their representatives to discuss and fix the specific items of economic construction and technique to be supplied by the Government of the P.R.C. to the Government of the Republic of Guinea and the methods of their implementation and to sign thereafter protocols.

Article VI

The executing organizations for this Agreement shall be the Ministry of Foreign Trade of the P.R.C. on the side of the P.R.C. and the Ministry of Planning of the Republic of Guinea on the side of the Republic of Guinea.

Article VII

This Agreement shall come into force on the day of its signing and remain in force for a period of twenty years.

Done in duplicate in Peking on the thirteenth day of September, 1960, in the Chinese and French languages, the text of both languages being equally authentic.

(Signed)
Yeh Chi-chuang
Plenipotentiary of the Government
of the People's Republic of China

(Signed)
Keita N'Famara
Plenipotentiary of the Government
of the Republic of Guinea

Source: Peking Review No. 37, 14 Sept. 1960.

Treaty of Friendship Between China and Ghana

The Chairman of the People's Republic of China and the President of the Republic of Ghana

Desiring to consolidate and further develop the profound friendship between the People's Republic of China and the Republic of Ghana, and

Being convinced that the strengthening of friendly co-operation between the People's Republic of China and the Republic of Ghana fully conforms to the fundamental interests of the peoples of the two countries, conduces to the enhancement of the friendship and solidarity between the peoples of the two countries as well as among Asian and African peoples, and is in the interest of world peace,

Have decided for this purpose to conclude the present Treaty.

Article I

The Contracting Parties will maintain and develop the relations of peace and friendship between the People's Republic of China and the Republic of Ghana.

Article II

The Contracting Parties decide to take the five principles of mutual respect for sovereignty and territorial integrity, mutual non-aggression, non-interference in each other's internal affairs, equality and mutual benefit, and peaceful co-existence and the Ten Principles laid down at the Asian-African Conference held in Bandung in 1955 as the principles guiding the relations between the two countries.

The Contracting Parties will settle all disputes between them by means of peaceful negotiation.

Article III

The Contracting Parties agree to develop the economic and cultural relations between the two countries in the spirit of equality, mutual benefit and friendly co-operation.

Article IV

The present Treaty is subject to ratification, and the instruments of ratification shall be exchanged in Accra as soon as possible.

The present Treaty shall come into force immediately on the exchange of the instruments of ratification and shall remain in force for a period of ten years.

Unless either of the Contracting Parties gives to the other notice in writing to terminate the present Treaty one year before the expiration of this period, the present Treaty shall remain in force indefinitely, subject to the right of either Party to terminate it ten years after it comes into force by giving to the other notice in writing of its intention to do so one year in advance.

Done in duplicate in Peking on the eighteenth day of August, nineteen sixty-one, in the Chinese and English languages, both texts being equally authentic.

(Signed)
Chou En-lai
Plenipotentiary of the People's
Republic of China

(Signed)
Kwame Nkrumah
Plenipotentiary of the
Republic of Ghana

Source: Peking Review No. 34, 25 Aug. 1961.

Sino-Congolese (B) Friendship Treaty

The Chairman of the People's Republic of China and the President of the Republic of the Congo (Brazzaville)

Desiring to maintain and further develop the profound friendship between the People's Republic of China and the Republic of the Congo (Brazzaville), and

Being convinced that the strengthening of friendly co-operation between the People's Republic of China and the Republic of the Congo (Brazzaville) conforms to the fundamental interests of the peoples of the two countries, helps promote the friendship and solidarity of the peoples of Asia and Africa and conduces to world peace,

Have decided for this purpose to conclude the present Treaty in accordance with the Five Principles of Peaceful Co-existence.

Article I
The Contracting Parties shall maintain and develop the peaceful and friendly relations between the People's Republic of China and the Republic of the Congo (Brazzaville).

Article II
The Contracting Parties undertake to respect each other's sovereignty, independence and territorial integrity.

Article III
The Contracting Parties undertake to settle through peaceful consultation any issue that may arise between them.

Article IV
The Contracting Parties agree to develop economic and cultural relations between the two countries in accordance with the principles of equality, mutual benefit and non-interference in each other's internal affairs.

Article V
The present Treaty is subject to ratification, and the instruments of ratification shall be exchanged in Brazzaville as soon as possible.

The present Treaty shall come into force on the date of exchange of the instruments of ratification and shall remain in force for a period of ten years. Unless either of the Contracting Parties gives to the other notice in writing to terminate the present Treaty one year before the expiration of this period, the present Treaty shall be automatically prolonged for another period of ten years, and shall thereafter be renewable accordingly.

Done in duplicate in Peking on October 2nd, 1962, in the Chinese and French languages, both texts being equally authentic.

(Signed)	(Signed)
Liu Shao-chi	Alphonse Massamba-Debat
Plentipotentiary of the People's	Plenipotentiary of the
Republic of China	Republic of the Congo
	(Brazzaville)

Source: *Peking Review* No. 3, 15 Jan. 1965.

Sino-Tanzanian Treaty of Friendship

The Chairman of the People's Republic of China and the President of the United Republic of Tanzania,

Desiring to consolidate and further develop the profound friendship between the People's Republic of China and the United Republic of Tanzania, and

Being convinced that the strengthening of friendly co-operation between the People's Republic of China and the United Republic of Tanzania conforms to the fundamental interests of the peoples of the two countries, helps promote the solidarity between them as well as among Asian and African peoples and the

common struggle against imperialism, and conduces to peace in Asia, Africa and the world,
Have decided for this purpose to conclude the present Treaty, the articles of which are as follows:

Article I
The Contracting Parties will maintain and develop the relations of peace and friendship between the People's Republic of China and the United Republic of Tanzania.

Article II
The Contracting Parties pledge to take the Five Principles of mutual respect for sovereignty and territorial integrity, mutual non-aggression, non-interference in each other's internal affairs, equality and mutual benefit, and peaceful co-existence as the principles guiding the relations between the two countries.

Article III
The Contracting Parties agree to develop economic and cultural relations between the two countries in the spirit of equality, mutual benefit and friendly co-operation.

Article IV
The Contracting Parties undertake to settle through peaceful consultation any issue that may arise between them.

Article V
The present Treaty is subject to ratification, and the instruments of ratification shall be exchanged in Dar es Salaam as soon as possible.
The present Treaty shall come into force on the date of exchange of the instruments of ratification and shall remain in force for a period of ten years. Unless either of the Contracting Parties gives to the other notice in writing to terminate the present Treaty one year before the expiration of this period, the present Treaty shall be automatically prolonged for another period of ten years, and shall thereafter be renewable accordingly.
Done in duplicate in Peking on February 20, 1965, in the Chinese, Swahili and English languages, all three texts being equally authentic.

(Signed)
Liu Shao-chi
Chairman of the People's
Republic of China

(Signed)
Julius K. Nyerere
President of the United
Republic of Tanzania

Source: *Peking Review* No. 9, 26 Feb. 1965.

China–Ghana Relations
Protocol on Dispatching Military Experts by the Government of The People's Republic of China to the Republic of Ghana
The Government of the P.R.C. and the Government of the Republic of

Ghana, for the purpose of strengthening the relations of friendship and co-operation between the two countries have, through friendly consultations, agreed as follows:

Article I

At the invitation of the Government of the Republic of Ghana, the Government of the P.R.C. dispatched, on September 30 and December 30, 1964, a military expert team to Ghana to help the Ghana Government train military personnel and teach them the use of weapons and equipment given by the Chinese Government to the Ghana Government.

Article II

It is agreed that the working period of the Chinese military experts in Ghana is two years. This period can be extended or shortened through consultations between the two sides if necessary.

Article III

The Chinese experts' passages to Ghana, their basic wages in Ghana and living allowances needed in Ghana shall be borne by the Chinese Government; while their return passage, the expenses of boarding, accommodation, transport and medical treatment during their work in Ghana shall be borne by the Ghana Government.

Article IV

The working and training plans shall be worked out by the Chinese military experts and the authorities concerned of the Ghana Government through consultations. The two sides should carry out the work in observance of the principles of mutual respect, co-operation and consultations. Should any personnel of either side act against the above principles, the two sides should solve the problem through consultations.

Article V

During their working period in Ghana, the Chinese experts should observe Ghana's laws and regulations, habits and customs; and shall not interfere in Ghana's internal affairs, nor ask for any privileges or special treatment. The Ghana Government shall render proper protection and assistance to the Chinese experts.

Article VI

The present Protocol shall be deemed to have come into force on September 30, 1964.

The Protocol is concluded in Accra on 5th August Nineteen Sixty Five.

Done in duplicate in the Chinese and English languages, both texts being equally authentic.

(Signed)
Huang Hua
Representative for the Government
of the P.R.C.

(Signed)
E.O. Baah
Representative for the
Government of the Republic
of Ghana

Source: Ghana Ministry of Information, *Nkrumah's Subversion in Africa*, Appendix B, p. 56, Accra, 1966.

Chinese Entry into the United Nations

1st Vote on the American Procedural Motion Results – 59 to 55 with 15 Abstentions

Against – 59
Afganistan, Alberia, Algeria*, Byelorussia, Bhutan, Burma, Burundi*, Bulgaria, Cameroun*, Canada, Ceylon, Chile, Congo(B)*, Cuba, Denmark, Egypt*, Ecuador, Ethiopia*, Finland, France, Guinea*, Equatorial Guinea*, Guyana, Hungary, India, Iraq, Iceland, Ireland, Kenya*, Kuwait, Libya*, Malaysia, Mali*, Mauritania*, Mongolia, Nepal, Nigeria*, Pakistan, Peru, Poland, Rumania, Sierra Leone*, Singapore, Somalia*, Sudan*, Sweden, Syria, Czechoslovakia, Trinidad and Tobago, Tanzania*, Ukraine, United Kingdom, Norway, Uganda*, U.S.S.R., Yemen, South Yemen, Yugoslavia, Zambia*.
* 19 African states

In favour – 55
Argentina, Australia, South Africa*, Bahrein, Saudi Arabia, Barbados, Brazil, Cambodia, Congo(K)*, Colombia, Central African Republic*, Costa Rica, Ivory Coast*, Dahomey*, Dominican Republic, United States, Spain, Fiji, Gabon*, Gambia*, Ghana*, Greece, Haiti, Guatemala, Honduras, Upper Volta*, Indonesia, Israel, Japan, Jamaica, Jordan, Lebanon, Lesotho*, Liberia*, Malawi*, Mexico, Luxemburg, Mauritius*, Nicaragua, Niger*, New Zealand, Panama, Paraguay, Philippines, Portugal, Rwanda*, Salvador, Swaziland*, Taiwan, Tchad*, Thailand, Uruguay, Venezuela, Malagasy, Bolivia.
* 17 African states

Abstentions – 15
Austria, Belgium, Botswana*, Cyprus, Iran, Italy, Laos, Malta, Morocco*, Netherlands, Qatar, Senegal*, Togo*, Tunisia*, Turkey.
* 5 African states.

2nd Vote – Albania Resolution Results – 76 to 35 with 17 Abstentions

In favour – 76
Afganistan, Albania, Algeria*, Austria, Belgium, Bhutan, Byelorussia, Burma, Botswana*, Bulgaria, Burundi*, Cameroun*, Canada, Ceylon, Chile, Cuba, Congo(B)*, Denmark, Ecuador, Egypt*, Ethiopia*, Finland, France, Ghana*, Britain, Guinea*, Equatorial Guinea*, Guyana, Hungary, India, Iceland, Ireland, Israel, Italy, Kenya*, Kuwait, Laos, Libya*, Malaysia, Mali*, Morocco*, Mauritania*, Mexico, Mongolia, Nepal, Nigeria*, Norway, Uganda*, Pakistan, Low Countries, Peru, Poland, Portugal, Rumania, Rwanda*, Senegal*, Sierra Leone*, Singapore, Somalia*, Sudan*, Syria, Sweden, Togo*, Czechoslovakia, Tunisia*, Trinidad and Tobago, Turkey, Ukraine, U.S.S.R., Tanzania*, Yemen, South Yemen, Yugoslavia, Zambia*, Iran, Iraq.
* 26 African states

Against – 35
South Africa*, Saudi Arabia, Australia, Bolivia, Brazil, Cambodia, Central

African Republic*, Chad*, Congo(K)*, Ivory Coast*, Costa Rica, Dahomey*, Dominican Republic, United States, Gabon*, Gambia*, Guatemala, Haiti, Honduras, Upper Volta*, Japan, Lesotho*, Liberia*, Malagasy*, Malawi*, Malta, Nicaragua, Niger*, New Zealand, Paraguay, Philippines, Salvador, Swaziland*, Uruguay, Venezuela.
* 15 African states.

Abstentions – 17
Argentina, Bahrein, Barbados, Cyprus, Colombia, Spain, Fiji, Greece, Indonesia, Jamaica, Jordan, Lebanon, Luxemburg, Mauritius*, Panama, Qatar, Thailand.
* 1 African state.

SELECT BIBLIOGRAPHY

Notes on sources
Much of the material utilised in this book can be found in publications accessible to research students. I have made extensive use of the facilities of the Press Library of the Royal Institute of International Affairs in London, and valuable press cuttings on economic, political, military and cultural events on China and African countries and regions are available.

I have also extensively made use of the B.B.C. Summary of World Broadcasts, Parts III and IV.

Also very useful were the regular publications of the U.S. Consulate General in Hong Kong – Surveys of China Mainland Press and Magazines; *Current Background* and *Current Scene*.

I also made use of the New China News Agency (Hsinhua) reports available in the School of Oriental and African Studies Library in London.

I had interviews and discussions with government and quasi-governmental officials in East Africa and London. The identities of some of them have already been disclosed. However, because of the nature of the information, I cannot disclose the identities of others.

Important periodicals
Peking Review, March 1958–December 1968. (Weekly)

Far Eastern Economic Review, Hong Kong, 1958–68. (Weekly)

The China Quarterly, March 1960–December 1968.
    Published by Congress for Cultural Freedom and later by the Contemporary China Institute of the School of Oriental and African Studies, London University.

Asian Survey, March 1961–December 1968.
    Institute of International Studies, University of California.

Books and articles
Attwood W.: *The Reds and the Blacks: A Personal Adventure*, Hutchinson, London, 1967.

Bass R. H.: 'Communist Fronts: Their History and Function' in *Problems of Communism*, May 1960.

Black C. E. and Thornton T. P.: *Communism and Revolution*, Princeton, New Jersey, 1964.

288 Select Bibliography

Black J. and Thompson K.: *Foreign Policies in a Changing World*, New York, 1963.
Brandt C. et al: *A Documentary History of Chinese Communism*, Allen and Unwin, London, 1952.
Brecher J.: *The New States of Asia*, Oxford University Press, London, 1963.
Brzezinski Z.: *The Soviet Bloc: Unity and Conflict*, Praeger, New York, 1960.
  ed.: *Africa and the Communist World*, Stanford University Press, Stanford, 1964.
Buchan A.: *War in Modern Society*, C. A. Watts & Co. Ltd, London, 1966.
Chen J.: *Mao and the Chinese Revolution*, Oxford University Press, London, 1967.
Cheng C. ed.: *Bulletin of Activities – The Politics of the Chinese Red Army*, Hoover Institution Publication, Stanford University Press.
Chester Chen J. ed.: *Mao*, Prentice Hall, New Jersey, 1969.
Clark G.: *In Fear of China*, Lansdowne Press, Melbourne, 1968.
Clos M.: In *Africa Report*, January *1965*.
Cottam R. W.: *Competitive Interference and 20th Century Diplomacy*, University of Pittsburgh Press, Pittsburgh, 1967.
Crabb C. Jr.: *The Elephants and the Grass*, Praeger, New York, 1965.
Cross J. E.: *The Nature and Politics of Guerilla War*, Doubleday, New York, 1963.
Crozier B.: *The Struggle for the Third World*, Bodley Head, London 1966.
Dalvi J. P.: *Himalayan Blunder: The Curtain Raiser to the Sino-Indian War of 1962*, Thacker and Co., Bombay, 1969.
Davidson B.: *The Liberation of Guiné*, Penguin, Harmondsworth, 1969.
Davies D.: 'China Earns from Hongkong' in *Far Eastern Economic Review* Vol. 40, No. 12, 20 June 1963.
Davies I.: *African Trade Unions*, Penguin, Harmondsworth, 1966.
Djilas M.: *Conversations with Stalin*, Harcourt Brace and World Inc., 1962.
Duffy J.: *Portugal in Africa*, Penguin, Baltimore, Maryland, 1963.
Eckstein A.: *Communist China's Economic Growth and Foreign Trade*, McGraw Hill, New York, 1966.
Fanon F.: *A Dying Colonialism*, Grove Press, New York, 1965.
Feis H.: *The China Tangle*, Princeton University Press, 1953.
Foreign Languages Press, Peking (F.L.P.P.): *Afro-Asian Solidarity Against Imperialism*, 1964.
  China and the Asian-African Conference, 1955.
  China Handbook, April 1957.
  'Long Live the Victory of People's War', article by Lin Piao, September, 1965.
  The Polemics On the General Line of the International Communist Movement, 1965.
  Selected Military Writings of Mao Tse-Tung, Second Edition, 1966.
  Selected Works of Mao Tse-Tung, Vols. I, II, III & IV, 1966.
  'Strategy: One Against Ten, Tactics: Ten Against One', article by Li Tse-Peng, 1966.
  Ten Glorious Years, 1959.
Fox R. C. et al: 'The Second Independence: A Case Study of the Kwilu Rebellion' in *Comparative Study in History and Society* Vol. VIII, 1965–6.

Select Bibliography 289

Garratee C.: in *Far Eastern Economic Review*, 25 August, 1960.
Ghana Ministry of Information: *Nkrumah's Subversion of Africa*, Accra, 1966.
Ghana Today, 7 November, 1962. Accra Publication.
Ghana Treaty Series Vol. II, 1961 and 1962.
Giap Vo Nguyen: *People's War, People's Army*, Praeger, New York, 1962.
Gittings J.: *The Sino-Soviet Conflict 1963–1967*, Oxford University Press, London, 1968.
Goldman M.: *Soviet Foreign Aid*, Praeger, London, 1967.
Goodrich L.: *Korea*, Council on Foreign Relations, New York, 1956.
Griffith W. E.: 'Africa in International Communism: The End of an Epoch' in *Survey* No. 54, January 1965.
The Sino-Soviet Rift, Allen and Unwin, London, 1964.
Guevara Che: *Guerrilla Warfare*, translated by I. F. Stone, Random House, New York, 1968.
Reminiscences of the Cuban Revolutionary War, Monthly Review Press, New York, 1968.
Che Guevara Speaks: Selected speeches and Writings, Grove Press, New York, 1967.
Halpern, A. M., ed.: *Policies Toward China*, McGraw Hill, New York, 1965. (Chapter by C. Legum.)
Hamrell S. and Witstrand C. eds.: *The Soviet Bloc, China and Africa*. (Articles by W.A.C. Adie and R. Lowenthal.), The Scandinavian Institute of African Studies, Uppsala, 1964.
Hinton H. C.: *Communist China in World Politics*, Houghton Mifflin, Boston, 1966.
Hoover Institution Publication: *Yearbook of International Communist Affairs*, Stanford, California, 1966 and 1968.
Horsley M.: *China's Way to Communism*, Allen and Unwin, London, 1968.
Huck A.: *The Security of China*, Chatto and Windus, London, 1970.
Hudson G.F.: 'Balance Sheet on Bandung', in *Commentary*, June 1955, p. 565.
Hudson G. F. et al: *The Sino-Soviet Dispute*, Praeger, New York, 1961.
Hsieh A. L.: 'The Sino-Soviet Dialogue' in *The Journal of Conflict Resolution*, June 1964.
Hsieh A. L.: *Communist China's Strategy in the Nuclear Era*.
Hsu Kai-yu: *Chou En-lai*, Doubleday, New York, 1968.
Lessing P.: *Africa's Red Harvest*, Michael Joseph, London, 1962.
Lewin P.: *Foreign Trade of Communist China*, Praeger, New York, 1964.
Lichtblau G. E.: *The Politics of African Trade Unionism*, Praeger, New York, 1967.
Lofchie M.: *Zanzibar: Background to Revolution*, Princeton University Press, New Jersey, 1965.
London K.: *Unity and Contradiction: The Communist Powers and Afro-Asian Nationalism*, Praeger, New York, 1962.
ed.: *New Nations in a Divided World*, New York, 1963.
Lowenthal R.: *World Communism: The Disintegration of a Secular Faith*, Oxford University Press, 1964.
Lyon P.: *Neutralism*, London University Press, London, 1963.
Mankekar D. R.: *The Guilty Men of 1962*, The Tulsi Shah Enterprises, Bombay, 1968.

290 Select Bibliography

Marshall S. L. A.: *The River and the Gauntlet*, William Morrow & Co., New York, 1953.
Martin L. W.: *Neutralism and Non-Alignment*, Praeger, New York, 1963.
Maxwell N.: *India's China War*, Jonathan Cape, London, 1970.
Mazingo D.: 'The Maoist Imprint on China's Foreign Policy' in *China Briefing*, University of Chicago Center for Policy Study, 1968.
Mizan Newsletter May 1964: *China, the Arab World and Africa*, Central Asian Research Center.
Mondlane E.: *The Struggle for Mozambique*, Penguin, London, 1969.
Morison D.: In *Problems of Communism*, July 1961.
Neilsen W. A.: *The Great Powers and Africa*, Pall Mall Press, London, 1969.
Neuhauser C.: *Third World Politics: China and the A.A.P.S.O. 1957–1967*, Harvard University Press, 1968.
Nkrumah K.: *Africa Must Unite*, Heinemann, London, 1963.
  Challenge of the Congo, Nelson, London, 1967.
  Dark Days in Ghana, PANAF Publications Ltd, Harmondsworth, 1968.
  I Speak of Freedom, Heinemann, London, 1961.
  Neo-Colonialism; The Last Stage of Imperialism, Nelson, London, 1965.
North R. C.: *Chinese Communism*, World University Library, London, 1966.
Nyerere J.: *Ujamaa: The Basis of African Socialism*, Oxford University Press, London, 1968.
Okello J.: *Revolution in Zanzibar*, East African Publishing House, Nairobi, 1967.
Ottaway D. & M.: *Algeria: the Politics of a Socialist Revolution*, University of California Press, 1970.
Pacific Affairs, Vol. 34, No. 3, 1961. Article by H. L. Boorman.
Paloncy E.: 'Build-Up of the Anti-Imperialist Front' in *Rude Pravo*, 21 March 1962.
Pellisier R.: *The Awakening of China 1793–1949*, Secker, London, 1967.
Pickles D.: *Algeria and France: From Colonialism to Co-operation*, Methuen, London, 1963.
Political Science Quarterly LXX, June 1965: 'Democracy and the Party System'.
Pomeroy W. J.: *Guerrilla and Counter Guerrilla Warfare*, International Publishers, New York, 1964.
Quandt W. B.: *Revolution and Political Leadership: Algeria 1954–1968*, The M.I.T. Press, Cambridge, Mass., 1969.
Ra'anan U.: *The U.S.S.R. Arms the Third World*, The M.I.T. Press, Cambridge, Mass., 1969.
Rees D.: *Korea: The Limited War*, Macmillan & Co. Ltd., London, 1964.
Reporter, 19 May 1955. Article by James Cameron.
Robinson J.: *The Cultural Revolution in China*, Pelican, Harmondsworth, 1969.
Rue J. E.: *Mao Tse-tung in Opposition*, Stanford University Press, 1966.
Scalapino R.: In *Foreign Affairs* Vol. 42, No. 4, July 1964.
Schatten F.: *Communism in Africa*, Allen and Unwin, London, 1966.
Schram S.: *Mao Tse-tung*, Pelican, Harmondsworth, 1967.
  The Political Thought of Mao Tse-tung, Pelican, Harmondsworth, 1969.
Tang Tsou: *American Failure in China*, University of Chicago Press, 1963.
  'Mao Tse-tung and Peaceful Co-existence' in *Orbis*, Spring 1964.
Tang Tsou and Halperin M.: 'Mao Tse-tung's Revolutionary Strategy and Peking's International Behaviour' in *American Political Science Review*, Vol. 59, No. 1, March 1965.

Thiam D.: *The Foreign Policy of African States*, Phoenix House, London, 1965.
The Times Survey Team: *The Black Man in Search of Power*, Thomas Nelson, London, 1968.
Townsend J. R.: In *Asian Survey* Vol. v, No. 1, January 1965.
Ulam A. B.: *Expansion and Co-existence: The History of Soviet Foreign Policy 1917–1967*, Secker & Warburg, London, 1968.
U.S. Department of State: *The China White Paper*, 1949, reissued by Stanford University Press, 1967.
Wesson R. C.: *Soviet Foreign Policy in Perspective*, Dorsey Press, Homewood, Ill., 1969.
Whiting A. S.: *China Crosses the Yalu*, Macmillan Co., New York, 1960.
Wint G.: *Communist China's Crusade*, Praeger, New York, 1965.
Wolfers A.: *Discord and Collaboration*, The Johns Hopkins Press, Maryland, 1962.
Zagoria D.: *The Sino-Soviet Conflict 1956–1961*, Princeton University Press, 1962.
'Sino-Soviet Friction in Underdeveloped Areas' in *Problems of Communism*, February 1961.
Zelman W. A.: *Chinese Intervention in the Korean War: A Bilateral Failure of Deterrence*, University of California Press, Los Angeles, 1967.

Yearbooks etc.

Africa Research Bulletin, Africa Research Bureau, London.
East Africa and Revenue Report, Common Services Organisation, Mombassa, Kenya, 1958–68.
External Trade of Nigeria, Federal Dept. of Statistics, Lagos, 1958–68.
External Trade Statistics of Ghana, Accra publication, 1958–67.
The Statesman's Yearbook, 1958–69, Macmillan & Co. Ltd, London.
Sudan Annual Foreign Trade Statistics, Dept. of Statistics, Khartoum, 1959–68.
U.A.R. Annual Statement of Foreign Trade, Dept. of Statistics and Census, 1959–67.
U.N. Economic Commission for Africa, Foreign Trade Statistics of Africa Series A, 1960–7.
Yearbook of the United Nations, 1950–64, New York.

INDEX

Abdar-Rahman Muhammad, 96
Abbas, Ferhat, 50, 51-2, 81, 100-1
Abboud, President, 29, 109, 125
Abdulahi Said, 154
Accra, inauguration of A.A.T.U.F. at, 46
Afghanistan, policy on admission of China to U.N., 285
Africa, concept of, as battleground for warring ideologies, 81-3
Africa, southern
  training of freedom fighters for, 232 n. 2
  wars of liberation in, 118, 250
  see also South Africa, Union of
African Heads of State conference, 115
African nationalism
  Chinese policy on, 56
  implications of Tan-Zam railway for confrontation in southern Africa, 250
African states
  attitude to Sino-Indian conflict, 107-11
  Chinese economic aid as instrument of foreign policy, 39-40
  Chinese reaction to series of coups d'état in, 183-4
  conference of Independent, 28
  emergence, strength of communist parties in, 96-8
  formulation of Chinese tactics and strategy in, 17-20
  implications of Sino-U.S. rapprochement for, 256-7
  independence achieved by, 21, 61-2
  policies of neutralism, 76
  policies on admission of China to U.N., 71-6, 285-6
  trade unionism in, 44-7
  see also Revolutionary movements *and under individual states*

Afro-Asian Economic Conference, 88
Afro-Asian Journalists' Conference, 167
Afro-Asian People's Solidarity Organisation
  changes in structure, administration, 95-6
  conferences, 14, 40, 41-3, 94-6, 121, 142-3 and n. 1, 165-7, 168-9 and nn. 1, 6
  constitution, objectives, 95-6
  establishment and membership of Secretariat, 43, 271
  establishment of Fund, 95-6
  financial support from China, 43-4
  inauguration, 59
  Sino-Soviet rivalry in, 94-8, 179
  split into Chinese, Soviet factions, 230-1, 266
  under Soviet domination, 239
Afro-Asian solidarity, Chinese concept of, 8
Afro-Asian Youth Conference, 44
Afro-Asian Writers' Organisation, 96, 230
Ahidjo, Ahmadou, 93-4, 173
Albania
  Chinese economic aid for, 40 n. 1
  communist ideology in, 182
  policy in Nigerian Civil War, 236
  policy on admission of China to U.N., 254, 285-6
Alexander, General, 80
Algeria
  Achievement of independence, 21, 75
  Chinese policy during internal conflicts, 6, 28-30, 47-8, 50-3, 58, 59-60, 129 and n. 2, 130, 148, 156, 219, 237, 259, 263, 264
  Communist Party in, 96-7
  death toll in war of liberation, 100-1 n. 6

Algeria (cont.)
diplomatic relations with China, 75, 192 n. 3, 274
economic, technical aid from China, 40 n. 2, 92, 154–6, 223–4, 239, 247, 262, 276; from France, 155; from Soviet Union, 155
exchange of delegations with China, 34, 35, 128, 269, 270
F.L.N. delegation at conference of Independent African States, 28
participation in A.A.P.S.O., 41–3, 271; in A.A.W.O., 230 n. 3
policy at second Non-Aligned Conference, 127
policy on admission of China to U.N., 285; on Second Bandung, 123, 133, 271
Sino-Soviet differences on support for war of liberation, 98–101
Soviet Union's policy towards, 51
support for Lumumbists in Congo, 177
trade unions in, 45–7
training of freedom fighters in, 130 n. 1, 170–1
Ali Sabri, 110
Ali Yata, 29
All-African People's Organisation, 46, 54, 64
All-African Trade Union Federation, 45, 46–7, 135
All-Black African Federation of Trade Unions, 46, 270
All China Athletic Federation, 97
All China Federation of Trade Unions, 36, 43, 45–7, 97
All China Journalists' Association, 36, 97
All China Students' Federation, 36, 97
All China Youth Federation, 36, 97
Angola
exchange of delegations with China, 34, 35, 232, 269, 270
liberation movement, 115, 170, 179, 232–3 and n. 2, 237, 239, 264
participation in A.A.W.O., 230 n. 3
representation on Secretariat of A.A.P.S.O., 271
Sino-Soviet differences on aid for liberation movement, 106–7
Arab-Israeli War, 1967, effects of
on Chinese influence in Middle East, 190–1

on Chinese relations with Tunisia, 238
on Chinese trade with Africa, 220–1
on Soviet prestige, 228–9
Arab nationalism
conflict with international communism, 22–6, 29–30
effects on Chinese foreign policy, 21–2
Arabic, Chinese broadcasts in, 9
Arang, Michael Dei, 144 n. 1, 145 n. 4
Argentina, policy on admission of China to U.N., 285–6
Asia–Africa Society, 97
Asian Solidarity Committee of China, 43
Aswan High Dam, 23, 123, 161
Atomic weapons see Nuclear weapons
Attwood, W., 163 n. 4
Australia, policy on admission of China to U.N., 285
Austria, policy on admission of China to U.N., 285
Aziz Sidqi, 161

Babu (Abdul Rahman Mohammad Babu), 136
Baghdad Pact, 48
Bahrein, policy on admission of China to U.N., 285–6
Bandung Conference 1955, 7–9, 21, 41, 43, 120, see also Second Bandung
Barbados, policy on admission of China to U.N., 285–6
Basutoland see Lesotho
Belgium, policy on admission of China to U.N., 285
Belgrade see Non-Aligned States, Conferences
Ben Bella, 128, 129, 130, 132, 155, 156
Ben Yussef Ben Khedda, 51
Bhutan, policy on admission of China to U.N., 285
Biafra see Nigeria
Bizerta, military base at, 170
Black Africa Youth, Trade Delegations to China, 34, 270
Bokasa, Colonel, 185
Bolivia, policy on admission of China to U.N., 285
Botswana
delegations to China, 270
policy on admission of China to U.N., 285
Boumediènne, Houave, 129, 133, 156 n. 1

294 Index

Bourguiba, Habib, President of Algeria, 81, 117, 124, 191
Bourguiba, Habib, Jnr., 190
Boutifliqa, Abdul, 129, 132, 133
Boxer Rising, 82
Brazil, policy on admission of China to U.N., 285
Budapest, Labour College at, 46
Bulgaria, policy on admission of China to U.N., 285
Burham Shahidi, 33, 48, 195
Burma
  Colombo Power, 8
  policy on admission of China to U.N., 285
Burundi
  Chinese distribution of arms to Congolese from, 177 n. 1
  diplomatic relations with China, 116-17, 119, 241, 242, 274
  exchange of delegations with China, 269, 270
  policy at second Non-Aligned conference, 127
  policy on admission of China to U.N., 285
Burundi, Queen of, 116
Byelorussia, policy on admission of China to U.N., 285

Cairo *see* Non-Aligned States, Conferences
Cambodia
  Chinese policy in, 174
  policy at second Non-Aligned conference, 127
  policy on admission of China to U.N., 285
Camerouп
  delegation to conference of Independent African States, 28
  diplomatic relations with China, 243-4, 253, 265, 274; with Taiwan, 71-2; with Soviet Union, 174
  effects of Chinese support for liberation movement, 48, 71, 170, 179
  exchange of delegations with China, 35, 269, 270
  participation in A.A.P.S.O., 41-3, 271; in A.A.W.O., 230 n. 3
  policy on admission of China to U.N., 75-6, 285; on Second Bandung, 126
  resistance to Chinese interference in, 118
  role of A.A.P.S.O. in liberation movement, 93
  Sino-Soviet differences on support for liberation movement, 53-4, 64-6
  students from, in China, 84-5
  trade with China, 150
  training of freedom fighters from, 147 n. 4, 172-3, 265
Canada
  aid for Tanganyika, 251
  policy on admission of China to U.N., 285
  training of Tanzanian pilots, 212-13 and n. 3
Casablanca Trade Fair, 1957, 9
Central African Republic
  diplomatic relations with China, 118, 162, 274
  economic, technical aid from China, 162, 276
  exchange of delegations with China, 35, 128-9, 269, 270
  policy on admission of China to U.N., 285-6
  repercussions of coup d'état in, 183, 185-6, 238, 263-4
  trade with China, 152 n. 1
Ceylon
  Colombo Power, 8
  participation in A.A.P.S.O., 271
  policy on admission of China to U.N., 285
Chad
  exchange of delegations with China, 35, 270
  participation in A.A.P.S.O., 41-3
  policy on admission of China to U.N., 285-6; on Second Bandung, 132-3
  students from, in China, 84-5
Chan Hiang-kang, 37
Chang Chuan-shih, 277
Chang Hsi-jo, 32
Chao Hsing Chih, 244
Chao Tsung-huan, 277
Chen Chia-kang, 9, 195
Chen Shu-yu, 277
Chen Yi, 50, 57, 64, 79, 97-8, 104, 116, 119, 126, 128, 129, 130, 150, 162, 171, 195, 235, 236 n. 1
Chi Wei-li, 37
Chiang Ching, 194 and n. 4
Chiang Ta, 197, 202

Index 295

Chile, policy on admission of China to U.N., 285
Chin Hui, 208
China
African students' complaints of racial discrimination in, 85 and n. 2
conflict between concepts of continuous revolution and national interest, 58–60
effect of admission to U.N. on foreign policy, 254
factors determining policy in Africa, 1–3, 13–14, 62–3
relations with Africa and other states, see under individual countries
representation at U.N. see under United Nations
representation on secretariat of A.A.P.S.O., 43, 271
role in advance of international communism, 10–13
see also Cultural Revolution, Sino-Indian Conflict, Sino-Soviet relations
China Council for the Promotion of International Trade, 36, 97
China Federation of Industry and Commerce, 97
China Federation of Literary and Art Circles, 36, 97
China Islamic Association, 9, 36, 43, 97
Chinese African People's Friendship Association, 36, 97
Chinese Committee for Afro-Asian Solidarity, 36, 97
Chinese National Women's Federation, 36, 45–6, 97, 116
Chinese Peace Committee, 36, 97
Chinese People's Association for Cultural Relations with Foreign Countries, 35, 97
Chinese People's Institute of Foreign Affairs, 35–6, 97
Chinese-Tanzania Joint Shipping Company, 198–9
Chou En-lai
at Bandung Conference, 8, 21, 43, 47
character of foreign policies, 254, 255
concept of revolution, 16, 40, 52–3, 106, 164, 169–70, 175 n. 1, 182–3, 188–9, 267
message to second A.A.P.S.O. conference, 94
philosophy of aid for developing countries, 152–3

policy in Algeria, 101 and n. 3; in Cameroun, 72; on independence of Guinea, 30–1; on Second Bandung, 131–2; on Taiwan Straits crisis, 50
pragmatism, 27
reception of delegates from A.A.W.O., 230; of Nkrumah following coup in Ghana, 186
relations with Nasser, 8
role during Cultural Revolution, 194 and n. 4
signature of economic agreement with Congo, 250
support for Ghanaian independence, 28
tour of eastern Europe, 12
visits to African countries, 117, 120, 123–6, 128–9, 135, 141, 143–4, 146, 158, 161, 162, 164, 271
Chou Poping, 208
Chou-Yang, 113–14
Chu Chang-fa, 277
Co-existence, Chinese concept of peaceful, 12, 22, 66–7, 120
Colombia, policy on admission of China to U.N., 285–6
Colonialism
Chinese fostering of revolution against, 15–17, 19–20; see also Revolutionary movements
Ghanaian concept of struggle against, 142
Commission for Social Relations with the Peoples of Africa, 36
Communism
Chinese policy of fostering, in Africa, 18
concept of Africa as battleground for conflict between Western ideology and, 15–17, 63–71
conflict with national interests, 10–13, 22–6, 29–30
control of secretariat of A.A.P.S.O., 43
defeat in Indonesia see Indonesia
reliance on people's organisations, 41
repression in Egypt see Egypt
rivalry for leadership of, in Russia, China, 10–13
strategy of uninterrupted revolution, 57–8
strength in African states, 96–8, 156 n. 4, 245–7
Communist and Workers' Parties, Moscow meeting, 1957, 14, 15

296   Index

Conakry, centre of All-Black African Federation of Trade Unions, 46
Congo (Congo-Kinshasa, Congo Leopoldville)
Algerian support for revolutionary movement, 130
Chinese policy during crises, 54–5, 71, 76–7, 102–4, 115, 117, 139 n. 1, 183
delegation to World Youth Festival, 44
diplomatic relations with China, 74, 233, 265; with Soviet Union, 233
effect of crises on Sino-Soviet relations, 63, 70–1
emergence of People's Republic, 249
exchange of delegations with China, 35, 84, 269, 270
Nkrumah's policy in, 79–80
participation in A.A.P.S.O., 271; in A.A.W.O., 230 n. 3
policy on admission of China to U.N., 75–6, 285–6
progress of revolutionary movement, 170, 174–7, 179, 233 and n. 1, 265
Sudanese support for nationalists, 174
training of freedom fighters for, 172
use of mercenary troops by Tshombe, 130 n. 4
Congo-Brazzaville
diplomatic relations with China, 117–18, 119 n. 3, 274
economic and technical aid from China, 3, 78, 156–8, 178–9, 221–3, 224, 239, 249–50, 260, 261–2, 276
exchange of delegations with China, 122, 128–9, 195–6 and n. 2, 221 n. 2, 250, 269, 270
flow of aid to freedom fighters through, 232 and n. 2, 239
internal conflicts, 222–3
involvement in Congo-Kinshasa conflicts, 176 n. 1, 177, 233 and n. 1
participation in A.A.W.O., 230 n. 3
people's militia as obstacle to army coup, 218 n. 5, 222–3
policy on admission of China to U.N., 285; on Second Bandung, 132; on second Non-Aligned conference, 127
relations with France, 225, 249
trade with China, 152 n. 1
treaty of friendship with China, 78, 122, 157, 281–2
Costa Rica, policy on admission of China to U.N., 285–6

Cuba
policy on admission of China to U.N., 285; on second Non-Aligned conference, 127
recognition of revolutionary government in Zanzibar, 136
Cuban missile crisis, effect on Sino-Soviet relations, 112, 178
Cultural missions *see* Delegations
Cultural Revolution, implications of, for Chinese foreign policy, 3, 181, 183, 189 and n. 5, 192–7, 220, 228, 231–2, 237, 238–9, 241, 267
Cyprus, policy on admission of China to U.N., 285–6
Czechoslovakia
implications of Soviet invasion, 1968, 217
policy on admission of China to U.N., 234, 285; on Nigerian Civil War, 234

Dacko, David, 162, 185
Daddah, President (of Mauritania), 247
Dahomey
diplomatic relations with China, 118, 162, 274
economic and technical aid from China, 162
exchange of delegations with China, 269, 270
policy on admission of China to U.N., 285–6
repercussions of coup in, 183, 185, 238, 263–4
Dalvi, J. P., 108 n. 2
Davies, I., 45 n. 1
Delegations, exchange of, between China and African states, 31–6, 44, 53–4, 63, 83–5, 106, 118, 121–2, 128–9, 195, 198, 204 and n. 4, 206, 214–15, 218, 221 n. 2, 224–5, 226, 232, 241, 244–5, 248, 250, 266–7, 269, 270
Denmark, policy on admission of China to U.N., 285
Diplomatic relations, Chinese cultivation of, 2, 4, 9, 18, 21, 27–9, 31, 38, 51, 59, 62, 71–6, 115–20, 124, 162, 184–92, 204, 208, 220, 224, 227, 233, 235, 238, 241–4, 253, 258–9, 259–60, 263–4, 265, 266, 274
Dien Bien Phu, implications of French defeat at, 98
Disarmament, similarity of Chinese, African opinion on, 78

Dominican Republic, policy on admission of China to U.N., 285-6
Dulles, John Foster, 7
Dunn, John, 6 n. 3
Dynamic Party of Eastern Nigeria, 234

East Africa
  growing importance in Chinese policy, 221
  mutinies of 1964, 125, 135, 138, 162-3, 175 n. 1, 179
East European states, aid for Guinea from, 40
Eckstein, A., 36-7 n. 4
Economic and technical aid for African States, Chinese policy on, 18, 39-40, 59, 63, 87-93, 118-19, 136, 137-41, 143-9, 152-65, 178-9, 197-213, 213-19, 219-20, 221-9, 241-2, 242-3, 244-57, 260-2, 276
Ecuador, policy on admission of China to U.N., 285
Egypt
  At Bandung Conference, 8, 21
  Chinese cultural mission, 1956, 9
  conflict between nationalists and communism, 39
  deterioration of relations with China, 22-7, 59, 96, 247
  diplomatic relations with China, 9, 21, 59, 192 n. 3, 227, 259, 274
  economic and technical aid from China, 21-2, 40, 224, 276
  military delegation to China, 34
  participation in A.A.P.S.O., 41-3, 271
  policy on admission of China to U.N., 285
  position of communist party in, 39, 96, 247
  Russian policy on aid for, 22, 23 n. 1
  trade with China, 9, 37, 39, 40, 86, 149, 152 and n. 2, 220, 224, 248, 259, 272-3
  United States' aid for, 212
  see also United Arab Republic
Eisenhower, Dwight D., 68, 69, 70
Equitorial Guinea see Guinea, Equitorial
Eretrean Liberation Front, 242
Ethiopia
  at Bandung Conference, 8, 21
  at conference of Independent African States, 28
  Chinese policy during dispute with Somalia, 237

diplomatic relations with China, 242-3, 274
economic and technical aid from China, 257, 262, 276
exchange of delegations with China, 9, 269, 270
foreign policies, 125 and n. 3
participation in A.A.P.S.O., 41-3
policy on admission of China to U.N., 285; on Second Bandung, 125, 126, 132, 271
reaction to U.S. intervention in Congo, 177
trade with China, 37

Feng Piao, 191-2
Fernando Po see Guinea, Equatorial
Fiji, policy on admission of China to U.N., 285-6
Finland, policy on admission of China to U.N., 285
Fitzgerald, Sir Patrick, 92
F.L.N. see Algeria
France
  attitude of communist party to Algeria, 99
  diplomatic recognition of China, 117-18, 259-60
  economic aid for Algeria, 155
  movement of colonies to independence, 30; see also individual states
  opposition to Nuclear Test Ban Treaty, 115-16
  policy on admission of China to U.N., 285
  relations with Congo-Brazzaville, 225, 249; with Khrushchev, 66, 259; with Mauritania, 225 n. 2
  see also Gaulle, Charles de
Freedom fighters, Chinese policy on training of, 130 n. 1, 146-8, 148-9, 156 n. 5, 170, 171, 172, 187, 232 and n. 3, 264-5, 277, 283-4
French Equatorial Africa, trade unions in, 45-7
Friendship Textile Mill in Tanzania, 199-202
Friendship with China societies see People's organisations

Gabon
  exchange of delegations with China, 269, 270

Index

Gabon (cont.)
 policy on Chinese admission to U.N., 74, 285–6
Gadafi, Moamer, 244
Gambia
 delegations to China, 270
 policy on admission of China to U.N., 285–6
Gaulle, Charles de
 Algerian policies, 58, 98–101
 implications of opposition to Nuclear Test Ban Treaty, 115–16
 policy on diplomatic recognition of China, 117–18, 259
 relations with Khrushchev, 66, 259
 see also France
Gbenye, Christophe, 176, 177
German Democratic Republic
 military aid for Zanzibar, 138
 recognition of revolutionary government in Zanzibar, 136, 137
Ghana
 at Bandung Conference, 8, 21
 at conference of Independent African States, 28
 Chinese support for nationalism in, 27–8
 delegation to World Youth Festival, 44
 diplomatic relations with China, 72, 73, 142–9, 241, 274
 economic and technical aid from China, 78, 80, 90–2, 93, 261, 276; from the Soviet Union, 91
 exchange of delegations with China, 32, 34, 35, 128–9, 269, 270
 objection to Chinese trade with South Africa, 150
 participation in A.A.P.S.O., 41–3, 271; in A.A.W.O., 230 n. 3
 policy on admission of China to U.N., 285; on Second Bandung, 124, 126, 271; on second Non-Aligned conference, 127; on Sino-Soviet dispute, 142–3, 147–8
 reaction to Algerian coup, 130
 repercussions of overthrow of Nkrumah, 183, 186–8 and nn. 2, 3, 220–1, 238, 264, 265
 students from, in China, 84–5
 support for Lumumbists in Congo, 177
 trade unions in, 45, 46
 trade with China, 37, 152, 220–1, 272–3
 training of freedom fighters, 106, 171, 172–3, 187, 277, 283–4
 treaties on friendship, cultural exchange with China, 78, 80, 84, 280–1
Ghana National Trading Company, 92
Gizenga, Antoine, 104, 175 n. 1
Gold Coast see Ghana
Goldman, Marshall, 23 n. 1
Gomulka, W., 12
Goodrich, L., 5 n. 2
Great Leap Forward, 39–40 and n. 1, 85, 89
Greece, policy on admission of China to U.N., 285–6
Guinea
 Chinese gift of grain to, 89–90
 Chinese policy on attainment of independence by, 30–1, 184
 cultural agreements with China, 84
 diplomatic relations with China, 31, 79, 84, 192 n. 3, 213–16, 274
 economic and technical aid from China, 3, 78, 90–1, 93, 144, 158–60, 178–9, 239, 248–9, 260, 261, 262, 276, 279–80
 exchange of delegations with China, 32, 33, 35, 44, 128–9, 214–15, 269, 270
 member of O.S.R., 215–16
 nationalisation of foreign companies in, 170
 participation in A.A.P.S.O., 271; in A.A.W.O., 230 n. 3
 people's militia as obstacle to army coup, 218 n. 5
 policy on admission of China to U.N., 285; on Second Bandung, 124, 132, 271; on second Non-Aligned conference, 127
 reaction to Algerian coup, 130
 relations with Morocco, 225; with Senegal, 216
 sources of communist aid for, 40
 support for Lumumbists in Congo, 177
 trade unions in, 45–7
 trade with China, 152 n. 1
 treaty of friendship with China, 78, 278
Guinea, Equatorial
 diplomatic relations with China, 241–2, 274
 exchange of delegations with China, 269, 270
 policy on admission of China to U.N., 285

Guinea, Portuguese (Guinea-Bissau)
  exchange of delegations with China, 232, 270
  liberation movement, 107, 115, 170, 179, 232-3, 237, 239, 264
  participation in A.A.W.O., 230 n. 3
Guinea-Mali Railway Project, 209, 215-16, 219, 245, 276
Guyana, policy on admission of China to U.N., 285

Haile Selassie, 125 and n. 3, 242; *see also* Ethiopia
Haiti, policy on admission of China to U.N., 285-6
Hanga, 136 and n. 5
Haykal, Muhammad Hasanayn, 109, 133-4
Hiang Tung-hui, 182
Ho Chi Minh, 6, 186
Ho Ching, 117
Ho Lung, 68 n. 3, 100
Ho Ying, 75, 131, 137, 138-9, 140, 197, 267
Honduras, policy on admission of China to U.N., 285-6
Hong Kong, importance in Chinese trading policies, 36-7
Hsiao Hsin-yu, 277
Hsin-hai of Revolution, 1911, 82
Hsinhua News Agency *see* New China News Agency
Hua Cheng-te, 191
Huang Chang, 52 n. 4
Huang Hua, 74-5, 118, 143, 144, 195, 254, 267
Huang Hung-sheng, 277
Hundred Flowers Campaign, 9-10, 13 and n. 2
Hungary
  Chinese economic aid for, 40 n. 1
  policy on admission of China to U.N., 285
  rising of, 1956, 12
Hy Yu-Chih, 83-4

Ibrahim Ohafa, 48
Iceland, policy on admission of China to U.N., 285
Imperialism
  Chinese assumption of leadership in struggle against, 10-13, 15-17, 113-15; *see also* Revolutionary movements
  similarity of Chinese, African opinion on, 78

Index 299

Sino-Soviet differences on policy towards conflict with, 63-71
Independent African States, Conference, 1958, 28
India
  Chinese policy towards, relations with, 4, 6, 25-6; *see also* Sino-Indian Conflict
  Colombo Power, 8
  implications of border clashes with China, 76, 81, 107-11, 263
  policy on admission of China to U.N., 285; on Korean War, 6; on Second Bandung, 126, 131, 132; on second Non-Aligned conference, 127
  relations with Tibet, 7 and n. 1; with U.A.R., 25-6
  representation on secretariat of A.A.P.S.O., 43, 271
  Russian policy on aid for, 22, 23 n. 1
  see also Indo-Pakistani War
Indo-China, Chinese policy in, 6; *see also* Vietnam, Vietnam War
Indo-Pakistani War, 1965
  Chinese policy during, 131, 180-1 and n. 1, 238
  U.N. role in, 255
Indonesia
  Colombo Power, 8
  effects of failure on communist coup, 131, 180, 238, 244
  participation in A.A.P.S.O., 43, 95-6, 271
  policy on admission of China to U.N., 285-6; on Second Bandung, 122-3, 126, 131
  Russian policy on aid for, 22, 23 n. 1
International Association of Democratic Lawyers, 230
International Conference of Free Trade Unions, 45-7
International Liaison and Organisation Departments of C.C.P., 35
International Organisation of Journalists, 44, 230
International Union of Students, 44
Iran
  participation in A.A.P.S.O., 271
  policy on admission of China to U.N., 285
Iraq
  Chinese policy on Kurdish struggle for independence, 72

Index

Iraq (*cont.*)
  conflict between communism and arab nationalism in, 24
  effects of revolution of 1958, 48-50
  participation in A.A.P.S.O., 43, 271
  policy on admission of China to U.N., 285
  relations with China, 24
Ireland, policy on admission of China to U.N., 285
Israel, policy on admission of China to U.N., 254, 285
Italy, policy on admission of China to U.N., 285
Ivory Coast
  delegation to World Youth Festival, 44
  exchange of delegations with China, 269, 270
  freedom fighters, 147 n. 4, 172, 265
  participation in A.A.W.O., 230 n. 3
  policy on admission of China to U.N., 74, 285-6

Jackson, Henry, 72
Jamaica, policy on admission of China to U.N., 285-6
Jansen, G. H., 108 n. 1
Japan
  policy on admission of China to U.N., 285-6
  representation on secretariat of A.A.P.S.O., 43, 271
Jen Min Jih Pao, 192
Jordan, policy on admission of China to U.N., 285-6
Juapong textile mill, Ghana, 145, 187, 221-2

Kali, Mr, 121
Kambona, Oscar, 32 n. 1
Kampala, Labour College in, 46
Kang Sheng, 65
Kano, Aminu, 234
Kapo, Hysni, 182
Kasavubu, 177
Kaunda, Kenneth, 206-7, 207-8
Kenya
  delegation to World Youth Festival, 44
  diplomatic relations with China, 116, 188-9, 192 n. 3, 274
  dispute with Somalia, 121-2, 154 and n. 2, 166, 237
  economic and technical aid from China, 149 n. 2, 162-5, 276

  exchange of delegations with China, 35, 269, 270
  mutiny, 125, 138, 162-3, 175 n. 1, 179
  participation in A.A.P.S.O., 41-3, 271
  policy on admission of China to U.N., 285; on Second Bandung, 132; on Sino-Indian conflict, 110
  recognition of revolutionary government in Zanzibar, 136
  relations with China, 83, 149 n. 2, 238, 264
  students from, in China, 84-5
  trade with China, 272-3
  U.S. attitude to trade unions in, 45
Kenya African National Union, 121, 164 and n. 1
Kenyatta, Jomo, 116, 163-5
Khalid Bakdash, 26-7
Khrushchev, Nikita
  anti-colonialism speech to U.N., 106
  effect of policies on Chinese activity in Africa, 258, 259
  fall, 181
  implications of foreign policies for China, 11, 12, 20, 48-50, 52, 56, 57, 62, 63-71, 112
  policy on Algeria, 52, 58 and n. 1, 99; on Taiwan Straits crisis, 50; on U.A.R., 24-5
  relations with France, 52, 66, 259
  visit to Peking, 48, 49
  see also Soviet Union, Sino-Soviet relations
Kida, H. N., 32 n. 1
Kissinger, Henry, 255
Kiwanuka, 35
Ko Hua, 89, 216
Korean War, 5-6, 181-2 and n. 1
Kuo Mo-jo, 42, 48, 195, 230
Kuomintang, U.A. support for, 4 and n. 1, 17; *see also* Taiwan
Kumasi pencil factory, 145, 187
Kurds, struggle for independence, 72
Kuwait, policy on admission of China to U.N., 285

Lai Ya-li, 216
Lansana Beavogui, 216
Laos, policy on admission of China to U.N., 285
Lebanon
  participation in A.A.P.S.O., 271

Lebanon (*cont.*)
  policy on admission of China to U.N., 285-6
Legum, Colin, 117 n. 1
Lesotho (formerly Basutoland)
  Communist Party in, 96
  delegations to China, 270
  participation in A.A.P.S.O., 271; in A.A.W.O., 230 n. 3
  policy on admission of China to U.N., 285-6
Li Fu-k'un, 277
Li Hsien-nien, 86 n. 9, 184, 195, 196 n. 1, 216
Liao Cheng-chih, 98
Liberia
  at Bandung Conference, 8, 21
  at conference of Independent African States, 28
  diplomatic relations with Taiwan, 71-2
  participation in A.A.P.S.O., 271
  policy on admission of China to U.N., 285-6; on Second Bandung, 126
Libya
  at Bandung Conference, 8, 21
  at conference of Independent African States, 28
  diplomatic relations with China, 244, 274; with Taiwan, 71
  exchange of delegations with China, 35, 269, 270
  participation in A.A.P.S.O., 41-3
  policy on admission of China to U.N., 285
  revolution, 1971, 244
  trade with China, 37 220, 273
Lin Piao, 57 n. 1, 178, 181 and n. 1
Liu Kan, 136 and n. 6
Liu Ning-yi, 167
Liu Shao-chi, 18-19, and n. 2, 56, 90, 101 n. 3, 171, 186
Lofchie, Michael, 135 n. 6
Lu Ting-yi, 99-100
Lumumba, Patrice, 54-5, 74, 79, 80, 104, 265
Lusinde, J. M., 210 n. 1
Luxemburg, policy on admission of China to U.N., 285-6

MacArthur, General Douglas, 5-6
Macmillan, Harold, 66
Madagascar *see* Malagasy
Mai Ch'ihua, 277

Malagasy
  delegation to World Youth Festival, 44
  exchange of delegations with China, 35, 270
  participation in A.A.P.S.O., 41-3; in A.A.W.O., 230 n. 3
  policy on admission of China to U.N., 285-6
  trade unions in, 45-7
Malawi
  attitude to Chinese offers of aid, 149 n. 2
  delegations to China, 270
  diplomatic relations with China, 119
  policy on admission of China to U.N., 285-6; on Second Bandung, 132-3
Malaysia
  policy on admission of China to U.N., 285
  question of admission to Second Bandung, 132
  trade with China, 38
Mali
  aid from Soviet Union, 216-17 and n. 1
  Chinese policy on Tuareg revolt, 174
  Chinese stress on importance in revolutionary movement, 184
  cultural agreement with China, 84
  delegation to World Youth Festival, 44
  diplomatic relations with China, 72, 192 n. 3, 274
  economic and technical aid from China, 3, 78, 92-3, 122, 158-60, 178-9, 215-19, 239, 244-5, 260, 261, 276
  effects of coup, 1968, 216, 217-19
  exchange of delegations with China, 33, 35, 122, 128-9, 218, 244-5, 269, 270
  member of O.S.R., 215-16
  nationalisation of foreign companies in, 170
  participation in A.A.W.O., 230 n. 3
  policy on admission of China to U.N., 72, 285; on Second Bandung, 124, 132, 271; on second Non-Aligned conference, 127
  relations with Morocco, 225
  support for Lumumbists in Congo, 177
  trade unions in, 45-7
  trade with China, 86, 152 n. 1, 244-5, 273
Malta
  economic aid from China, 257
  policy on admission of China to U.N., 285-6

302 Index

Mankekar, D. R., 108 n. 2
Mao Tse-tung
    address to A.A.P.S.O. conference, 41-2
    comments on U2 incident, 69
    'east wind' speech, 15
    policy on Algeria, 50, 101
    presentation as leader of international communism, 12-13, 192-4 and n. 1
    pronouncements on foreign policy, 3-4, 6, 11
    reception for Egyptian military delegation, 34
    relations with Khrushchev, 49
    speech on American Negro, 120-1
Mao Tun, 96
Massemba-Debat, Alphonse, 117-18, 122, 157, 222-3
Matsu, Chinese policy on, 50
Mauritania
    diplomatic relations with China, 119, 192 n. 3, 224, 239, 266, 274
    dispute with Morocco, 225 and n. 2, 266
    economic and technical aid from China, 3, 224-5, 247, 261, 266, 276
    exchange of delegations with China, 33, 35, 224-5, 269, 270
    mediation in relations of China and Cameroun, 244
    member of O.S.R., 215-16
    policy on admission of China to U.N., 285
    relations with France, 225 n. 2
Mauritius
    diplomatic relations with China, 241, 274
    exchange of delegations with China, 35, 269, 270
    policy on admission of China to U.N., 285-6
    trade unions in, 45-7
Maxwell, Neville, 7 n. 1, 108 n. 2
May Day rallies, presence of African delegates at, 34
Mboya, Tom, 162-3
Mexico, policy on admission of China to U.N., 285
Mikoyan, Anastas, 91
Military aid
    Chinese, for African liberation movements, 100, 101 and n. 1, 138-9 and n. 5, 146-8, 148-9, 156 and n. 5, 172-3, 187, 212-13, 218 and n. 5,

222-3, 232-3 and nn. 2, 3, 264, 277, 283-4
    from Soviet Union to Egypt, 228, 229
    see also Freedom fighters, Revolutionary movements
Militia, development of, as obstacle to army coups d'état, 218 and n. 5, 222-3
Mintoff, Dom, 257
Mobutu, General, 177, 233 and n. 1, 265
Modibo Keita, President, 24, 122, 124, 159-60, 216, 217, 218, 276
Mondlane, Eduardo, 172 and n. 3
Mongolia
    Chinese economic aid for, 40 n. 1
    participation in A.A.P.S.O., 271
    policy on admission of China to U.N., 285
    Russian retention of Outer, 11-12 n. 4
Morocco
    at conference of Independent African States, 28
    attainment of independence, 6, 21
    basis of Chinese policy in, 28, 29-30
    Chinese aid for Red Cross in, 40 n. 2
    Chinese policy during dispute with Algeria, 237
    Communist Party in, 96
    diplomatic relations with China, 51, 192 n. 3, 259, 274
    dismantling of U.S. bases, 170
    dispute with Mauritania, 225 and n. 2, 266
    exchange of delegations with China, 9, 32, 33, 35, 128-9, 269, 270
    participation in A.A.P.S.O., 41-3, 271; in A.A.W.O., 230 n. 3
    policy on admission of China to U.N., 253, 285; on Algerian war of independence, 101 n. 1; on Second Bandung, 123-4, 126, 132-3, 271
    relations with Mali, Guinea, 225
    trade unions in, 45-7
    trade with China, 9, 29 n. 3, 37, 38, 86, 89, 149, 150 and n. 1, 220, 259, 272-3
Moumie, Félix, 28, 53-4, 73, 93-4, 105
Mouvement National Congolais *see* Congo
Mozambique
    economic and technical aid from China, 233
    exchange of delegations with China, 172, 232, 270

Index 303

Mozambique (cont.)
   liberation movement, 115, 170, 172, 232–3 and n. 2, 237, 239, 264
   participation in A.A.P.S.O., 271; in A.A.W.O., 230 n. 3
Mulele, Pierre, 175–6 and nn. 1, 2, 233 n. 1
Muslims see China Islamic Association

Nan Han-Chen, 88
Nasser, Gamal Abdul
   acceptance of U.S. aid, 212
   policy on non-alignment, 127, 161, 227; on Second Bandung, 123, 129; on Sino-Soviet conflict, 108–9
   relations with Chou En-lai, 8
   views on Communism, 22–7, 39
   see also Egypt, United Arab Republic
National Day, presence of African delegations at Chinese, 34
Negroes of North America, Mao Tse-tung's speech on, 120–1
Nehru, Pandit, 7, 43, 107–11
Nepal, policy on admission of China to U.N., 285
Netherlands, policy on admission of China to U.N., 285
Neutralism among African states, 18; see also Non-Aligned States
New China News Agency, 76
New Zealand, policy on admission of China to U.N., 285–6
Ngendandumwe, Premier, 119
Ngouabi, Marien, 223, 249
Nicaragua, policy on admission of China to U.N., 285–6
Niger
   exchange of delegations with China, 33, 269, 270
   freedom fighters, 147 n. 4, 172, 265
   participation in A.A.W.O., 230 n. 3
   policy on admission of China to U.N., 75, 285–6; on Sino-Indian conflict, 110
   trade with China, 273
Nigeria
   aid from U.S., 91, 272–3
   Chinese policy during Civil War, 233–7, 239–40, 243
   diplomatic relations with China, 38, 220, 233, 235, 243, 253, 274
   economic and technical aid from China, 257, 260
   effects for China of coup in, 183
   exchange of delegations with China, 33, 34, 35, 269, 270
   participation in A.A.P.S.O., 41–3, 267
   policy on admission of China to U.N., 72, 285; on Second Bandung, 132–3
   purchase of military planes from Soviet Union, 234 and n. 2
   trade unions in, 45–7
   trade with China, 37, 38, 86, 149, 220, 248
Nimeiry, Jaafar, 246–7, 262
Nixon, Richard, 253, 254, 255–6
Nkrumah, Kwame
   acceptance of U.S. aid for Volta Dam, 212
   implications of overthrow, 183, 186–8 and nn. 2, 3, 238, 264, 265
   militant anti-colonialism, 28
   objection to Sino-Soviet competitive tactics in Africa, 142–3, 168–9 and nn. 1, 6
   pan-Africanism, 54, 80 and n. 2, 145–6
   policy on African nationalism versus international communism, 24; on Chinese aid for revolutionary movements, 146–8, 148–9; on Congo crisis, 79–80; on coup in Algeria, 148; on French Cameroun, 54; on Nuclear Test Ban Treaty, 148; on Second Bandung, 124, 144; on Sino-Indian conflict, 108–9; on Vietnam War, 148, 183
   relations with China, 54, 73, 80–1, 91
   support for, in Guinea, 213–14
   support for restoration, 188 and n. 2
Non-Aligned States, conferences of, 108, 122, 123, 127–8; see also Tshombe
North Korea
   Chinese economic aid for, 40 n. 1
   participation in A.A.P.S.O., 271
   policy in Nigerian Civil War, 236
North Vietnam see Vietnam
Northern Elements Progressive Union of Nigeria, 234
Norway, policy on admission of China to U.N., 285
Noumazalay, Ambroise, 195
Nuclear Test Ban Treaty, 112, 115–16, 120–1, 148, 167–8
Nuclear weapons
   attitudes to Chinese making of, 127
   calls for cessation of tests, 42–3, 148
   concept of nuclear umbrella, 17
   see also Nuclear Test Ban Treaty

Nyerere, Julius
  policy on African nationalism versus international communism, 24; on training of freedom fighters, 172
  reaction to competition between great powers for influence in Africa, 134–5, 165
  relations with China, 74–5, 137
  visit to China, 122, 140–1, 204, 213

Obi, Chike, 234
Obote, Milton, 122
Oginga Odinga, 83, 116, 162, 163–4 and n. 1, 188–9, 238, 264
Okello, John, 135 n. 6, 136
Okotie-eboh, Festus, 86
Olenga, Nicholas, 177
Olympio, President, 130
Omar Oussedik, 52
Organisation of African Unity
  formation, 171
  Liberation Committee, 171, 232
  policy on Rhodesia, 197–8 and n. 3
Organisation of Senegal River States, 215–16
Ottaway, D. and M., 129 n. 2
Ouambi, Ernest, 244
Ousman Ba, 216

Pakistan
  Colombo Power, 8
  Chinese relations with, 180–1
  participation in A.A.P.S.O., 271
  policy on admission of China to U.N., 285; on Second Bandung, 131
  see also Indo-Pakistan War
Pan-Africanism, Nkrumah's concept of, 54, 80 and n. 2, 145–6
Panama, policy on admission of China to U.N., 285–6
Paraguay, policy on admission of China to U.N., 285–6
Peng Teh-huai, 52, 57
People's organisations
  communist, Chinese reliance on, 33, 41, 165–9, 179, 266–7
  effects of Sino-Soviet conflict on activities, 93–8, 165–9, 179, 229–31, 239, 266–7
Peru, policy on admission of China to U.N., 285
Philippines, policy on admission of China to U.N., 285–6

Pickles, Dorothy, 98 n. 3
Pien Chih-hai, 277
Poland
  independent nature of communism in, 12
  policy on admission of China to U.N., 285
Political Science and Law Association of China, 36, 97
Port Arthur, return to China, 11–12 n. 4
Portugal
  policy on admission of China to U.N., 254, 285
  reaction to Nigerian Civil War, 237
  territories in Africa see under individual areas
Portuguese Guinea see Guinea, Portuguese

Quandt, William B., 129 n. 2
Quassim, General, 24, 53
Quatar, policy on admission of China to U.N., 285–6
Quemoy, Chinese policy on, 50; see also Taiwan

Racial approach in African affairs, conflict over, 85 and n. 2, 96, 121, 166 and n. 6, 168–9, 179
Racial discrimination, African students' complaints of, in China, Soviet Union, 85 and n. 2
Raoul, Alfred, 223, 250
Rashidi, Kawawa, 137, 139
Rashidov, 42
Red Cross
  Chinese donations to, in Tunisia, Morocco, 40 n. 2
  national society in China, 97
Red Guards, 194 and nn. 4, 5, 207, 241
Rees, David, 5 n. 1
Research Commission for African Subjects, 36
Retail trade in Southern Africa, Chinese-Western rivalries in, 210–11 and n. 1
Revisionism
  African trade unions' attitudes to, 142
  Chinese accusations of, against Soviet Union, 112
  Chinese assumption of leadership in struggle against, 113–15
Revolutionary movements in Africa
  Chinese policy on support for 2, 13–14,

Index   305

Revolutionary movements in Africa (*cont.*)
15–17, 18–19, 21, 22–3, 27–8, 40 n. 2, 42, 43, 47–8, 49–50, 52–3, 55–8, 59–60, 98–107, 115, 146–8, 156–8 and n. 4, 164, 169–70, 231–2, 259, 260, 264–6
implications of Biafran surrender, 236 n. 3
see also under individual states
Rhodesia
delegations to China, 270
participation in A.A.W.O., 230 n. 3
policy during Nigerian Civil War, 237
repercussions of unilateral declaration of independence, 204–5
Rio Muni *see* Guinea, Equatorial
Roberto, Holden, 170–1 and n. 4
Rumania, policy on admission of China to U.N., 285
Rwanda
Chinese policy on Tutsi revolt, 116–17
delegations to China, 270
diplomatic relations with China, 242, 274
participation in A.A.W.O., 230 n. 3
policy on admission of China to U.N., 285; on Second Bandung, 132

Saka Bashorun, Nigerian trade unionist, 234
Salvador, policy on admission of China to U.N., 285–6
Saudi Arabia, policy on admission of China to U.N., 285
Schatten, F., 95 n. 1
Scott-Thompson, 80 n. 2
Second Bandung Conference, Proposed exclusion of Soviet Union, 126–7, 128, 129, 130–1, 132, 156, 178, 227
negotiations for, 122–32, 144, 263, 271
postponement, 133–4, 141, 162, 180, 238, 263
Sekou Touré *see* Touré
Self-reliance, Chinese concept of, 2, 89, 152–3, 260
Senegal
delegation to World Youth Festival, 44
diplomatic relations with China, 74, 119, 190, 242, 253, 274
exchange of delegations with China, 33, 34, 35, 84, 269, 270
member of O.S.R., 215–16
participation in A.A.P.S.O., 41–3

policy on admission of China to U.N., 72, 253, 285
reaction to U.S. intervention in Congo, 177
relations with Guinea, 216; with Taiwan, 74
trade with China, 273
Senghor, President, 216
Sharmarke, Dr, 121–2, 125
Shehu, Mehmet, 182
Shen Kuang-wu, 277
Sierra Leone
diplomatic relations with China, 242, 253, 274
exchange of delegations with China, 35, 269, 270
participation in A.A.W.O., 230 n. 3
policy on admission of China to U.N., 285
trade with China, 273
Sihanouk, Samdech Norodom, 174, 186 n. 3
Singapore
policy on admission of China to U.N., 285
question of admission to Second Bandung, 132
trade with China, 38
Sino-Indian conflict
effect of Khrushchev's policy during, on Sino-Soviet relations, 112, 178
Ghanaian policy during, 142
repercussions in Africa, 107–11, 142–3, 166, 263
Sino-Soviet relations
and policies on aid for African states, 1, 4, 10–14, 22–7, 48, 52, 56–7, 59–60, 63–71, 88, 89, 98–107, 149, 154 and n. 2, 161–2, 171–2, 226, 227, 260–1, 262, 264
attitudes in African states towards dispute, 47, 142–3, 263
border clashes, 251, 255
disputes at third A.A.P.S.O., conference, 142–3 and n. 1
effects of conflict on people's organisations, 93–8, 165–9, 179, 229–31, 239, 266–7
effects of Congo crisis on, 63
implications of Sino-U.S. rapprochement, 256
international factors determining deterioration of, 57, 59–60, 112, 178; *see also* Khrushchev

306 Index

Sino-Soviet relations (*cont.*)
 repercussions of Sino-Indian conflict, 112, 178
 significance of loan repayments, 86, 113 n. 1, 143 n. 5, 275
 worsening through proposed Russian exclusion from Second Bandung, 126–7, 128, 129, 130–1, 132
Solod, Ambassador, 79
Somalia
 aid from Soviet Union, 225–6 and n. 1
 Chinese policy during disputes with Ethiopia, Kenya, 121–2, 154 and n. 2, 166, 237
 cultural agreement with China, 84
 diplomatic relations with China, 72, 83, 192 n. 3, 239, 274
 economic and technical aid from China, 121–2, 225–6, 245, 261–2, 276
 exchange of delegations with China, 34, 34, 121, 226, 269, 270
 participation in A.A.P.S.O., 271; in A.A.W.O., 230 n. 3
 policy on admission of China to U.N., 285; on Second Bandung, 125, 132, 271
 students from, in China, 84–5
 support for Lumumbists in Congo, 177
 trade with China, 152 n. 1
Somaliland, British, French, Italian, participation in A.A.P.S.O., 41–3
Soumialot, Gaston, 176, 177
South Africa, Union of
 attitude to Tan-Zam Railway, 251
 Chinese policy in, 56, 209–10
 Communist Party in, 96
 diplomatic relations with Taiwan, 71
 exchange of delegations with China, 35, 270
 not at Bandung Conference, 21
 participation in A.A.P.S.O., 271; in A.A.W.O., 230 n. 3
 policy on admission of China to U.N., 285; on Nigerian Civil War, 237
 trade with China, 86, 149–50, 272–3; with Soviet Union, 149–50
 training of freedom fighters for, 232 n. 2
 Western-Chinese rivalries in retail trade, 210–11 and n. 1
South West Africa
 exchange of delegations with China, 270
 participation in A.A.P.S.O., 271; in A.A.W.O., 230 n. 3
South Yemen *see* Yemen

Soviet Union
 African students' complaints of racial discrimination in, 85 and n. 2
 Chinese desire to exclude, from Second Bandung, 126–7, 128, 129, 130–1, 132, 156, 178, 227
 Chinese policy on detente with U.S., 17
 contribution to people's organisations, 93, 165–6, 167, 239
 economic and technical aid for African states, 22–6, 40, 91–2, 144–5, 154 and n. 2, 155, 216–17 and n. 1, 225–6 and n. 1, 227–8, 264
 effects of Arab-Israeli War on prestige, 228–9
 extent of support for Nkrumah, 188 and n. 2
 financial support for A.A.P.S.O., 43–4
 implications of technological advances, 13, 15, 17, 50
 influence in north Africa, 39, 48–9, 224, 227–8, 239, 259, 262
 military aid for Zanzibar, 138
 policy on admission of China to U.N., 285; on Algeria, 51, 52, 58 and n. 1, 99; on Congo crisis, 102–4, 175, 176, 177, 233; on French Cameroun, 53–4, 174; on Nigerian Civil War, 234–6 and n. 2; on Sudan, 246–7
 reaction to formation of Tanzania, 136–7
 refusal to sponsor Tan-Zan railway, 205
 representation on Secretariat of A.A.P.S.O., 43, 271
 suspicion of Sino-U.S. rapprochement, 256
 trade unions' policy towards developments in Africa, 45
 trade with South Africa, 150
 see also Khrushchev, Sino-Soviet relations
Spain, policy on admission of China to U.N., 285–6
Stalin, Joseph, 10–11 and n. 1, 12, 16–17
State Council's Commission for Cultural Relations, 35
Students from African states
 accusations of racial discrimination against, 85 and n. 2
 funds for study in Soviet bloc countries, 43
 scholarships to China, 84–5

Index 307

Sudan
    at Bandung Conference, 8, 21
    at conference of Independent African States, 28
    Chinese policy on southern rebels, 72, 173-4, 236-7, 240, 242, 266
    Communist Party in, 96, 245-7
    cultural agreement with China, 84
    diplomatic relations with China, 29, 72, 192 n. 3, 259, 274
    economic and technical aid from China, 245-7, 262, 276
    exchange of delegations with China, 9, 32, 33, 35, 269, 270
    participation in A.A.P.S.O., 41-3; in A.A.W.O., 230 n. 3
    policy on admission of China to U.N., 285; on Second Bandung, 125, 132, 271
    relations with Soviet Union, 246, 262
    support for Lumumbists in Congo, 174, 177
    trade with China, 29 n. 3, 37-8, 39, 151, 220, 259, 272-3
Sudan African National Union, 173-4
Suez Canal, nationalisation of, 169-70
Suez Crisis, 1956, 9, 40
Summit Conference, 1960, 66, 69-70
Sun Chun-yueh, 277
Sun Hung-wen, 277
Sun Yat Seṅ, 82
Swaziland
    delegations to China, 270
    participation in A.A.W.O., 230 n. 3
    policy on admission of China to U.N., 285-6
Sweden
    aid for Tanzania, 251
    policy on admission of China to U.N., 285
Syria
    conflict between Communism and arab nationalism in, 24
    participation in A.A.P.S.O., 43
    policy on admission of China to U.N., 285
    support for Eritrean Liberation Front, 242
    union with Egypt, 24; see also United Arab Republic

Taiping rising, 82

Taiwan
    foreign policies of nationalist regime in, 62
    international status, 7, 17, 57 and n. 1, 71-2, 74, 105, 188, 190, 252-6, 74
    policy on admission of China to U.N., 285; on Sino-Indian conflict, 112
Taiwan Straits crisis, 48, 50
Tanganyika
    attitude to trade unions in, to revisionism, 142
    diplomatic relations with China, 74-5, 134, 274
    exchange of delegations with China, 35, 135, 269, 270
    mutiny, 125, 135, 138, 162-3, 175 n. 1, 179
    policy on Sino-Indian conflict, 110
    trade with China, 37, 272-3
    see also Tanzania
Tanganyika Federation of Labour, 135
Tanko, 234
Tan-Zam Railway Project, 161, 204-13, 242, 248, 250, 252 and n. 1, 261, 262, 276
Tanzania
    Canadian aid for, 212-13 and n. 3
    Chinese aid for liberation movement, 172, 184, 212-13, 264-5
    Chinese diplomacy in, 134-41, 197-213
    Chou En-lai's visit, 129, 271
    diplomatic relations with China, 192 n. 3
    economic and technical aid from China, 3, 78, 199-202, 202 n. 1, 239, 251-2, 260, 261, 276
    exchange of delegations with China, 137, 184, 198, 204 and n. 4
    flow of aid to freedom fighters through, 172, 232 and n. 2, 236, 239, 264-5
    formation of union, 136
    participation in A.A.P.S.O., 271; in A.A.W.O., 230 n. 3
    policy on admission of China to U.N., 285; on Second Bandung, 132, 141; on second Non-Aligned conference, 127
    reaction to Algerian coup, 130, 132
    response to Chinese aid, 178-9
    support for Lumumbists in Congo, 176 n. 1, 177
    trade with China, 152 n. 1, 198, 248
    treaties on friendship with China, 78, 140, 282-3

308 Index

Tanzania People's Defence Force, 212, 213 n. 1
Tawia Adamafio, 80
Technical assistance for African states *see* Economic and technical aid
Textile factories *see* Friendship Textile Mill, Juapong
Thailand, policy on admission of China to U.N., 285-6
Tibet
  relations with India, 7 and n. 1
  U.A.R. policy on, 25-6
Tito, Marshal, 127
Togo
  delegation to World Youth Festival, 44
  exchange of delegations with China, 35, 269, 270
  overthrow of President Olympio, 130
  policy on admission of China to U.N., 75, 285
  trade with China, 273
Touré, Ahmed Sekou, 30-1, 40, 46, 74, 77-9, 81, 89-90, 109-10, 124, 158-9, 213-14, 215, 249
Trade with African states
  Chinese competition with western interests, 210-11 and n. 1
  development of Chinese policies, 9 and n. 1, 18, 21, 29 n. 3, 33, 36-9, 59, 63, 85-7, 141, 149-52, 179, 198, 219-20, 220-1, 244-57, 262-3, 272-3
Trade unionism, trade unions
  alignment of African, in Sino-Soviet dispute, 47
  attitudes in Russia, to developments in Africa, 45
  competition for control of, in Africa, 44-7
  sponsorship of African students to go to China, 84-5
  World Federation, 44-7, 229, 231, 245-7
  see also individual states
Trans-Sahara roads project, 155
Trinidad and Tobago, policy on admission of China to U.N., 285
Tshombe, Moise, 128, 130 n. 4, 139 n. 1, 176-7, 233 and n. 2, 265
Tunisia
  at conference of Independent African States, 28
  attainment of independence, 6, 21
  attitude to Chinese foreign policies, 124
  Chinese donations to Red Cross in, 40 n. 2

Chinese policy in, 28-9
Communist Party in, 96
deterioration in relations with China, 238
diplomatic relations with China, 28, 117, 124, 189-91, 241, 274; with Taiwan, 71
exchange of delegations with China, 9, 32, 33, 35, 269, 270
participation in A.A.P.S.O., 41-3, 271
policy on admission of China to U.N., 253, 285; on Algerian war of independence, 101 n. 1; on Second Bandung, 132-3, 271
trade with China, 37, 272-3
U.S. attitude to trade unions in, 45
Turkey, policy on admission of China to U.N., 285
Tutsi revolt in Rwanda, 116-17

U2 incident, effects of, 68-9
Uganda
  Chinese support for independence movement, 48
  delegation to World Youth Festival, 44
  diplomatic relations with China, 75, 192 n. 3, 274
  economic and technical aid from China, 225-6, 276
  exchange of delegations with China, 34, 35, 269, 270
  independence, 75
  mutiny, 125, 135, 138, 162-3, 175 n. 1, 179
  participation in A.A.P.S.O., 41-3, 271; in A.A.W.O., 230 n. 3
  policy on admission of China to U.N., 285; on Second Bandung, 132
  recognition of revolutionary government in Zanzibar, 136
  students from, in China, 84-5
  support for revolutionaries in Congo, 176 n. 1
  trade with China, 272-3
Ukraine, policy on admission of China to U.N., 285
Union de Populations du Cameroun *see* Cameroun
Union of African Students in China, 84-5
Union of Chinese Writers, 36, 97
United Arab Republic
  at conference of Independent African States, 28

Index 309

United Arab Republic (*cont.*)
  Chinese Embassy in, during Cultural Revolution, 194-5
  Chou En-lai's visit, 1965, 129
  cultural agreements with China, 84
  deterioration in relations with China, 22-7, 59, 96, 239, 247
  diplomatic relations with China, 192 n. 3, 274
  economic and technical aid from China, 160-2, 226-9, 262, 276
  exchange of delegations with China, 32, 33, 34, 35, 269, 270
  influence of Soviet Union, 39, 48-9, 224, 227-8, 239, 259, 262
  policy on Second Bandung, 123, 126, 129, 132, 271; on Sino-Indian conflict, 108-9, 110
  relations with India, 25-6
  support for A.A.P.S.O., 95, 271; for Lumumbists in Congo, 177
  trade unions in, 45-7
  trade with China, 9, 37, 39, 40, 86, 149, 152 and n. 2, 220, 224, 248, 259, 272-3
  see also Egypt, Nasser
United front, Chinese strategy of, 6, 7-8
United Kingdom
  financial aid for Tanzania, 197-8 and n. 1
  policy on admission of China to U.N., 285; on Sino-Indian conflict, 108-9
  relation of trading and foreign policies, 36
United Nations
  admission of China to, 4, 28, 62, 71-6, 119, 162, 173, 207 n. 2, 242, 243, 252-5, 258-9, 277, 285-6
  membership of newly independent African states, 62-3
  operations in Congo, 101-4
  role in Indo-Pakistan War, 255
United States of America
  aid for African states, 91, 212, 251
  attitude during Nigerian Civil War, 234-6 and nn. 1, 1
  changing policy on Chinese admission to U.N., 252-5, 285-6
  Chinese fostering of antipathy to, in Africa, 19-20, 185-6
  detente with U.S.S.R., 17
  effects of trading embargos, 36-7 and n. 4
  military alliances in Asia, 114

policy on Baghdad Pact, 48-9; on Congo crisis, 63, 101-4, 177 and n. 3; on Taiwan Straits crisis, 50
  reaction of trade unions in, to developments in Africa, 45
  relations with China, 4, 7, 17, 125, 151, 253, 255-7
Upper Volta
  Chinese delegation to, 269
  effects for China of coup in, 183
  policy on admission of China to U.N., 285-6
Uruguay, policy on admission of China to U.N. 285-6

Venezuela, policy on admission of China to U.N., 285-6
Vietnam, North
  Chinese policy in, 6
  participation in A.A.P.S.O., 271
  policy in Nigerian Civil War, 236
Vietnam, South, participation in A.A.P.S.O., 271
Vietnam War
  Chinese policy on, 6, 181 and n. 1
  effects on Chinese support for revolutionary movements in Africa, 178, 231
  implications of intensification, 183, 238
  Nkrumah's attempt to mediate in, 148, 183
Volta Dam, U.S. aid for, 212

Wang, Comrade, 236 n. 1
Wang Hsien-chen, 277
Wang Ken-fa, 277
War, Chinese view of Marxist-Leninist concepts, 47, 67-9
Whiting, Allen, 6 n. 1
Women's Federation of the P.R.C., 36, 45-6, 97, 116
Women's International Democratic Federation, 44
World Bank
  aid for Tanzania, 251
  refusal to finance Tan-Zam Railway, 205, 206
World Congress of Women, Moscow, 1963, 167
World Federation of Democratic Youth, 44
World Federation of Trade Unions
  in struggle for control of unions in Africa, 44-7
  leader from Suda, 245-7

Index

World Federation of Trade Unions (*cont.*)
  Soviet domination of, 229
  split into Chinese, Soviet factions, 231
World Peace Council, 44, 168, 229–30, 231
World Youth Festival, 1959, 44
Wu Meng-ch'un, 277

Yakasai, 234
Yang Shuo, 54
Yang Te-yeh, 277
Yemen
  participation in A.A.P.S.O., 271
  policy on admission of China to U.N., 285
Yemen, South
  policy on admission of China to U.N., 285; on Nigerian Civil War, 235
Yen Len, 277
Youlou, Fulbert, 117, 156, 158
Yousef el Sebey, 43
Yu Chao-li, 24, 64
Yugoslavia, policy on admission of China to U.N., 285

Zambia
  diplomatic relations with China, 118, 192 and n. 3, 204, 208, 274
  economic and technical aid from China, 3, 203, 250–1, 271; *see also* Tan–Zam Railway
  exchange of delegations with China, 206, 269, 270
  participation in A.A.P.S.O., 271
  policy on admission of China to U.N., 285
Zanzibar
  Communist Party in, 96
  diplomatic relations with China, 116, 274
  economic and technical aid from China, 136, 197, 203
  exchange of delegations with China, 269, 270
  participation in A.A.P.S.O., 41–3
  revolution, 116, 125, 135–6 and n. 6, 170, 175 n. 1, 179
  students from, in China, 84–5
  union with Tanganyika, 136; *see also* Tanzania
Zelman, W. A., 5 n. 3